AF381151

Picasso–El Greco

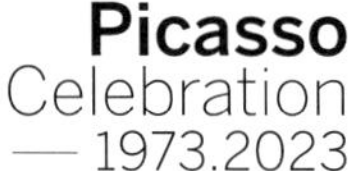

Picasso
Celebration
— 1973.2023

**The exhibition and accompanying publication were created
in collaboration with the Embassy of Spain in Switzerland**

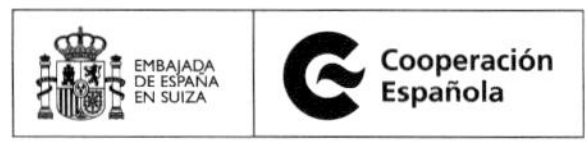

Picasso–El Greco

Edited by
Carmen Giménez and
Josef Helfenstein

With essays by
Gabriel Dette, Carmen Giménez,
Javier Portús, and Richard Shiff

HATJE CANTZ

kunstmuseum basel

In memory of Francisco Calvo Seraller
(1948–2018)

Contents

Josef Helfenstein

Foreword

Pablo Picasso (1881–1973) changed the course of European art history many times in his long career. Few artists are as internationally famous or as thoroughly researched; few are as synonymous with the European avant-garde, especially Cubism. But is there anything new to discover in his work? For Carmen Giménez and the curatorial team that worked with her on this exhibition, the answer is a resounding yes. The exhibition looks at Picasso's influences and sources of inspiration and, in doing so, examines a link between two artists that spans more than three centuries in the history of painting.

Nearly all experts agree that Picasso's enthusiasm for El Greco (1541–1614) is clearly visible in his work, but most tend to focus on the early years up to and including the Blue Period. Our exhibition offers a new reading: that Picasso's interest in El Greco was not only more intense but considerably more prolonged than is generally assumed. Both his Cubist paintings and those from his Classical period reveal clear affinities with El Greco. Even after World War II and until the end of his life, Picasso was still making explicit allusions to the Greek-Spanish master.

The El-Greco-Picasso nexus has, since the nineteen-fifties, been situated within the *longue durée* of Spanish painting. To date, however, there has been no in-depth exploration of Picasso's rich engagement with El Greco's work. Of course it would not do justice to either artist to suggest some kind of simple, linear development from El Greco to Picasso. Rather, the present exhibition offers an experimental and at times associative analysis of Picasso's intimate dialogue with an artist he regarded both as a role model and an equal. It is fascinating to observe the young Picasso shifting from the imitational stance evident, for example, in the drawing he signed "Yo El Greco" in 1899 to the artistic self-confidence of a painting like *Yo–Picasso* from 1901 (private collection). Toward the end of his life, Picasso engaged with the Old Masters with the same confident directness, but seventy years had elapsed, and he was now a world-famous artist. A particularly incisive example is the 1967 painting *The Musketeer* in the last part of the exhibition (cat. 66), which he "signed" on the back "Domenico Theotocopulos van Rijn da Silva"—an extraordinary amalgam of the surnames of El Greco, Rembrandt, and Diego Velázquez.[1] From this sometimes paradoxical position he was able to give new impetus not only to the art of painting—with explicit reference to his revered masters—but also to himself as an artist who was in some ways removed or alienated from his time.

El Greco's Rehabilitation
El Greco was probably the earliest of the many artistic influences that Picasso drew on in his youth. His interest in him was sparked at the end of the nineteenth century when the family settled in Barcelona in 1896. There the teenager moved in a circle of open-minded artists who were instrumental in reviving interest in the neglected Old Master. Tellingly, El Greco's rediscovery was not the work of art historians but of writers,

artists, and critics. Nor did the first sparks of this initiative come from Spain, but from French artists like Édouard Manet and, later, Paul Cézanne.

In 1898 Spain lost the Spanish-American War and with it, its last important colonies. Many Spanish intellectuals and cultural figures reacted to the geopolitical fall of the former colonial power by turning to the Spanish Golden Age for inspiration; the artists of the Spanish School enjoyed considerable importance in this era marked by nationalism and a search for identity, including within progressive, reformist circles. When the third centenary of Velázquez's birth was celebrated with great pomp and ceremony in 1899, Francisco de Goya and El Greco, though still controversial, were also becoming increasingly central figures in the national discourse.

What gave El Greco so much sway over the avant-garde imagination? From a nineteenth-century perspective he stood out among the other artists of the Spanish School. His long-overlooked work, barely known beyond the Iberian Peninsula until after the Napoleonic Wars, revealed intriguing departures from the classical ideals of his contemporaries. Many artists saw in him a champion of radical expression—in form, in color, and in subject matter— one of the great individualists in the history of European painting. El Greco was indeed deeply unconventional, not least because his biography provided him with three different traditions with which to work (Greek-Byzantine, Venetian, and Spanish) and from which to create his own unique visual language. Even today he continues to fascinate us, partly because, unlike artists such as Titian and Velázquez, so little is known about his life and work; revelatory documents are comparatively rare. The legends surrounding him made him an ideal target for the projections of artists rebelling against the academy, although as we now know, much of their romanticizing had little basis in historical truth. What is certain, however, is that almost three centuries after his death, El Greco inspired an entire generation of young artists—among them Picasso—in their fight against conventional fin-de-siècle conceptions of art.

Picasso's engagement with his Spanish predecessors would occupy him all his life. The three Spanish artists most important to him were El Greco, Velázquez, and Goya. All were leading figures of their times, and all three viewed artistic

authority, and in particular the demands of the academy, with no small skepticism.[2] Among the many artists who threw themselves into studying El Greco in the late nineteenth century, Picasso was one of the most perceptive. Cézanne, Henri de Toulouse-Lautrec, and the anonymous creators of what was then called primitive art were all important points of reference for Cubism, but it was El Greco who laid the ground for Picasso's later development as an artist. According to Romuald Dor de la Souchère, Picasso even stated plainly that Cubism was "Spanish in origin" and that he, Picasso, had invented it. He is also said to have pointed to the Spanish influence on Cézanne—especially El Greco's. The master of Toledo may have been a "Venetian painter," but he was "Cubist in construction."[3]

The Exhibition
The exhibition at the Kunstmuseum Basel is the first to focus exclusively and on such a grand scale on El Greco's influence on Picasso's work. Experts have long agreed that El Greco's controversial paintings had a profound impact on the young Picasso, but we would like to show that his interest and inspiration lasted on and off right up until the end of his life. From the nineteen-fifties onward, Picasso's appropriation of old masters, including works by El Greco, resembles a dialogue with the classical history of painting in which he can be seen asserting his own historical significance. The period between 1950 and 1963 is also dominated by an engagement with the painting of the past more generally; it was at this time that Picasso painted variations on works by Gustave Courbet, Eugène Delacroix, Velázquez, and Manet. After the death in 1954 of his great friend and rival Henri Matisse (who was also a close neighbor in the South of France), Picasso became more acutely aware of his intellectual loneliness and increasingly saw himself as the last master of the classical European painting tradition.

The exhibition comprises about thirty pairs of works by El Greco and Picasso. These juxtapositions allow us to trace a fascinating artistic conversation—what Picasso imagined as a timeless dialogue.[4] Beside a core group of works from the Kunstmuseum collection, we show outstanding loans from prestigious museums and private collections all over the world. In this way we not only open up new perspectives on Picasso and his work but also offer insight into the extraordinary and less widely-known oeuvre of El Greco. In addition, the exhibition sheds light on the importance of Picasso's dialogue with El Greco for the development of twentieth-century avant-garde art as a whole.

The Kunstmuseum Basel has a superlative collection of art from all phases of Picasso's oeuvre; this collection forms the basis of the project. When it comes to El Greco, the situation is very different. The Öffentliche Kunstsammlung Basel has only one work, acquired in 1935, and although it is from El Greco's studio, it cannot be attributed to him with any certainty (cat. 55). Beyond Basel, the work of this radical Old Master is scattered in museum collections, churches, and monasteries across the world; without the generous support of many of these institutions, the exhibition could never have come to fruition. Thanks to them, we can present the local and international public with masterpieces by El Greco—many of them never previously shown in Basel—alongside those of Picasso. The exhibition also takes us beyond Picasso to explore El Greco's influence on Modernism and to invite visitors to discover an artist who, for various reasons, was long consigned to the shadows.

1 See *Picasso: Tradición y vanguardia; 25 años con el Guernica*, ed. Francisco Calvo Serraller and Carmen Giménez, exh. cat. Museo Nacional del Prado and Museo Nacional Centro de Arte Reina Sofia (Madrid, 2006), pp. 64–65. See also the analysis offered by Carmen Giménez in this catalogue.

2 Jonathan Brown, "Picasso and the Spanish Tradition of Painting," in *Picasso and the Spanish Tradition*, ed. Jonathan Brown (New Haven, 1996), pp. 1–25.

3 "Nous devons rechercher les influences espagnoles chez Cézanne . . . l'influence de Greco sur son œuvre . . . Greco: un peintre vénitien, mais cubiste dans la construction!" Picasso, as recalled by Romuald Dor de la Souchère, *Picasso à Antibes* (Paris, 1960). Quoted in Francisco Calvo Serraller, "Picasso et l'école espagnole," in *Picasso et les maîtres,* ed. Pierre Vallaud, exh. cat. Galeries nationales du Grand Palais (Paris, 2008), p. 64.

4 As Picasso said to Hélène Parmelin, "I have a feeling that Delacroix, Giotto, Tintoretto, El Greco and the rest, as well as all the modern painters, the good and the bad, the abstract and the non-abstract, are all standing behind me watching me at work." Hélène Parmelin, *Picasso Plain: An Intimate Portrait* (London, 1963), p. 77.

Acknowledgments

When, in a meeting ten years ago, Carmen Giménez came up with the idea of an exhibition juxtaposing the work of El Greco and Picasso, none of us knew what form it would take—or whether it would even happen. It wasn't until the summer of 2015, when it became clear that I would become director of the Kunstmuseum Basel in the fall of the following year, that Carmen's dream began to assume a more concrete form. In early 2017 we held a series of meetings to develop a concept for the exhibition. It was soon obvious that Picasso's lifelong engagement with El Greco would have to be presented thematically rather than chronologically. As a result, we had some very precise ideas about the items we hoped to borrow for particular juxtapositions. Despite the difficult circumstances created by the pandemic, we were fortunate and privileged enough to enjoy the generous support of many colleagues in Europe, the United States, and Asia. Our special thanks go to them, without whom this project would never have been possible.

Carmen Giménez would like to dedicate this exhibition to the memory of her longtime friend Francisco Calvo Serraller, with whom she developed the idea for this project as well as many others. Their collaboration on El Greco and Picasso began in 1987 when they organized the exhibition *From El Greco to Picasso* at the Musée du Petit Palais. In 2006, several projects and almost twenty years later, they co-curated *Picasso: Tradition and Avant-Garde*—presented simultaneously at two Madrid venues, the Museo del Prado and the Museo Reina Sofía—in which Picasso was directly confronted with the artistic tradition that preceded him: Titian, Tintoretto, Rubens, Zurbarán, Velázquez, Ribera, Goya . . . The exhibition revealed that Picasso's creative dialogue with the Old Masters was a thread that ran throughout his life. Another joint curatorial project followed at the Guggenheim in New York in 2006–07 with the exhibition *Spanish Painting from El Greco to Picasso*. Sadly, Francisco Calvo Serraller did not live to see the present Picasso–El Greco project realized. As a result, it is not only a tribute to his legacy and friendship but also a conclusion to all the exhibitions he curated jointly with Carmen.

Carmen Giménez and Josef Helfenstein

**We would like to thank the following individuals
and institutions for their generous support:**

Picasso Family
Fundación Almine y Bernard Ruiz-Picasso
  para el Arte
Maya Widmaier-Picasso
  and Diana Widmaier Picasso
Claude Ruiz-Picasso
Paloma Ruiz-Picasso
Picasso Administration

Lenders To The Exhibtion
CANADA
The Montreal Museum of Fine Arts:
  Stéphane Aquin, Marie-Dailey Desmarais
FRANCE
Musée de Picardie, Amiens: Laure Dalon
Musée d'Art Moderne de la Ville de Paris:
  Fabrice Hergott
Musée du Louvre, Paris: Jean-Luc Martinez,
  Laurence des Cars
Musée national Picasso, Paris:
  Laurent Le Bon, Cécile Debray
Musée des Beaux-Arts de Strasbourg:
  Paul Lang
GERMANY
Museum Frieder Burda, Baden-Baden:
  Henning Schaper
Staatliche Museen zu Berlin – Preussischer
  Kulturbesitz, Nationalgalerie, Museum
  Berggruen: Gabriel Montua
Staatliche Museen zu Berlin – Preussischer
  Kulturbesitz, Gemäldegalerie: Michael
  Eissenhauer, Dagmar Hirschfelder
Museum Ludwig, Cologne: Yilmaz Dziewior
HUNGARY
Ludwig Museum – Museum of
  Contemporary Art, Budapest: Julia Fabényi
Szépművészeti Múzeum, Budapest:
  László Baán

ITALY
Peggy Guggenheim Collection, Venice:
  Karole Vail
SPAIN
Church of Santa María la Mayor, Andújar
  (Diocese of Jaén): Don Pedro Montesinos
Museu Picasso, Barcelona: Emmanuel
  Guigon
Fundación Hospital Ntra. Sra. de La
  Caridad – Memoria Benéfica de Vega
  (FUNCAVE), Illescas: José Manuel Tofiño
Museo Nacional del Prado, Madrid:
  Miguel Falomir, Javier Portús, Javier Barón
Museo Nacional Thyssen-Bornemisza,
  Madrid: Guillermo Solana, Paloma Alarcó
Patrimonio Nacional, Colecciones Reales,
  Madrid: Ana de la Cueva, Leticia Ruiz
  Gómez
Church of San Ginés de Arlés, Madrid
  (Archdiocese of Madrid): Don José Luis
  Montes
Museo Picasso, Málaga: José Lebrero
Museo del Greco, Toledo: Carmen Álvarez
  Nogales, Rosa Becerril Sánchez,
  Juan Antonio García Castro
Parish Church of San Nicolás de Bari –
  Archdiocese of Toledo; Museo de Santa
  Cruz, Toledo: Anastasio Gómez Hidalgo,
  Rvdo. Sr. Don José Luis Pérez de la Roza,
  Fernando Fontes Blanco
SWITZERLAND
Fondation Beyeler, Riehen/Basel: Sam Keller
Gottfried Keller-Stiftung, Bundesamt für
  Kultur, Bern
UNITED KINGDOM
Glasgow Museums, Stirling Maxwell
  Collection: Duncan Dornan
The National Gallery, London: Gabriele
  Finaldi
The Pittas Collection – El Greco, London
Tate, London: Frances Morris, Matthew
  Gale, Achim Borchardt-Hume (1965–2021)

UNITED STATES OF AMERICA
  The Baltimore Museum of Art:
    Christopher Bedford
  The Nelson-Atkins Museum of Art, Kansas
    City: Julián Zugazagoitia
  The Metropolitan Museum of Art, New York:
    Max Hollein, Dita Amory
  Solomon R. Guggenheim Museum, New
    York: Richard Armstrong, Tracey Bashkoff
  Kate Ganz Family Trust, New York
  Philadelphia Museum of Art: Timothy Rub
  National Gallery of Art, Washington, D.C.:
    Kaywin Feldman, Harry Cooper

We also warmly thank all lenders who prefer to
remain anonymous.

Our sincere thanks go to the authors of the
catalogue:
  Gabriel Dette
  Carmen Giménez
  Javier Portús
  Richard Shiff

We are also grateful for the remarkable commitment
of the staff of the Kunstmuseum Basel, without
whom the exhibition would never have been
possible. We would particularly like to thank:
  Lara Baltsch
  Gabriel Dette
  Matthias Fellmann
  Monique Meyer
  Olga Osadtschy

In particular, we wish to thank Ana Mingot in Spain
for her invaluable support.

Thanks also go to all those who gave us their
active and generous support through the long
and complicated process of bringing the exhibition
and catalogue to fruition and in helping us trace
some of the exhibits:
  Juan Alfonso Martos y Azlor de Aragón,
    Duke of Granada de Ega, and
    Fátima Bláquez de Lora y Lora
  Juan Ariño
  Olivier Berggruen
  Tobia Bezzola
  Cesar Borja
  Manuel Borja-Villel
  Marco Francioli
  Marcos Giralt
  José Guirao
  Florence Half-Wrobel
  Dolores Jiménez-Blanco
  Guillaume Kientz
  James Macdonald
  Margot McGreevy
  María Celsa Nuño García
  Santiago Olabarri
  Christine Pinault
  Frédéric Prot
  Nancy Rosen
  Beat Wismer
  Miguel Zugaza

**The exhibition was made possible
by the generous support of:**

CREDIT SUISSE

Credit-Suisse (Schweiz AG)

SULGER-STIFTUNG
Sulger-Foundation

L. + Th. La Roche Foundation

Pierrette Schlettwein

Dorette Gloor

HEIVISCH

Peter & Simone Forcart

Bérengère Primat

Trafina Privatbank AG

The exhibition was made possible thanks to support
from the Mobilière Cooperative Jubilee Foundation.

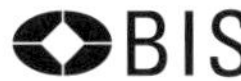

Bank for International Settlements

Isaac Dreyfus-Bernheim Foundation

Anonymous sponsors

Foundation for the Kunstmuseum Basel

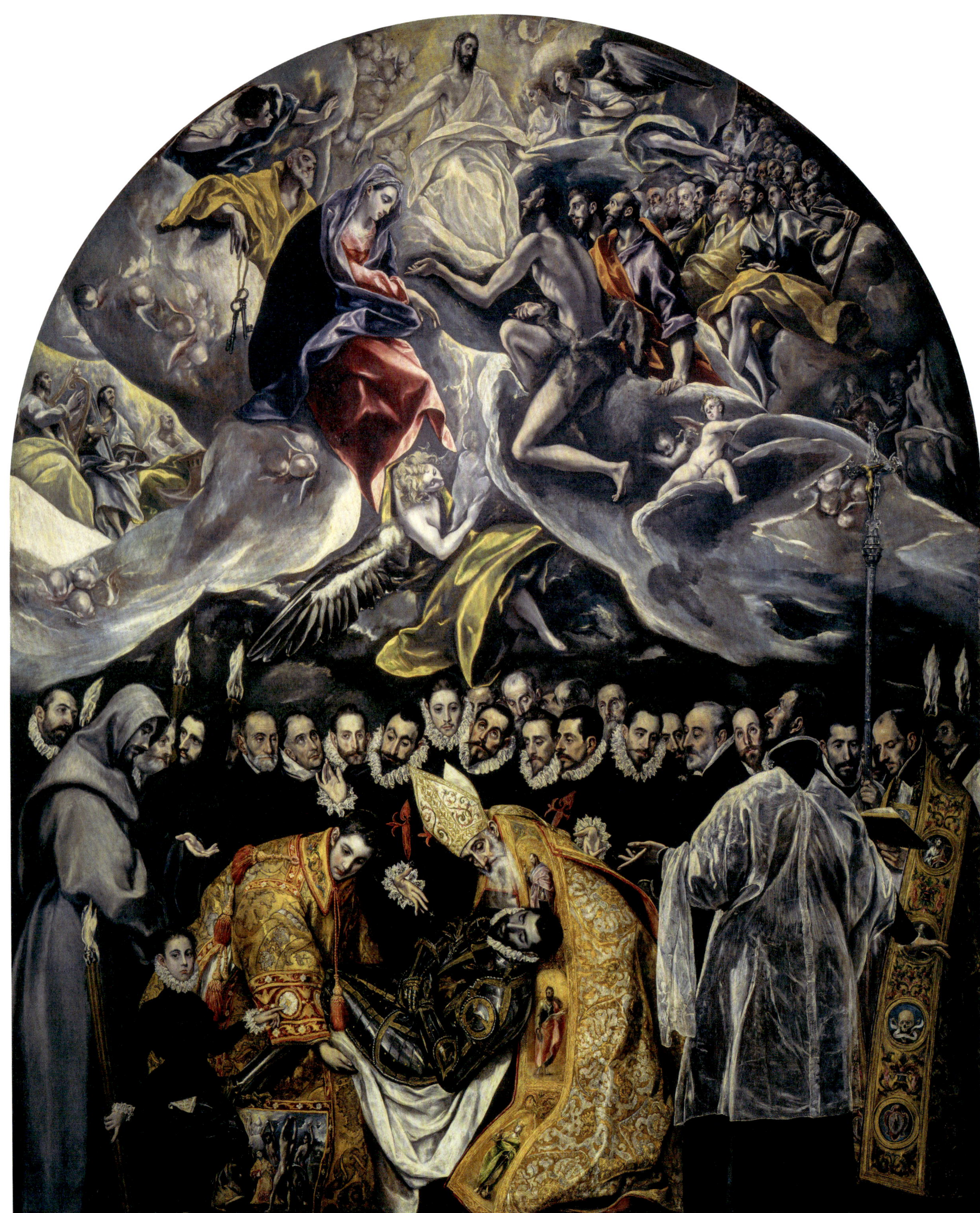

Carmen Giménez

Picasso – El Greco

To me there is no past or future in art. If a work of art cannot live always in the present it must not be considered at all. The art of the Greeks, of the Egyptians, of the great painters who live in other times, is not an art of the past; perhaps it is more alive today than it ever was.
—Pablo Picasso[1]

The year 2023 marks the fiftieth anniversary of the death of Pablo Picasso. More than four centuries have passed since El Greco died. The gap in time between them seems, because it is, immense. But great art is atemporal, oscillating constantly between the past and the present. Picasso understood this better than anyone else in the twentieth century. The most avant-garde artist of his era maintained the most enriching dialogue with historical precedents. Again and again, he dipped into the glories of bygone periods, taking what he wanted to shape the development of his genius. Of special fascination is his far too often scanted, particularly profound and consequential relation to El Greco. A chance to explore that dramatic confluence of old and new, here in our own present that is already slipping into the past, opens doors to expanded comprehensions of what mattered in and to modern art and cannot cease to nurture future possibilities. Looking back, in this case, models looking forward.

↖
[Fig.1] El Greco, *The Burial of the Count of Orgaz*, 1586–88
Oil on canvas, 480 × 360 cm
Iglesia de Santo Tomé, Toledo

The young Picasso was trained in the strictest academic tradition. His father, a conventional painter, encouraged him when he was fourteen to enroll in Barcelona's Escuela de Bellas Artes and, later, at seventeen, at Madrid's Real Academia de Bellas Artes de San Fernando, where he received unbeatable marks in his entrance exam. Yet his letters and the drawings from that time show that instead of attending art classes at the Academia, he spent his days copying the Old Masters at the Museo del Prado:

> The museum of painters is beautiful: Velázquez is first class. Some of Greco's heads are magnificent. Murillo is not always convincing. Titian's [Mater] Dolorosa is good; there are some beautiful Van Dyck portraits and a *Betrayal of Christ*; Rubens has a painting (*The Brazen Serpent*) that is a wonder; a few small, very good paintings of some drunks by Teniers, but I do not remember anything else just now.[2]

A sheet of drawings from this time includes a telling line of invocation: "El Greco, Velázquez, *inspirarme!*"—inspire me! (cat. 6). Another sketch, this one inscribed with the words *Yo El Greco* (I, El Greco), makes the identification even clearer (cat. 5); these are unequivocal statements from a young student of seventeen, who—despite the general indifference or animosity toward El Greco at that time—already saw in El Greco the origins of a struggle he himself would pursue: the liberation of modern painting from dogma. Francisco Bernareggi, a young Argentine painter who accompanied him on his visits to the Prado, recalled in his memoirs how people dismissed them as "Modernistas!" for copying El Greco, and Picasso's father chided them in response: "You're taking the wrong path!"[3]

With the possible exception of Diego Velázquez who had kept three of his portraits in his private collection, the fact is that El Greco had no followers of any importance for centuries following his death. Only his son Jorge Manuel and a few more or less obscure painters produced copies of the master's works. It is true that El Greco enjoyed fame from the time he settled in Spain in 1577 until his death in 1614, but soon after, his critical reputation declined as a local myth began to circulate about the wild pictorial distortions that characterized his final years.

It was not until well into the nineteenth century that El Greco's reputation began to revive—especially in France. The writer Théophile Gautier had exalted his work in his *Voyage en Espagne,* published in 1843, and as the century progressed, El Greco's paintings once again began to circulate and interest French artists, collectors, and connoisseurs. The realist painters were the first to appreciate him. Édouard Manet, encouraged by his close friend, the artist Zacharie Astruc (who came to own as many as five works attributed to El Greco), undertook his legendary trip to Spain in 1865. After Madrid, Manet went on to Toledo—doubtless at Astruc's urging—where he admired many El Greco masterpieces, including the monumental *Burial of the Count of Orgaz* (1586–88) in the church of Santo Tomé (fig. 1). Edgar Degas was equally intrigued, acquiring two El Grecos for his own collection.[4] Other Impressionists—as well as a few naturalists, post-Impressionists, and Symbolists—were also drawn to the artist from

Crete; he was an important influence on Henri de Toulouse-Lautrec as well as Paul Gauguin and the latter's young followers in the Pont-Aven group. French art critics and writers, among them Théodore Duret, Joris-Karl Huysmans, and Maurice Barrès, also gave El Greco extensive attention.[5]

In Spain, it was mainly the group of forward-looking artists in Cataluña—including Santiago Rusiñol, Ramon Casas, and Isidre Nonell, among others—that promoted the rediscovery of El Greco. Other Spanish artists of that generation, such as Darío de Regoyos and Ignacio Zuloaga, also took part. The first grand El Greco retrospective took place at the Prado in 1902, followed in 1908 by Manuel B. Cossío's seminal monograph. That same year the German critic Julius Meier-Graefe went to Spain with the aim of examining Velázquez. The account he published in 1910 described his discovery of El Greco as a revelation—"probably the most important experience any of us could have"[6]—and rated him above Velázquez. Two years later, in 1912, Wassily Kandinsky and Franz Marc also declared their admiration in the almanac *Der Blaue Reiter.*

Raphael is a great master, Velázquez is a great master, El Greco is a great master, but the secret of plastic beauty is located at a greater distance: in the Greeks at the time of Pericles.
—Pablo Picasso[7]

Born in 1541 in the Kingdom of Candia, present-day Crete, El Greco trained as an icon painter in the post-Byzantine tradition. The island was part of the Republic of Venice at

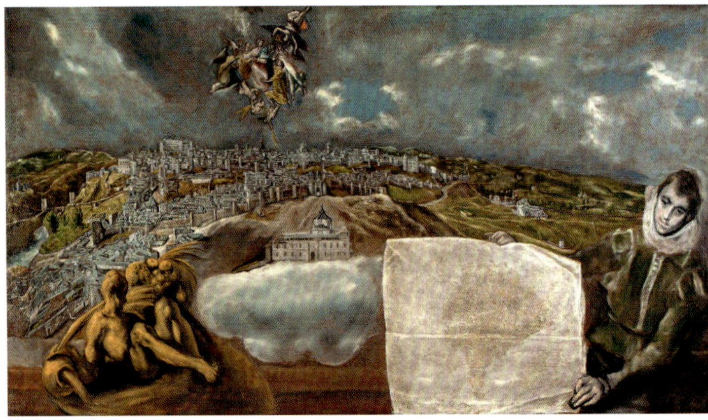

[Fig. 2] El Greco, *View and Plan of Toledo,* ca. 1600–10
Oil on canvas, 132 × 228 cm
Museo del Greco, Toledo

the time, and El Greco, like most Greek artists of his day, moved to Venice when he was still a young man. There he discovered the works—and workshops—of Titian and Tintoretto and began to absorb the complexities of the Italian Renaissance canon. His art began to convey complex narratives, and a new spatial dimension entered his work. This marked a departure from the two-dimensional space of traditional icons in which figures seemed to hover in an undefined space. The switch from tempera to oil paint, which took longer to dry, also allowed him to paint with far greater subtlety.

After three years in Venice, instead of returning to Crete, El Greco moved to Rome in 1570. With an introduction from the famous miniaturist Giulio Clovio, he joined the group of artists working under the patronage of Cardinal Alessandro Farnese. Two years later, the powerful cardinal dismissed him. This was the first time, though certainly not the last, that El Greco alienated a powerful patron to the detriment of his career. He opened a studio and started painting portraits and small-scale religious works but was unable to secure major commissions. This inability to gain a foothold in Rome is often attributed to El Greco's criticism of Michelangelo, who had died in 1564 but remained an outsized presence in the Eternal City. Though El Greco voiced admiration for Michelangelo's talent in drawing and sculpture, he had dared to criticize the Sistine Chapel frescoes for their "faulty" use of color, which made potential patrons wary of his taste and skill.[8]

Well, I was there once. . . . Do you really know it? Now that I think of it, I don't know what's so wonderful about it. It's what I like least of Michelangelo. It's all the same, whether it's the Holy Father or an angel's wing or a slave. Everything is all on the same scale and in the same proportion. The truth is, I don't understand it.
    —Pablo Picasso, looking at a color photograph
    of the Sistine Chapel[9]

In Rome, El Greco was in touch with the large community of Spaniards, especially Luis de Castilla, son of the dean of Toledo's cathedral, Diego de Castilla, who later gave him his first commission in Toledo. He moved to Spain in 1576 with his assistant Francesco Preboste, drawn by Philip II's construction of the Royal Monastery of San Lorenzo de El Escorial. Philip

the Prudent, as he was known, was the richest, most powerful leader in Europe. A devotee of the arts and patron of Titian, he was nonetheless having difficulties finding good artists to execute the large paintings for the new royal palace and monastery complex. Titian had died in 1576, and Tintoretto along with other Italian masters were unwilling to come to Spain. Navarrete el Mudo, Philip II's choice to decorate the basilica at the heart of the complex had died in 1579.

The Escorial monastery is home to the first major painting El Greco executed in Spain, his *Adoration of the Name of Jesus* (ca. 1577–79; cat. 16). It commemorates the 1571 defeat of the Ottomans at the battle of Lepanto by the allied forces of Spain, Venice, and the Italian States led by the Pope. El Greco shows the King of Spain, the Doge of Venice, and the Pope—the alliance—kneeling in the foreground. Philip II, dressed in black and wearing a ruff, is a conspicuous presence, which suggests that the work was either commissioned by the king or painted to catch his eye. And indeed, one year after the painting's delivery, Philip II commissioned El Greco to paint a major altarpiece for the basilica at the Escorial, *The Martyrdom of Saint Maurice and the Theban Legion* (fig. p. 42). When El Greco delivered it two years later, the painting was not well received; the king ordered its removal from the saint's chapel and commissioned a replacement by Rómulo Cincinnato, a mediocre painter whose version still hangs there today.

El Greco had violated the highest standard of Counter-Reformation taste, privileging style over content. Instead of drawing attention to the main subject matter—the decapitation of Saint Maurice and his companions—El Greco focused on the saints as they weighed the decision to accept martyrdom. The elegant stance of these figures was deemed a distraction, for Philip II prized beauty only so long as no articles of faith were compromised. This royal rejection could well be what saved El Greco from years of court service—a role Velázquez performed fifty years later—and bestowed on El Greco the opportunity to embrace his artistic flamboyance. Nonetheless, a continued dialogue between the monastery's architect Juan de Herrera and El Greco would certainly have enriched the Escorial.

After his attempt to secure royal patronage, El Greco now settled permanently in Toledo, a city with "a distinguished past, a prosperous present, and an uncertain future" (fig. 2).[10] It had ceased to serve as the seat of the Spanish monarchy in 1561, the year Philip II moved the court to Madrid, but the clergy's upper hierarchy remained, preserving Toledo as a bastion of devout reactionary Catholicism, a counter-weight to the excesses of papal indulgence. El Greco arrived there at a time when his style of painting was falling out of fashion in Rome. Had he stayed in the Eternal City, he would surely have had to make concessions to the waning of Mannerism, the growing influence of Caravaggio and Carracci, and the return to Renaissance naturalism inspired by classical antiquity. In the relative isolation of Toledo, however, El Greco could forge a style of his own, one that struck a unique balance between the essential post-Byzantine tradition of his earliest training in Crete and the techniques he had learned in Italy. His art embodies one of the most complex and fantastic evolutions to be found in the history of art. As the art historian Jonathan Brown stresses, it was in Toledo that El Greco invented a way of painting whose bold defiance of the classical canon went unmatched until the late nineteenth century.[11] He reclaimed a Byzantine approach with an emphasis on verticality over depth and a liberal use of inverted perspective in which, distinct from linear perspective, the vanishing point converges on the viewer rather than in the painting. He also applied what he had learned in Venice, namely how to create a sense of depth by gradually changing his colors in a dappling of light and shade. Ultimately, once rescued from oblivion, El Greco provided Picasso with the lead he needed to make a permanent break with the art of the past and the pillars of traditional representation.

I had already seen a few of his paintings, which impressed me very much. That was when I decided to take a trip to Toledo, and it left a profound impression on me. It's probably owing to his influence that my human figures from the blue period became elongated.
    —Pablo Picasso[12]

The critic Gustave Coquiot—who organized Piccasso's first show at the Galerie Vollard in 1901 and was an early Paris friend of the art-ist—was the first to link El Greco to Picasso's Blue Period. In an essay published in 1914, he

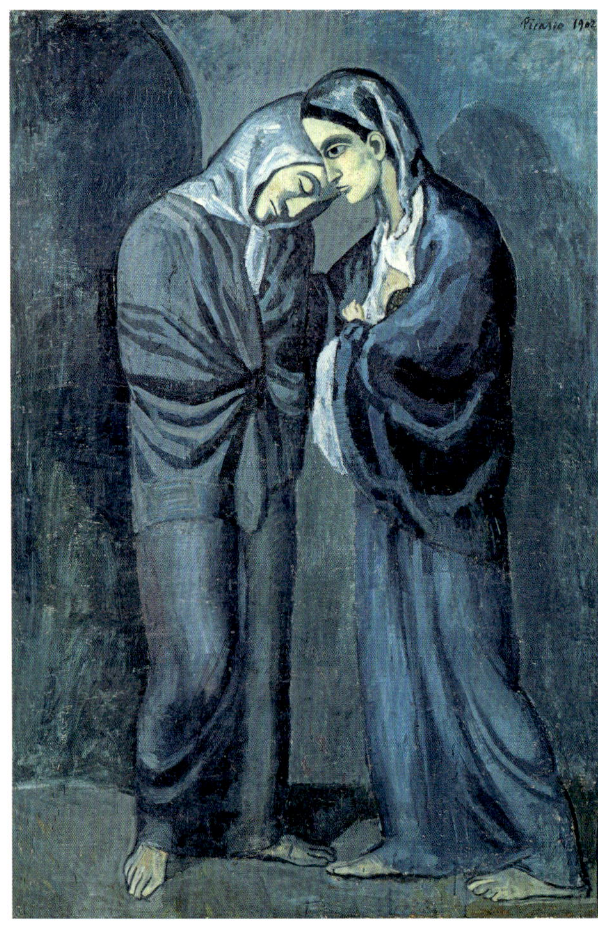

[Fig. 3] Pablo Picasso, *The Two Sisters,* 1902
Oil on panel, 152 × 100 cm
The State Hermitage Museum, Saint Petersburg

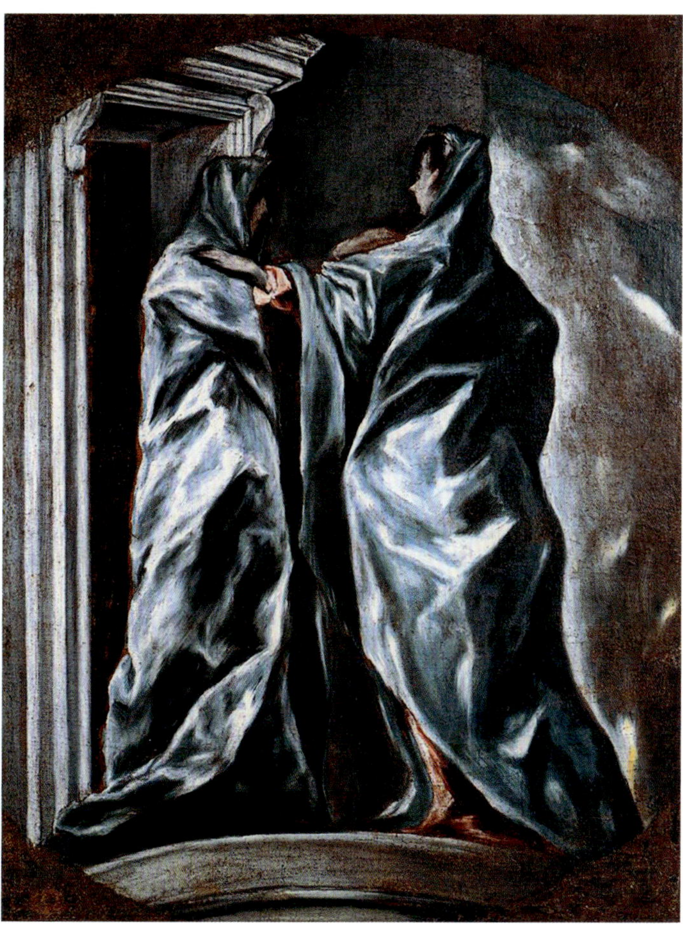

[Fig. 4] El Greco, *The Visitation,* 1609–13
Oil on canvas, 98 × 72 cm
Dumbarton Oaks, Washington, D.C.

recalled his impressions of the artist at the time, describing a studio packed with reproductions of El Greco's paintings:

> He returns from a trip to Spain laden with extraordinary portraits that are, truthfully, very curious. Yet this does not last; he is always running after an originality; and as he suddenly fell in love with El Greco, he placed photographs of the incredible paintings of this Master all around the walls of his room, he innovates the blue period.[13]

The Blue Period, with its symbolic, sentimental, almost monochromatic works filled with elongated, mannerist figures so reminiscent of El Greco, began in 1901 after a traumatic event: the suicide in February 1901 of Picasso's close friend Carles Casagemas. The twenty-year-old Catalan artist and poet shot himself in a café in Paris, despairing over his unrequited love for a model, Germaine Gargallo. Picasso was temporarily in Spain at the time, and when the news reached him, he was devastated. The two friends had studied together in Barcelona and later shared a Paris studio. That summer in Paris Picasso began work on a depiction of his friend's funeral, *Evocation (The Burial of Casagemas)* (cat. 17). His large, elongated monochrome painting bore the clear influence of El Greco's *Burial of the Count of Orgaz,* which he had seen that February in Toledo.[14] He drew on its compositional device of dividing his canvas into two separate realms, the earthly from the heavenly, but deliberately ignored its religious content. Under a cloudy sky with no depth, reminiscent of El Greco, Picasso captured the purity and radical approach of the artist from Crete while inverting the religious aspect of the earlier work and replacing the concept of heaven with one of sexual pleasure and procreation.

Other paintings of the same period are almost literal reflections on El Greco. Picasso's 1902 composition *The Two Sisters* (fig. 3) is strikingly close to *The Visitation* of 1609 (fig. 4), a work painted some three hundred years earlier. This work distills El Greco's palette to a single chromatic range of gray and silvery blue, applied with such nuance that the monochrome becomes virtually polychrome. In tones ranging from purest white to deepest black, shapes are arranged in folds that are almost abstract. But while El Greco depicted a scene from scripture—the visit the pregnant Virgin Mary paid to her cousin Elizabeth, who was pregnant with the future

Saint John the Baptist—Picasso described his
subjects as "a Saint-Lazare whore and a mother"
in a letter to his friend Max Jacob of July 1902.[15]
Picasso's women, shown in profile, stand arm in
arm and greet each other, enveloped in chiaro-
scuro infused with mystical restraint. The painter
appropriates the main elements of El Greco's
work but makes them blasphemous—"as God
does nothing to help fallen women in distress,"
as Picasso's friend and biographer Pierre Daix
put it.[16] El Greco's *Visitation* was hidden away
in Toledo's convent of Santa Clara de Daimiel
until the late 1920s or early 1930s, when the
nuns there sold it to the art dealer Arthur Byne.[17]
Picasso had to have seen the painting on his trip
to Toledo in February 1901.

In 1904 Picasso made the momentous decision to leave Spain and return to Paris, this
time permanently. The move from Barcelona
introduced a more colorful palette into his work,
with an abundance of pinks and oranges, and
the influence of El Greco receded somewhat.
Yet glimpses are present in works such as
Family of Acrobats with Monkey (1905), today in
the Gothenburg Museum of Art, which recalls
numerous depictions of the Holy Family by
El Greco. In 1905, Picasso visited the Salon
d'Automme, where he was profoundly moved
by encounters not only with Jean-Auguste-
Dominique Ingres, whose *Turkish Bath* (1862)
was on public view for the first time, but also
with the sensational new works of the Fauves,
particularly Henri Matisse and André Derain.
In this defining experience, he realized that
Impressionism and Symbolism were coming to
an end and the old mimetic link between art and
nature appeared to have been broken. Fauvism
and Expressionism called for a radical change
from the prevailing naturalism, and art increasingly sought to reflect an inner world of spiritual
concerns. Picasso readily took up the challenge.

*Furthermore, it is the realisation that counts. From this point
of view, it is true that Cubism is Spanish in origin, and it was
I who invented Cubism. We should look for Spanish influence
in Cézanne. . . . Observe El Greco's influence on him. A
Venetian painter but he is a Cubist in construction.*
    —Pablo Picasso[18]

In the winter of 1906–07, Picasso began work
on his first Cubist painting—a new, large canvas almost square in format: 243.9 by 233.7

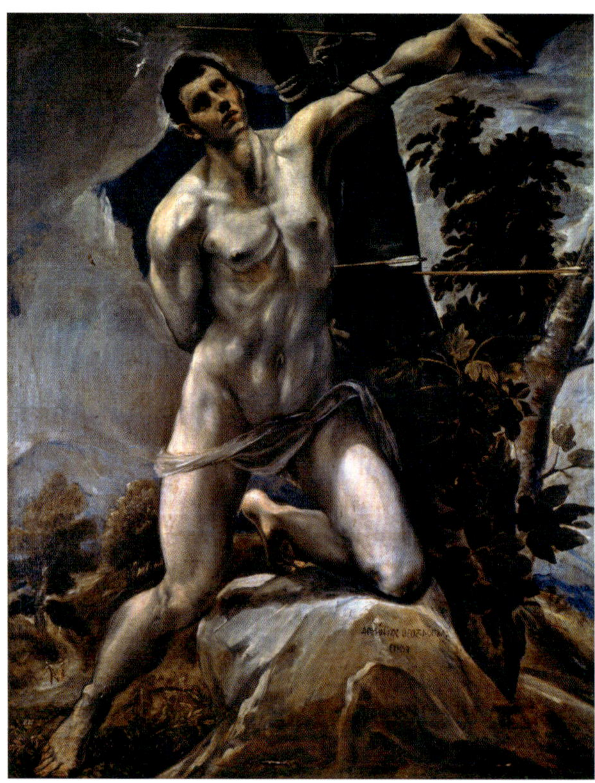

[Fig.5] El Greco, *The Martyrdom of Saint Sebastian,* 1576–79
Oil on canvas, 191 × 152 cm
Sacristy of the Cathedral, Palencia, Spain

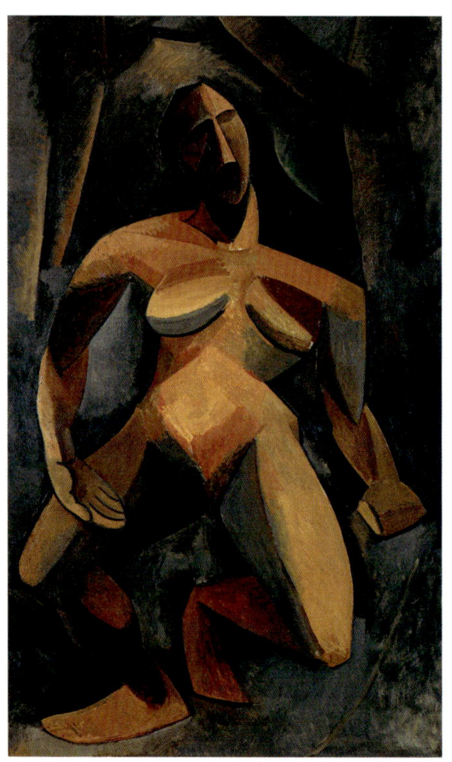

[Fig.6] Pablo Picasso, *Dryad,* 1908
Oil on canvas, 185 × 108 cm
The State Hermitage Museum, Saint Petersburg

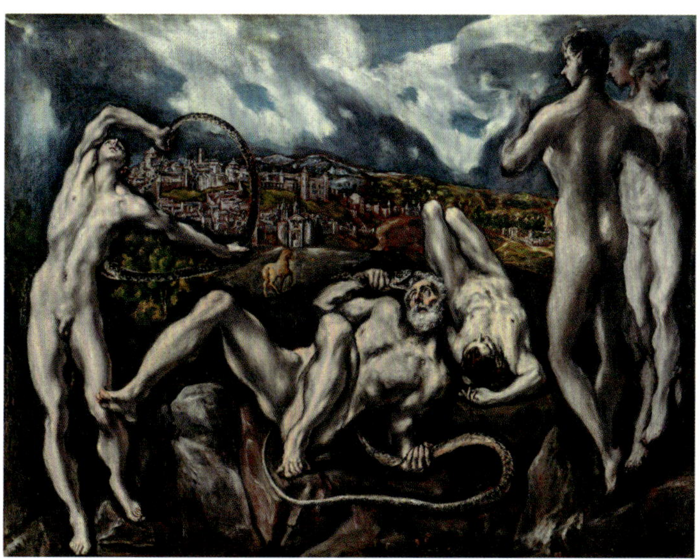

[Fig.7] El Greco, *Laocoön,* ca. 1610–14
Oil on canvas, 137.5 × 172.5 cm
National Gallery of Art, Washington, D.C., Samuel H. Kress Collection

centimeters. Making a permanent break from the relentless paradigm of naturalist art, *Les Demoiselles d'Avignon* (1907; fig. p. 62) reflects his fascination with Iberian art and his response to the work of Cézanne, one of the artists to best incorporate and transmit El Greco's influence. Cézanne imbued his compositions with a similar pictorial quality, vindicating the intrinsic value of painting, indifferent to any real representation of objects. Picasso was surely familiar with the three monumental versions of *The Bathers* that engaged Cézanne until his death in 1906. These are now at the Kunstmuseum in Basel, Philadelphia, and London, respectively. (See also fig. p. 73.) In these works all the elements are on a single plane, and the insistence on creating volume with color heralds, with El Greco's blessing, the arrival of Cubism (figs. 5, 6).

The affinity of *Les Demoiselles d'Avignon* to the work of El Greco—especially to *The Vision of Saint John*, known then as *The Opening of the Fifth Seal* (fig. p. 67)—is so striking (not just at a visual level but also "spiritually and psychologically," as John Golding noted) that it is hard to imagine Picasso did not have it mind.[19] Indeed, he knew the work, for by 1906 it was hanging in the Paris home of his acquaintance Ignacio Zuloaga, who had recently purchased it in Spain.[20] The *Demoiselles*—"the first modern art painting," as Pierre Daix called it—borrowed more from it than just the idea of the square canvas.[21] In *The Vision of Saint John,* the horizon dissolves and is replaced by swirling forms and spiritual bodies that break free from traditional composition and perspective. Nothing short of a radical challenge to the traditional ways of portraying the body in space, the painting proposed a path for Picasso toward the destruction of the perspective inherited from the Renaissance: discoloration, a cancellation of space, and a deliberate confusion of the plane.[22]

In the year he spent working on the canvas, Picasso produced hundreds of preliminary drawings and paintings (cats. 27, 28). These show that he originally conceived the figure on the left as a man, a medical student entering the brothel, and only later turned it into a fifth woman. Below the figures is a small arrangement of fruit, including the curved rind of a piece of watermelon. As Jonathan Brown has pointed out, one of the sketches places the crescent shape directly beneath the central figure, who "rises up

weightlessly against a fragmented blue sky . . .
reminiscent of one of the most familiar images of
Catholic Spain, the Immaculate Conception suspended over a half moon."[23] The blasphemy of
the brothel setting is exacerbated by demystifying
that most Spanish of all virgins, who—instead of
treading lightly on a moon (cat. 26) or trampling
the snake of mortal sin—hovers over a fleshy,
suggestive slice of watermelon.

The women emerge from brown, white, and
blue curtains in a room where the lack of depth
pushes their bodies toward the viewer. Reprising
El Greco's use of pictorial space, everything
in the work is on the same plane. In his essay
"Variations on El Greco," Aldous Huxley described a similar approach:

> On earth, as in heaven, there is hardly room to swing
> a cat. Moreover, unlike Tintoretto and the baroque
> artists of the seventeenth century, El Greco never
> hints at the boundlessness beyond the picture-frame.
> His compositions are centripetal, turned inwards
> on themselves. He is the painter of movement in a
> narrow room, of agitation in prison. This effect of
> confinement is enhanced by the almost complete
> absence from his paintings of a landscape back-
> ground. The whole picture-space is tightly packed
> with figures, human and divine; and where any chink
> is left between body and body, we are shown only
> a confining wall of cloud as opaque as earth, or of
> earth as fluidly plastic as clouds.[24]

In *The Vision of Saint John,* as in so many of his
works, El Greco portrayed the spiritual realm as
already present in the spirit of men, conveying
the *essence* of the world rather than imitating its
appearance. The world he created is based on a
vision so that, as Christian Zervos noted, it mattered little if a cloud happened to cut an angel in
two.[25] Compositionally, all the different elements
on the canvas claim the same value and are articulated in accordance with the pictorial forms and
construction.

The *Demoiselles* ushered in Picasso's Cubist
period, the first stage of which—Analytic
Cubism—focused on highlighting the two-
dimensionality of the canvas. Neither flat nor
three-dimensional, Picasso's subjects were broken down into geometric fragments that gradually accumulate, building up an image. In 1920,
Picasso's art dealer Daniel-Henry Kahnweiler
described the transformation thus:

> Much more important, however, was the decisive
> advance which set Cubism free from the language

previously used by painting. This occurred in
Cadaqués (in Spain, on the Mediterranean near the
French border) where Picasso spent his summer [in
1910]. Little satisfied, even after weeks of arduous
labor, he returned to Paris in the fall with his unfinished works. But he had taken the great step; he had
pierced the closed form."[26]

Picasso approached the portrayed form and its
place in space by ignoring the technique that had
been used since the Renaissance. Kahnweiler
continued:

> Instead of beginning from a supposed foreground
> and going on from there to give an illusion of depth
> by means of perspective, the artist begins from a
> definite and clearly defined background. Starting
> from this background the painter now works toward
> the front by a sort of scheme of forms in which each
> object's position is clearly indicated, both in relation
> to the definite background and to other objects.[27]

The final destination was the viewer. In contrast
with the traditional art experience, viewers now
had to reconstruct the image in their minds
using the elements on display. Picasso created an
illusion of relief and depth that relied less on perspective and more on shading—on the difference
between darkness and light. Solely concerned
with the intrinsic qualities of the painting itself,
rather than its ability to portray a subject, he
reduced his palette to an almost monochromatic
range, with a preference for browns, grays, and
creams, and did so with such intensity that it
made Clement Greenberg describe Analytic
Cubism as a sort of "orgy of shading."[28]

*Who would believe that Dominico Greco put his hand to
his paintings many times and retouched them over and
again to leave the colors unblended and distinct, and left
rough blotches [of paint] to affect virtuosity? I call this
working very hard for a poor result.*
—Francisco Pacheco[29]

The painter Francisco Pacheco (in addition to
being the teacher and father-in-law of Diego
Velázquez) authored an influential set of "lives"
of the Spanish painters. Tellingly, after making
a personal visit to El Greco's studio in 1611, he
used the term "crueles borrones" (cruel stains,
or rough blotches) to describe the myriad brushstrokes scattered across the surface of El Greco's
work. Instead of the polished finish of the central
Italian style that prized concise drawing and
strong lines, El Greco used a Venetian sketching

technique, in which layered patches of colored brushstrokes rather than line define the form and provide depth and luminosity. A precise, complex, and perfectly planned technique in which nothing is left to chance, it relies on an internal structure to add volume (see fig. 7). The compositional logic arises from the juxtaposition of colors to create a blurred, vague image in which the shading creates depth. El Greco used a light layer of orange-reddish primer as a medium tone that remained visible in certain parts of the painting or became transparent under the subsequent application of color glazes. It was a key internal preparatory step for the structural coherence of his works, in which it is perfectly clear what lies under the volumes. As conservator Rafael Alonso Alonso puts it, "everything is explained in . . . loose and simple brushstrokes."[30]

He was singular in every way, and as extravagant as his paintings . . . which were capricious enough to bewilder anyone who was sufficiently well informed to ponder their extravagance . . . because the dissonance between his paintings is such that they do not appear to be by the same hand.
    —Jusepe Martínez, quoted by Manuel B. Cossío[31]

The words of Martínez (carefully spliced together by Cossío in his 1908 study) clearly reflect what many of El Greco's contemporaries found jarring about his painting: that it was "singular" and "extravagant," that there was "dissonance" between his works. Picasso, on the other hand, was praised for many of the same traits. He "is justly accused," wrote Zervos, "of that extreme variety of mind from which everyone has benefited."[32] Singularity and stylistic diversity and a wide range of styles are traits that El Greco and Picasso shared. And those traits—which their contemporaries recognized, albeit in different ways—were ultimately "for everyone's benefit."

In Picasso's case, this plurality of styles set him free as he progressed. As the German critic Carl Einstein wrote, Picasso, "had to realize that a style is ultimately a prejudice, a limitation, and every artwork a fragment, one may not succumb to the style of a single work, the challenge is always to seek the new, not to idolize fetishes. Otherwise art becomes cowardice, a prison, rather than a path to revolt and to freedom."[33] In El Greco's case, his unique way of painting came at least in part from having experienced a wide variety of styles, or *manners,* beginning with his early training as a painter of icons in Crete to the time he spent in Venice and even Rome, though he did not stay there long. In Spain, after his brief period at El Escorial, he found his place in Toledo where,

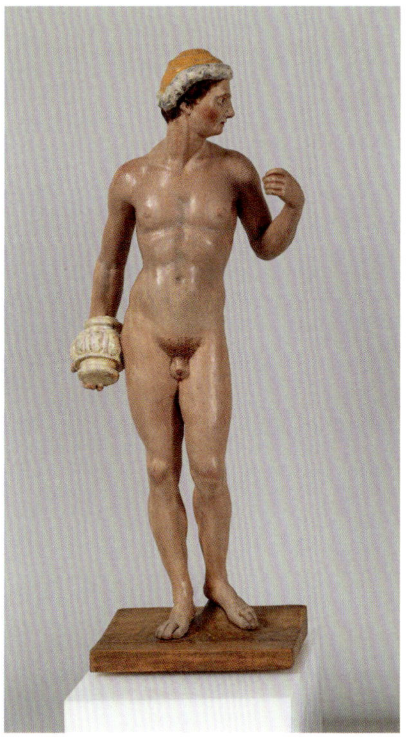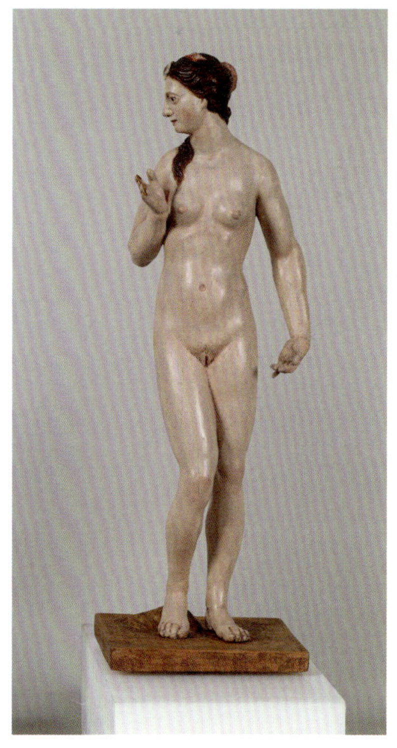

[Fig. 8] El Greco, *Epimetheus,* ca. 1600–10, and *Pandora,* ca. 1600–10
Wood (polychrome), height: ca. 43 cm each
Museo Nacional del Prado, Madrid

through a constant exploration of different
schools, he was able to develop his own multifaceted, flamboyant style.

Pacheco had been the first to describe El
Greco as someone "who was singular in every
way, as was his painting." Upon visiting the
artist's studio, he was greatly surprised to find a
cupboard full of clay models.[34] Like archetypes,
these sculptural models allowed El Greco to
reproduce and study different effects in his
pictorial compositions; he would even hang them
from the ceiling to examine their foreshortened
perspective. He very likely came to this practice
in Venice, where Titian and Tintoretto made
regular use of it. El Greco also used sculpture
when creating architectural models; these were
probably based on versions made in advance
from clay or some other material that he would
then carve in wood and include in the altarpieces
he designed (fig. 8).

Little more than three hundred years later, the
photographer Brassaï was similarly astonished
when he discovered that Picasso had been quietly
working on sculpture in Boisgeloup. He had met
Picasso in December 1932 when he was commissioned to photograph in the artist's ateliers
in Paris and Boisgeloup for *Minotaure,* the new
Surrealist newspaper. It was the beginning of

a long professional relationship that developed
into a friendship.[35] Brassaï recounts a nighttime
visit to the studio, where in the glow of the head-
lights of Picasso's Hispano Suiza, he had his first
glimpse in a large stall of "the dazzling whiteness
of an entire people of sculptures."[36] (See fig. 9.)

It is telling that both Picasso and El Greco
kept a space next to their studios to collect what
no doubt contributed great meaning to their
works. In the case of Picasso, his sculptural vision
largely shaped his pictorial production, and
vice versa. (Some artists such as Julio González
even considered his approach to art to be closer
to that of a sculptor than a painter.[37]) El Greco
included wooden figures in the architecture of
his altarpieces, but he also used small models
made of plaster, clay, and wax in order to study
poses and light effects for his paintings and thus
infuse his paintings with a sculptural vision. Or
was it his painting that influenced his sculptures?
Both forms of inspiration seem to have applied,
moving easily between the plane of his canvas
and three-dimensional space.

In Pacheco's account of visiting the master's
workshop, El Greco's son Jorge Manuel, on the
instructions of his old and weary father, brought
their visitor to a sort of storage annex, a building
next to their apartments. Here Pacheco reported

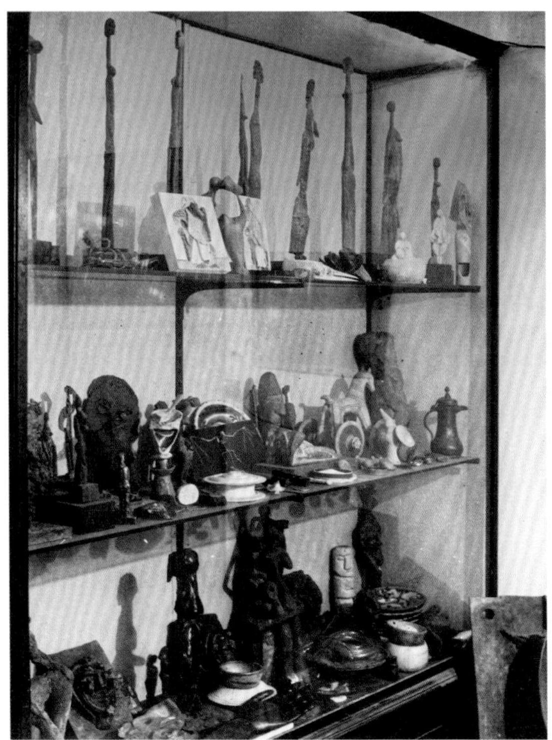

[Fig. 9] Brassaï
Vitrine with sculptures and other objects at
the studio on rue des Grands-Augustins, Paris,
October 25, 1943 (printed ca. 1950)
Silver gelatin print, 23.5 × 17.5 cm
Musée national Picasso, Paris

seeing a number of small paintings (none larger
than about three feet, he said) and discovered—
again to his surprise—that these were reproductions of all the works that El Greco had painted
to date. By arranging the various versions in
sequence in his studio, El Greco could draw on
them as compositional models for related works.
A posthumous studio inventory includes a count
of two hundred prints and 150 drawings.[38] These,
too, seem to have served as a starting point for El
Greco's own compositions, which he could then
modify as needed and adapt to suit his style and
objective.

Indeed, nearly all of El Greco's major works
exist in multiple versions—almost in anticipation
of Andy Warhol's Factory, where repetition and
serial work were part of the artist's idiosyncratic
vision.[39] One well-known example of El Greco
producing multiple works is *The Agony in the
Garden,* a version of which is housed in Santa
Maria la Mayor in Andujar (1600; cat. 19). He
approached this subject in two series of paintings
that differed in terms of format and composition.
Picasso relied on a similar method, often producing multiple variations on a single theme in the
apparent hope of exhausting every possibility the
painting's object or subject might have to offer.

Another of El Greco's recurring motifs is
Christ Driving the Traders from the Temple, and
its multiple versions shed light on the nature
of his transformation.[40] The differences between the versions can be seen mainly in their
architectural backgrounds. In the final version
(1610–14)—painted in the last years of his life
and now in Madrid (cat. 56)—El Greco moved
the action from the temple's portico to the interior sanctuary, shrinking the space and bringing
the main figures into the foreground. It is an
almost unreal, phantasmagorical scene, lit by
the glistening, gleaming light that characterizes
his final works. An architectural niche in the
background corresponds with a real building, the
Iglesia de la Caridad in Illescas. The painting's
exaggerated, elongated architectural backdrop in
grisaille stands out against a palette that includes
carmines, yellows, lead grays, liquid blues, and
ochres in the lower portion of the painting. Any
reference to perspective has been suppressed,
and coloring is limited to strong flashes of
light. Pure colors are intensified thanks to their
proximity to black and white, a technique that
El Greco used often, for example in the *Pietá*

of 1581 (in the Stavros Niarchos Collection in
Paris), where he defines the monochromatic
figure of Christ with a strong black contour,
separating it from its surroundings.

Picasso used a similar technique in 1930
when he painted *Crucifixion* (cat. 57), a work
seldom exhibited in his lifetime because he kept
it in his personal collection until his death. The
figures are shaped with contrasting forms that
differ in terms of color and size or even their
linear or curved brushstroke. Longinus, presented in mannerist perspective, appears as a tiny
figure on a horse, stabbing a minuscule lance
into the central figure of Christ, who fills the full
height of the painting. The austere black and
white of Christ silences the colors around, and
the lack of shading flattens the crucified figure
and pushes it forward to separate it starkly from
its surroundings.

In *Saint Martin and the Beggar* (cat. 63)—
one of El Greco's first compositions to include
a landscape—the figure on horseback is not
minuscule but heroic. That he painted five
versions of the work testifies to its popularity.
The work presents a young, refined nobleman
on a splendid white Arabian horse from a low
viewpoint that gives the figures monumentali-
ty. Far in the distance is the recognizable Tagus
River landscape, finely depicted, with Toledo's
distinctive Alcántara bridge. It is the same landscape of the Saint Sebastian in the Prado and
of the Metropolitan Museum's *View of Toledo*
(fig. p. 32), produced in the last years of his
life. The different versions of the *View of Toledo*
constitute his only full foray into the genre of
landscape. El Greco took an interpretative rather
than a literal approach to the subject, moving
the buildings as he saw fit in order to capture the
essence of the city rather than render it realisti-
cally. The heavy sky heralds a violent storm, and
Toledo is illuminated by a flash of lightning.

Picasso, too, produced only one pure landscape, which he painted in Vallauris on December 22, 1950. *Paysage d'hiver, Vallauris* (Winter
Landscape, Vallauris; cat. 64) conveys the tem-
porary death of nature: a bleak landscape of bare
trees whose twisted, skeletal branches and trunks
appear tormented. He loaned the painting for a
few months to Matisse, who gave it pride of place
over the mantle in his house in Cimiez. Though
Matisse wanted to keep the painting, Picasso did
not consent to an exchange.

The modern idea of the artist was born in the Italian Renaissance, as painters, architects, and sculptors began to lay claim to a social status that transcended the modest place of artisans and craftsman. El Greco was extremely invested in this redefinition of the visual arts. Though financial troubles plagued him throughout his career, he wanted to be considered a gentleman, an artist, and a man of learning. A portrait he painted of his son, Jorge Manuel, around 1603 fully embodies this idea of the gentleman artist (fig. 10). In 1950 Picasso produced his own version of the work—*Portrait of a Painter (After El Greco)* (fig. 11)—borrowing the Old Master's warm browns and ochres to portray a typical gentleman of the Spanish Golden Age. In El Greco's painting, Jorge Manuel's elegant garments signal that he is a refined member of the upper classes, while the proud display of brushes and palette underline the idea of painting as a noble profession. An intense self-portrait Picasso made some three hundred years later, in 1906, also shows the young artist holding a palette in his left hand but wearing a simple work shirt (cat. 25). The conspicuous absence of brush near the palette suggests that, for Picasso, painting is a mental rather than a manual process. "Painting's universal nature makes it speculative," El Greco had said of painting—thereby elevating it to a speculative or cognitive process comparable to philosophy.[42] In Toledo El Greco spent time mainly with scholars and poets, including Luis de Góngora, Hortensio Félix Paravincino, and Jose de Valdivieso. In this he was much like Picasso, who preferred the company of writers and poets over painters. Max Jacob, Alfred Jarry, André Salmon, Pierre Reverdy, Maurice Raynal, and Guillaume Apollinaire numbered among his companions.

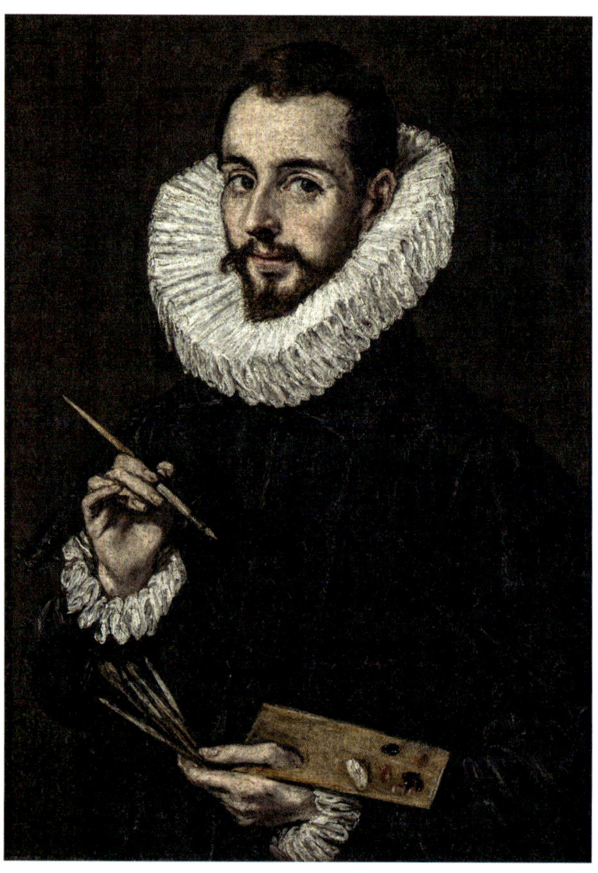

[Fig. 10] El Greco, *Portrait of a Painter (Jorge Manuel Theotocopuli),* 1597–1603
Oil on canvas, 74 × 50.5 cm
Museo de Bellas Artes, Sevilla

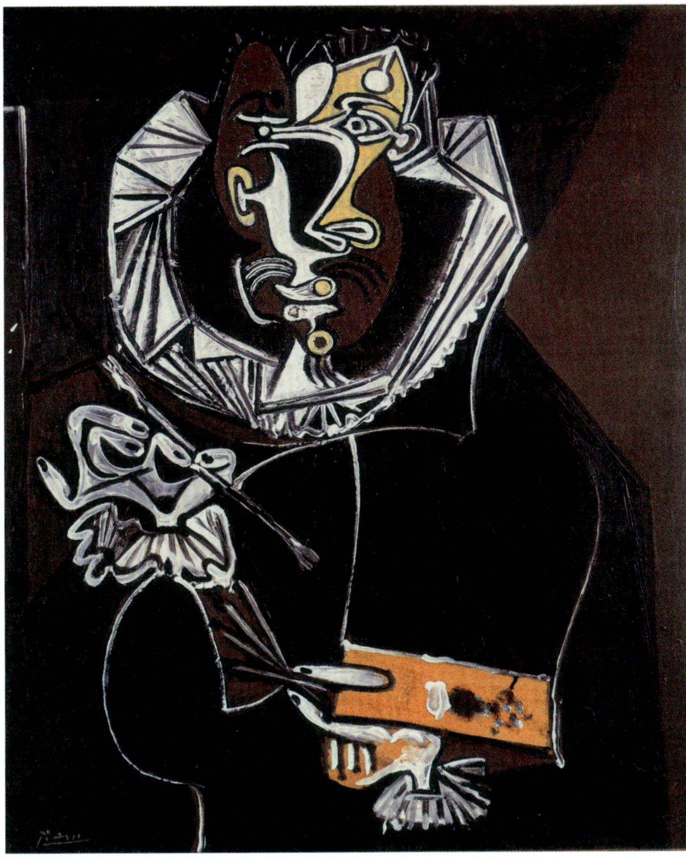

[Fig. 11] Pablo Picasso, *Portrait of a Painter (after El Greco)*
Vallauris, February 22, 1950
Oil on panel, 100.5 × 91 cm
Collection of Angela Rosengart, Lucerne

In his final years, El Greco created several pictorial ensembles known as *Apostolados*—"Apostle groups"—that included individual images of the twelve apostles and an image of Christ the Savior. Together with his workshop he completed at least six such groups, each showing a figure at half-length with his particular attribute, looking either to the right or to the left, and Christ looking straight at the viewer. Dressed in brightly colored cloaks and tunics, the apostles are set against neutral, dark backgrounds devoid of specific spatial references. The emphasis is on style over features, with the figures frontally illuminated in a bright light that falls on their faces and attributes. El Greco winnowed these canvases down to the essential, focusing attention on the expressions of his subjects—their looks, gestures, and especially their hands. Compared to the apostles of conventional depictions, who quietly carry their symbols, cloaks, or books, El Greco's apostles have expressive hands. José Álvarez Lopera captured it perfectly when he described them as "full of energy and quite massive but, above all, lost in thought, oblivious to everything." The group is "an expression of a particular collective mood. Seen on their own, these images lose some of their intensity. Each one draws part of its power from its relationship to the others, which multiplies their expressive qualities."[44]

The complete ensemble in the collection of the Museo del Greco in Toledo is considered the best *Apostolado* of them all. Painted in the master's own hand, with minimal input from his studio assistants, the set of thirteen paintings is rhythmically composed, marked by unsurpassed dynamism. It is also unique in that it is the only extant *Apostolado* to contain a *Saint Bartholomew* (cat. 44). (In all the other series, El Greco substituted Saint Luke, who although he was not one of the original apostles, was the patron saint of painters.) Saint Bartholomew faces left, his torso turned gently to the right. The geometric folds in his cloak are practically Cubist, revealing the structure of this marvelous, monochrome, almost abstract, painting. The similarity to Picasso's Cubist portraits across a chasm of three centuries is astonishing. El Greco's free, almost spontaneous brushstrokes are reminiscent of what Deleuze wrote of El Greco:

> Thus, in themselves, [the figures] no longer have to do with anything but "sensations"—celestial,

infernal, or terrestrial sensations. Everything is made
to pass through the code; the religious sentiment is
painted in all the colors of the world. One must not
say, "If God does not exist, everything is permitted."
It is just the opposite. For with God, everything is
permitted. It is with God that everything is permitted, not only morally, since acts of violence and infa-
mies always find a holy justification, but aesthetically,
in a much more important manner, because the
divine Figures are wrought by a free creative work,
by a fantasy in which everything is permitted.[45]

In 1955, Picasso told his dealer Kahnweiler
that he especially admired El Greco's portraits
(fig. 12).[46] Defined by a typically Spanish aus-
terity, El Greco's late portraits are marked by
continence and distance while also retaining a
Venetian succulence where the depths of the
blacks and the rich variety of whites contrast
radically with the neutral background. El Greco's
portraits showed the gentlemen of Toledo in a
way that distinguished them from the detached,
idealized, and conventional court portraits of
his day. His sitters express personal feelings. El
Greco looked at his sitters closely, analytically,
probing deeply in order to shed light on their
personalities. He bestowed a new typology on the
Spanish School—the psychological portrait—
and he did so, in part, by means of an important
aesthetic resource: the asymmetrical face. The
eyes, placed at different levels, accentuate imme-
diacy and truth, forging a new path in realism,
one that reached Picasso by way of Velázquez
and the seventeenth-century Spanish Masters.
At times, Picasso takes this facial asymmetry to
an extreme, transforming this device into a de-
formation that verges on monstrosity (cat. 68).

You are what you keep.
  —Pablo Picasso

Velázquez died unexpectedly at the age of sixty-
one, in 1660 before he had time to clear his
studio or organize his things. Alongside minor
works by Titian, Jacapo Bassano, and Ribera,
three magnificent portraits by El Greco were
found stored in the painter's rooms. All are now
in the Prado: *Portrait of a Doctor* (1582–85), *An
Elderly Gentleman* (1587–1600; cat. 58), and *Saint
Thomas* (1608–14). Velázquez had learned how to
work color from El Greco, had drawn on his im-
pressionistic exuberance, and had embraced the
psychological aspect of his portraits. If Velázquez

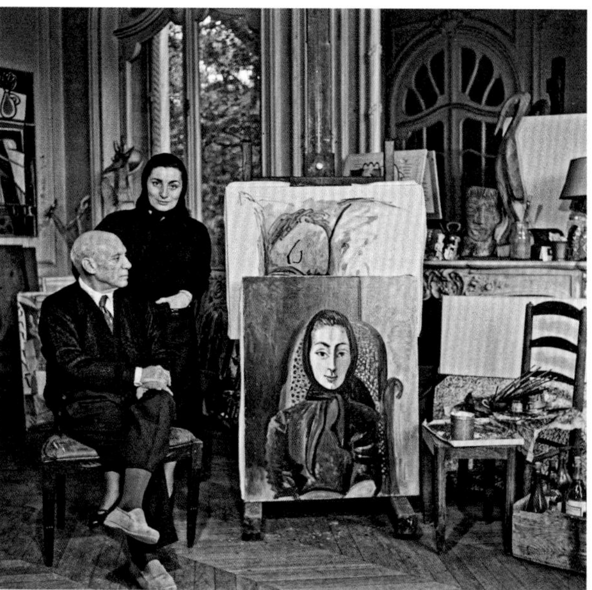

[Fig. 12] Edward Quinn
Pablo and Jacqueline Picasso with the painting
*Portrait de Jacqueline au rocking-chair et à la
mantille noire*, La Californie, Cannes 1955

admired Venetian painting, he came to it through El Greco. His nature as a painter, like El Greco's, was essentially analytical and anti-decorative. As Christian Zervos noted when comparing the work of the younger to the older master:

> Simply put, the work of these two men offers only contrasts. In Velázquez, an important effort, but one limited in its scope by the embrace of the physical; in El Greco, a propensity to elevate transcendent states of consciousness. By thinking deeply about himself, El Greco also worked for the future. He bequeathed to [Velázquez] not systems, methods, recommendations or instructions [which would have] deprived him of all possible initiative, but rather an apprenticeship in freedom and the strength to emancipate himself from conventional views of habit.[47]

And in this manner El Greco opened the door to modern art.

In the 1950s and early 1960s, Picasso appears to have leaned more toward Velázquez, painting at least forty-four variations of *Las Meninas*. In the 1960s, Kahnweiler told Brassaï, "Picasso has recovered somewhat from his great passion for El Greco. . . . He still likes certain portraits . . . but likes his compositions much less."[48] But nothing in Picasso is obvious, and his statements can rarely be taken as maxims. Shortly afterward, in a 1966 conversation with the Argentine journalist Roberto Otero, Picasso turned the tables once again: "What does everybody see in Velázquez these days? I prefer El Greco a thousand times more, he was really a painter!"[49]

A year later, when he was eighty-six, recovering from an operation, and inexorably drawing closer to death, Picasso painted *The Musketeer* (cat. 66). He dated the front of this painting in his usual manner—"Mougins, 28.3.67"—but placed a remarkable signature on the back of the painting: "Domenico Theotocopulos van Rijn da Silva"—in other words, El Greco (Domenikos Theotokopoulos), Rembrandt (van Rijn), and Diego Rodríguez (de Silva) y Velázquez. Here were the lesser-known names of three painters so famous that they were typically identified by one name alone. (And it is no coincidence that Picasso's first surname, Ruiz, has also been forgotten over time.) There was of course no need to meld his own name onto this extraordinary tribute, no need to announce in any obvious way that Picasso considered himself to be on par with these three masters. And yet he was clearly placing himself "squarely within the tradition to which he felt he belonged throughout his life."[50]

El Greco more often than not signed his paintings, usually in the lower right-hand corner. Often he would place his name on a piece of paper, on a book, a step . . . and though the signature evolved over time, he always signed his paintings with his full birth name in Greek letters. A year before leaving Rome for Spain, the young El Greco painted a version of *Christ Driving the Money Changers from the Temple* (fig. p. 37). In the bottom right-hand corner, instead of his signature, he included four portraits—of Titian, Michelangelo, Clovio, and Raphael—a visual signature to secure his place among the immortals. In *The Muskeeter*, Picasso's own tribute to the Old Masters, he infused the work with an immediate urgency full of impetuous, hurried, material, sensual, and quick brushstrokes that invoked his inheritance and yet seemed to implore time to hold still.

1 From an interview with Marius de Zayas (1923). A translation approved by Picasso was published as "Picasso Speaks," *The Arts* (May 1923), excerpted in Herschel B. Chipp, *Theories of Modern Art* (Berkeley and Los Angeles, 1984), p. 264. Unless otherwise noted, all translations from the Spanish are by Tony Beckwith.

2 "El museo de pinturas es hermoso: Velázquez de primera; de El Greco unas cabezas magníficas; Murillo, no me convence en todos sus cuadros; Tiziano tiene una Dolorosa muy buena; Van Dick unos retratos y un Prendimiento de Jesús, de órdago; Rubens tiene un cuadro (La serpiente de fuego) que es un prodigio; Teniers unos cuadros pequeños muy buenos, de borrachos, ahora no recuerdo más." Picasso to Joaquim Bas, November 3, 1897, Fundació Palau, Caldes d'Estrach, partially translated in *Pablo Picasso Retrospective*, ed. William Rubin, exh. cat. Museum of Modern Art, New York (Boston, 1980), p. 18.

3 Diego Pro, *Conversaciones con Bernareggi* (Tucumán, 1949), p. 21.

4 Degas bought *Saint Dominic in Prayer* (1600–10) from Astruc in 1896; it is now in the Boston Museum of Fine Arts. His other El Greco, *Saint Ildefonsus* (1603–05) (similar to cat. 36), was purchased at the estate sale of the celebrated painter Jean-François Millet, who kept it above his bed until his death; that painting is now in the National Gallery of Art in Washington DC.

5 In 1912 Barrès published his influential book *Greco ou Le secret de Tolède* (Paris, 1912).

6 Julius Meier-Graefe, *Spanish Journey*, trans. J. Holroyd-Reece (New York, 1926) p. 128.

7 Felipe Cossío Del Pomar, *Con los Buscadores del Camino* (Madrid, 1932), p. 109, quoted in Dore Ashton, *Picasso on Art* (Boston, 1988), p. 165.

8 El Greco wrote toward the end of his life: "Michelangelo did not know how to paint portraits or represent hair or imitate human fleshtones. . . . And as for imitating colors as they appear to the eye, it cannot be denied that this was a fault with him." Quoted in Xavier de Salas, *Miguel Angel y El Greco* (Madrid, 1967), p. 38, translated in Jonathan Brown, "El Greco and Toledo," in *El Greco of Toledo*, ed. Jonathan Brown, exh. cat. Museo del Prado, Madrid, et al. (Boston, 1982), p. 88.

9 Roberto Otero, *Forever Picasso: An Intimate Look at his Last Years*, trans. Elaine Kerrigan (New York, 1974), pp. 189–90.

10 Jonathan Brown and Richard L. Kagan, "View of Toledo," in *Figures of Thought: El Greco as Interpreter of History, Tradition, and Ideas*, ed. Jonathan Brown (Washington, DC, 1982), pp. 18–vii.

11 Brown 1982 (see note 8).

12 Brassaï, *Conversations with Picasso*, trans. Jane Mary Todd (Chicago and London, 1999), p. 199. Originally published as *Conversations avec Picasso* (Paris, 1964).

13 Gustave Coquiot, *Cubistes, futuristes, passéistes: Essai sur la jeune peinture et la jeune sculpture* (Paris, 1914), pp. 147–48.

14 Picasso would later return twice to *The Burial of the Count of Orgaz*: in an illustrated poem (1957–59) and a homonymous "sacrilegious illustration" (1968).

15 Picasso to Max Jacob, July 13, 1902, reproduced in Jaime Sabartés, *Picasso Documents Iconographiques* (Geneva, 1954), p. 70, translated in Marilyn McCully, ed., *A Picasso Anthology: Documents, Criticism, Reminiscences* (Princeton, 1982), p. 38.

16 Pierre Daix, *Picasso* (Paris, 2007), p. 62.

17 José Álvarez Lopera, catalogue entry, in *Picasso Tradición y Vanguardia*, ed. Francisco Calvo Serraller and Carmen Giménez, exh. cat. Museo Nacional del Prado and Museo Nacional Centro de Arte Reina Sofia (Madrid, 2006); English edition, *Picasso: Tradition and Avant-Garde* (Madrid, 2006).

18 Picasso, as recalled by Romuald Dor de la Souchère, the first curator of the Musée Picasso, Antibes, in Romuald Dor de la Souchère, *Picasso in Antibes*, trans. W. J. Strachan (New York, 1960), p. 14.

19 The painting, *The Vision of Saint John* (1608–14), now hangs at the Metropolitan Museum in New York; it has also been called *The Fifth Seal of the Apocalypse*. See John Golding, "Les Demoiselles d'Avignon and the Exhibition of 1988," in *Picasso's Les Demoiselles d'Avignon*, ed. Christopher Green (Cambridge, 2001), pp. 15–30.

20 Zuloaga probably learned of the painting from the writer Pío Baroja and the painter Darío de Regoyos, who had seen it in 1905 in Cordoba, where it was on sale for 2,500 pesetas. Zuloaga later came with Auguste Rodin and Ivan Shchukin (brother to the great Russian collector Sergei Shchukin) and bought it for a thousand pesetas. Zuloaga would go on to become Franco's favorite artist, and though Picasso was seeing much of Zuloaga in his early Paris years, the friendship did not last.

21 The El Greco canvas was cut some time after its completion.

22 Francisco Calvo Serraller, "Picasso et L'école espagnole," in *Picasso et les Maîtres*, ed. Pierre Vallaud, exh. cat. Grand Palais, Paris, et al. (Paris, 2008), p. 64.

23 Jonathan Brown, *Picasso and the Spanish Tradition* (New Haven and London, 1996), p. 75. The sketch is in the collection of the Kunstmuseum Basel. (See cat. 27.)

24 Aldous Huxley, "Variations on El Greco," in *Themes and Variations*, rev. ed. (London, 1954), p. 181.

25 Christian Zervos, *Les Oeuvres du Greco en Espagne* (Paris, 1939), p. xlviii.

26 Daniel-Henry Kahnweiler, *The Rise of Cubism*, trans. Henry Aronson (New York, 1949), p. 10. Originally published as *Der Weg zum Kubismus* (Munich, 1920).

27 Ibid., p. 11.

28 "And then the Cubist pointed out that the illusion of relief and of depth depended much more importantly on shading than it did on perspective—differences of dark and light. And Analytic Cubism was one kind of orgy of shading, as it were, for its own sake." Clement Greenberg, *Homemade Esthetics: Observations on Art and Taste* (London, 2000), p. 126.

29 "Quién creerá que Dominico trajese sus pinturas muchas veces a la mano . . . para dar aquellos crueles borrones para afectar valentía? A esto llamo yo trabajar para ser pobre." Francisco Pacheco, *Arte de la pintura* (1649) (Madrid, 1990), p. 483; translations from Brown 1982 (see note 8), p. 132 and Elizabeth Gilmore Holt, ed., *A Documentary History of Art* (New York, 1958), vol. 2, p. 218.

30 Rafael Alonso Alonso, "El Greco Conservado: Las restauraciones y la técnica pictórica de las obras del Museo de El Greco," in *Domenikos Theotokopoulos 1900 El Greco*, exh. cat. Consejo Nacional para la Cultura y las Artes, Museo del Palacio de Bellas Artes (Mexico City, 2009), p. 86.

31 "Fue en tiso singular y de extravagante condición como sus pinturas . . . y éstas, tan caprichosas, que pondrían en confusión a cualquiera bien entendido para discurrir su extravagancia . . . porque son tan disonantes unas de otras, que no parecen ser de una misma mano." Jusepe Martínez, *Discursos practicables del Nobilisimo arte de la Pintura* (ca. 1675), quoted in Manuel B. Cossío, *El Greco* (Madrid, 1908), p. 478.

32 "Est justement accusé de cette extrême variété d'esprit dont tout le monde a bénéficié." Christian Zervos, "Lendemain d'une exposition," *Cahiers d'Art*, no. 6 (July 1926), p. 119.

33 Carl Einstein, "Pablo Picasso" (1931) in *Die Kunst des 20. Jahrhunderts*, 3rd ed. (Berlin, 1931), p. 113; included in Carl Einstein, *A Mythology of Forms: Selected Writings on Art*, ed. and trans. Charles Haxthausen (Chicago and London, 2019), p. 223.

34 The posthumous inventory of El Greco's property included some thirty figures of wax or clay and twenty of plaster—surely the ones Pacheco describes. There were also small, polychrome wooden figures such as the Christ in the Tabernacle at the Hospital de Tavera and the two beautiful carvings (of Epimetheus and Pandora) at the Prado (see figs. 8 and 9).

35 In fact, Picasso only allowed Brassaï to photograph his work in preparation for the book *Les Sculptures de Picasso* (1949).

36 Brassaï 1999 (see note 12), p. 16.

37 The sculptor Julio González went so far as to call Picasso a sculptor even when he was painting: "Picasso . . . Il peint toujours mais il ne pense qu'à la sculpture." (He is always painting but he thinks of nothing but sculpture.) In Julio Gonzalez, "Picasso sculpteur," *Cahiers d'Art*, nos. 6–7 (1936), p. 189.

38 Francisco de Borja de San Román y Fernández, *El Greco en Toledo o nuevas investigaciones acerca de la vida y obras de Dominico Theotocópuli* (Madrid, 1910), p. 195, cited in Brown 1982 (see note 8), p. 122.

39 On a visit to Toledo, Andy Warhol called El Greco "the god of painting." Quoted in Fernando Arrabal, *El Greco* (Madrid, 2018), p. 53.

40 These include *Christ Cleansing the Temple* (before 1570), at the National Gallery, Washington, DC; *Christ Driving the Money Changers from the Temple* (c. 1570–75), at the Minneapolis Institute of Art; *The Purification of the Temple* (ca. 1600) at the Frick Collection in New York; *Christ Driving the Traders from the Temple* (1600) at the National Gallery, London; and *La expulsión de los mercaderes* (1610–14) in the Church of San Ginés, Madrid.

41 Quoted in Arrabal 2018 (see note 39), p. 8.

42 "La pintura por ser tan universal se hace especulativa." Quoted in Fernando Marias Franco and Agustin Bustamante Garcia, *Las ideas artísticas de El Greco (comentarios a un texto inédito)* (Madrid, 1981), p. 151.

43 José Clemente Orozco, *An Autobiography* (Austin, Texas, 1962), p. 157.

44 José Álvarez Lopera, *El Greco: La obra esenciel* (Madrid, 1993), p. 212, quoted in Leticia Ruiz Gómez, "La galería de retratos del Greco: Los apostolados," in *El Greco: Los Apóstoles; Santos y "locos de Dios,"* exh. cat. Museo de Guadalajara and Antiguo Convento de la Merced, Ciudad Real (Toledo, 2014), p. 88.

45 Gilles Deleuze, *Francis Bacon: The Logic of Sensation*, trans. Daniel W. Smith (London and New York, 2003), pp. 9–10.

46 Daniel-Henry Kahnweiler, "Entretiens avec Picasso au sujet des Femmes d'Alger," *Aujourd'hui: Art et Architecture*, no. 4 (September 1955), pp. 12–13, excerpted in McCully 1982 (see note 15), p. 251.

47 Zervos 1939 (see note 25), p. lviii.

48 Brassaï 1999 (see note 12), p. 348.

49 Otero 1974 (see note 9), p. 80. See also Otero, *Recuerdo de Picasso* (Madrid, 1984), p. 32: "¿Qué tiene la gente con Velázquez últimamente? Yo prefiero a El Greco mil veces: ¡ése sí que era un pintor de verdad!"

50 Francisco Calvo Serraller, "Picasso frente a la historia," in Serraller and Giménez 2006 (see note 17), p. 62.

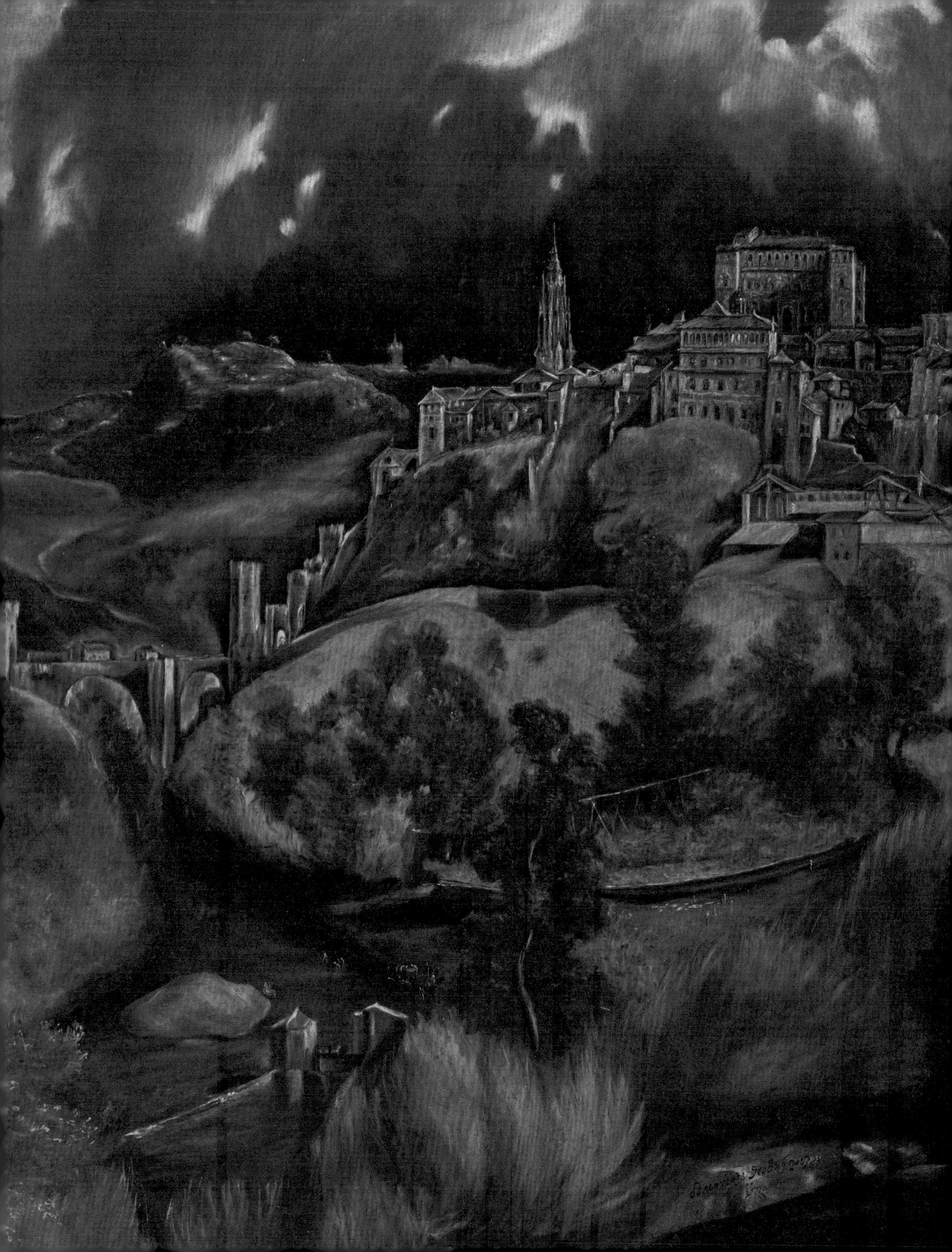

Gabriel Dette

El Greco: Fame, Disfavor, and Rediscovery

Crete gave him life and the painter's craft,
Toledo a better homeland, where through
Death he began to achieve eternal life.

These lines by the influential scholar, preacher, poet, and Trinitarian monk Fray Hortensio Félix Paravicino (1580–1633) conclude a sonnet on the death, on April 8, 1614, of Domenikos Theotokopoulos, better known as El Greco.[1] The highly educated Paravicino, a keen art lover, had met El Greco in the last years of the painter's life. This epitaph and three slightly earlier sonnets he devoted to him distill his impressions into a celebration of the artist and his work.[2] One of these addresses "Divino Griego" directly, expressing amazement over the portrait he painted of Paravicino in 1609; the likeness surpassed nature so utterly, he wrote, that the poet's soul could not decide whether the man or the portrait served as a fitter dwelling place.[3] That portrait hangs today in the Museum of Fine Arts, Boston, and has lost none of its charisma (fig. p. 63). More than four hundred years after its completion, it continues to work its magic, as Richard Shiff's essay in this exhibition catalogue attests (pp. 60–79).

Paravicino was not the only contemporary to pay tribute to El Greco and his art.[4] According to an account written in 1612 by Toledan historian and professor of theology Francisco de Pisa, El Greco had a wide circle of admirers. In the (un-published) follow-up volume to his *Historia o descripción de la imperial ciudad de Toledo,* Pisa names *The Burial of the Count of Orgaz*—completed for the parish church of Santo Tomé in 1588—as one of the best paintings in Spain; people came from far and wide to admire it, and even the Toledans never tired of looking at the picture, because you could always find something new in it and it was full of portraits of famous city dignitaries.[5] Like Paravicino, Pisa was hardly impartial—he too was having his likeness painted by El Greco at the time of writing[6]—and yet his words ring true today, for the painting is now widely acknowledged to be one of El Greco's masterpieces. It too has maintained its power over the centuries. Just how much the young Pablo Picasso was able to discover in such portraits, or in a painting like *The Burial of the Count of Orgaz,* is one of the topics Carmen Giménez takes up in her essay (pp. 14–31). (See also cats. 15–18.)

Paravicino's sonnet at the tomb of El Greco draws a direct line between the painter's artistic achievement and the "better homeland" he found in Toledo (fig. 1). It was here that—after spells in Venice and Rome, and a brief intermezzo in Madrid—the native of Crete would spend the second half of his life, although it had probably not been his original plan to stay. He came to the city some time in or before the summer of 1577, after being commissioned to paint *The Disrobing of Christ* for the cathedral sacristy and provide altarpieces for the monastery church of Santo Domingo el Antiguo.[7] For centuries a political and intellectual hub in Spain, Toledo

El Greco, *View of Toledo* (detail), ca. 1599–1600
Oil on canvas, 121.3 × 108.6 cm
The Metropolitan Museum of Art, New York, bequest of Mrs. H. O. Havemeyer, 1929

had lost its status as a royal seat a few years
before El Greco's arrival, when Philip II—king
of the Spanish Empire since 1556—moved the
royal court to Madrid and finally to the nearby
Escorial, where he started to build a new mon-
astery-palace complex in 1563. Toledo, however,
remained an important religious and intellectual
center, thanks to its powerful and influential
archdiocese and famous university; it continued
to prosper economically and offered a wide range
of opportunities for artists.[8]

In El Greco's three and a half decades in
Toledo, he rose to become a busy and acclaimed
artist, whose flourishing studio kept up with the
city's demands for paintings and was soon one of
the most prolific. His impressively varied port-
folio included large and lavish altarpieces after
his own design for churches and private chapels
in and around Toledo (cat. 50), several portraits
of members of the local elite (cats. 53, 58, 63),
and some small-scale devotional pictures and
images of saints (cats. 4, 38, 41). This versatility
allowed him to satisfy a broad range of clients,
from clerical institutions to scholars, dignitaries,
and private individuals, while at the same time
asserting himself with a degree of success on the
free art market.[9] Most of his clients and patrons
seem to have come from the intellectual milieu
of learned clerics, doctors of law, city dignitaries,
and members of the university; some of them
became friends.[10]

If this sounds like a classic success story of
uninterrupted and lasting glory, there was also
another side to El Greco's career. During his
time in Toledo, he also suffered some painful
setbacks, not least his rejection by Philip II,
from whom he had hoped to secure favor and
patronage. Moreover, despite a large number of
commissions, he was beset by long periods of
financial difficulties and often conducted lengthy
lawsuits against his clients, demanding adequate
remuneration and recognition. These did not
always end to his advantage and sometimes led
to long delays in payment.[11] Paravicino's praise
for El Greco was by no means universally shared
during his lifetime. And soon after his death,
his reputation became increasingly mixed until
eventually it was turned around altogether. The
barbs published by the Spanish art biographer
Antonio Palomino in 1724 would be echoed
for generations: that El Greco was prone to
indecent extravagance—"extravagancia"—and

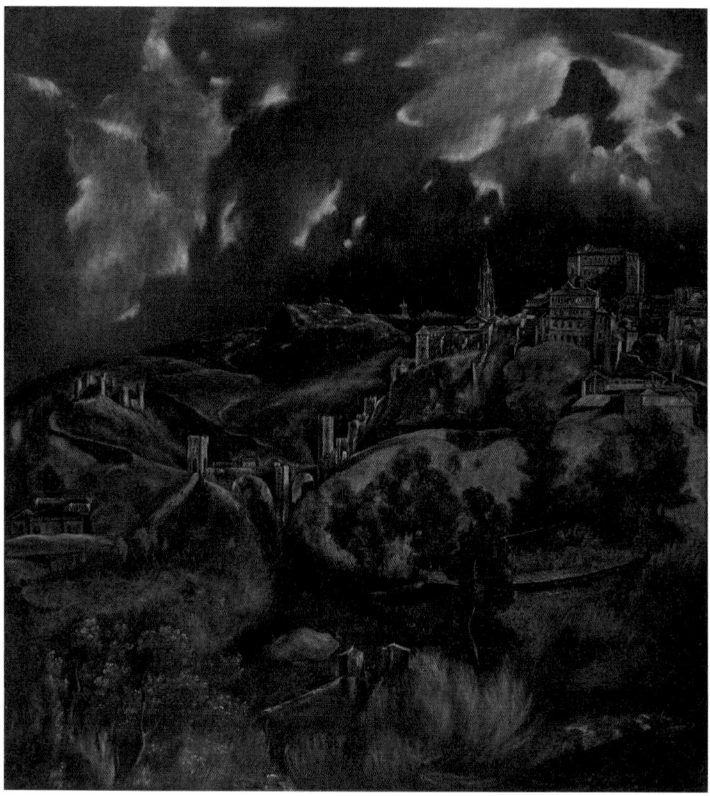

[Fig. 1] El Greco, *View of Toledo*, ca. 1599–1600
Oil on canvas, 121.3 × 108.6 cm
The Metropolitan Museum of Art, New York, bequest of Mrs. H. O. Havemeyer, 1929

that "whatever he did well, no one did better, and what he did badly, no one did worse."[12] As Javier Portús details in his chapter on El Greco's critical reception (pp. 46–59), El Greco's route into the canon of Spanish art—and, beyond that, into the collective consciousness of a broad and interested public—was long and circuitous; myths, speculation, misconception, and political appropriation persisted even into the twentieth century.[13]

Stations of a Life: From Crete to Toledo
Domenikos Theotokopoulos was born in 1541 in Crete, in the harbor city of Candia, today Heraklion.[14] Although Crete had been a colony of the Republic of Venice since the early thirteenth century, it had become a center of Greek post-Byzantine culture after the conquest of Constantinople in 1453 and the fall of the Byzantine Empire.[15] The young Domenikos, whose father was a tax collector for the Venetian authorities, trained as an icon painter in his homeland and must have completed his apprenticeship by September 1563, because a document from this time describes him as "maestro."[16] No details are known of his teachers or his first years of work, but his 1566 painting *The Passion of Christ* was appraised before a lottery for the

unusually high sum of seventy ducats, suggesting that the young painter was not only skilled but also appreciated.[17]

Icon painting on Crete tended to follow long-standing Byzantine Orthodox traditions, which involved as authentic a reproduction as possible of established sacred images and left little room for artistic innovation. But the island's close ties to—and cultural exchange with—Venice had also encouraged a degree of outside stimulus that led to the development of hybrid images.[18] This hybridity can also be seen in the early work of El Greco, whose interest in Italian motifs is evident from early in his career. *Saint Luke Painting the Virgin* (fig. 2)—signed "ΧΕΙΡ ΔΟΜΗΝΙΚΟ" (by the hand of Domenikos) and generally accepted as one of the artist's early works—is a good example. The composition features a kind of ingenious icon-within-an-icon; the Madonna and child being painted by Luke correspond closely with the traditional *Hodegetria* (a common Madonna type in Orthodox art), but the figures of the hovering angels and the artist-evangelist follow Italian models, which El Greco would have known from prints. The Italian influence is also evident in some of the furnishings and still-life elements such as the painting utensils on the footstool.[19]

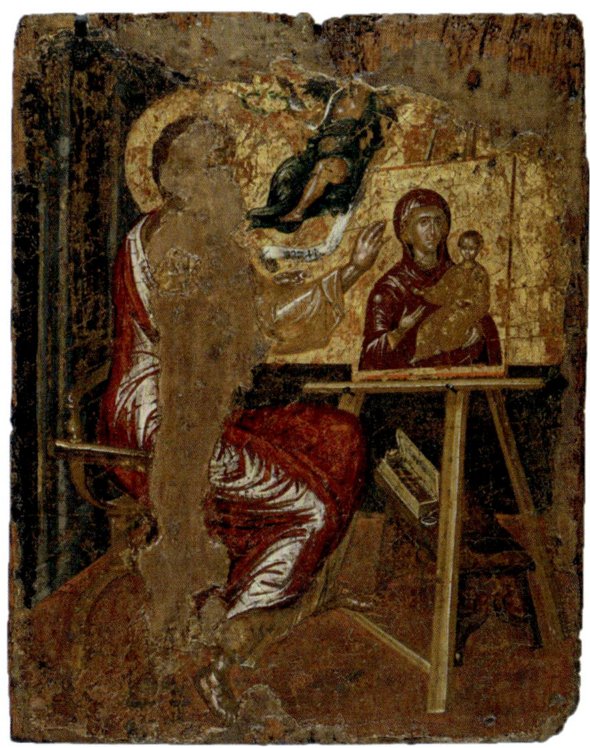

[Fig. 2] El Greco, *Saint Luke Painting the Virgin,* ca. 1560–67
Tempera and gold on canvas attached to pine panel, 41.6 × 33 cm
Benaki Museum, Athens

It was probably in the spring of 1567 that Domenikos left Crete for Italy, the cradle of this new approach to art. His first stop was Venice, where his stay was documented, for the first and only time, in the summer of 1568.[20] The prosperous republic, one of the most important centers of Renaissance painting alongside Florence and Rome, opened new horizons to him. Thanks to artists like Titian, Jacopo Bassano, Jacopo Tintoretto, and Paolo Veronese, there was a burgeoning art scene in Venice in the second half of the sixteenth century, and El Greco seems to have learned quickly and deeply from what he saw of these masters. Having come to Italy as a fully trained and established *maestro* himself, he now relearned his craft from scratch. Within only a few years, he had acquired a profound knowledge of oil painting, perspective, the proportions and depiction of figures, and the principles of composition and color.[21] It is unclear whether this process of assimilation took place at one of the city's big painting workshops, or whether El Greco taught himself by studying the vast quantity of art available to the public in Venice. In late 1570, newly arrived in Rome, he was introduced as a talented "disciple of Titian" in a 1570 letter of recommendation from the artist Giulio Clovio (1498–1578; fig. 3) to Clovio's employer Cardinal Alessandro Farnese, but scholars have disputed that designation.[22]

There is no dispute, however, that El Greco's intense engagement with the works of Titian, Tintoretto, and others made a strong impression on him and would continue to influence his work throughout his life. If we compare the Minneapolis version of *Christ Driving the Money Changers from the Temple,* probably painted soon after 1570 (fig. 4), with a work like *Saint Luke Painting the Virgin* from his time on Crete, the extent to which he had absorbed the art of late Renaissance Italy is immediately apparent. Even if he had not yet abandoned the smaller format familiar to him as an icon painter, the change is evident in the painting's luminous Venetian colors, its architectural backdrop receding into the perspectival distance, and the sophisticated poses of the figures, both clothed and nude. El Greco was also alluding explicitly to the tradition in which he now saw himself; the four august gentlemen grouped at the painting's lower right bear the unmistakable features of Titian, Michelangelo, Raphael, and—in a special nod to

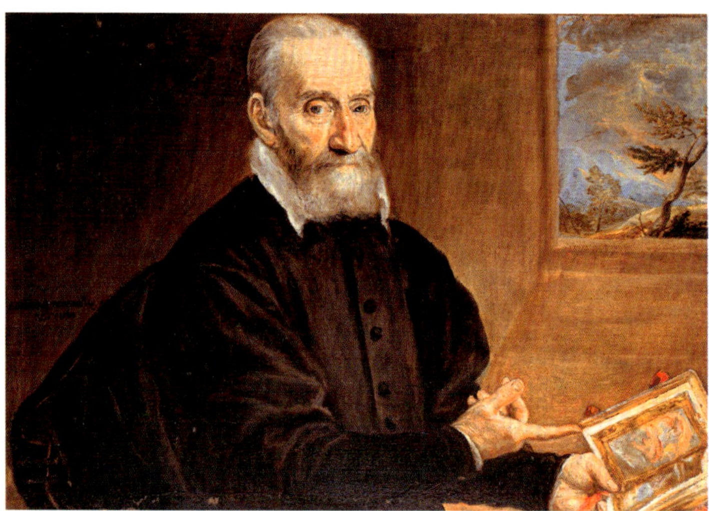

[Fig. 3] El Greco, *Portrait of Giulio Clovio,* ca. 1570–72
Oil on canvas, 58 × 86 cm
Museo e Gallerie Nazionali di Capodimonte, Naples

his own friend and patron—Clovio, whose miniatures were highly prized at the time.[23]

By the time El Greco painted this work, he had left Venice and joined the Roman court of Cardinal Farnese, a celebrated patron of the arts. We can only speculate about his reasons for the move. Perhaps he hoped for better access to commissions. (Venice was dominated by a small group of celebrity artists, while Rome after Michelangelo's death in 1564 offered a different playing field.) Quite probably he was also attracted by the prospect of complementing his grasp of Venetian art with first-hand knowledge of the latest achievements in Roman art.[24] He certainly made the most of his journey, stopping along the way to see artworks, among other places, in Padua, Vicenza, Mantua, Parma, Bologna, Florence, and Perugia. We see this from the marginal annotations in his own copy of the second edition of Giorgio Vasari's *Lives,* which he acquired later via the Roman artist Federico Zuccari. These contain many careful observations on Italian artists and paintings that he had clearly seen firsthand.[25]

El Greco's access to Palazzo Farnese and his growing friendship with Clovio provided ideal conditions for gaining a foothold as an artist in Rome. Clovio was well connected, and the rich and powerful Cardinal Farnese wielded considerable influence both at the papal court and in the city. El Greco found entry into a select circle of artists, writers, and educated patrons.[26] Those he met included the cardinal's librarian—the great humanist, antiquarian, and collector Fulvio Orsini—who later added paintings by El Greco to his collection. El Greco also came into contact with the large Spanish community in Rome.[27]

Just as he later would in Toledo, El Greco belonged to a flourishing group of intellectuals and art lovers, but he seems to have had little talent for making the most of such opportunities. Only two years after his arrival in Rome, an unknown incident led to his expulsion from the cardinal's circle; something compelled him to leave Palazzo Farnese. The art theorist Giulio Mancini, writing some forty years after El Greco left Rome, claimed that El Greco had insulted Michelangelo's *Last Judgment* in the Sistine Chapel, offering to paint his own, better version in its place. It is plausible that Alessandro Farnese—as someone who greatly appreciated Michelangelo—might have found such presumption unpardonable, but the veracity of this tale is, on the whole, questionable.[28]

All the same, it contains a grain of truth. For in the long-running theoretical rivalry between *disegno* and *colorito*—with the Florentines and Romans claiming the authority of rigorous composition, as exemplified by Michelangelo, and the Venetians championing the dazzling effects of paint, with Titian—El Greco largely sided with the colorists. This is clear from the notes he left in the margins of his Vasari. ("I hold the imitation of color to be the greatest difficulty of art."[29]) To be sure, El Greco's feelings about Michelangelo were ambivalent. Although he prized him highly as a sculptor and draftsman, and although echoes of his work are to be found in several of his paintings (cats. 16, 50), he had strong reservations about Michelangelo's skills as a painter.

All this suggests that in Rome, if not before, El Greco gave considerable attention both to the theory and practice of Mannerism and to contemporary discourses about the impact on the arts of the Council of Trent, which had concluded in 1563. This is confirmed by the extensive list of books and pamphlets on these subjects found in his posthumous inventory.[30]

After his expulsion from the Farnese circle in 1572, El Greco joined the Roman painters' guild, the Compagnia di San Luca, registering not under his full birth name, but as Dominico Greco, a reference to his Greek origin and the name he would use from then on.[31] He set up a studio of his own; there are records of two assistants working here, one of whom, Francesco Preboste (1544–ca. 1607), accompanied El Greco to Spain and remained in his workshop for the rest of his life.[32] Little is known of El Greco's commissions in Rome, but it seems to have been during his time here that he came into demand as a portrait painter (fig. p. 177). It was also in Rome that he started to produce modified variations of his own compositions.[33] This practice of repetition would be an important feature of El Greco's work in Toledo as well (cats. 19, 20). Indeed, it is evident from the 1610 painting *Christ Driving the Traders from the Temple* (cat. 56) that he was still

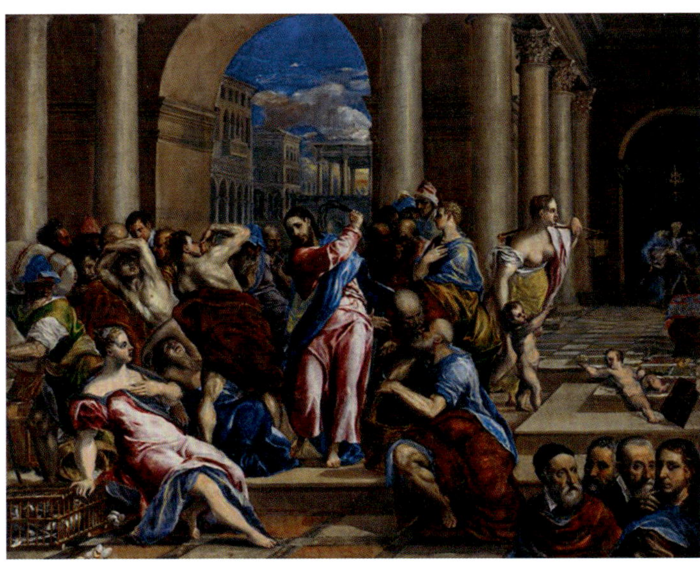

[Fig. 4] El Greco, *Christ Driving the Money Changers from the Temple,* ca. 1570
Oil on canvas, 115.57 × 147.32 cm
Minneapolis Institute of Art, William Hood Dunwoody Fund

reworking compositions from his years in Italy at the end of his life. The artist and theoretician Francisco Pacheco (1564–1644), who visited him in his studio in Toledo in 1611, even reported that El Greco showed him miniature versions of all his compositions, which he kept as models for variations; the large number of paintings listed in the posthumous inventory suggest that this was at least partly true.[34]

Over the next five years or so, El Greco tried with moderate success to establish himself in Rome, but his effort to find patrons was less successful. Then, probably in the spring of 1577, he set off for yet another country, Spain. The hope, clearly, was that the Spanish network he had come to know in Rome would facilitate his entry to the Iberian Peninsula. Among his connections was Luis de Castilla, whose influential father, Diego was dean of the chapter house of Toledo Cathedral. And indeed, in the summer of 1577, Diego de Castilla commissioned El Greco's first works in Toledo—the *Disrobing of Christ* and the important altarpieces for Santo Domingo el Antiguo, including the *Assumption of the Virgin* now in Chicago (fig. p. 44).[35]

El Greco in Spain: Success and Setbacks
El Greco had by now arrived at the view that, as an artist, he was more than a mere craftsman—a position that reflected his decade of socialization in the great capitals of Italian art. But in Spain, different rules applied. This is clear from the contractual terms customary there at the time, according to which the fee for a commission was not usually agreed up front but only after the work had been completed—and evaluated—by a previously named appraiser. Such an arrangement tended to disadvantage the artists who (down payment aside) bore the full burden of the financial risk; they had to pay for materials and for their assistants without knowing whether they would manage to recoup their expenses. If, after delivery, the price named turned out to be unsatisfactory, they had a choice: either accept it anyway or become embroiled in a long and costly lawsuit whose outcome was far from certain— and which led to an inevitable delay in payment even if the court decided in their favor. Legal disputes were common between business partners at the time, but prior to El Greco's arrival, it was not a risk that many artists in Toledo were willing to take.[36]

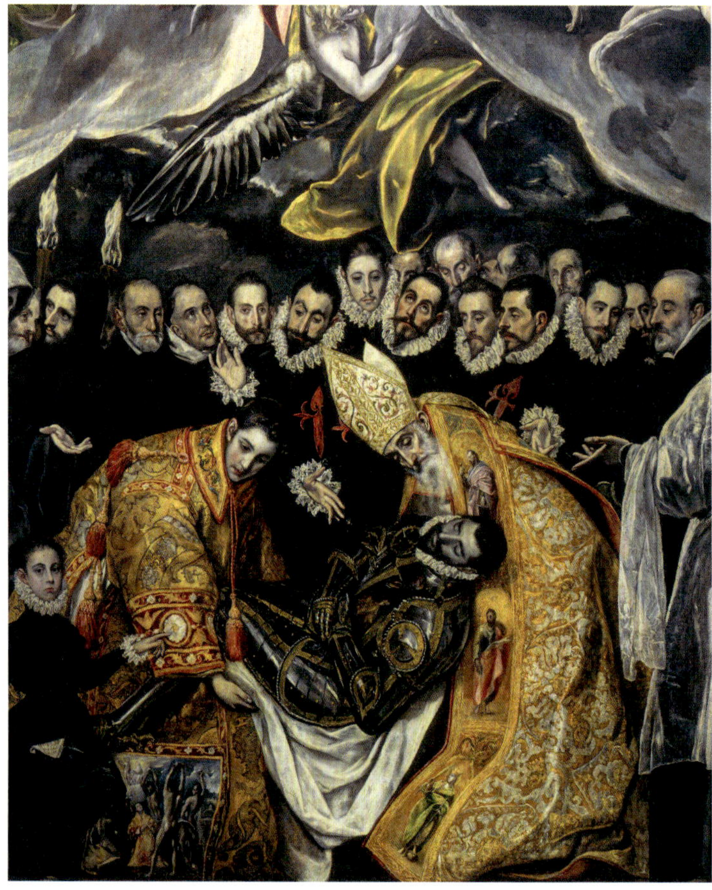

[Fig. 5] El Greco, *The Burial of the Count of Orgaz* (detail), 1586–88
Oil on canvas, 480 × 360 cm
Iglesia de Santo Tomé, Toledo

The newcomer had no such qualms. After lawsuits over his first two commissions of 1577, he continued to take his clients to court over almost every major commission until the end of his life. (Upon his father's death, El Greco's son, the Toledo-born Jorge Manuel [1578–1631], inherited not just his father's studio but also the last of these lawsuits, a dispute with the Hospital de Tavera.[37]) These embroilments have been cited as evidence of El Greco's belligerence and generally irascible character—playing into attempts to brand him as a social outsider—but the truth was more complex. El Greco refused to accept the injustice of the system. On the one hand, he needed as much income as possible to cover the expenses of his studio, and on the other hand, as suggested above, the injustice of underpayment cut against his notion of his status as an artist.[38] Even the influential Antonio Palomino (in his rather unflattering 1724 "life" of El Greco) gave him credit on this front, saying that all artists owed him "eternal thanks" for his pioneering achievements in the battle for artistic independence.[39]

I shall dispense with a detailed list of El Greco's many commissions in Toledo, some of which are listed in the chronology at the end of this catalogue alongside the main landmarks of his career (pp. 176–88). Instead I should like to take a closer look at *The Burial of the Count of Orgaz* (fig. 5), this time as an example of some of the ways in which El Greco aroused the wonder of his contemporaries while at the same time challenging their habits of looking.

This vast painting—almost five meters high and more than three and a half meters wide— depicts a miracle fabled to have taken place two hundred and fifty years before El Greco's time. According to legend, when Gonzalo Ruiz de Toledo, Count of Orgaz was to be buried in 1327, Saint Stephen and Saint Augustine themselves descended from heaven to take part in the rites, rewarding him for his philanthropy and piety by laying his body to rest with their own hands. The 1586 contract between El Greco and his client, priest Andrés Núñez of the parish church of Santo Tomé, set out in detail what was to be included in the painting: those who had presided over the mass (that is, the priest and other clerics), the two saints carrying the count's body, a large group of onlookers, "and above all this . . . an open heaven of glory."[40]

Although El Greco conscientiously ticked all the boxes—the program of the finished painting meets all Núñez's stipulations—he was also ingenious enough to find room for maneuver within the terms of the contract and put his own spin on the legend. The first thing that strikes the viewer is the strict division into an earthly and a heavenly realm, each in its markedly different style of painting. The lower half of the canvas is remarkable both for its realism—evident, for example, in the rendering of the various materials: the rich cloth of the liturgical robes, the shiny armor of the dead count—and for its clearly structured composition. The upper half, however, with Christ enthroned at the center, takes the form of a powerfully expressive, mystically charged, spiritual vision. In the ethereal, almost immaterial banks of clouds populated by slender and elongated saints in complicated poses, the earthly laws of nature seem to have been suspended. Between these two spheres, the row of onlookers are arranged with their heads all on a level, as in a frieze, following the principle of isocephaly— from the Greek words *isos* (equal) and *kephalos* (head). In use since antiquity, this compositional technique would have been familiar to a trained icon painter, but it was also part of the standard Italian Renaissance repertoire. The central group of the two saints carrying the count's body was presumably inspired by paintings such as Titian's *Entombment of Christ* (completed some six decades earlier for the Gonzagas in Mantua and now in the Louvre). As for the "heaven of glory"—for which no further details were specified in the contract—El Greco chose to set Christ among all the saints in a composition that bears similarities to Venetian depictions of the Last Judgment.[41]

The most radical aspect of El Greco's reinterpretation of the legend of the Count of Orgaz, however, is undoubtedly the translation of the historical miracle story into the viewers' present. All those attending the funeral ceremony are dressed in late-sixteenth-century clothes; the dead count's ceremonial armor and the saints' chasubles are similarly contemporary in style.

It seems plausible, then, that Francisco de Pisa's *descripción* was right and that El Greco really did place several real-life Toledans, with their distinctive pointy beards and ruffs, among the onlookers. To date the only figure to have been identified with full certainty is the white-bearded scholar Antonio de Covarrubias y Leiva, portrayed in profile toward the right (near the officiating priest, who is sometimes assumed to portray Núñez).[42] A deeply learned member of Toledo's upper echelons, Covarrubias was a close friend and patron of the artist (cat. 53). As the boy in the foreground on the left (often said to be El Greco's son Jorge Manuel) indicates with his eloquently pointing finger, the miracle depicted here is not only of historical importance. Rather, the salvation of the soul through the practice of good works and the veneration of the saints—a salvation vividly represented in the painting by the special treatment the count receives from the saints in reward for his philanthropy in life—is held up as an example to be followed by every believer. In this way, *The Burial of the Count of Orgaz* serves to illustrate some central tenets of Counter-Reformation faith.[43]

As this brief overview shows, El Greco was not only a tremendously skilled and creative painter; he also had a sound intellectual grounding, an extensive knowledge of contemporary Italian art and art theory, and a grasp of how to answer the Council of Trent's call for theological clarity in religious art. More important, he knew how to combine all these things. In this *The Burial of the Count of Orgaz* is by no means an isolated case in El Greco's religious oeuvre. Such reinterpretations and modernizations of traditional subjects were not, however, always appreciated.

In the case of *The Madonna of Charity*—part of an iconographically and theologically complex commission for the high altar of the Hospital de la Caridad in Illescas completed in 1605 (fig. 6)—El Greco's client even went so far as to write an open letter of protest.[44] As he had portrayed the onlookers in *The Burial of the Count of Orgaz,* El Greco depicted the people seeking protection under Mary's mantle as contemporary members of the upper class (with El Greco's son Jorge Manuel allegedly among them once again). The presence of so much earthly wealth, however, was deemed inappropriate for an institution dedicated to the care of the poor, and a particularly lengthy court case ensued over the purchase and payment of the altarpiece; in the course of it, the hospital authorities called for El Greco to remove the portraits and replace them with more "decent" figures.[45] El Greco did not, in fact, comply—in 1607 he agreed to an out-of-court settlement that was not exactly to his advantage

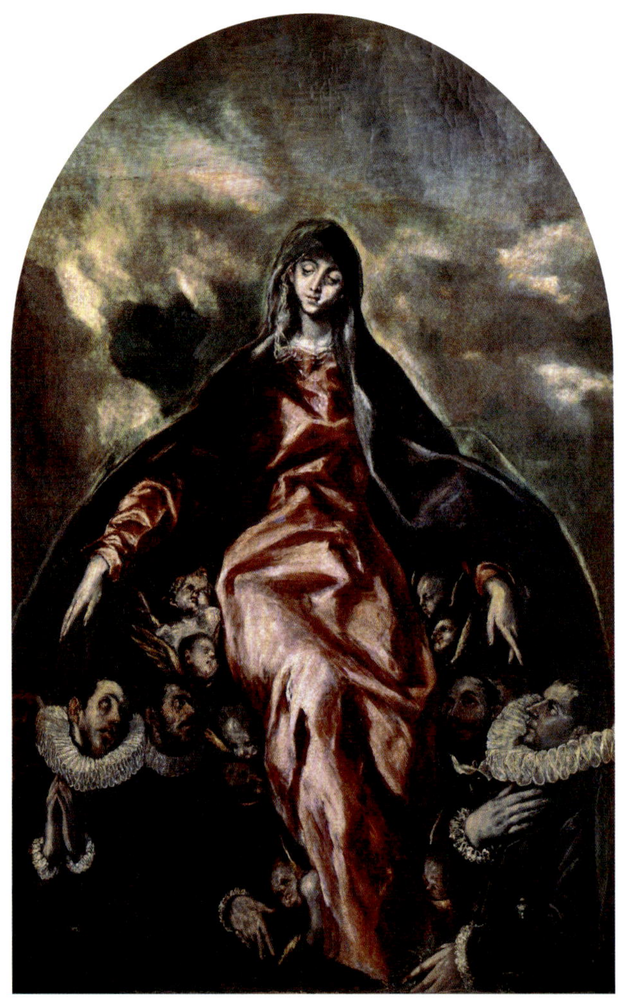

[Fig. 6] El Greco, *The Madonna of Charity,* 1603–05
Oil on panel, 155 × 124 cm
Hopital de la Caridad, Illescas, Toledo

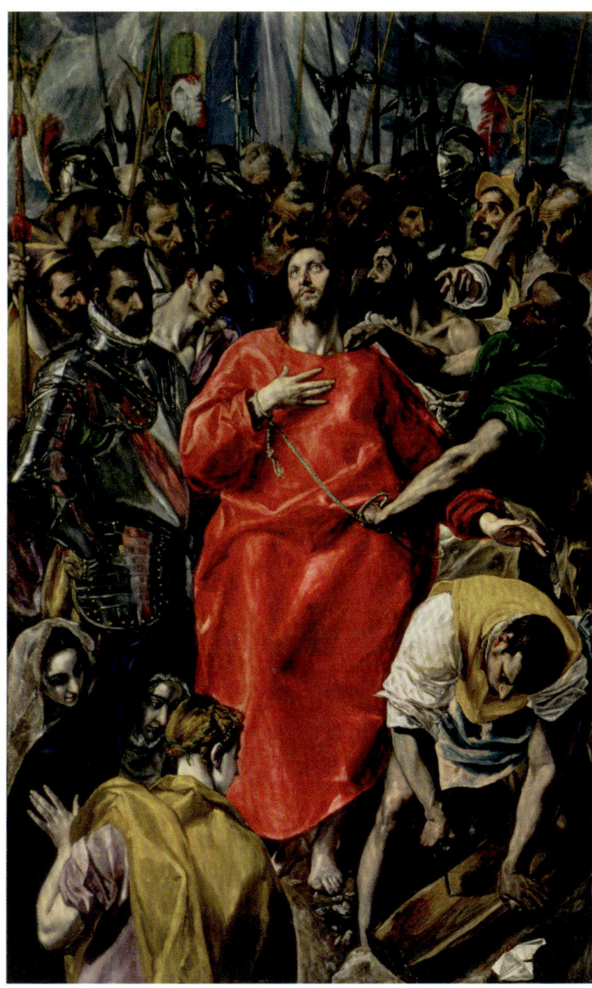

[Fig. 7] El Greco, *The Disrobing of Christ,* 1577–79
Oil on canvas, 285 × 173 cm
Sacristy of the Cathedral of Toledo

and the request was dropped.[46] Soon after his death, however, the requested modifications were made by another artist, who painted out the disputed figures and put a group of beggars in their place. It was only when the painting was restored in 1985 that these changes were reversed.[47]

Twenty-five years before, El Greco's two most important early commissions in Spain had provoked similar troubles and partial or even outright rejection. The aforementioned *Disrobing of Christ* (fig. 7), commissioned in 1577 for the sacristy of Toledo Cathedral, was criticized by the cathedral's official appraisers on several counts. Among other things, the heads of some of the minor figures were censured for being larger than that of Christ; the contemporary nature of the henchmen's armor was found to be inappropriate; and it was pointed out that the three Marys in the left foreground, introduced at the painter's own initiative, were not mentioned in the relevant verses of the Gospel of Matthew.[48] Here too, El Greco did not undertake the requested revisions. And since, here too, the real origin of the dispute was of a financial rather than a theological nature—the primary purpose of the list of objections being to justify the low valuation—it is possible that they were to some extent tactical.[49] Nevertheless, apart from being commissioned to create the elaborate frame for *The Disrobing of Christ* (ordered once the dispute had been settled), El Greco received no further direct commissions from the rich and powerful archbishopric.[50]

The Failed Court Painter

Rather more serious was the fallout from El Greco's brief interlude with Philip II. Their relations got off to an auspicious start but ended in fiasco. Soon after El Greco's arrival in Spain, he produced a painting with the king in mind entitled *The Adoration of the Name of Jesus* (ca. 1577–79; cats. 16, 18)—a complex work whose precise interpretation is still debated today. It is possibly an allegory of the 1571 victory of the Holy League over the Ottoman fleet at the Battle of Lepanto. It is not known whether the *Adoration*—which prominently features Philip II—was painted at the king's request or whether it was done as a kind of job application, a bid for royal favor. But with its Venetian composition (Titian, in particular, is a clear influence), its vivid colors reminiscent of Roman Mannerism, and its Michelangelo-like nudes on the right, the painting certainly demonstrates El Greco's will to present himself in his best and most advanced light to Spain's leading potential patron.[51]

El Greco won his first royal commission (or perhaps his second, if one counts the *Adoration*) in 1579 or 1580. Philip II was on the lookout for suitable successors to his court painter Juan Fernández de Navarrete, whose death in 1579 had paused the extensive work underway at the basilica of the Escorial. He engaged El Greco to paint a *Martyrdom of Saint Maurice* (fig. 8) for the altar of a side chapel but was displeased with the result. Once again, El Greco failed to profit from a favorable situation, just as he had lost the favor of Cardinal Farnese eight years earlier in Rome. Although the painter was paid handsomely for the work, without the usual haggling (the eight hundred ducats far surpassed his usual earnings), the king expressed his rejection in another way: by placing the painting in a less prominent location than the chapel for which it was intended and by calling in the elderly Florentine artist Romulo Cincinnato to create a new altarpiece in its place.[52]

Thus El Greco saw his only chance of royal patronage snatched from him. Never again would he receive a commission from the king. Instead he settled down to life and work in Toledo. What had gone wrong? In his effort to commend himself as a worthy successor to Navarrete, El Greco had pulled out all the stops of his artistic talent. His efforts culminated in another idiosyncratic iconographical interpretation. (Rather than focus on the act of holy martyrdom itself—which in his painting takes place quite literally in the background—the composition foregrounds the heroic refusal of the condemned soldiers and their leader, Saint Maurice, to save their lives by abjuring their faith.) By including a likeness of Philip II and other figures in contemporary dress among Saint Maurice's companions, El Greco again infused the work with topical relevance, opening up a symbolic link between the martyr's steadfastness and Philip himself in his fierce Counter-Reformation battle to uphold Catholicism as the "One True Faith."

El Greco's failure seems to have stemmed from his belief that his innovations and reinterpretations would be understood and appreciated by Philip and his advisers; he obviously had little sense of the king's actually very different tastes

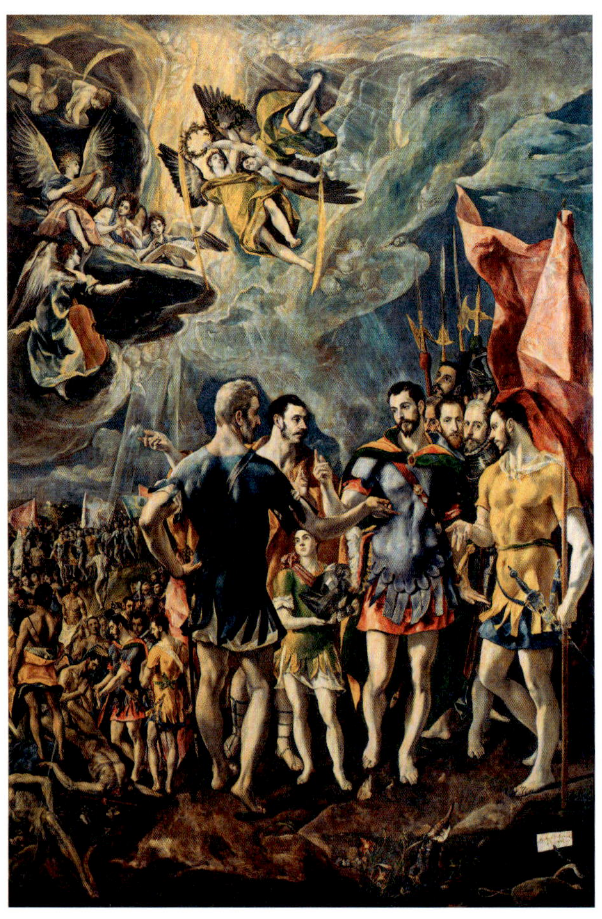

[Fig. 8] El Greco, *The Martyrdom of Saint Maurice and the Theban Legion*, 1580–82
Oil on canvas, 445 × 294 cm
Patrimonio Nacional, San Lorenzo de El Escorial

and priorities. Philip had expected clear yet exalted images—images that spoke directly to the viewers and strengthened their faith, in the spirit of the Council of Trent's insistence on the reform of religious art. An unnecessarily complex and intellectually discursive composition was less to his taste, and the addition of such incongruous elements as contemporary figures with no historical legitimation was seen to distract from the substance of the narrative.[53] As royal adviser Fray José de Sigüenza wrote in his history of the construction of the Escorial:

> [The painting] did not please his Majesty (unsurprisingly) because it pleases few, although they say it has much art, and that its author knows a great deal. . . . A bad painting can deceive the senses of the ignorant with adornment or appearance and thus it is pleasing to the ignorant and those of little understanding. And following this . . . the saints should be painted in such a way that our desire to pray to them is not

destroyed; rather, they should inspire devotion, since this ought to be the principal effect and aim of painting.[54]

A "Modern" Old Master? Appropriation and Misconception

If El Greco's paintings continue to captivate viewers—even in an age when Counter-Reformation art theory and the niceties of Christian iconography have become largely alien to the general public—it is above all thanks to their unique combination of individual style and expressive power, a hallmark instantly recognizable to modern eyes, distinct from all other art of the period (fig. 9). An important aspect of this is El Greco's rejection (increasingly marked toward the end of his life) of natural anatomical proportions and poses in favor of fluid, elongated figures charged with tension; the quivering spiritual emotions of these figures seem to spill over onto inanimate elements such as architecture, landscape, and sky. Also central is El Greco's Venetian use of color, further enhanced by his remarkably free and individual method of applying paint. Seemingly random brushstrokes—sometimes overlapping, sometimes merging, and often sparse enough to reveal the hue of the underlying canvas—create vibrant, amorphous patches of color in which shape, detail, and materiality seem almost to melt away.[55]

Looking, for example, at the robes of El Greco's apostles (cats. 42, 44, 46)—or the way, in the Budapest *Saint Mary Magdalene*, the hard line of the Magdalene's cloak glances off the similarly painted rock face behind her (cat. 41)—we can understand Picasso's alleged remark that El Greco was "a Cubist in construction."[56]

What modern viewers value as a mark of artistic expression, however, met with rather less approval in the years following El Greco's death. Francisco Pacheco expressed incomprehension over his method, disparaging the way he applied his paint in "crueles borrones" (cruel stains, rough blotches).[57] Antonio Palomino, for his part, explained that El Greco's "ludicrous" style was the result of a desperate attempt to

distinguish his art from that of his (supposed) master Titian, insinuating that he had fallen prey to madness at the end of his life.[58] Even into the twentieth century there were debates about whether El Greco's elongated figures might not be the result of astigmatism or some other pathological condition.[59]

However understandable, then, the enthusiasm with which El Greco was greeted at the turn of the twentieth century by a generation of young artists in search of new means of expression—among them Picasso—it is important to remember that this aesthetic annexation was in part based on a distorting and anachronistic point of view. That is not to say that El Greco's art is undistinguished by individuality and expressiveness, but only that he was committed to the traditions of Italian painting and certainly made no conscious effort to revolutionize or abandon them.

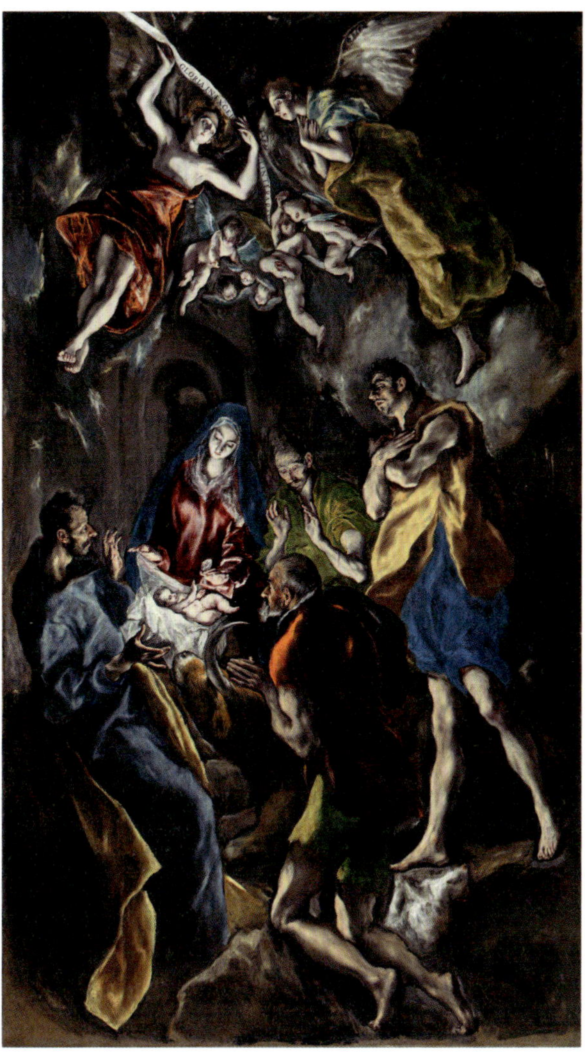

[Fig. 9] El Greco, *The Adoration of the Shepherds,* 1612–14
Oil on canvas, 319 × 180 cm
Museo Nacional del Prado, Madrid

Modern reception of most of El Greco's work
generally fails to take into account the context
in which it came into being. The circumstances
surrounding the creation of each of El Greco's
individual religious paintings were highly specific. Some of the particularly pronounced elon-
gations, for instance, can be explained at least in
part by the simple fact of their original locations.
In all cases, the intended effect would have been
quite different from that achieved on museum
walls today. As Ingrid Rowland has put it, a
monumental altarpiece like his *Assumption of the
Virgin* (1577–79; fig. 10) belongs in "the soaring,
sunlit, whitewashed chancel of Santo Domingo,
rather than a dark, squat windowless gallery of
the Art Institute of Chicago."[60] *The Resurrection
of Christ* from the Prado (cat. 50) is another good
example. This almost three-meter high painting
was originally conceived for the upper register of
the retable of the high altar in the church of the
Colegio de Doña María de Aragón in Madrid.[61]
Here it would have been positioned at more than
one and a half times its own height; accordingly,
the proportions were designed to be viewed from
below. Similarly, many of El Greco's paintings
were left unfinished, so that they appear freer and
more open than he presumably intended. This
may apply, for example, to some of the apostles
in the exhibition (cat. 44),[62] but also to the *Vision
of Saint John* (fig. p. 67), another painting that
was most certainly well known to Picasso.[63]

Centuries after his death, El Greco was declared a visionary prophet of Modernism, but
during his lifetime, the situation had been quite
the reverse. His highly individual and increasingly abstract style was out of step with his time. In
Rome and elsewhere the pendulum had swung
back. Soon Mannerism had been superseded,
and naturalism was sweeping across Europe. One
of the first naturalists—a certain Michelangelo
Merisi, known as Caravaggio (1571–1610)—had
already died by the time El Greco was painting
his last works. The older painter witnessed the
change with his own eyes. Even in Toledo, there
was no overlooking it; in 1611, the artist Juan
Bautista Maíno arrived from Rome, where he
had been directly influenced by the work of
Caravaggio. A year before, a young boy called
Diego Rodríguez de Silva y Velázquez began
his apprenticeship with Francisco Pacheco.[64] It
would not be long before he dominated early seventeenth-century Spanish art. Velázquez (1599–

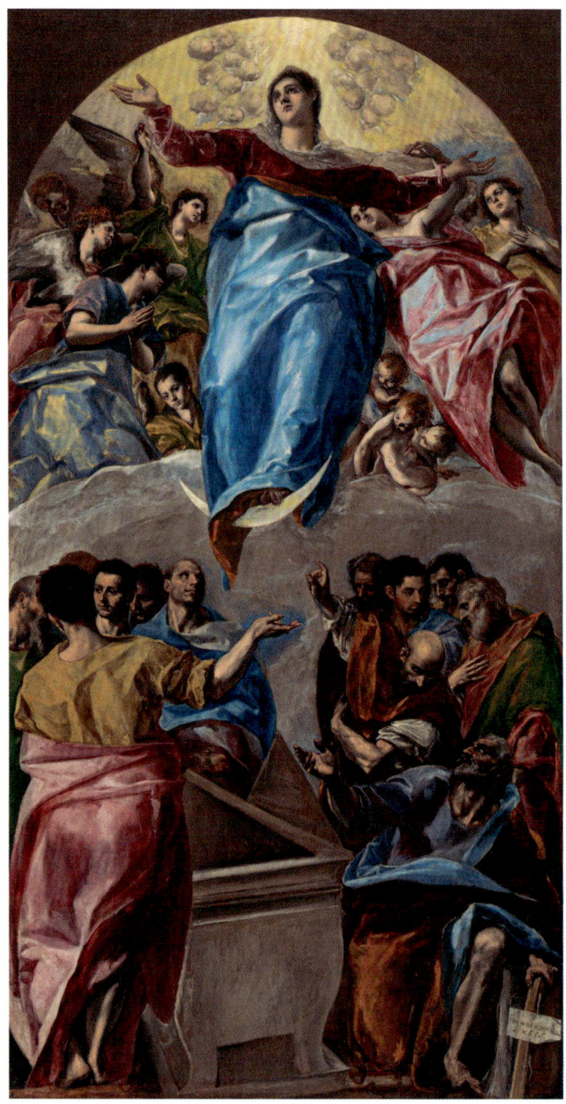

[Fig. 10] El Greco, *The Assumption of the Virgin*, 1577–79
Oil on canvas, 403.2 × 211.8 cm
The Art Institute of Chicago, gift of Nancy Atwood Sprague
in memory of Albert Arnold Sprague

1660) may have admired El Greco's work—at
least the portraits, of which he even owned three
examples—but the future had caught up with
El Greco. After his death he became a kind of
phantom, and it would be almost three centuries
before he was rediscovered.

1   "Creta le dio la vida, y los pinceles / Toledo, mejor patria donde empieza / a lograr con la muerte eternidades." Hortensio Félix Paravicino, "Al tumulo deste mismo Pintor, que era el Grego de Toledo," in *Obras posthumas, divinas y humanas de Don Felix de Arteaga* (Madrid, 1641), p. 74. Lines translated in Jonathan Brown, "El Greco and Toledo," in *El Greco of Toledo,* exh. cat. Museo del Prado, Madrid, et al. (Boston, 1982), p. 75.

2   Manuel B. Cossío gathers the four sonnets in an appendix to his major study *El Greco* (Madrid, 1908), pp. 659–61. Nina Mallory includes two in her annotated translation of Antonio Palomino, *Lives of the Eminent Spanish Painters and Sculptors* (Cambridge, 1987), p. 86nn20–22.

3   "In spite of twenty-nine years of acquaintance, [my soul] doubts which is the body that it should inhabit, perplexed between your hand, and that of God." Hortensio Félix Paravicino, "Al mismo Griego en un retrato que hizo del Autor," in ibid., p. 660; translated in Palomino 1987 (see note 2), p. 86n20. See also Dawson W. Carr, "Zu El Grecos Portraits," in *El Greco,* ed. Sylvia Ferino-Pagden and Fernando Checa Cremades, exh. cat. Kunsthistorisches Museum Vienna (Milan, 2001), p. 94.
     For discussions of El Greco's portraits of Paravicino and the relationship between the two men, see Fernando Marías, *Greco: Biographie d'un peintre extravagant,* trans. Marie-Hélène Collinot (Paris, 1997), pp. 258–60, and its English edition, *El Greco: Life and Work; A New History,* trans. Paul Edson and Sander Berg (London, 2013); Fernando Marías, *El Greco in Toledo* (London, 2001), p. 57; David Davies, "El Greco's Portraits: The Body Natural and the Body Politic," in *El Greco,* ed. David Davies, exh. cat. The Metropolitan Museum of Art, New York, et al. (New Haven, 2003), pp. 259–60.

4   The Cordoban poet Luis de Góngora (1561–1627) also wrote an epitaph for El Greco in 1614, a sonnet entitled "Inscripción para el sepulcro de Dominíco Greco." See Cossío 1908 (see note 2), p. 662.

5   Francisco de Pisa, *Apuntamientos para la II parte de la descripción de la imperial ciudad de Toledo* (Toledo, 1976), pp. 66–67; Sarah Schroth, "Burial of the Count of Orgaz," in *Figures of Thought: El Greco as Interpreter of History, Tradition, and Ideas,* ed. Jonathan Brown (Washington, DC, 1982), pp. 3, 15n7; Marías 1997 (see note 3), p. 185.

6   El Greco, *Portrait of Dr. Francisco de Pisa,* ca. 1610–14, Kimbell Art Museum, Fort Worth, TX, AP 1977.05.

7   Rebecca J. Long, "El Greco's Altarpieces: Artistic Ambition and Legal Frustration," in *El Greco: Ambition and Defiance,* ed. Rebecca J. Long, exh. cat. Grand Palais, Paris, and The Art Institute of Chicago (Chicago, 2020), pp. 39–40; Marías 1997 (see note 3), p. 126.

8   See Richard L. Kagan, "The Toledo of El Greco," in Brown 1982 (see note 1), pp. 35–73 (esp. pp. 35–50); Richard L. Kagan, "*Urbs Sacra:* The Demand for Art in El Greco's Toledo," in Long 2020 (see note 7), pp. 63–71 (esp. pp. 64–67).

9   An overview of the most important commissions can be found in the catalogue's chronology, pp. 175–78.

10   Kagan 1982 (see note 8), pp. 61–72; David Davies, "El Greco's Religious Art: The Illumination and Quickening of the Spirit," in Davies 2003 (see note 3), pp. 66–68; Kagan 2020 (see note 8), pp. 68–69.

11   A detailed account of El Greco's lawsuits and the historical context can be found in Richard L. Kagan, "El Greco and the Law," in *Figures of Thought: El Greco as Interpreter of History, Tradition, and Ideas,* ed. Jonathan Brown (Washington, DC, 1982), pp. 79–90.

12   Antonio Palomino, *El Museo Pictórico, y Escala Óptica: El Parnaso Español Pintoresco Laureado con las Vidas de los Pintores, y Estatuarios Eminentes Españoles* (Madrid, 1724), p. 286 (in the El Greco chapter), p. 323 (in the Velázquez chapter). See also Palomino 1987 (see note 2), pp. 83, 142.

13   This topic is covered in detail by José Álvarez Lopera, *El Greco: Textos, documentos y bibliografía,* vol. 2 of *De Ceán a Cossío: La fortuna crítica del Greco en el siglo XIX* (Madrid, 1987); Eric Storm, *The Discovery of El Greco: The Nationalization of Culture versus the Rise of Modern Art (1860–1914)* (Eastbourne, 2016), esp. pp. 7–20, 45–49, 105–18, 153–64; Marías 1997 (see note 3), pp. 11–21; Michael Scholz-Hänsel, "Wie der Blitz?' Ambiguitäten, produktive Missverständnisse und konstruierte Perspektiven in der El Greco-Rezeption," in *El Greco und die Moderne,* ed. Beat Wismer and Michael Scholz-Hänsel, exh. cat. Museum Kunstpalast, Düsseldorf (Ostfildern, 2012), pp. 196–211 (esp. pp. 196–200); and Jonathan Brown, "The Redefinition of El Greco in the Twentieth Century," in *El Greco: Italy and Spain,* ed. Jonathan Brown and José Manuel Pita Andrade (Washington, DC, 1982), pp. 29–32.

14   El Greco named Candia as his place of birth at a court appearance in 1582; in a document from October 31, 1606, he gives his age as sixty-five. See Xavier Bray and Louis Oliver, "Chronology," in Davies 2003 (see note 3), pp. 32.

15   John H. Elliott, "El Greco's Mediterranean: The Encounter of Civilisations," in Davies 2003 (see note 3), pp. 19–21.

16   Nicos Hadjinicolaou, "Zwischen post-byzantinischem Griechentum und westlicher Modernität," in Ferino-Pagden 2001 (see note 3), p. 59.

17   Marías 1997 (see note 3), pp. 38–41, where all written sources quoted from El Greco's time in Crete are reproduced in full.

18   For a more detailed account, see Irene Leontakianakou, "Western Elements in Icon Painting in Regions under Venetian Rule and the Work of Theotokopoulos," in *Perceptions of El Greco in 2014,* ed. Nicos Hadjinicolaou and Panayotis K. Ioannou (Athens, 2019), pp. 29–47; Enrico Maria Dal Pozzolo, "The Young Domenikos and the Self-Construction of an Artistic Language," in *Creative and Imaginative Powers in the Pictorial Art of El Greco,* ed. Livia Stoenescu (Turnhout, 2016), pp. 148–52.

19   See Ferino-Pagden 2001 (see note 3), p. 126, cat. 1. See also the introduction to the early works from Crete in *Greco,* ed. Réunion des musées nationaux, exh. cat. Grand Palais, Paris, and The Art Institute of Chicago (Paris, 2019), p. 77, cat. 1; Leontakianakou 2019 (see note 18), pp. 260–61.

20   In August 1568, El Greco's name appears in a letter by the Duke of Candia (now in the state archives of Venice), which indicates that he must have been in the city at that time. See Ana Carmen Lavín, "New Information Concerning El Greco's Sojourn in Italy," in Hadjinicolaou 2019 (see note 18), pp. 260–61.

21   Keith Christiansen, "El Greco in Italy," in Long 2020 (see note 7), pp. 18–19; Fernando Marías, *El Greco in Toledo* (London, 2001), pp. 39–41.

22   Christiansen 2020 (see note 21), p. 18; Sylvia Ferino-Pagden, "El Greco: Einleitende Bemerkungen zu Leben und Werk," in Ferino-Pagden 2001 (see note 3), p. 21. A new (seventeenth-century) source has recently emerged that repeats Clovio's claims; see Lavín 2019 (see note 20), pp. 257–61.

23   Leticia Ruiz Gómez, "Zum malerischen Stil El Grecos: Eine Annäherung," in Ferino-Pagden 2001 (see note 3), p. 102; in Ferino-Pagden 2001 (see note 22), p. 23; Christiansen 2020 (see note 21), p. 20.

24   Christiansen 2020 (see note 21), p. 19.

25   Marías 1997 (see note 3), pp. 78–83.

26   For a detailed account of relations between El Greco and Giulio Clovio, see José Riello, "El Greco and Giulio Clovio: Three Gazes," in Long 2020 (see note 7), pp. 29–37. For other artists in Rome at the same time as El Greco, see Christiansen 2020 (see note 21), pp. 21–26.

27   Christiansen 2020 (see note 21), pp. 22–23; Elliott 2003 (see note 15), pp. 22–23. For a detailed account of the Spanish community in sixteenth-century Rome, see Marías 1997 (see note 3), pp. 118–23.

28   Guilio Mancini, manuscript written ca. 1617–21, in *Considerazioni sulla pittura,* ed. Adriana Marucchi and Luigi Salerno (Rome 1956), vol. 1, pp. 230–31. For a refutation, see Christiansen 2020 (see note 21), p. 22; Marías 1997 (see note 3), pp. 113–14.

29   Brown 1982 (see note 1), p. 133. For detailed discussions of El Greco's feelings about Michelangelo's art and his remarks on Vasari, see Karin Hellwig, "El Greco's Giorno as an Early Commentary on Vasari's Vita of Michelangelo (1568)," in Stoenescu 2016 (see note 18), pp. 129–45; Brown 1982 (see note 1), pp. 129–34.

30   A transcription of the inventory is provided in Marías 1997 (see note 3), pp. 312–13.

31   Riello 2020 (see note 26), p. 29.

32   Ruiz Gómez 2001 (see note 23), p. 105.

33   Ibid., pp. 102–5; Marías 2001 (see note 21), pp. 43–44. For the practice of variations, see Guillaume Kientz, "Greco et l'image: Invention et variation," in *Réunion des musées nationaux 2019* (see note 19), pp. 14–25; also his related text: idem., "El Greco and the Image: Between Invention and Variation," trans. Antony Shugaar, in Long 2020 (see note 7), pp. 73–81; Leticia Ruiz Gómez, "El Greco's Workshop in Spain," in Long 2020 (see note 7), pp. 86–91.

34   Ruiz Gómez 2001 (see note 32), p. 86.

35   For an account of these first commissions in Toledo, see Brown 1982 (see note 1), pp. 95–98.

36   Kagan 1982 (see note 11), pp. 81–82, 88; Long 2020 (see note 7), p. 40.

37   Long 2020 (see note 7), pp. 39–40, 47.

38   Kagan 1982 (see note 11), pp. 79, 88; Long 2020 (see note 7), p. 49.

39   Palomino 1724 (see note 12), p. 286. "All masters of this art, therefore, owe eternal thanks to Dominico Greco for being the first to take up arms with such success in defense of the immunity of our art from taxes, for later judgments were based on this sentence." Palomino 1987 (see note 2) p. 84.

40   See Marías 2001 (see note 21), p. 79, and Schroth 1982 (see note 5), p. 1.

41   Schroth 1982 (see note 5), pp. 9–14, with reference to Tintoretto's *Last Judgment* in Santa Maria dell'Orto in Venice.

42   See Brown 1982 (see note 1), p. 127. It is impossible to confirm whether the man gazing out of the painting above Saint Stephen's head is, as often assumed, a self-portrait of El Greco. This is due to an absence of available images for comparison. For other speculative identifications, see Francisco Calvo Serraller, *El Greco: The Burial of the Count of Orgaz* (London, 1995), pp. 19–21.

43   Davies, "El Greco's Religious Art," in Davies 2003 (see note 3), pp. 62–63.

44   For an account of this commission, see Marías 1997 (see note 3), pp. 235–44. For the ensuing legal disputes, see Kagan 1982 (see note 11), pp. 87–88.

45   Marías 2001 (see note 21), p. 89.

46   Kagan 1982 (see note 11), p. 88.

47   Rafael Alonso Alonso, "Zur Restaurierung von El Grecos Gemälden," in Ferino-Pagden 2001 (see note 3), pp. 113–23 (esp. pp. 113–14).

48   Long 2020 (see note 7), pp. 7–8.

49   Kagan 1982 (see note 11), pp. 84–86; Marías 1997 (see note 3), p. 134.

50   Kagan 1982 (see note 11), p. 86; Long 2020 (see note 7), p. 41.

51   See Marías 1997 (see note 3), p. 126; Long 2020 (see note 7), pp. 43–44; Ferino-Pagden 2001 (see note 3), p. 140, cat. 7 (Leticia Ruiz Gómez).

52   Carmen Garcia-Frias Checa, "Das Martyrium des hl. Mauritius und sein Schicksal im Escorial," in Ferino-Pagden 2001 (see note 3), pp. 77–78.

53   Ibid., pp. 78–81; Marías 1997 (see note 3), pp. 151–54; Felipe Pereda, "El Greco, Religious Painter: Success and Failure," in Long 2020 (see note 7), pp. 53–56.

54   Fray José de Sigüenza, *Fundación del Monasterio de El Escorial,* MS, part 2, discourse 7, folio 122, Biblioteca di San Lorenzo de El Escorial, Madrid, Sig. &-II-22, quoted in Pereda 2020 (see note 7), p. 56.

55   For an overview of El Greco's technique, see Ruiz Gómez 2001 (see note 23), pp. 100–06.

56   Picasso, as recalled by Romauld Dor de la Souchère, *Picasso in Antibes,* trans. W. J. Strachan (New York, 1960), p. 14, quoted in Robert S. Lubar, "Narrating the Nation: Picasso and the Myth of El Greco," in *Picasso and the Spanish Tradition,* ed. Jonathan Brown (New Haven and London, 1996), p. 30.

57   Francisco Pacheco, *Arte de la pintura,* ed. Bonaventura Bassegoda i Hugas (Madrid, 1990), pp. 440–41 and 483. See Yannis Hadjinicolaou, "El Greco's *Borrones:* A European Practice and Theory," in Hadjinicolaou 2019 (see note 18), pp. 383–401 (esp. pp. 386–87).

58   "El Greco, however, seeing that his paintings were confused with those of Titian, tried to change his manner, but with such extravagance that he managed to make his painting ludicrous and contemptible, as much for his disjointed drawing as for the harshness of its coloration." Palomino 1724 (see note 2), pp. 286, 323; translated in Palomino 1987 (see note 2), p. 84.

59   See for example David Katz, *War El Greco astigmatisch? Eine psychologische Studie zur Kunstwissenschaft* (Leipzig, 1914).

60   Ingrid Rowland, "Irresistible El Greco," *New York Review of Books,* June 19, 2014.

61   Long 2020 (see note 7), p. 45.

62   Marías 2001 (see note 21), p. 111.

63   See the discussions in this volume by Richard Shiff and Carmen Giménez, esp. pp. 66 and 21–22. See also John Richardson, "Picasso's Apocalyptic Whorehouse," *New York Review of Books,* April 23, 1987.

64   Dawson W. Carr, "Painting and Reality: The Art and Life of Velázquez," in *Velázquez,* ed. Kate Bell, exh. cat. The National Gallery, London (New Haven, 2006), pp. 26–27.

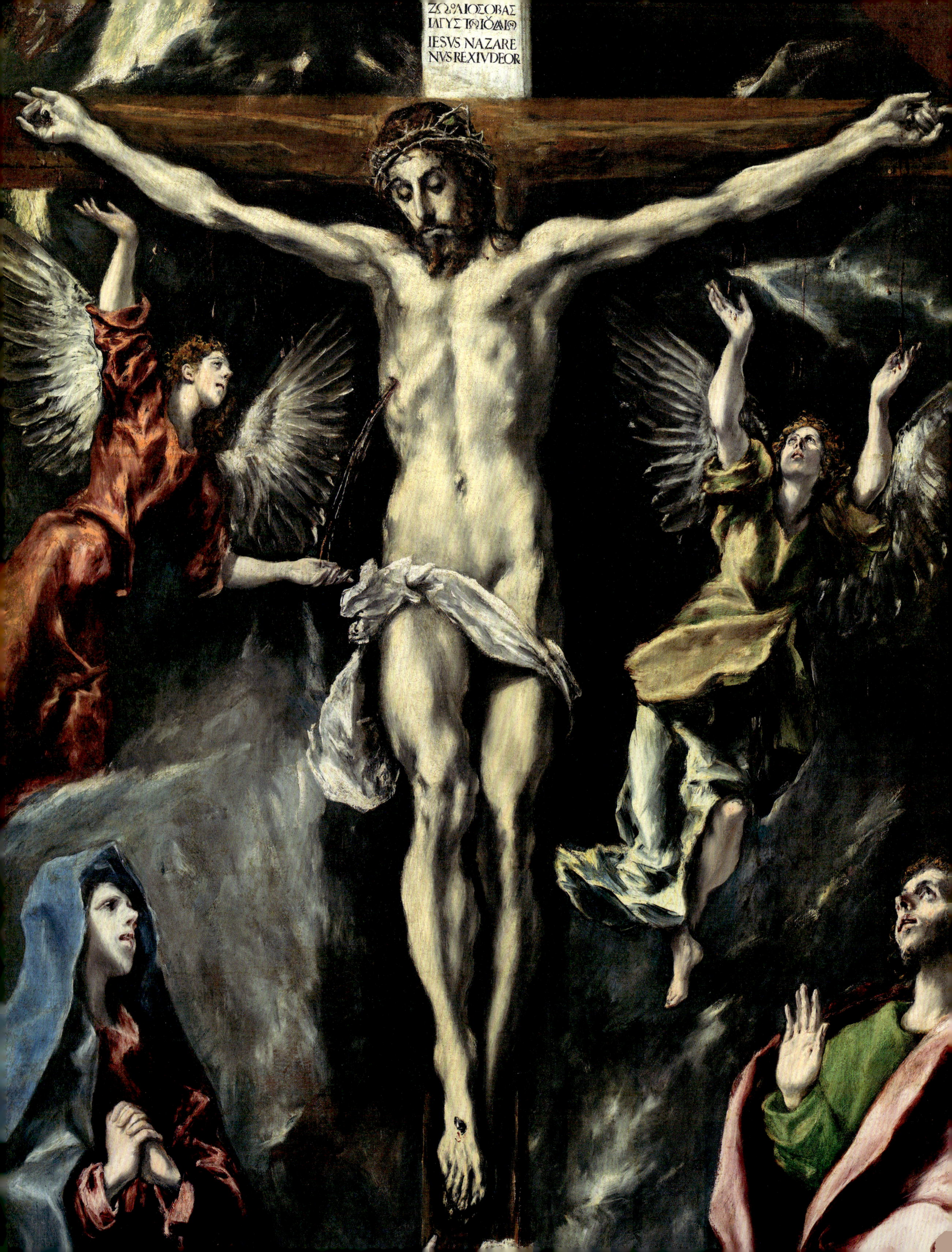
ΖΩ Ρ ΛΙΟΣΟΒΑΣ
ΙΛΓΥΣ ΤΩΙΟ ΔΑΙΩ
IESVS NAZARE
NVS REX IVDEOR

Javier Portús

El Greco and the Canon of Spanish Painting in the Time of Picasso (1895–1910)

While in La Coruña in 1894–95, Pablo Picasso filled a sheet of paper with lively sketches of distinct figures, several of them satirical. The themes of this sheet, now at the Museu Picasso in Barcelona, were prestige and artistic and literary fame (fig. 1). The Venus de Milo appears on the far left, on a high pedestal flanked by two putti. At center right is a bust of Velázquez, with a glimpse of the cross of Saint James, set atop a painter's palette with maulstick and brushes. (To dispel any doubts about his identity Picasso wrote the Old Master's name beside it.) The façade of a classical temple presides over the upper right corner, while the lower right is devoted to the bust of a man with an open book. (Inscriptions identify him as Cervantes and his book as *Don Quixote.*) Putti and eschatological figures cavort at the center of the sheet, including a cupid aiming his arrow at a woman. It is interesting that Picasso was so keen to clarify the identities of his characters, for Velázquez and Cervantes were the major figures in the Spanish cultural canon of the day.[1] Ten years earlier, when the new home of the Ateneo de Madrid opened its doors, portrait reliefs of the same men adorned the façade, flanking King Alfonso X of Castile himself (fig. 2).

In his early teens at the time, Picasso would have been absorbing this canon firsthand even as he experimented with the charms of caricature. Very soon a new figure—El Greco—would appear

in his private pantheon and eventually even supersede the young artist's interest in Velázquez.

Various forces buttressed Diego Velázquez's dominant position in the Spanish canon in the closing years of the nineteenth century. Both at home and abroad, these affected exhibition policies, historiographic activity, artistic practices, and the painter's symbolic presence in urban space. That process culminated the year of the third centenary of the artist's birth, 1899, when a prime portion of the Museo del Prado was given over entirely to his work. Up until then the great basilical hall had housed masterpieces by several different artists. Now the space was cleared for the paintings of Velázquez, which hang there to this day. The hanging was organized according to modern criteria, with works placed at a distance from each other and arranged in chronological order, allowing viewers to appreciate the artist's stylistic development.

This new curatorial approach reflected a landmark event in Velázquez studies: the appearance the previous year of the major monograph by the painter and scholar Aureliano de Beruete.[2] This study was itself part of a golden age for such publications. The first edition of Carl Justi's *Velázquez y su siglo* (Velázquez and His Century) had appeared in 1888, followed by *The Art of Velázquez* by Robert A. M. Stevenson in 1895. In short, three of the pillars upon which modern Velázquez studies rest had appeared within less than fifteen years. Around the same time, public monuments honoring the Spanish master propagated his fame, not only in Spain. An equestrian

←
El Greco, *The Crucifixion* (detail), 1597–1600
Museo Nacional del Prado, Madrid

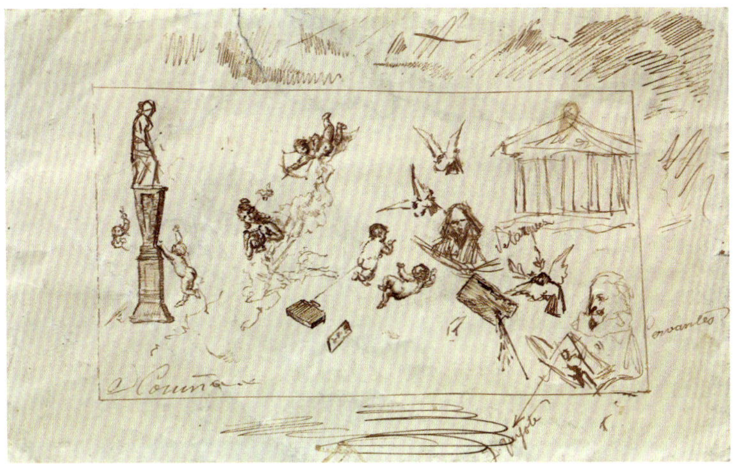

[Fig. 1] Pablo Picasso, *The Pantheon,* 1894–95
Pen on paper, 13 × 20.7 cm
Museu Picasso, Barcelona

statue by Emmanuel Fremiet was erected outside the Louvre in Paris in 1893, and 1899 saw the installation of the seated bronze by Aniceto Marinas at the main portal of the Prado, where it remains today.[3]

Velázquez's place at the pinnacle of Spanish art history was largely due to the interest that artists of successive periods had taken in his work. This appreciation began in Spain in 1780 with no less a figure than Franciso Goya. In the next decades it spread to Europe and America, as the opening of the Prado in 1819—among other factors—drew more and more visitors to the Iberian Peninsula. Art movements began to emerge that were particularly receptive to Velázquez's naturalism, leading ultimately to the Impressionists.[4] In 1904, the elderly Claude Monet told the art dealer Paul Durand-Ruel that he was planning to fulfill his wish to "go to Madrid to see the Velázquez paintings."[5] Many of his fellow painters had already made their pilgrimages to the Prado for the same reason. In 1882, John Singer Sargent quoted *Las Meninas* directly when he painted *The Daughters of Edward Darley Boit* (The Museum of Fine Arts, Boston). By 1900, the lines connecting the museum in Madrid, Velázquez, and modern painting were so much taken for granted that the artist Charles Ricketts could say that "the Prado is a museum for painters and has become a Mecca for many modern artists."[6]

Other Spanish painters had previously shared the limelight with Velázquez. Bartolomé Esteban Murillo was highly prized from the seventeen-fifties on, a factor that contributed to making his work more widely represented than Velázquez in European collections and museums. Murillo's fame peaked in 1852, when his *Immaculate Conception of Los Venerables* (now in the Prado) fetched a record price at auction. Around the same time, however, John Ruskin cast a shadow over the painter's reputation when he savaged Murillo's depiction of two beggar boys in the Dulwich Collection for "its mere delight in foulness."[7] As I will show later in this essay, something similar happened to Velázquez—a rise to the top followed by a sudden fall from grace. Each artist enjoyed a different kind of prestige; Velázquez's art included many elements that could be used by more restless nineteenth-century painters, whereas Murillo's influence was more limited; his reputation had been great-er among collectors and the general public than among artists.

There were other artists in addition to Murillo, but they were accorded a different type and degree of esteem. The work of Jusepe Ribera was very highly regarded during his lifetime and possessed sufficiently solid values to ensure last-ing appeal. The fact that he spent his art career in Italy and that his works found their way into collections and museums all over Europe made him the best-known Spanish artist of the seven-teenth and eighteenth centuries. Although his reception in his native country was ambivalent for a while, the nineteenth century saw him take

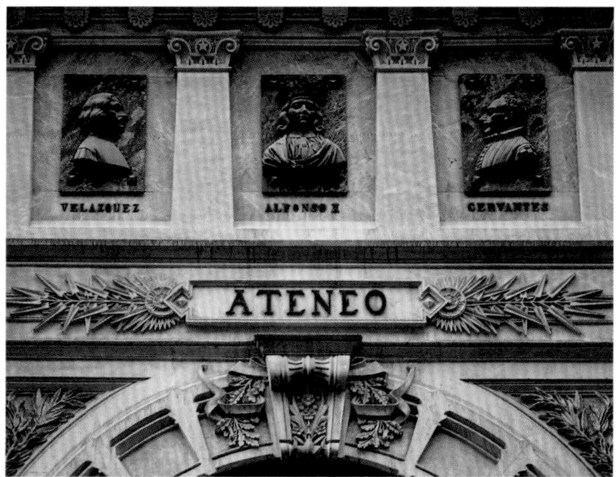

[Fig. 2] Detail of the façade of the Ateneo Científico, Literario y Artístico de Madrid (1884)

his place in the canon there. This acceptance was aided by the realism, harshness, and expressivity of his style, attributes that were compatible with contemporary characterizations of the Spanish experience.

Matters were quite different with Francisco de Zurbarán. His works were not seen in the rest of Europe until after Napoleonic forces withdrew from the Iberian Peninsula in 1814. With the 1838 opening in the Louvre of King Louis Philippe's Galerie espagnole, however, Zurbarán caught the attention of the general public, collectors, and European painters. He was the exhibition's surprise discovery and, from then on, the values most closely associated with the Spanish School would unfailingly include the "mysticism and asceticism" that were more apparent in his paintings than in the works of any other painter. This helped, in time, to make room in the histories of the school for artists who shared similar characteristics. These included Luis de Morales and, later, El Greco.

As the nineteenth century progressed, Europeans looked beyond the artists of the so-called Golden Age and became increasingly interested in Goya—an almost contemporary painter, whose work influenced many important artists, particularly Édouard Manet. Goya was originally known for his prints, particularly the *Caprichos*; but as his paintings began to appear in European collections and museums, and as more and more foreigners came to Madrid to visit the Prado, it became increasingly obvious that he

was an interesting painter. His presence in the Louvre was also a decisive factor. A proliferation of Goya monographs ensued, including books by Charles Yriarte, Paul Lefort, and Paul Lafond.[8]

As studies have pointed out, Europe's nineteenth-century "discovery" of Spanish painting involved two key elements: its previous "invisibility" and the immense appeal (once it became better known) of its naturalism. The limited exposure was because very few paintings made their way beyond Spanish borders and relatively few foreigners visited the country until after the Napoleonic Wars. Once Spanish painting became better known, the fact that the naturalism embraced by its masters proved compatible with the ideals of some of the nineteenth century's most important cultural movements helped facilitate its assimilation and appeal. From then on it was acknowledged as a "school" (though that is a largely arbitrary concept), and in time a dual phenomenon emerged. On one hand, the number of interesting Spanish artists, periods, and subjects increased. On the other— as the case of Murillo shows—the prestige of individual artists within that school fluctuated.[9]

The most important addition to the Spanish canon—the induction of El Greco—occurred in the late nineteenth century in a very swift process led chiefly by artists and art critics. Other important writers participated as well, and museum curators and collectors soon followed. All indications suggest that Velázquez himself had admired El Greco's portraits and kept some in his studio. At the same time the two artists' respective conceptions of painting differed in important ways. Whereas the court painter from Seville spent his entire career reviving what in his time was called "an imitation of the natural," the master from Toledo preferred to explore the expressive and emotional possibilities of painting, which at times led him to what critics long characterized as chromatic and formal "distortions." To be sure, several nineteenth-century artists like Manet understood how to combine a taste for Velázquez with a lively interest in El Greco, but others were more pronounced in their preferences.[10] Those who continued to embrace the illusionist approach to painting—among them, many Impressionists and adherents of related movements—claimed Velázquez. Later in the century—as younger artists fought to "free" painting from the illusionist corset, giving greater autonomy to form and color and greater emphasis to expressivity—the quest for precursors led many of them to the work of El Greco.

After the turn of the century, although most artists, art historians, and collectors could combine an appreciation for both painters, El Greco came to replace Velázquez in several important ways. This was apparent, for example, in the preferences contemporary painters expressed after 1900; most were far more interested in El Greco. That substitution was most vividly expressed by the German critic Julius Meier-Graefe, who arrived at the Prado in the spring of 1908 and expressed his disappointment in Velázquez; he did not see the structural solidity in his paintings that he had expected to find. His encounter with El Greco, on the other hand, prompted him to become one of his most enthusiastic champions. Meier-Graefe's *Spanische Reise,* a travel memoir published in 1910, was extremely influential in making El Greco's work better known in German-speaking countries, thanks not only to the book's abundance of favorable comments but also to its twenty or so photographs of the Old Master's works. (An English edition followed in 1926.)

In his book Meier-Graefe described his encounter with El Greco as a spontaneous event, something almost akin to revelation. Scholars have noted that it was more complicated, however, and also had something to do with the author's rivalry with Carl Justi, one of Velázquez's greatest champions.[11] As an art critic, Meier-Graefe was moreover very open to post-Impressionist trends; this made him particularly receptive to the values of El Greco's painting that were so compatible with the ideas of more restless and innovative contemporary artists, including Paul Cézanne. (Not only did Meier-Graefe quote Cézanne several times in his travel book, but he later devoted a monograph to him.) In his reading of El Greco, Meier-Graefe emphasized both its formal-structural and expressive values, assessing these very shrewdly for example in the extensive analysis he gave the *Crucifixion* in the Prado (fig. 3)—a work he claimed only Rembrandt could match. His discussion even offered a sketch outlining the formal coherence of the altarpiece's composition (fig. 4).[12]

Given its emphasis on El Greco, *Spanische Reise* frequently cites the scholarship of Manuel

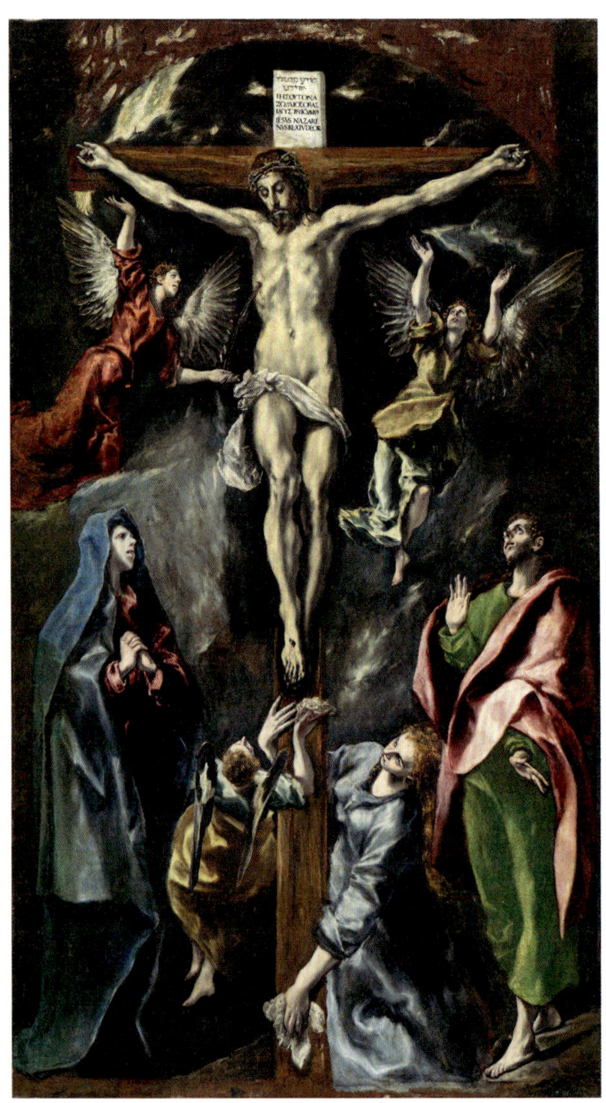

[Fig. 3] El Greco, *The Crucifixion,* 1597–1600
Oil on canvas, 312 × 169 cm
Museo Nacional del Prado, Madrid

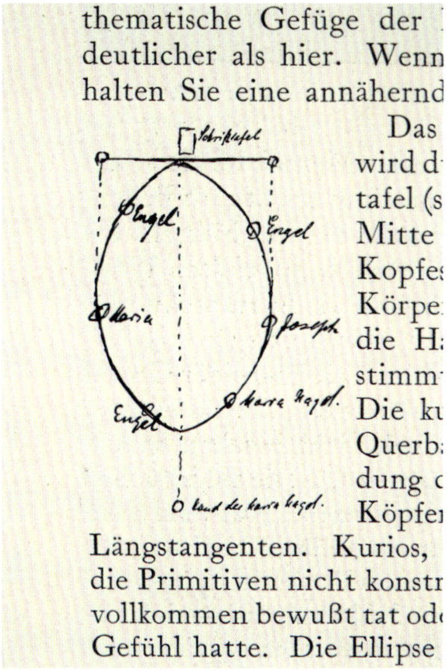

thematische Gefüge der
deutlicher als hier. Wenn
halten Sie eine annähernd
Das
wird d
tafel (s
Mitte
Kopfe:
Körpe
die H:
stimm
Die kı
Querb:
dung (
Köpfe
Längstangenten. Kurios,
die Primitiven nicht konstr
vollkommen bewußt tat od
Gefühl hatte. Die Ellipse

[Fig. 4] Julius Meier-Graefe, Sketch of El Greco's *The Crucifixion,* in *Spanische Reise* (Berlin, 1910), p. 250

Bartolomé Cossío, whose multivolume 1908 monograph on the Old Master had just been published.[13] Cossío's study is also emblematic of the above-mentioned process of substitution—although in his case, El Greco was "replacing" Murillo, not Velázquez. (Though written in Spanish and published in Spain, it had originally been commissioned by an English publisher, who had asked for a monograph on Murillo.)

Meier-Graefe's book also mentions Cossío's friend and fellow scholar Aureliano de Beruete, albeit not so much for his monumental Velázquez study as for his distinguished private collection. He owned two notable El Grecos: the *Portrait of an Old Man* (cat. 1), considered by some to be a self-portrait at the time, and the *Purification of the Temple* (fig. 5). Lavishing particular praise on the second of these, Meier-Graefe claimed that Beruete's "Grecos exceed all expectations."[14] And so Cossío and Beruete had thus met with the distinguished German critic in Madrid in the spring and early summer of 1908 after he reached out to them on the basis of their shared passion for the master of Toledo.

Their approaches were quite different, however. Meier-Graefe considered El Greco from a deeply formalist perspective, identifying what distinguished him from Velázquez in order to understand and explain El Greco's values. His two Spanish counterparts, on the other hand, sought to underscore the very thing that linked the painters. The German critic compared El Greco favorably to Rembrandt and Rubens and appreciated the internal order and structural coherence of his paintings; whereas Cossío and Beruete considered him squarely within the Spanish tradition, focusing not only on formal aspects but also on the content of his works.

These two main lines of approach in fact endured in subsequent critical reception of the artist as well (figs. 6, 7, 8). Certainly they would have been familiar to artists like Picasso who was drawing lessons at that time about the formal construction of some of El Greco's works and harnessing their iconic power and their ability to connote a particular moment in history.

Beruete was keeping an eye on El Greco's evolving reputation abroad. The first edition of his Velázquez monograph, published in 1898, while acknowledging El Greco as a key figure in the history of painting, had "affirmed" that he was "completely unknown outside Spain."[15]

Eight years later, the English edition, stated: "Until just a few years ago, El Greco was unknown outside Spain. Now, his name is familiar to painters and critics . . . and he is considered the precursor of modern art."[16] Monet had recently made his long-planned trip; Beruete, reporting to the painter Joaquín Sorolla, wrote: "Claude Monet was here . . . his eyes looking very lively and young. He does not say much and is quite direct. He admired El Greco, Velázquez, and especially Goya. Nothing else moved him."[17]

El Greco's influence on early modern art has long been a subject of interest and has generated a significant number of publications and exhibitions in recent decades, the present volume included.[18] Perhaps less known to enthusiasts of modern art is the story of El Greco's journey to critical reception in Spain. For it would take several hundred years before the painter born on Crete came to occupy an important position in the histories of Spanish art.

Indeed, El Greco's critical fortunes in Spain had been ambivalent until right up to the end of the nineteenth century. Though he experienced setbacks during his lifetime—most notably Philip II's reservations about one of his most ambitious works, *The Martyrdom of Saint Maurice and the*

Theban Legion (fig. p. 42)—he had nonetheless made a name for himself among his clients in Toledo. Here he received important commissions for the rest of his career and developed his extraordinarily personal style, which earned him the admiration, among others, of contemporary poets such as Luis de Góngora and Hortensio Félix Paravicino. After his death in 1614, however, the dominant aesthetic ideas in the country changed dramatically. His work was forgotten, except for his portraits, which Velázquez admired. Word of his conduct, however, lived on, and he was often cited as an example of a painter who had defended his dignity and his art, even to the point of suing his clients. His name was often invoked in subsequent writings on the worth of the painter's profession.[19]

During the eighteenth century few artists— neither those devoted to the "beautiful ideal" nor those who advocated a return to nature in the twilight of the 1700s—found a precedent to embrace in El Greco. And in the first half of the nineteenth century, his position in Spanish painting was at best obscure. Indeed, because he was born and trained abroad, his standing as a "Spanish" painter was challenged on several occasions. An 1824 catalogue of paintings exhibited at the Prado described him as a "singular

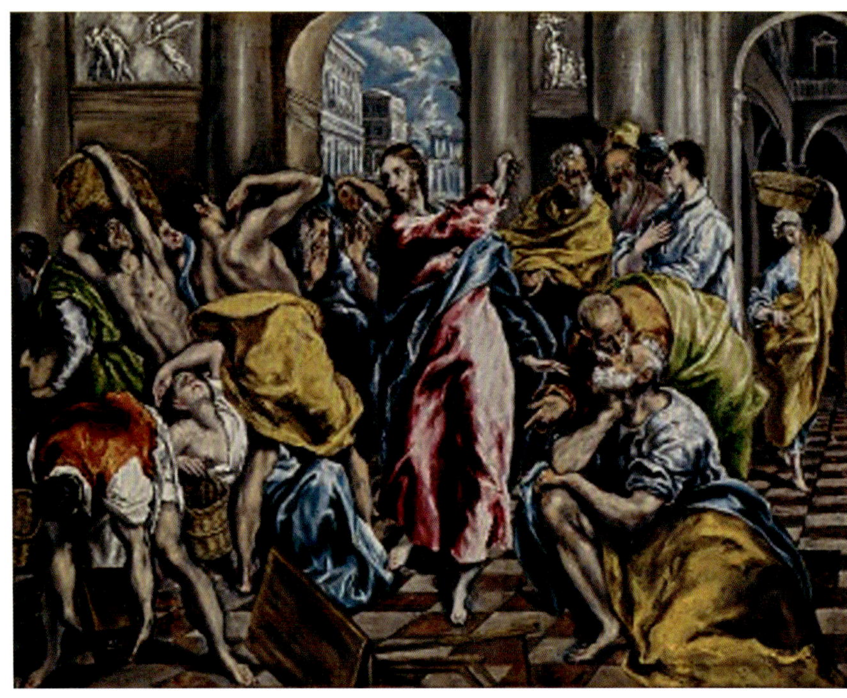

[Fig. 5] El Greco, *The Purification of the Temple*, 1595–1600
Oil on canvas, 41 × 52 cm
The Frick Collection, New York

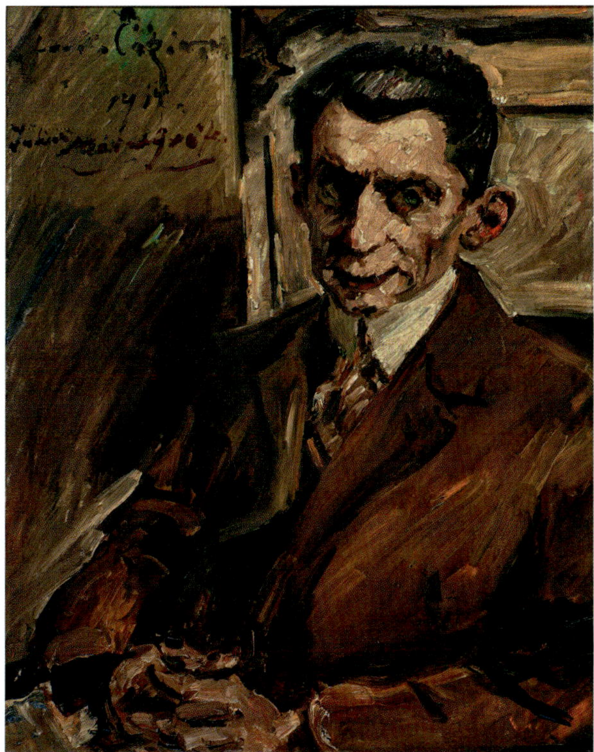

[Fig. 6] Lovis Corinth, *Julius Meier-Graefe,* 1912
Oil on canvas, 90 × 70 cm
Musée d'Orsay, Paris

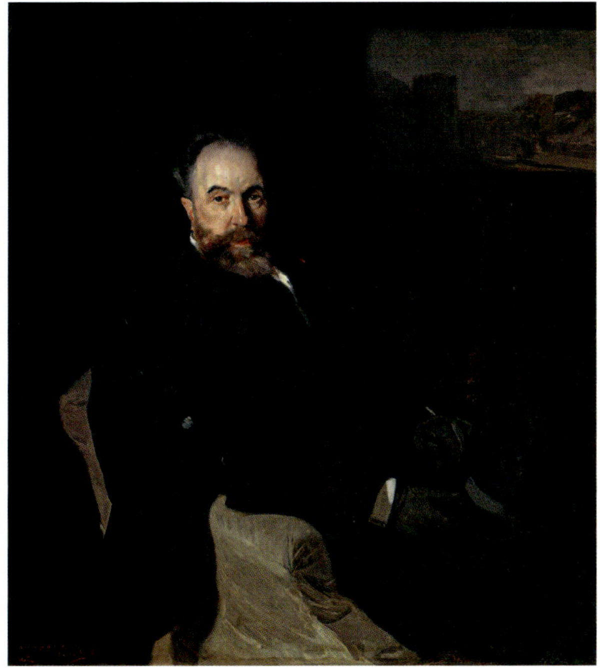

[Fig. 7] Joaquín Sorolla, *Aureliano de Beruete,* 1902
Oil on canvas, 115 × 110 cm
Museo Nacional del Prado, Madrid

painter" of "the Venetian school," and the Italian label dogged him at the Prado as late as 1900.[20]

Several important events in the 1830s drew new attention to his work, however, paving the way for greater recognition and revival. One was the aforementioned opening in 1838 of the Spanish gallery at the Louvre, which displayed El Greco's *Christ on the Cross Adored by Two Donors* (ca. 1590) and a few portraits.[21] Though Zurbarán and Goya drew more critical attention in this context, El Greco was noticed as well; moreover, in a collection identified specifically with Spain, El Greco's inclusion helped associate him more clearly in the public mind with the concept of Spanish painting.

In Madrid, too, the painter's visibility was on the rise. In 1832, Ferdinand VII purchased *The Holy Trinity* of 1577–79 from the painter Valeriano Salvatierra, making it the first large-scale history painting by El Greco to enter the Spanish royal collection and go on view at the Prado. Three years later the Spanish government began its program of seizure and sale of the property of religious institutions, leading to the creation of new museums to accommodate the thousands of works of art that had changed hands. One of these was the Museo Nacional de la Trinidad, which opened in Madrid in 1837 with some fifteen hundred paintings confiscated from monasteries and convents in the city and surrounding towns. The intention was to complement the Prado's own holdings in Spanish painting and fill its gaps; in El Greco's case, the acquisitions included several devotional pieces, plus five works he painted for the Colegio de Doña María de Aragón in Madrid, one of his more ambitious projects.[22] With the Revolution of 1868 and the ensuing nationalization of the Prado it was soon decided that the Museo de la Trinidad would be incorporated into the Prado. In fact, most of the paintings remained at the Trinidad site until the 1880s, when they were scattered around the country. But several of the El Grecos from Doña María de Aragón were among the hundred or so paintings that from 1868 on were gradually transferred to the Prado.

In the 1830s and 1840s, as various events brought Spanish painting into the spotlight, several publications appeared in a variety of forms to document its history. The most influential of these included widely-read travel books by Richard Ford and Théophile Gautier, as well

as Louis Viardot's writings on the Prado and
other Spanish museums, and William Stirling-
Maxwell's extensive, scholarly *Annals of the Artists
of Spain*.[23] Their authors had first-hand knowledge not only of Spain but also of the locations
of its important paintings. And, significantly, all
of them made important references to El Greco.
It is true that their accounts of him echoed
the traditional historiography—for example in
calling El Greco a "flamboyant" artist whose
production consisted of some highly considered
paintings and others that were disconcerting.
(Stirling-Maxwell described him as fluctuating
between "reason and madness."[24]) But apart from
their specific critical opinions, they nonetheless
helped consolidate El Greco's presence within the
"Spanish School." Stirling-Maxwell embedded
him into a scholarly account of the evolution of
Spanish painting, while Ford and Gautier, working within the lighter "travel" genre," intertwined
El Greco with the historical landscape of Spain.

Within the general parameters of the Spanish
School, moreover, El Greco was gaining his own
special status as a representative of the "Toledo
School."[25] Gregorio Cruzada Villaamil, deputy
director of the Museo de la Trinidad, designated
him as its founder.[26] The distinguished historian
of Spanish art was nonetheless speaking for many
of his colleagues when he wrote that El Greco's
"errant, crazy style of painting" was a source not
only of "great beauty to emulate" but also "many
defects from which to escape."[27]

In France, 1869 marked the year that the
Histoire des peintres de toutes les écoles (A History
of Painters of All Schools) brought out its volume
on Spain. Here, too, it was clear that the Greek-
born master from Toledo had found a place in
the history of Spanish painting. The book—part
of a high-profile fourteen-volume project edited
by Charles Blanc (and also issued in English
and German)—was specifically limited to artists
deemed part of the *école espagnole*. And indeed,
Paul Lefort's chapter on El Greco constituted
one of the longer segments. Lefort accorded El
Greco a very important place, singling him out
as "the founder of a new, truly national, truly
Spanish School: The ascetic and realist school."
And, just as significantly, Lefort identified the
"mystical exaltation and religious naturalism" of
the local Spanish milieu as the main factor that
had allowed El Greco to let go of his Venetian
ways and undertake a radical change in his style.[28]

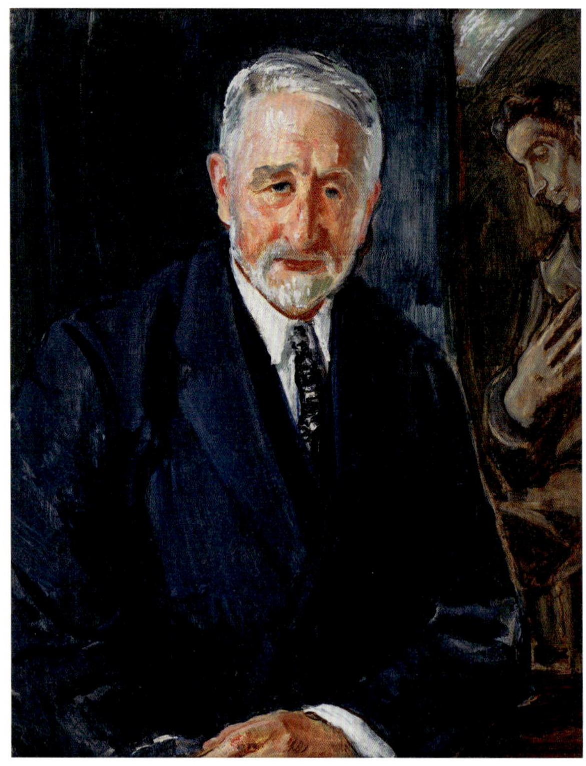

[Fig. 8] Maurice Fromkes, *Manuel Bartolomé Cossío,* ca. 1925
Oil on canvas, 74 × 56 cm
Museo Nacional del Prado, Madrid

Soon this process linking the painter's stylistic transformation to the "spirit" of his new country of residence found a solid foothold in art historiography and the popular imagination alike.

The next decades saw a revival of interest in the pictorial values of El Greco's painting and the appropriation of those values by the more daring artists. Parallel to this there was also a process of "nationalization" of his work, as scholars and cultural figures sought formal characteristics and content that could be linked not just to the concept of Spanish painting but to the actual historical definition of "Spain" itself.

This phenomenon should be viewed through a larger prism that takes several factors into account: the fact that interest in Spanish art had been building in Europe and America for decades;[29] the availability of ever more sophisticated instruments for historical-artistic analysis; and, at a local level, a "national" awareness among many of the period's most active intellectuals. Concurrent with the emergence of significant nationalist movements in the Basque Country, Catalonia, and Galicia, general reflection throughout Spain began to turn on themes of the nation, its history, its definition, its problems, and how to solve them. Significantly, within this context—and at this unique moment in Spanish cultural history—El Greco essentially became naturalized "citizen" of Spain. Certainly he came to be the focus of lively interest among some of the country's most prominent thinkers. In a number of cases, moreover, the varied interpretations of his work became woven into a broad reflection on Spanish national character.[30]

A two-sided process emerged from this, with the each side at times acting autonomously. On one hand, the extraordinary formal and chromatic singularity and remarkable structural coherence of El Greco's painting made him uniquely influential in the development of painting from the late nineteenth century on. At the same time, his works became charged with new national and historical content—to the point that his oeuvre now stood, alongside that of Goya, as one of the most important bodies of work within the entire history of Spanish painting.

Within Spain itself, these aspects were not necessarily mutually exclusive.[31] One of the first collectives to embrace El Greco (not only in Spain but in all of Europe) was a group of Catalonian artists with close links to Paris, along with the Basque painter Ignacio Zuloaga and, occasionally, Picasso. Several of them, including Zuloaga and Santiago Rusiñol, were early collectors of El Greco and made myriad (implicit and explicit) references to his art in theirs. Their efforts to revive him even fueled an initiative to erect a statue to the Old Master, which was unveiled in the Catalan seaside town of Sitges in 1898 (fig. 9). (At the time only Murillo and Ribera had been similarly honored in Spain. Velázquez took his seat before the Prado the next year.) Elsewhere in Europe, various artists, historians, and collectors had shown some interest in El Greco, but not—yet—on a scale that matched the revival promoted by painters and critics with ties to Catalonia.[32]

Two of the primary groups in Spain that were encouraging national introspection at the time were the Institución Libre de Enseñanza (The Free Institution of Education) and the so-called Generación del 98. Both advocated critical analysis of Spain—its current conditions, historical character, and attempts to improve the country—based on deep knowledge of the situation. Founded as a progressive project in 1876 in Madrid, the Institución was the seat of "Spanish Krausism"—a broad progressive cultural and educational movement based on the thought of the philosopher Karl Christian Friedrich Krause (a contemporary of Hegel's). As for the "generation" of contemporary writers and thinkers that emerged circa 1898—around the time that Spain lost its remaining colonies in America—many of those intellectuals had in fact studied at the Institución.

The new attention accorded El Greco was also reflected in major literary works published in the late nineteenth and early twentieth centuries, one of the golden ages in the history of the Spanish novel. Here the painter is often mentioned in connection with Toledo, then a city in the process of becoming one of Europe's best-known "memory places." (With its intact urban layout, Toledo was steeped in the past and easily stood for the history of the country itself—an appealing backdrop for commenting on Spain's social, religious, and intellectual complexities.) Indeed, the construction of the myth of El Greco underway in Spain at the time was inseparable from Toledo's own wealth of connotations, and they mutually enriched each other over time.[33] Benito Pérez Galdós set the last part of his 1891 novel *Ángel Guerra* in Toledo, allowing the author to refer to El Greco's works and occasionally draw comparisons with the characters in his story. And in Pío Baroja's important novel *Camino de perfección* (Pathway of Perfection), published ten years later, a visit to see El Greco's portrait of Cardinal Tavera and, most particularly, his painting *The Burial of the Count of Orgaz* forms the basis of a climacteric episode.[34]

Manuel Bartolomé Cossío (fig. 8), art historian and Krausist educator, stands out among those who paved the way for El Greco's transformation into a quintessentially *Spanish* figure entirely identified with Toledo. A leading member of the reformist Institución Libre de Enseñanza, he published a history of Spanish painting in its *Boletín* in 1886 that claimed a deep connection between "the People" (*el pueblo*) and the artistic expression of their times; painting was nothing less than "the result of the unfolding of the overall history of the People." This thinking was influenced, among other currents, by the positivism of the French historian and critic Hippolyte Taine.[35] In the spirit of these ideas, Cossío described the evolution of Spanish painting as an interaction between constant foreign influences (Flemish and Italian) and the Spanish personality; it reached its peak in the seventeenth century with

the emergence of an entirely Spanish style. "El Greco, Ribera, Zurbarán, Velázquez, and Murillo are the most original and representative painters in Spain." Here was Cossío acknowledging El Greco as a very pillar of the Spanish School and referring to him as "the highest example of Spanish painting."[36]

The far-reaching reflection on and research into El Greco carried out both in Spain and the rest of Europe in the following years culminated in the publication of Cossío's 1908 monograph, a watershed event in the historiography of Spanish art.[37] Exemplary in its documentary wealth and marked by its author's determination to examine most of the artist's paintings and compare their details, the book's narrative style and intellectual honesty won it a wide audience. It was also a product of its time in the sense that it relied on ideas that are now considered a priori, such as the belief that the artist's "soul" was infused with the essence of the country's history. In Cossío's opinion, El Greco was not just a *part* of the history of Spanish painting; he was also a *symbol* of the country and its historical character and was "deeply and intimately identified with Spain's very nature and soul."[38]

Cossío underscored the role of Toledo in that process of identification, describing the relation-

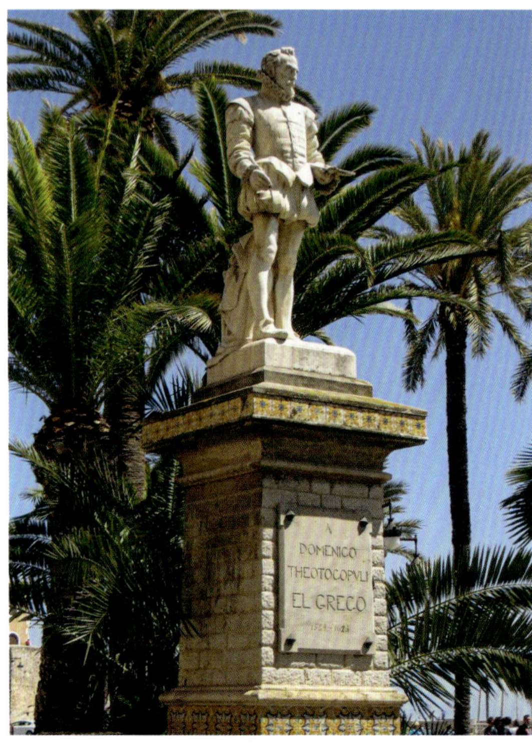

[Fig. 9] Josep Reynés, Monument to El Greco, 1898
Sitges ((Province of Barcelona)

ship between the painter and his city as a sort of communion:

> Toledo needed a painter who was both a genius and skilled enough to understand the city's character and identify with its history; one who could translate the melancholy mood and prevailing pessimism of the times and even the cold local color with great sincerity; one whose works would rival in beauty Toledo's trove of artistic gems. That painter was El Greco.[39]

But Cossío's transformation of El Greco into a "Spanish painter" was not based solely on the artist's identification with the city where he spent most of his career; there was also a stylistic consideration involved. Beruete had already compared El Greco to Velázquez and, in so doing, helped to incorporate him into the history of Spanish painting.[40] Beruete pointed out that the two painters shared a similar approach to color, which in turn linked them to the Venetians. Cossío went further, claiming that it was not just their use of color but their "realism" that formed the basis of their connection, "in the sense . . . of an essentially human intimacy at an ordinary, everyday level, with no preconceived selection of heroic or transcendental types."[41] In other words, in order to present El Greco as a "Spanish painter," he relied on one of the criteria that had been used for a century to characterize the "Spanish School" as a whole. During the nineteenth century, this concept was infused with new, positive connotations; it was used whenever there was a need to describe the Spanish masters. And, at a time when the importance of contextual factors as a means to explain the process of artistic creation was ranked very highly, it was presented as a way to explain El Greco's painting within the context of the Spanish tradition.

Cossío also relied on another characteristic: "mysticism." The term had been applied to Spanish painting for decades, which meant that there were two reasons to include El Greco in its history. The allusion to mysticism moreover allowed Cossío to present a reasoned justification of El Greco's more "advanced" style, which up until then had been the main source of critics' reservations about his painting. Cossío cited *The Burial of the Count of Orgaz* as an example of the coexistence of both styles in his work (fig. p. 14); describing the values of the painting's lower and upper zones—its "realist" and "mystical" portions—as part of the same reality.[42] For him (and for many intellectuals at the time), these were the two faces of the Spanish culture as a whole: the realism expressed in the depiction of the members of Toledan society attending the count's funeral and the mysticism and spirituality that illuminate the upper, heavenly section and extend and distort the painter's forms.

Cossío's monograph quickly became a definitive reference work for El Greco. Its vast wealth of documentary facts and shrewd critical insight still make it essential reading. In addition to its many contributions to "objective" scholarship, the book also contains some critical judgments that placed the painter from Crete at the very heart of Spain's artistic culture. Since its publication, El Greco has been a fixture in the history of Spanish painting, in the "Spanish" sections of great museums, and in exhibitions of Spanish art.

In the last century, two main factors have contributed to loosening the "corset" of that essentially Spanish label. The first involved changes in the categories of art history, specifically a more international approach to studying the Baroque and Mannerist styles—changes that have done much since the 1920s to secure El Greco's position on a broader, supranational stage. The second factor of course was his profound influence on modern art. This accorded him a place in an entirely different (though not necessarily incompatible) milieu, one that reached well beyond Spain. It has helped all of us gain a better understanding of his painting and has profoundly enriched our layered readings of his work.

1 *Museu Picasso: Catàleg de pintura i dibuix* (Barcelona, 1984), cat. MPB110.255.
2 Aureliano de Beruete, *Velázquez* (Paris, 1898).
3 Alisa Luxemberg, "Regenerating Velázquez in Spain and France in the 1890s," *Boletín del Museo del Prado* 35 (1999), pp. 125–51.
4 María de los Santos García Felguera, *La fortuna de Murillo* (Seville, 1989), pp. 415–43.
5 Ibid., pp. 415–43.
6 Charles Ricketts, *The Art of the Prado* (Boston, 1907), p. 46.
7 Referring to Murillo's *Invitation to a Game of Argolla* (1665–70), Ruskin described its two boys as "ragged and vicious vagrants that Murillo has gathered out of the street" and blasted the painting on moral grounds. "We all know that a beggar's bare foot cannot be clean; there is no need to thrust its degradation into the light." John Ruskin, "The Nature of the Gothic," in *The Stones of Venice* (London, 1907), vol. 2, pp. 212–13. See also García Felguera 1989 (see note 4), p. 76.
8 Nigel Glendinning, *Goya and His Critics* (New Haven, 1977).
9 See Javier Portús, *El concepto de pintura española: Historia de un problema* (Madrid, 2012).
10 Javier Barón, *Greco et les modernes* (Paris, 2019), pp. 83–89.
11 Martin Warnke, "El viaje a España de Meier-Graefe," in *Historiografía del arte español en los siglos XIX y XX* (Madrid, 1995), pp. 349–54; idem. "Julius Meier-Graefes 'Spanische Reise': Ein kunsthistorischer Paradigmwechsel," in *Kunst in Spanien im Blick des Fremden*, ed. Gisela Noehles-Doerk (Frankfurt, 1996).
12 "I believe that only Rembrandt can hold his own beside El Greco's Crucifixion." Julius Meier-Graefe, *Spanische Reise* (Berlin, 1910), p. 254.
13 Manuel Bartolomé Cossío, *El Greco* (Madrid, 1908).
14 Meier-Graefe 1910 (see note 12), p. 32. See pp. 48–49 for the extensive description of the *Purification*.
15 Beruete 1898 (see note 2), p. 67.
16 Aureliano de Beruete, *Velázquez* (London, 1906), p. 45.
17 Quoted in *Aureliano de Beruete*, exh. cat. Caja de Pensiones (Madrid, 1983), p. 89.
18 See, among others, José Álvarez Lopera, "El 'descubrimiento' de El Greco y el desarrollo de la pintura moderna," in *Hommage à El Greco*, ed. István Barkóczi, exh. cat. Szépművészeti Múzeum (Budapest, 1991); Francisco Calvo Serraller, "El Greco y la pintura contemporánea," in *El Greco: Su revalorización por el Modernismo catalán*, ed. José Milicua, exh. cat., Museu Nacional d'Art de Catalunya (MNAC) (Barcelona, 1996); Gary Tinterow and Geneviève Lacambre, eds., *Manet/Velázquez: The French Taste for Spanish Painting*, exh. cat. The Metropolitan Museum of Art, New York, and Musée d'Orsay, Paris (New Haven, 2003); Robert S. Lubar, "La presencia de El Greco en el arte español del siglo XX," in *El Greco*, ed. José Álvarez Lopera (Barcelona, 2003), pp. 445–62; Beat Wismer and Michael Scholz-Hänsel, eds., *El Greco and Modernism*, exh. cat. Museum Kunstpalast (Dusseldorf, 2012); Javier Barón, ed., *El Greco y la pintura moderna*, exh. cat. Museo del Prado (Madrid, 2014); and Barón 2019 (see note 10).
19 José Manuel Pita Andrade, *Dominico Greco y sus obras a lo largo de los siglos XVII y XVIII* (Madrid, 1984). See, among other sources, Antonio Palomino's short biog-

raphy of El Greco in *Lives of the Eminent Spanish Painters and Sculptors* (1724), trans. Nina Ayala Mallory (Cambridge and New York, 1987), pp. 82–86.
20 Luis Eusebi refers to El Greco as a "singular painter" in his *Catálogo de los cuadros que existen colocados en el Real Museo de Pinturas del Prado* (Madrid, 1824), p. 34. On the "Italian label," see, for example, Pedro de Madrazo, *Catálogo de los cuadros del Museo del Prado de Madrid*, 8th ed. (Madrid, 1900). See Leticia Ruiz Gómez, *El Greco en el Museo Nacional del Prado: Catálogo razonado* (Madrid, 2007), pp. 13–18.
21 Notice no. 253–260, 1838 (included in the "Écoles espagnoles"). See Jeannine Baticle, "The Galerie Espagnole of Louis-Philippe," in Tinterow 2003 (see note 18), p. 187.
22 José Álvarez Lopera, *El Museo de la Trinidad: Historia, obras y documentos* (Madrid, 2009).
23 Richard Ford, *A Handbook for Travellers in Spain and Readers at Home* (London, 1845); Théophile Gautier, *Voyage en Espagne* (Paris, 1843); Louis Viardot, *Les Musées d'Espagne: Guide et memento de l'artiste et voyageur* (Paris 1860); William Stirling-Maxwell, *Annals of the Artists of Spain*, 3 vols. (London, 1848). See José Álvarez Lopera, *De Ceán a Cossío: La fortuna crítica del Greco en el siglo XIX* (Madrid, 1987).
24 Stirling-Maxwell 1848 (see note 23), vol. 1, p. 285.
25 Viardot 1860 (see note 23), pp. 109–10.
26 Gregorio Cruzada Villaamil, *Catálogo provisional, historial y razonado del Museo nacional de Pintura y Escultura* (Madrid, 1865), p. 163.
27 Ibid., p. 164.
28 Paul Lefort, "Dominico Theotocopuli, surnommé Le Greco," in *Histoire des peintres de toutes les écoles: École espagnole*, ed. Charles Blanc (Paris, 1869), p. 7 of the eight-page fascicule on El Greco.
29 See Enriqueta Harris, "El Greco's 'fortuna crítica' in Britain" (1995), reprinted in *Spanish Art in Britain and Ireland, 1750–1920*, ed. Nigel Glendinning and Hilary Macartney (Woodbridge, 2010), pp. 240–54; Inge Reist and José Luis Colomer, eds., *El Greco Comes to America: The Discovery of a Modern Old Master* (New York and Madrid, 2017).
30 José Álvarez Lopera "El Greco: Los caminos de la rehabilitación," in Milicua 1996 (see note 18), pp. 28–30; Eric Storm, *El descubrimiento del Greco: Nacionalismo y arte moderno (1860–1914)* (Madrid, 2011); and *The Discovery of El Greco: The Nationalization of Culture and the Rise of Modern Art* (Chicago, 2016).
31 Francisco Calvo Serraller, *La invención del arte español: De El Greco a Picasso* (Barcelona, 2013), pp. 137–46.
32 Milicua 1996 (see note 18).
33 On Toledo and El Greco at the time, see Jesús Carrobles, "Toledo y El Greco a comienzos del siglo XX," in *El Greco: Toledo 1900*, ed. Ana Carmen Lavín, exh. cat. Zaragoza et al. (Madrid, 2008), pp. 20–37.
34 Álvarez Lopera 1987 (see note 22), pp. 340–42, 493–96. See also Rafael Alarcón, "El Greco," in *Temas literarios hispánicos*, ed. Leonardo Romero Tobar (Zaragoza, 2013), vol. 1, pp. 111–41.
35 Juan Carlos Sánchez Illán, *La nación inacabada: Los intelectuales y el proceso de construcción nacional (1900–1914)* (Madrid, 2002), p. 77.
36 All passages from Manuel Bartolomé Cossío, *Aproximación a la pintura española* (1886) (Madrid, 1985), pp. 34, 57, 107.

37 See José Álvarez Lopera, "El Greco de Cossío: Gestación y primeras reacciones críticas," in *El Greco: The First Twenty Years in Spain*, ed. Nicos Hadjinicolau (Rethymno, 2005), 261–77; Javier Portús, "Manuel B. Cossío y El Greco," in *El arte de saber ver: Manuel B. Cossío, la Institución Libre de Enseñanza y El Greco*, ed. Salvador Guerrero (Madrid, 2016), pp. 81–118.
38 Cossío 1908 (see note 13), p. 198.
39 Ibid., p. 112.
40 Beruete 1906 (see note 16), pp. 44–47.
41 Cossío 1908 (see note 13), p. 197.
42 Ibid., p. 44.

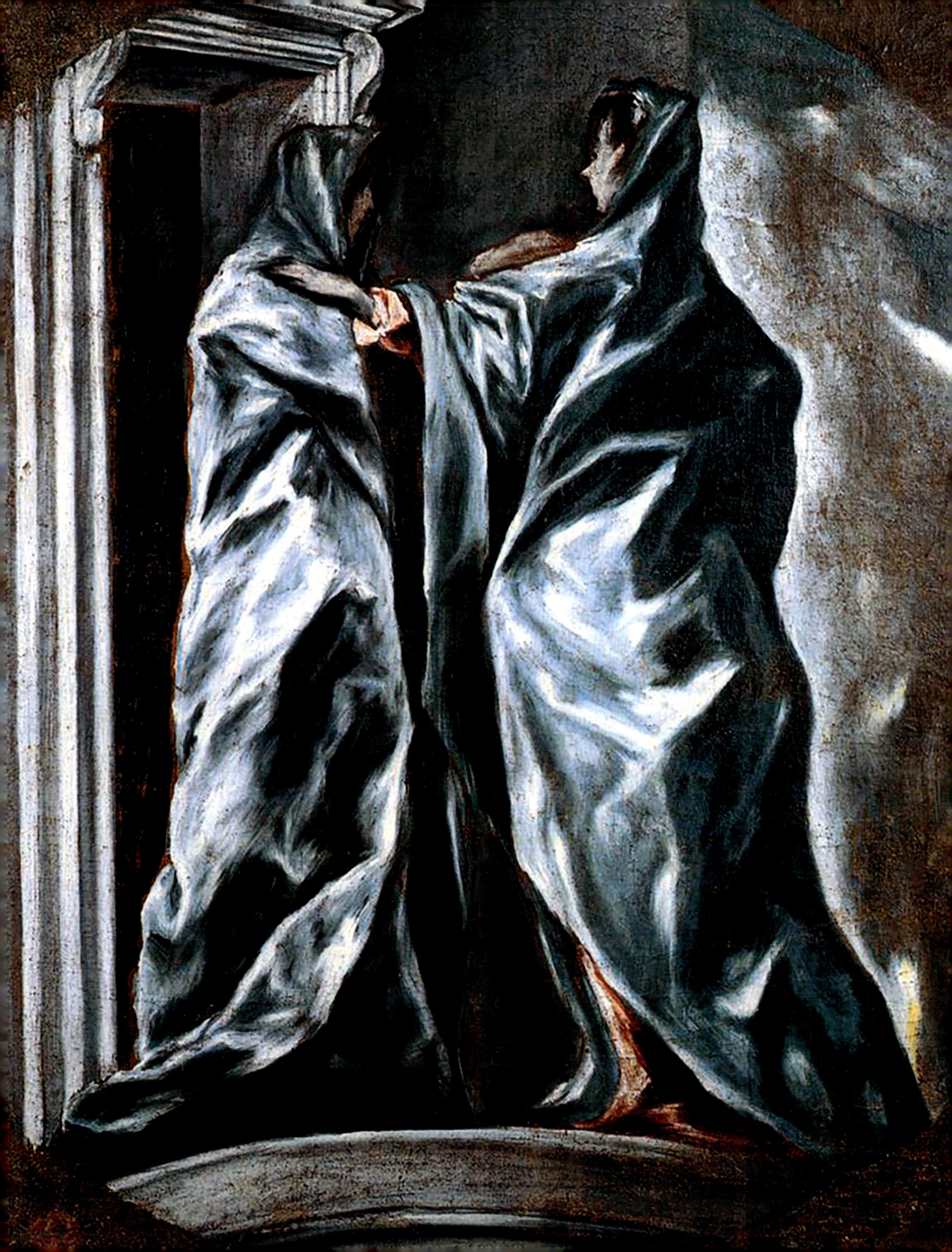

Richard Shiff

Magic

To Deny a Future

Why preface an assertion of cause or motivation with the phrase "not by chance"? I can hear myself saying, without self-consciousness, "It was not by chance that my methods proved effective." Yet I might have been making fortunate guesses that, by chance, arrived at a desirable end.[1] Is the existential difference detectable?

Imagine two events, A and B, for which the discernible context establishes no more than their temporal coincidence, contiguity, or succession. To propose that a causal relation exists—that A entails B, or B is the logical result of A—overdetermines a chance situation that might exist just as well with no determination, its end in itself. To the amorphousness of an array of chance occurrences, causation introduces an orderly narrative, a convincing history, even a mythology. By this finality, this decisiveness, causation denies chance a future.

In support of causal ends, the qualification "not by chance" adds rhetorical emphasis along with redundancy. Yet "not by chance" backtracks, for it protests too much. It eliminates in advance the threat that chance—its entropic disorder —might intervene in lieu of an explanation. Chance cannot be a cause. It explains nothing.

Interpretation of art or of any human endeavor amounts to a science of supposition.

←
El Greco, *The Visitation* (detail), 1609-1613
Oil on canvas 98 x 72 cm
Dunbarton Oaks, Washington, D.C.

"I suppose . . . " announces both a guess and a proposition. The edgy sexual ambiguity of Pablo Picasso's *Demoiselles d'Avignon* (1907; fig. 1) leads a wary critic into a morass of interpretation initiated by others: "It is perhaps *not by chance* if [a masculinized demoiselle] took on so much importance . . . "[2] "Not by chance," the critic writes. This is a supposition. How logically coherent, culturally germane, or psychologically compelling must a phenomenon be to have appeared "not by chance"?

A Small World of Meaning

In 1901, in Spain and in France, Picasso drew from numerous sources of sensory, emotional, and intellectual stimulation, among them the art of El Greco. His memorial to his suicided friend Carles Casagemas—*Evocation (The Burial of Casagemas)* of 1901 (cat. 17)—recalls El Greco's *Burial of Count Orgaz*, with its division of earthly and heavenly realms (fig. p. 14). Picasso visited the El Greco site around the time of Casagemas's death.[3] But interpretation requires no such precision in timing. Given Picasso's nationalistic identification with the recently lionized El Greco, any discernible formal analogies, Picasso to El Greco, would hardly be considered accidental. Picasso's identities were nevertheless eclectic and complex; and on the French side, also in 1901, he parodied Édouard Manet's *Olympia,* converting the reclining courtesan from white to black, European to African. In a subsequent drawing, he himself became the courtesan, a Moorish one—again, European to African.[4]

Such derivations, invocations, and instances
of visual wit and even whimsy, if convincingly
set into a cultural context, appear purposeful.
Most occurrences, however, including those that
have acquired contextual meaning, will seem in
relation to the totalizing history of *all* events no
more than coincidental. Things that exist, without
discernible effect on history as recorded, have
at least beaten the odds of never existing at all.
Significance, "meaning," occupies a small world.
What does it *mean*, interpretive critics ask, as they
transition from selective description to speculative analysis?[5]

Picasso's 1901 was also Sigmund Freud's
1901. This year marked the initial appearance, in
two installments in a medical journal, of Freud's
most widely read publication, *Psychopathology
of Everyday Life*. His study distinguished two
mentalities in relation to the play of chance: one,
a mind conscious of innumerable chance events
and the potential for chance association, accepting all phenomena without insisting on attributing meaning to any, no matter how attractive the
connections; the other, a life of the unconscious
that, as Freud argued, knows nothing of chance.
Whatever strikes the unconscious bears meaning.
Freud defined the life of the unconscious—
comprising fantasies, dreams, illusions, and imaginative associations—as ruled by causal relations
from the start. Every turn of unconscious thought
has its purpose, its reason, its connection to every
other thought. By this definition, the play of the
unconscious resembles the generation of a critical
discourse in which every factual observation
becomes the symptom of an explanatory order
awaiting articulation.

"I believe in outer (real) chance," Freud
wrote, "but not in inner (psychic) accidents. With
the superstitious person the case is reversed: he
knows nothing of the motive of his chance and
faulty actions, he believes in the existence of
psychic contingencies; he is therefore inclined
to attribute meaning to external chance, which
manifests itself in actual occurrence, and to see in
the accident a means of expression for something
hidden outside of him."[6] Where others accept
chance, letting sleeping dogs lie, the superstitious
person imposes the rationality of the psychic unconscious on the chaos of conditions and events,
perceiving causality in every aspect of the external
world. This is an egocentric, paranoid position.
The science of interpretation, motivated by inner

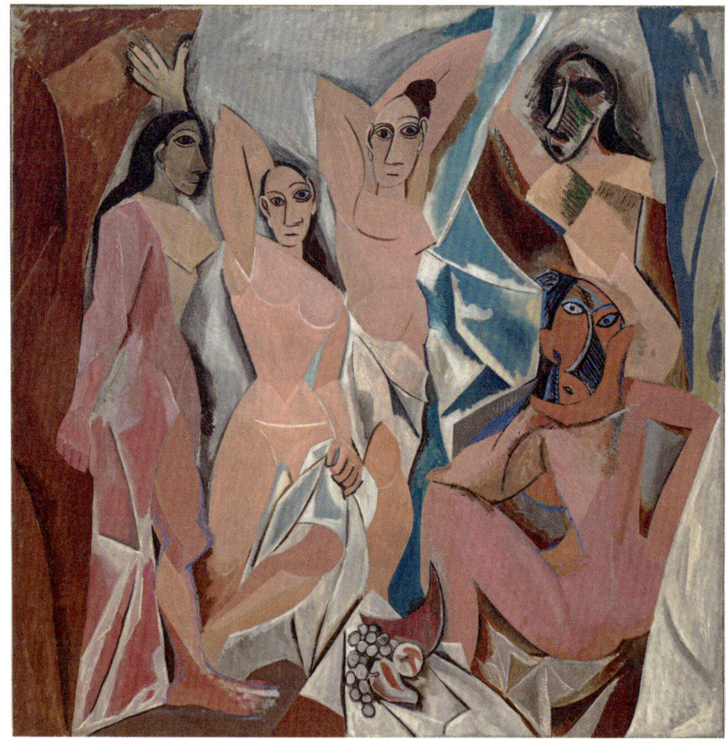

[Fig.1] Pablo Picasso, *Les Demoiselles d'Avignon,* 1907
Oil on Canvas, 243.9 × 233.7 cm
The Museum of Modern Art, New York

needs as it investigates outer phenomena, is similarly paranoid. Hence, the common objection to hypotheses advanced by a critic's intellectual rivals: such proposals merely "reflect the fantasies of their originators."[7] Yet does not *every* interpretation reflect a fantasy? Often a collective fantasy, the promotion of a prevailing theory. Historiography, the history of history, adopts as its object of study the collective fantasies of an era—its theories of political order, social formation, aesthetics, sexuality, magic, whatever.

Any relation between what Freud and Picasso were thinking in 1901 would constitute a chance configuration, at least for Freud and Picasso, who had no fantastical "cause" to take an interest, each in the other, at that moment. Let's assume, nevertheless, on the basis of cultural context, biography, witness accounts, and personal statements, that Picasso was superstitious in Freud's sense of the concept. This becomes an interpreter's working supposition. In fact, Picasso may well have been "the most superstitious of twentieth-century artists."[8] He criticized Georges Braque, his sometime partner in formal innovation, for lacking the superstition that grounded his own aesthetic practice.[9] Picasso's superstitious beliefs become a guide, but an ironic one, for non-believing interpreters.

Causal Form

In 1908, the German critic Julius Meier-Graefe spent six days on site in Madrid at the Escorial contemplating El Greco's *Martyrdom of Saint Maurice and the Theban Legion* (1580–82; fig. p. 42). He sought a logic of form and composition to explain its sensory force:

> You fight with this picture. What happened to me was that every morning in front of the picture I had to recognize as ridiculous excuses the explanations which at night, away from the picture, I had thought out for myself. The picture stood there like a spirit whom you are trying to kill with a pistol. . . . The picture stood there, fortified against all attacks.[10]

Meier-Graefe's knowledge of normative composition was proving inadequate to establishing the cause or origin of El Greco's transformative power.

Decades later, at the Boston Museum of Fine Arts, the first cultural institution I visited regularly, I experienced a minor version of the phenomenon Meier-Graefe described, as I, too, fixated on El Greco. In my case, it was his relatively modest portrait of a personal friend, *Fray Hortensio Félix Paravicino* (1609; fig. 2)—much easier to grasp than the complexities of the *Saint Maurice*. I was wondering what distinguished art of high aesthetic quality from objects of mere

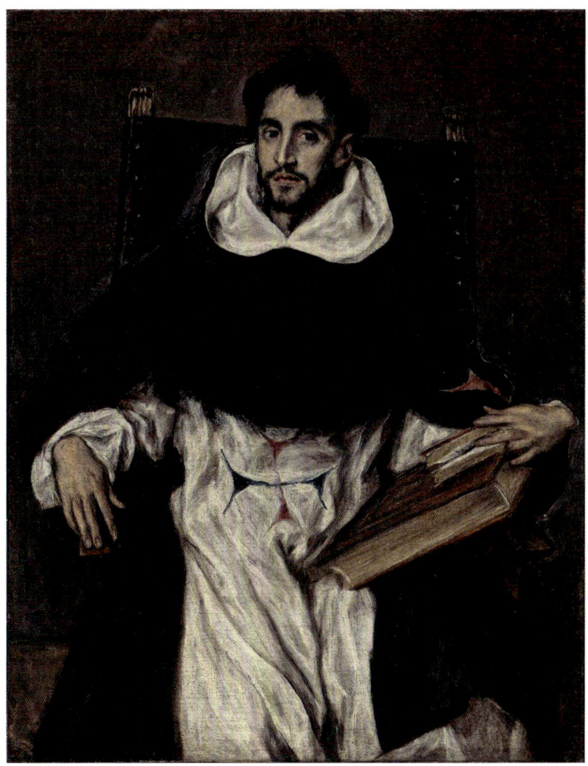

[Fig. 2] El Greco, *Fray Hortensio Félix Paravicino,* 1609
Oil on canvas, 112.1 × 86.1 cm
Boston Museum of Fine Arts, Isaac Sweetser Fund

antiquarian or sentimental interest. Why were canonical works so canonical? Barely familiar with the history of art at the time, I had little idea of the irony of El Greco's having been demeaned for many years for the eccentricity of his forms, then having become central to what was nominally my own tradition. What I observed about myself was that I returned to *Fray Hortensio* repeatedly, finding it the most magnetic image in the galleries. I can recall what fascinated me: a tension established by the crossed axes of the figure, the vertical of the torso, and the horizontal spread of the arms. A concert of diagonals complicated this organic geometry—the tilt of the figure's right hand, the compensatory tilt of the left hand extended by the book, and the tilt of the head with its complementary diagonal within the lower folds of the friar's Trinitarian habit. The central emblem, a blue-and-red Maltese cross with its own axes and tilts, all exquisitely animated by the painter's touch, epitomized the general vectorial play.

A cultural historian might argue that it was *not by chance* that I appreciated the compositional subtlety of El Greco's portrait, despite the uninformed circumstances of my encounter. Granted, the emotional reaction I experienced could not have depended on an identification with the Trinitarian order (or any monastic order), nor with the physical type. Nothing in my past would have generated more than the most general emotional link to this human subject. Nor could my perception of the representation have been related to El Greco's glorification during the nineteenth and early twentieth centuries by the likes of Meier-Graefe, which established him in art history as a profound spiritual presence and an innovative master of form. I knew nothing of these peripheral historical matters. The argument would be that I had unconsciously acquired a Western sensitivity to the type of formal order evident in El Greco, induced by multiple examples, albeit lesser ones, unavoidable in my cultural environment. This argument—that individuals are shaped unknowingly by the culture of others—is both commonplace and inherently paranoid.

Having no academic understanding of El Greco at the time, I *felt,* to the contrary, that my affinity for the image of the friar was personal, not cultural—a chance discovery, *my* discovery, within a vast array of art.[11] In retrospect, I realize that I could have fixated on Picasso in a nearby

gallery in the same museum, his *Standing Figure* of 1908 (fig. 3); it might have inadvertently prepared me for subsequent encounters with the *Demoiselles d'Avignon,* Picasso's work of the previous year. But I preferred El Greco. Through *Fray Hortensio* as intermediary, I was falling under the spell of Western art and its sense of formal order. Focusing on any object from the Western tradition might have accelerated this fall, even one from Boston's extensive Egyptian collection, African as much as European-Mediterranean. Yet if El Greco was merely demonstrating a version of Western practice that had been thoroughly assimilated into the whole, to me, his painting seemed uniquely "magical." Let this word resonate with all its common, colloquial senses. An event or phenomenon is *magical* when causal explanations fail it. To delve into the anthropological nuances of belief in magic, indulging in academic protocols, would impose an authoritative terminology on minimally describable qualities of an experience recalled years after the fact. Let the vague suggestiveness stand.

Was there nevertheless a reason for Picasso's art in Boston having been—for me, at that time—less of a sensory and emotional draw? In 1908, when Picasso painted *Standing Figure,* he was *falling out* of the same spell of Western art that I, decades later, was falling into as I gazed on *Fray Hortensio.* As a source of instruction in canonical Western anatomy, perspective, and pictorial composition, El Greco's image would serve much better than Picasso's, which confuses figure and ground, especially around the upper torso. Like my chance falling into El Greco, the *falling out* that befell Picasso, his turn from the standards of the European West, was an accident that happened—yet not *entirely* by chance. Whenever we discuss an event analytically, we cannot confine causation to chance alone. To repeat: chance is not a cause.

Chance Magic
Now, a novelistic conceit: in 1907, visiting the ethnographic collection at the Trocadéro in Paris, perhaps on a whim, Picasso experienced an unprecedented moment of metanoia, a totalizing reorientation of his mentality. His experience was so singular that, it might be argued, no concatenation of diverse causal factors—the "context" dear to historians—will explain it. Like

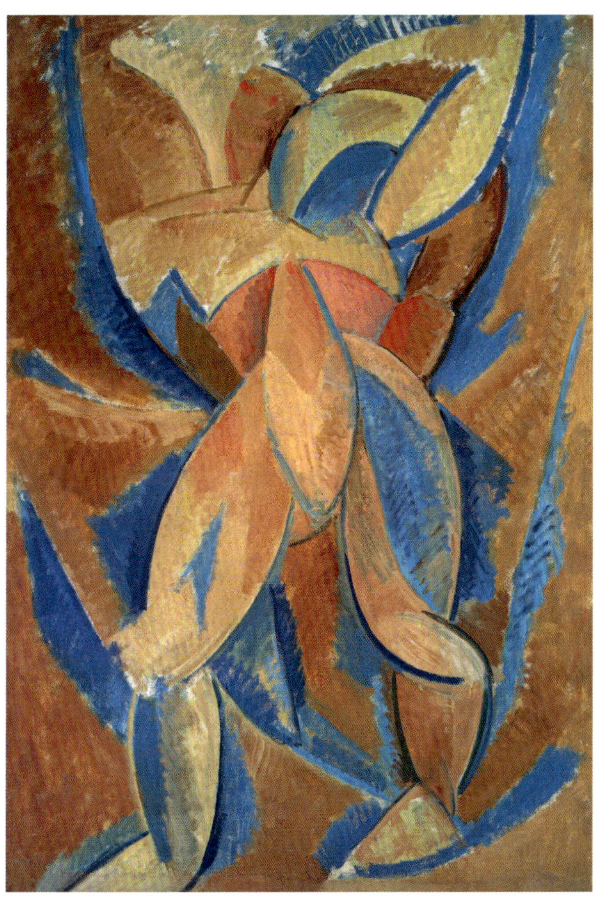

[Fig.3] Pablo Picasso, *Standing Figure,* 1908
Oil on canvas, 150.2 × 100.3 cm
Boston Museum of Fine Arts, Juliana Cheney Edwards Collection

William Rubin and others before me, like Picasso before Rubin and the others, I propose dating the artist's *falling-out* to this Trocadéro moment, notwithstanding many previous prodromal indications.[12] No person, instruction, protocol, or habit acted as Picasso's guide to the event. As if the truth of the world suddenly appeared in a dream taken for real, the unnamable and indescribable showed itself; and no cultural or social circumstances mitigated the transformative experience. At the Trocadéro, Picasso fell out of his European context. To fall is to undergo an accident.

Many of Picasso's peers as well as their predecessors had been seeking escape from the restrictions imposed by traditional, academic training in the arts, emblematic of a repressive social structure.[13] Subsequent to the fall, Picasso completed *Les Demoiselles d'Avignon* with reconfigured African-Oceanic types; he left them brutally juxtaposed to his preexisting Iberian-European types. His exit from normative practice was so abrupt that even his like-minded colleagues were mystified, some of them assuming that the work must have been abandoned unfinished.[14] As Picasso later described his Trocadéro conversion, it followed from a chance occurrence. Chance disrupts the biographic logic of a life, just as the *Demoiselles,* a case of historical chance in material form, disrupted the canonical history of painting.

Having gone to the Trocadéro to revisit the historical collections, Picasso, as he indicated to Rubin around 1970, "virtually stumbled upon the ethnological material" by entering the opposite wing of the building, passing through "the wrong door."[15] If the cause of his experience was truly the non-cause known as chance, Picasso could have had no inkling of his emotional reaction. Chance demolishes the psychological defenses established by reason and conscious intention. Yet Rubin's analysis introduces a not-by-chance qualifier, referring to Picasso's abrupt confrontation with non-Western material as a "logical continuation of the search that had [first] taken him to the [art-historical wing]. . . . What could be more logical than that this 'revelation' should have taken place in an ethnological museum?" There, the "ritual function" of the objects was evoked by the mode of display.[16] History and museal practice disarm chance by converting its appearances to signs or symptoms, references to a relational order.[17]

My own interpretive specificity follows Picasso's recollections. But it is not precisely "Picasso." The documentation of his falling-out is secondhand, consisting of accounts by André Malraux, Françoise Gilot, and others (like Rubin) that set Picasso's speech within quotation marks, as firsthand statements of fact, not mere paraphrase. The strict veracity of these recollections—first Picasso's belated account of what he had been thinking years before, then his witness's memory years afterward—has occasionally been questioned.[18] The challenges, however, come from a minority, while the majority of interpretive commentators accept the quoted statements. A question arises: Why have so many critical minds been willing to rely on statements with so much potential for inaccuracy? The obvious answer: because the statements confirm what the critics are predisposed to believe, their collective fantasy. Like belated Freudians, it suits them to acknowledge Picasso's irrational superstition, because they can use it to bring cause and reason to their interpretations.

To judge by its sustained invocation, the most convincing statement from Picasso-at-a-remove is the memoir by Malraux, who in 1974 quoted the artist's words from a conversation of 1937. Picasso is recorded as saying: "When I went to the old Trocadéro, it was disgusting. . . . The smell. I was all alone. . . . Something was happening to me, right? The masks . . . were magic things" (*des choses magiques*). In his telling, Picasso stands alone in a second sense, as the only one who perceives magic or spirit in the African and Oceanic objects, as opposed to deriving principles of structure from them. "We all of us"—the likes of Braque, André Derain, and Henri Matisse—"loved fetishes."[19] At least once, however, at the Trocadéro in 1907, Picasso felt no love. He responded with fear. The others, hardly superstitious, were taking mental notes on design from their casual engagements with exotic objects. They were translating non-Western magic into European form.

Picasso could have followed El Greco as a precedent in resisting the lure of normative Western convention. Many scholars have proposed El Greco as a potent "influence," arguing that aspects of his *Vision of Saint John* (1608–14; fig. 4), a work Picasso knew, appear in the *Demoiselles*.[20] Some of Picasso's contemporaries believed that El Greco acquired cultural significance not as a formal cause but because he embodied magical chance. An early French commentator, who characterized the Greek-Venetian-Spanish artist as "eager for liberation" from all inherited methods, offered this account:

> In [Toledo's] environment of mystical exaltation and religious naturalism, El Greco transformed his beautiful Venetian harmony to the point of despoiling it. His design becomes tortured; his figures exaggerate their gestures and expression; his coloration develops singular hues and strikingly violent contrasts of value; his canvases assume the appearance of passionate, disorderly studies.[21]

A "despoiled," "tortured" image that nevertheless transfixes its viewer in wonder must be magical (at least in the colloquial sense). El Greco had mastered "Venetian harmony" yet converted this epitome of the Western tradition to something other, explicable only by a critic's resort to "mystical exaltation," the magic of religious believers. With or without religion, Picasso had his complex array of superstitions, which exposed him to the terror of non-Western fetishes. His *Demoiselles,* whether or not a convincing formal analogue to El Greco's *Vision of Saint John,* becomes its *magical* analogue. But this comparison holds only with a shift from El Greco's culture to Picasso's.

Despite the religiosity—or because of it—El Greco's paintings could not, to European eyes, be fetishes. A non-Western fetish becomes a mere curiosity to those disinclined to respect and fear its magical powers. To Picasso's non-superstitious cohort, "the masks were just like any other pieces of sculpture"; Matisse hardly distinguished between the art of sub-Saharan regions and works from ancient Egypt, long assimilated into the Western canon.[22] According to Malraux's report of his words, Picasso alone registered the "magical" function of African and Oceanic fetish-objects:

> They were [defensive] weapons. To help people no longer be subject to spirits, to become free. . . . If we give a form to the spirits, we become free. The spirits, the unconscious (people weren't yet talking about this much), emotion—all the same thing. . . . *Les Demoiselles d'Avignon* must have come to me that very day, but not at all because of the forms.[23]

Here, Picasso insists on distinguishing an experience of form, structure, or design from an encounter with magic, spirit, or affect. Form responds to causal logic; the force of spirit appears as magical chance.

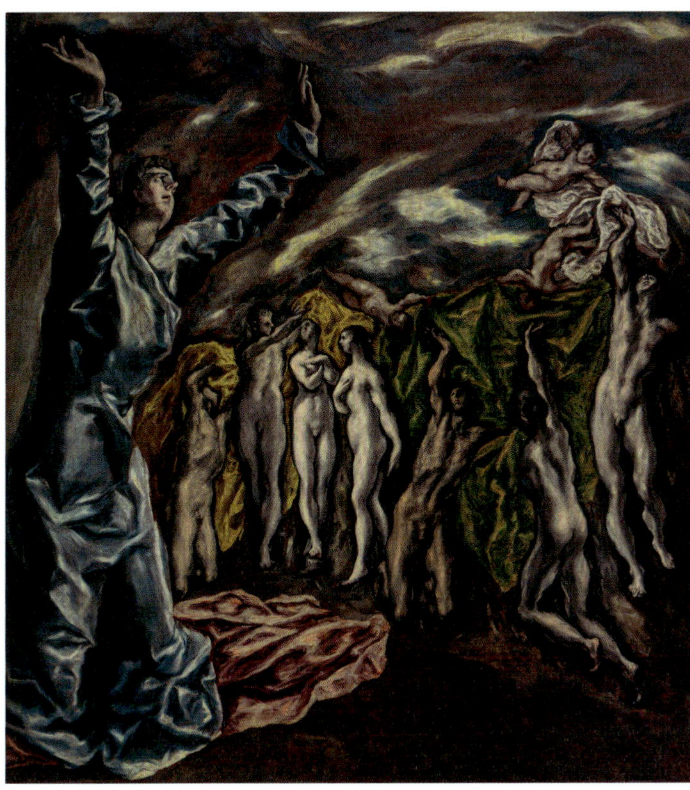

[Fig. 4] El Greco, *The Vision of Saint John,* ca. 1608–14
Oil on canvas, 222.3 × 193 cm
The Metropolitan Museum of Art, New York, Rogers Fund, 1956

Musing over his creative reactions to his emotional states, Picasso often finessed the differential gap between cause and chance. According to André Salmon, who argued that formal design superseded symbolism and allegory, Picasso had acknowledged a measure of rationality in the compositional violence of African and Oceanic objects. Non-Western art, by Salmon's account, nourished a developing "science" of painting, exemplified by the *Demoiselles.*[24] Formal cause prevailed over the chance magical encounter. But Picasso hedged the attribution of conscious intention to his aesthetic choices; in 1946, he claimed that art derives from "calculations that are frequently unknown to the author himself . . . calculation that precedes intelligence. . . . The condition of discovery is outside ourselves."[25] The dreamlike logic of expressive form that lies beyond the reach of the rational mind may be ready at hand within the superstitious mind—in its paranoia, it becomes receptive to magic. By anachronistic projection, Picasso in 1937 referred to the psychology of the unconscious to justify his Trocadéro experience of 1907. At either of the two moments, 1937 and 1907, Picasso's sense of his superstitiousness aligned with Freud's "psychopathology of everyday life."

Fetish-form
To give spirit a form, the form of one's own invention—to become conscious of unconscious impulses, attributing them to external causes—was to appropriate the spiritual or magical force, converting an offensive threat to a personal defensive protection.[26] Internal fears and anxieties become externalized in fetish-form, only to be internalized again in some strategic configuration. A fetish-object facilitates this process of safeguarding its maker or possessor. "We become free," as Picasso told Malraux.

Picasso's consciousness—or his unconscious—was already free enough, primed to recognize fetish-objects in the Trocadéro as fetishes rather than mere objects. With this "revelation," instead of perceiving form, Picasso felt spirit. Having been startled, even threatened, by spirit, he adopted form as a defensive weapon. In appropriating the magical power of alien objects, "giv[ing] a form to the spirits," he seized his chance, took control of his fate, mastered his superstitious fear—whether of the sexual power of women, of venereal disease, or of death.[27]

With this homeopathic remedy, incorporating the maleficent spirits, Picasso altered the look of his *Demoiselles,* most astonishingly in the masklike faces of the two figures to the right. The resultant disharmony was antithetical not only to European classicism and academicism but to Golden Age primitivism as well. The aggressive sexuality of Picasso's women brokered no tempering by allusion to European religion, mythology, or moralizing. The abrupt juxtapositions in a composition of divergent figural types, only tenuously integrated, confounded and even terrorized the artist's aesthetic allies.[28] But Picasso had "protection," having assimilated the violence as his own.[29] Leo Steinberg's description captures both the sexuality and the idiosyncrasy: "The space of the *Demoiselles* is a space peculiar to Picasso's imagination. Not a visual continuum"—conforming to academic norms—"but an interior apprehended on the model of touch and stretch, a nest known by intermittent palpation, or by reaching and rolling, by extending one's self within it."[30]

For the *Demoiselles* and related works, Picasso had previously appropriated some formal features of archaic Iberian sculpture (fig. 5).[31] And, it seems, he may well have been stimulated by some of El Greco's formal devices, present in many examples of this predecessor's work. Convention dictated that figures ought to project, while grounds recede. But El Greco often collapsed this distinction by illuminating the folds and billows of enveloping drapery to the point of causing a figure to seem encased in a cocoon of contoured edges—acute, halated edges that impinge on the spatial presence of the bodies they "ground," as they establish a corporeal limit or border. (Compare the knifelike, projective contours in *The Visitation* of circa 1609–13 [see p. 58] or *The Penitent Magdalene,* 1576 [cat. 41], to the similar effects of drapery in the *Demoiselles.*) To the extent that archaic Iberian sculptures and El Greco's paintings stimulated Picasso's formal innovations, all accorded with the identity politics of the time; these sources were appropriate to Picasso as a Spaniard and hardly required an act of appropriation in turn. Some critics of the day continued to object to El Greco's errancy. The Iberian figures were crude by most standards. Such violations nevertheless appealed to Europeans who were engaged in romancing the countercultural—a means of acquiring freedom without need of soliciting spirits. A French writer described El Greco's images as "exaggerated,"

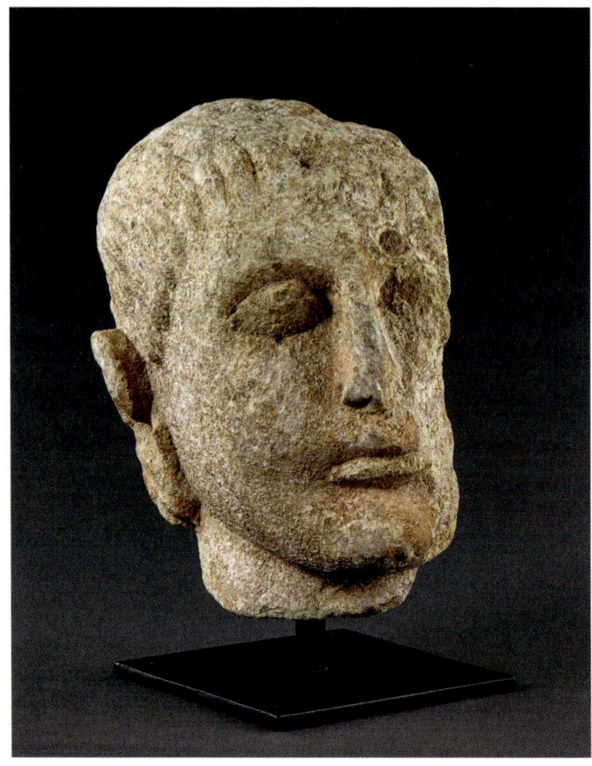

[Fig. 5] Iberian culture, Male head, ca. 300 BCE
Limestone, 20 × 17.5 × 13 cm
Musée du Louvre, Paris

"crude," "excessive," "undisciplined," and "painful," all in appreciation, not disparagement.[32]

If Picasso was drawn to homegrown European resistance to the Western norm, this cultivated otherness paled in relation to what he derived from the non-Western works at the Trocadéro. Reports of liberated sexuality and terroristic atrocities fueled the European colonialist romance with "dark" sub-Saharan Africa and distant Oceania. But the force that Picasso *felt*— alone in the dim light and musty atmosphere— could not have been the result of this avalanche of public information.[33] *Art nègre* (the collective descriptor for colonialist appropriations) acted at that Trocadéro moment not as an inspiration to formal innovation but as a fetish. No specific work should be enlisted to illustrate what Picasso saw; *this would reduce the magic to an inventory of form.*[34] Believe in the fetish. A fetish reserves its magical power for whoever takes hold of it.

How did Picasso take hold? The obvious way—physically. "You have to be very physical with Picasso," Rubin told Steinberg in 1972.[35] The artist had an importunate habit of handling objects and manipulating them as a way of discovering their formal secrets, their physical being. Recall Steinberg's description of the space of the *Demoiselles* as "an interior apprehended on the model of touch," preceded by a generalization: "Picasso's thinking is tenaciously three dimensional."[36] The Trocadéro, as a museum, prohibited touching the three-dimensional objects. Previously, however, Picasso had been fascinated enough by an African sculpture in Matisse's possession to have "held it in his hand the entire evening."[37] There are many such anecdotal accounts of Picasso's restless, inquisitive hands. Having placed "some little straws between his fingers, he had to create something."[38] At a bistro, he "molded bread into little figures."[39] Presented with an unfamiliar object, "he would hold it at a certain angle and then change the angle."[40] Trying on another man's hat, appropriating it, he experienced "a new transformation of himself."[41]

When representing a human figure by drawing or painting it, Picasso was transforming it in his mind as much as manipulating its image by hand. Whatever he handled, directly or indirectly, he was appropriating—mentally, physically, emotionally. Such gestures defused the potential dangers of a thing external to himself, a thing in the world. Returning to Picasso's 1937 memory of 1907: "What I called 'the whole of it,' or life, or—I don't know—the earth?—everything that surrounds us, everything that is not us—[is] hostile."[42] Picasso appropriated and translated into his own idiom the form of an object—but only after having been emotionally affected by it. Its magic and its form were distinct experiences, the first spontaneous, the second reflective. Reasonable enough. But is there a limit to this distinction? Handling an object with fetish qualities, investigating its form, Picasso fetishized it. Such an action collapses the habitual division between spontaneity and reflection, the illogic of chance and the logic of cause.

The Whole of It
I've taken the novelistic liberty of stressing Picasso's "revelation" (his word, apparently) during a chance encounter with "magic" at the Trocadéro.[43] Now, a second interpretive liberty, as I assert a not-by-chance "logical" analogy, hinged on the language of wholes and parts. Picasso's apprehensive reference to "'the whole of it,' or life . . . everything that surrounds us, everything that is not us" evokes his manner of physical engagement with the whole of an object, his physical mode of appropriating the totality of a living thing, and all of life, in all its conceptual parts—appropriating the magic or fetish-quality of things in the world.

Whether to the same point or not, in 1912, Salmon wrote suggestively that Picasso "wants to give us a representation of the whole [*représentation totale*] of man and things . . . outside the laws of academicism and the anatomical system, in a space rigorously in line with the spontaneous freedom of [bodily] movements."[44] The laws of academic representation maintain "everything that surrounds us" at its proper distance, offering the viewer a disengaged analytical perspective, the view of science. Later, using language that became common to the advocates of modernist pictorial design—with expressive form dependent only on itself ("un fait plastique en soi")— Salmon displaced one distance, one objective science, by another. He established a lineage of autonomous formal abstraction leading from El Greco, Paul Cezanne, and others to Picasso.[45]

As a sophisticated historian of pictorial form, Steinberg used his formal analysis as a lead into thematic and psychological content. He rejected

the sterile autonomy of Salmon's "Cubism,"
along with the allied thinking of "modernist"
critics like Alfred H. Barr, Jr. and Clement
Greenberg.[46] He offered a fundamentally different view of the anti-academic nature of Picasso's
Demoiselles. It represented "a terrifying desubli-
mation of art. The picture breaks the triple spell
of tradition—idealization, emotional distance,
and fixed-focus perspective—the tradition of
high-craft illusionism which conducts the specta-
tor-voyeur unobserved to a privileged seat."[47] For
Steinberg, it was not one formal logic substitut-
ing for another, Cubism displacing academicism,
but one psychology displacing another. And
if, for both artist and viewer, the focus was no
longer fixed, a "picture" could represent "the
whole"—perhaps in the way that we "view" spirit
and life as fully existent from any position we
assume (a fetish offers universal protection at any
place, at any time). Picasso was not redrawing
the scientific order of perspective, as in so-called
"Cubist perspective" or the "Cubist grid"; he
was withdrawing from every manifestation of the
inherited system of visual analysis, all of it.

Relevant to my claim that a spiritual sense of
the "whole of life" is analogous to the aesthetic
appreciation of a totalizing representation,
Steinberg stressed the capacity of the tactile
sense to collaborate with vision and its optics.
Against both nature and the science of the body,
Picasso had *hands that see*. The superstitious
person can regard such magic as a fact; to the rational mind, it becomes metaphorical. Steinberg
wrote of an "embrace gifted by sight," vision
being accorded the flexible extension of a pair of
arms; this was a "bent vision," facilitating the aim
to "make recto and verso cohabit."[48] As if antic-
ipating the quasi-physical reach of Steinberg's
tropes, Picasso stated in 1956: "The problem is
how to pass, to go around the object and give
a plastic expression to the result. All of this
[studio work] is my struggle to break with the
two-dimensional aspect."[49] If in the *Demoiselles*,
Picasso (like El Greco before him) had compact-
ed figure and ground, crumpling and faceting
his supportive two-dimensional surface, some
of his figural work that followed developed an
alternative kind of totalizing pictorial magic.
It was sorcery in the sense that vision became
empowered to perceive what nature had assigned
to touch. What the paranoid logic of the unconscious might have allowed was now being toler-

ated within Picasso's quotidian studio practice.
The spirit-magic of the *Demoiselles* evolved into a
form-magic, a consequence of appropriating the
fetish.

Circumfiguration

Arguing analytically, Steinberg offered a prime
example of Picasso's transformation in pictorial
thought, without insisting that it was the first
of its kind. I follow his lead but in pursuit of
different interests. The work of mutual regard is
Bather, 1908–09 (fig. 6).[50] At a glance, it appears
as an awkwardly postured female figure in a
traditional pictorial setting, pressed into zones
of color that denote beach, sea, and sky. Magic,
however, disdains the fixity of such mundane
order.

View Picasso's painting as a microcosmic
depiction of the cosmic "whole of it," of "life," of
all there exists to be experienced in a volumetric
body that can feel its own being as well as its interaction with its environmental surround. From
the outside, perhaps from the inside, Picasso
represented more than a momentary angle on the
figure and more than a perspective on the scene,
whether fixed or mobile.[51] This is not to imply
that several views emerge in succession or that
multiple perspectives have become simultaneous.
We would then be observing a collection of parts
rather than "the whole of it . . . everything that is
not us." Here, via Malraux, I take Picasso at his
word: his concern was much more than an analysis of representational form; he felt compelled to
deal with "the whole of it."

Only by the power of pictorial magic—a
transference of Picasso's inner imaginings to an
external fetish, his art object—could he "give a
form to the spirits." Spirits occupy "the whole,"
have possession of "everything." The magic of
the fetish transcends analytical methods. As a
view from outside Picasso's world of superstition,
my interpretation imposes conventional elements
of analysis on the constituent forms of his *Bather,*
which may cause it to appear like a collection of
moving parts, even a machine. This is the system
that the painting suggests to me, but only when—
tautologically—I attempt a systematic analysis.
System in, system out. Fantasy in, fantasy out.
Analysis may describe how the *Bather* looks but
not so much how I *feel* while looking at it. I am
not Picasso and cannot restage his totalizing
magic. *Bather* has not been my Trocadéro. Fifty-

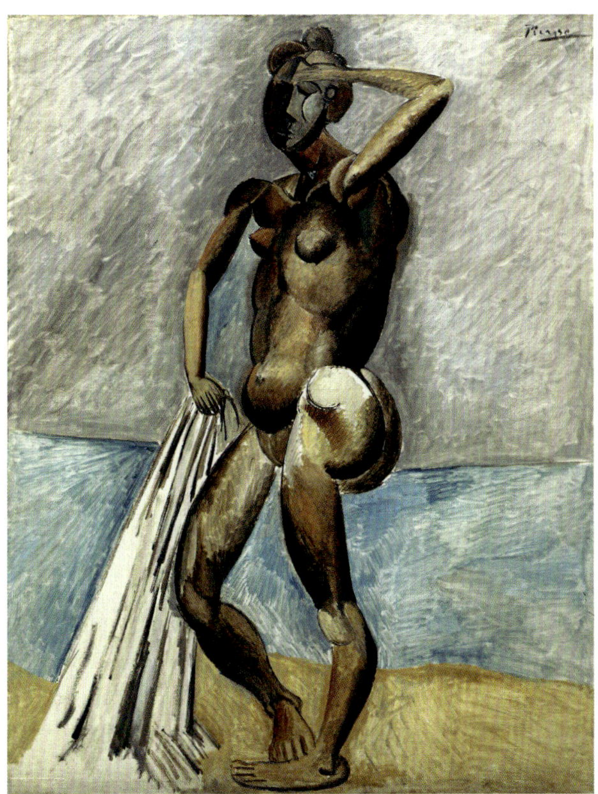

[Fig. 6] Pablo Picasso, *Bather,* 1908–09
Oil on canvas, 130 × 97 cm
The Museum of Modern Art, New York, Reinhardt Smith Bequest

plus years after the *Demoiselles* and the *Bather,* I discovered a magic analogous to Picasso's (but without the fright) when viewing El Greco's *Fray Hortensio.*

Now, one-hundred-plus years later, it is easy enough to perceive the head of *Bather* as both frontal and profile. This look became familiar through Picasso's subsequent decades of painting. Other features of *Bather* may remain somewhat alien. At the level of the hips, a contrapuntal sequence of segments of circles generates an arc or wave that extends from the figure's compact right hand around and across the belly, which is itself in three-quarter view (or a combination of frontal and profile). The wave continues on to the buttocks, of which both halves show in profile. The "back" half, seemingly larger and longer than the "front" half, cradles it, instead of being obscured by it. As a result, much of the figure's backside becomes accessible to a normative viewing position, face on. Though in profile, the buttocks swing around to compete with the figure's pubic triangle in occupying a frontal plane. It is as if Picasso reached back and had as firm a grasp of the back of the body as of its front—all of it subject to circumspection. As for the central torso, it seems to offer a three-quarter view from the front, rotating around to a three-quarter view from the back, pictorial left to pictorial right. Such rotation reveals more than would be available to a fixed perspective or an orthogonal mapping; it corresponds to an intuitive visualization of the experience of the hand's touch. Add one three-quarter view to another three-quarter view, and the sum is a whole body with a half somehow held in reserve. I fantasize that Picasso's figuration generates such sensory plenitude that a whole body includes superfluous parts.

The visible surface of this torso, like the hip area, circumnavigates the axis of a cylindrical volume.[52] Much of the figure's right profile shows at the pictorial left, as if the torso were torqued around. Also, some of the figure's right dorsal area shows at the pictorial *right,* a perspectival contradiction. Little of the figure, if any of it, remains hidden from view. What space does the nominal back occupy, the entirety of it? Has it migrated to the front? If so, then a contiguous volume of atmospheric sky, wave of sea, and strip of beach ought to have been pulled around to the front as a necessary accompaniment. To imagine the back of the body hidden from view entails visualizing the three contiguous zones of its environment as in back of the back, equally concealed. A pictorial environment shares the condition of whatever figure it contains.

Of relevance to these speculations is one of Picasso's own, regarding Cezanne. He claimed that pressure exerted on depicted objects by the surrounding areas, the nominal background, would account for the extraordinary volumetric presence of Cezanne's apples.[53] In painting, a contour separates a figure from its ground. Usually regarded as a feature of the figure, a contour can also be a feature of whatever *impinges* on a figure. Pictorially, the trace of a human figure's side or back, present at the very edge, pressures its front. A figure, alive, is perpetually turning. To deny this is to extinguish the life of the form. Cezanne often reiterated the contoured edges of bodies and objects, stressing them by materially thickening them. What results is an extra dimension, corresponding to a perspective that passes beyond the normative edge, encompassing a surplus, as if every edge amounted to a lost profile that revealed just a bit of what lies behind and around. Cezanne observed in 1906: "I think I could be occupied [painting] for months without changing position, leaning now a bit to the right, now a bit to the left."[54]

In a painting of three bathers (1879–82; fig. 7), which Matisse acquired in 1899, Cezanne thickened many of the depicted edges, including the right shoulder of a striding figure seen from the back. This accented contour contributes a sliver of volumetric substance that wraps around the torso, from its unseen front to its fully exposed back. The shoulder and upper body of the bather abut an environment of bright yellow hatch marks with additions of white, representing generic vegetation. These colors project forward aggressively. In luminous competition with the adjacent figure, their effect recalls El Greco's draperies and streaks of cloud.

To imagine a scenario in which Picasso rendered both figure and ground as fully articulated volumes is to grasp his spatial sense of Cezanne.[55] Picasso may have imagined Cezanne as standing in sympathy with his own longstanding effort: "I've painted on curved surfaces. I've painted [on] spherical balls. It's amazing, you make [the image of] a bottle. It slips away from

you; it turns around the ball."[56] Composing his *Bather,* a compound of solid and space, Picasso risked having the forms slip away from him, even though his hands could "see" all 360 degrees of a volumetric form. I suppose that what appears as a three-quarter view at one moment can slip into lost profile at the next.

Picasso struggled because pictures, like fetishes, are magical; they have forces and spirits within themselves. A critic like Meier-Graefe did not shy away from attributing power to objects of art; in response to El Greco's *Saint Maurice,* he wrote: "You fight with this picture."[57] It was not a metaphor. The forms of a painting remain independently active—turning to face, turning away—all the more when viewed by a superstitious artist attuned to the magic. Picasso's portraits often manifest facial features that—by structural design? by animated will?—migrate from their normative "home" positions, expanding their expressive possibilities. In a portrait of 1939 (cat. 59), the bridge of Jaume (Jaime) Sabartés's nose appears in profile but with one nostril remaining frontal. To the extent that the nose does in fact function as profile, it appears to have moved askew of the central vertical axis of a head that orients, but just barely, a mobile mouth and chin. If a nose in profile is half a nose, and a frontal nose is the whole of a nose, then, combining the two, Picasso's portrait of Sabartés is somehow a three-quarter view that fails to align with normative three-quarter perspective. The facial features shift from full to half to three-quarter, never coalescing. Under such circumstances, whatever spirit inhabits Sabartés's portrait preserves its spontaneity. It becomes antithetical to a photographic view, necessarily stilled and limited. Anti-photographically, "Sabartés" remains alive in his image. Call it magic.

Picasso's *Bather* exhibits analogous perspectival shifts within the whole of the body, and an instance of migration appears not in the figure's face but in the nominal background. The blue-green of the sea travels upward to occupy a segment of sky between the figure's right arm and torso, a willful pictorial contradiction.[58] Picasso's art shares this chromatic displacement with the practices of Cezanne and Matisse before him. Although relatively unobtrusive, the effect parallels the more disturbing migration of the features and qualities of Picasso's bodies, as they slip around or are being pulled around a virtual

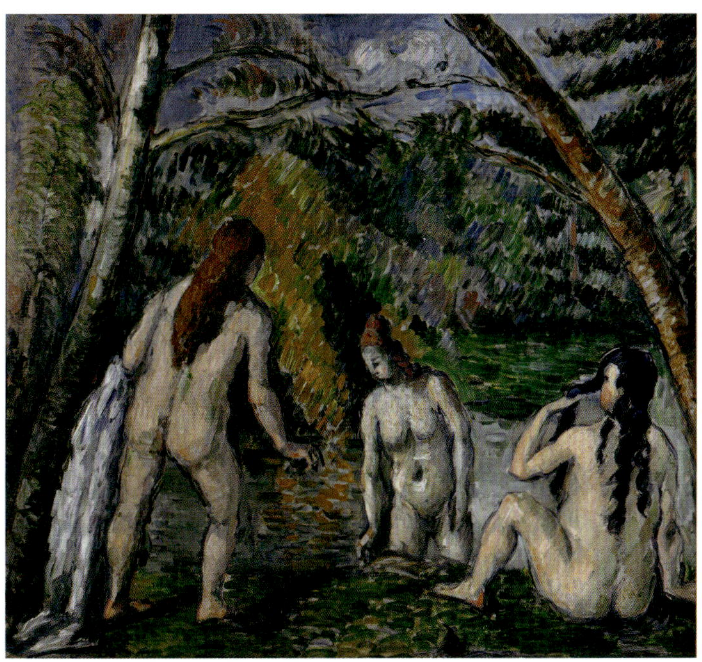

[Fig. 7] Paul Cezanne, *Bathers,* 1879–82
Oil on canvas, 55 × 52 cm
Musée de la Ville de Paris, Musée du Petit-Palais
Gift of Mr and Mrs Henri Matisse, 1936

central axis. Think of a Picasso figure as a rotating cylinder. If seen from the front, its back will show around the turn; if seen from the back, its front will show.[59]

Recall also the brute juxtaposition of El Greco-like, sharp-edged drapery in the *Demoiselles. Bather* has no such drapery but has a towel, rigid and creased; on striking the level of the beach, it angles into a fold, both stiff and pliant, a rudimentary channel, a vessel-like element of an incipient organic system. The towel assumes something of the form of the two legs beside it, bent at the ankles. Coincidentally—but is it mere coincidence?—Picasso's bent towel resembles the same motif linked to Cezanne's striding bather, who holds a towel parallel to her left leg (see figure 7). A flexible fold or angle is the first step in converting a straight line to a circle or rounding a plane into a volume.[60] When investigated by mobile, flexible hands, volumes lose all front-to-back and left-to-right differentiation. For a painter who faces the grid-like rigidity of a flat surface plane, volume affords a magical release. Volume was Picasso's freedom.

At this point, a reductive summation: The fetish-magic that Picasso encountered—his chance, not his cause—became his liberating form (representing "the whole of it"). His form protected him from a world of hostile spirit ("the whole of it"). The spirits were those his superstitious mind projected. The forms owed their existence to Picasso's acts of appropriation—not of other forms but of the magic.[61]

A Cylindrical Coda
I like to think that Picasso, by appropriating El Greco's drapery folds with their illuminated edges, aids in any continuing interpretation of El Greco. We understand phenomena through other phenomena. Many artists have alluded to aspects of Picasso's circumfiguration, and each offers, if only inadvertently, a bit of instruction about this source of inspiration.

In the art of Jasper Johns, circumfiguration shifts from volume to plane. Johns rotates graphic signs. These are "figures" in the sense of numbers, letters, and even pictures of bodies (like the figures in an illustrated book), but in most instances they are not bodies themselves. Johns's magic—virtual—relates to illusions and paradoxes, whereas Picasso derived his magic—actual—from spirituality and superstition.

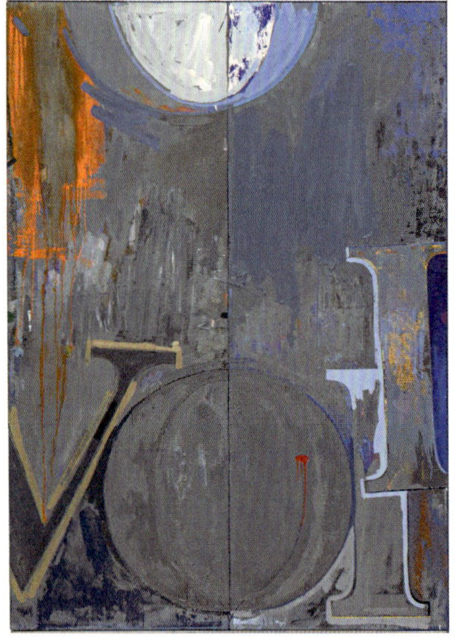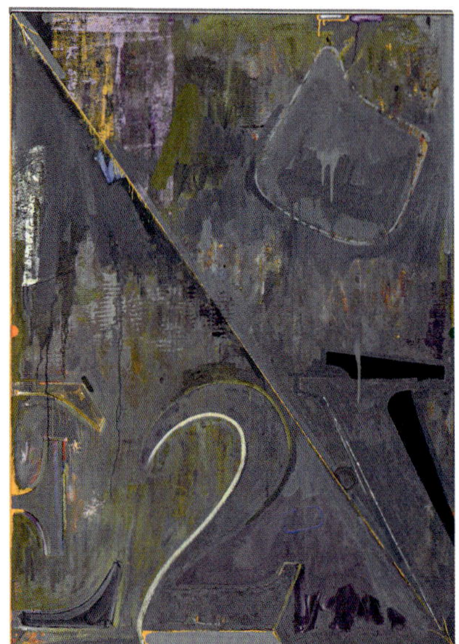

[Fig. 8] Jasper Johns, *Voice 2*, 1971
Oil and collage on three canvases, 183 × 127 cm each
Kunstmuseum Basel

A geometrical emblem suited to both artists might be the cylinder, not as a solid but as a surface that rotates around an axis.

Johns's *Voice 2* (1971; fig. 8), painted while Picasso was still active and productive, is one of a number of works that, whether consisting of multiple panels or a single panel divided into discrete segments, implies a continuous rotational sequencing. Each of the three separate panels of *Voice 2* can function as the initial unit, as long as a certain orthographic integrity is maintained.[62] As in a film loop or a repeating performance, if a middle or end segment of the whole appears first, then the narrative sequence eventually passes fully around, back to the beginning segment. By using familiar signs (well-understood graphic configurations) as his subject or "model," Johns can be assured that his viewer will grasp the nature of the perceptual game. A common word or inscription will be recognized even when its terminal part precedes its inaugural part. "CE," followed by "2," followed by "VOI" is legible as "VOICE 2." *Voice 2* enacts circumfiguration, but it does so as a curiously planar cylinder, not a volumetric one.[63]

Voice 2 exhibits another structural wrinkle. The "VOI" panel has a symmetrical vertical division; the "CE" panel has a symmetrical horizontal division, and the "2" panel has a symmetrical diagonal division. Johns highlights the type of structural order and taxonomy that my analytical distinction of frontal, three-quarter, and profile perspectives also deploys. Yet with Picasso such categorical divisions never quite fit the magic. Johns puns; Johns plays with paradox; Johns inverts, reverses, and mirrors. He turns images front to back and inside out.[64] A knowledge of linguistic tropes and optical phenomena can guide the interpretation of his art to a reasonable degree by following common logic. Even paradox finds its place in logic—but not Picasso's paradoxes.

Johns found himself in "sympathy" with the art of Marcel Duchamp and the definitional dilemmas that his so-called Readymades generated.[65] He learned as well from the example of John Cage, a Duchampian type who composed readymade music. But Picasso eventually became dominant among Johns's select company of antecedents.[66] Then there is Cezanne, whom both Picasso and Johns viewed as a model. Cezanne's art, Johns said in admiration, "makes looking equivalent to touching."[67] He could have observed the same in Picasso's art, and perhaps he did. If not, he seems to have thought it. And it was *thought*, not magic, that Johns perceived in Picasso. Called to comment on Picasso's *Woman in a Straw Hat* (1936; fig. 9), Johns found it "full

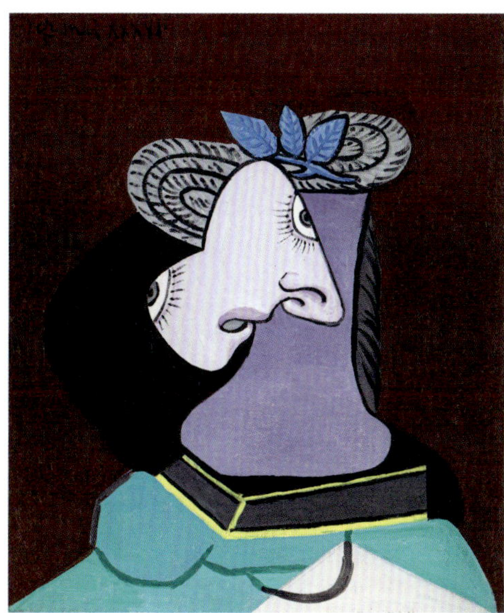

[Fig. 9] Pablo Picasso, *Woman in a Straw Hat,* 1936
Oil on canvas, 61 × 50 cm
Musée national Picasso, Paris

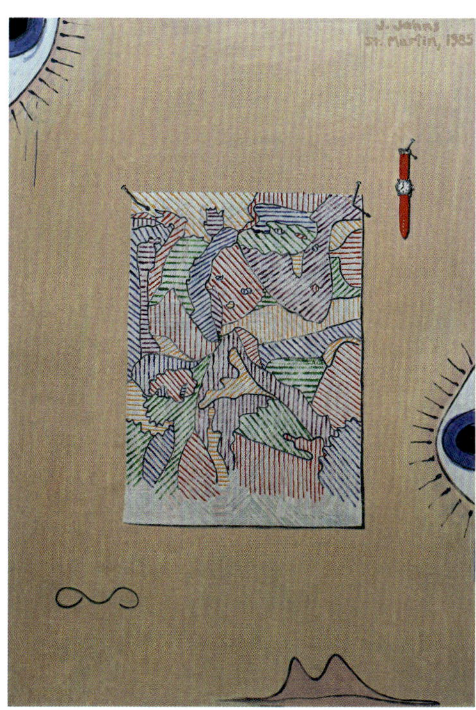

[Fig. 10] Jasper Johns, *Untitled (A Dream),* 1985
Oil on canvas, 190.5 × 127 cm
Collection of Robert and Jane Meyerhoff, Phoenix, MD

of interesting"—and he pauses—"Interesting—what? Thoughts, I guess."[68] Thoughts, rather than forms.

Thoughts may be the more magical of the two. Johns mused over his own mind as a source of magical thinking, thoughts beyond his control and understanding. "I don't know if it's out of choice or out of necessity—how my mind must move," he remarked, as if his thinking (perhaps Picasso's too) was more unconscious than conscious.[69] "How my mind must move" is nearly passive voice, as in "how my mind must be moved." It could be moved by logical cause; it could be moved by illogical chance. Along related lines, Johns had once entertained a thought experiment: "Make something, a kind of object, which as it changes . . . offers no clue as to what its state or form or nature was at any previous time."[70] With no evident cause or motivation, the changes would occur as if by chance—or by magic.

Among the common-domain signage that Johns adopted as his own cause, his own chance, were paintings by Picasso—readymade graphic configurations circulating in the culture. Having "chanced" upon a book illustration of *Woman in a Straw Hat* in 1984, Johns reproduced the image in many variations, and elsewhere he adopted to new purposes its meandering, migrating features, shifted to the edges of the warped plane of the face. Johns recalled that Picasso's construction led him "to use the rectangle of the paper as a face and attaching features to it."[71] He responded planometrically to Picasso's stereometric operation. At times, he appropriated the Picasso face as the irregular shape it was. On other occasions, he stretched it taut into a rectangular form, leaving a central reserve suited to drawing and painting other figures and faces.

Untitled (A Dream) (1985; fig. 10) exemplifies Johns's interpretation of Picasso's figuration. It renders obvious that Picasso had turned volumetric bodies inside out, inverting the relation of features to face, contained to container. This inside-out maneuver amounted to a variant way of turning around the edges, volumetrically. In *Untitled (A Dream),* the features become the frame, the container. With blank "skin" now largely relieved of its burden of displaying facial features, it becomes available for any other signage. Johns "tacks" to the newfound surface a trompe-l'oeil drawing sheet displaying an image of a figure derived from Matthias Grünewald's *Isenheim Altarpiece,* rotated into an inverted position.[72]

I need to stress a difference: while Picasso derived forms from El Greco and later revisited the well-known compositions of several European masters, he remained primarily an observer of life in three dimensions. He thought like a sculptor working in space. A sheet of sketches indicates that Picasso's migrating features may have derived from the appearance of a live but sleeping woman, observed from an odd angle.[73] Johns, to the contrary, works from culture, not life. His manipulation of facial features during the nineteen-eighties developed from one or more images that others had already projected onto a plane.[74]

In *The Bath* (1984; fig. 11), Johns appears to have divided Picasso's *Woman in a Straw Hat* into two segments that would reconstitute the whole if adjoined; one would need to be passed around the other to facilitate the proper linkage. To speak of two segments may, however, be misleading, for each visible fragment becomes conceptually a whole if we imagine that its absent portion has been concealed by the lateral trompe-l'oeil framing of the bathtub scene. To imagine two "Picassos" rather than one encourages visualizing the passage from one to the other, either as two copies of the painting in two different positions or as one and the same painting at two different times, having shifted location within a stable pictorial environment. As optical phenomena, the two images might be occupying two moments in the turn of a cylindrical plane that curves around a vertical axis—perhaps Johns's peculiar way of confronting the slippage around a volume that obsessed Picasso.[75] Whereas Johns would render an imagined cylinder planar, Picasso would give a planar projection the sense of a cylinder.

Suited to *The Bath,* Johns generates a second type of slippage, caused by melting. He had heard anecdotally that Picasso wondered why he never melted in a warm bath, like a lump of sugar.[76] *The Bath* is a work in wax encaustic. By applying heat, Johns could alter either the whole of it or selective parts. Picasso here may be a cause that Johns chooses to accept—"how my mind must move" (it moves toward Picasso). When Johns melts his representation of Picasso's representation of a face, he imposes on Picasso's

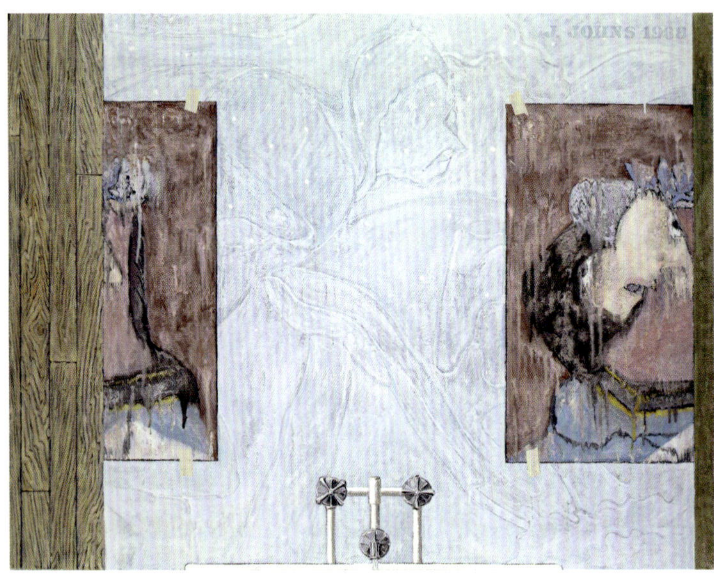

[Fig. 11] Jasper Johns, *The Bath,* 1984
Encaustic on canvas, 122.5 × 153 cm
Kunstmuseum Basel, acquired with funds from
the Friends of the Kunstmuseum Basel

form a new instantiation of chance, for melting allows the colors and contours to flow, uncontrolled. Yet the visual forms assume the character they *must* assume, given the temperature, viscosity, and force of gravity. These are nature's controls. An interpreter can either analyze the science, the physics of it, or accept the chance, the magic of it.

"Picasso" (the image of *Woman in a Straw Hat*) melts in Johns's *Bath* in the way that Johns's mind moves, as it "must"—freely, unpredictably—more unconsciously than consciously. Yet the unconscious (in a Freudian sense) is not only ruled by cause, it is also susceptible to the chance influence of spirits. I might call this the condition of spirit-paradox, which both Picasso and Johns address in their art. Spirit is cause and chance at once. In 1984, Picasso's imagery offered something of a Trocadéro moment for Johns, by releasing facial features from their acculturated order. In turn, Johns released the soul of matter within the image he appropriated. He let loose a migration of the material qualities of encaustic, an activation of its inherent physicality. Johns played materialist empiricist to Picasso's spirit-worker. But this binary distinction hardly proves stable in the hands and thought of such artists.

Johns's art accommodates no readymade classification. More representational than abstract, it depicts cultural signs that are already abstractions. Johns has explored aspects of Picasso's circumfiguration without exhausting his predecessor's potential, demonstrating that this magic continues to haunt the practice of art and its history. Critical generalities—Cubism, Surrealism—fail to align with or contain the forms that Picasso invented. What Johns has done to Picasso has normalized neither of these two historical agents. El Greco does not rest much easier. I ask knowledgeable colleagues: Is El Greco Renaissance, Mannerist, or Baroque? Does the sense of spirituality that his art projects accord with the theological doctrine of his era? Or does his idiosyncratic form reveal a soul at once transcendent and deviant? I receive no definitive replies. Cezanne, too, is a master who fails to fit.[77] A master of what? I venture that Cezanne, with his brutish strokes, attempted to record sensation as a flow of unmediated data, all the while preserving the raw emotion of his reaction, both to the view itself and to its emergence on the canvas. But this characterization, a complex of order and chance, leaves Cezanne's mode of figuration no less resistant to definitive analysis.

Picasso, like El Greco and Cezanne before him, like Johns after him, enters the field of art not as logical, formal cause but as magical chance. For Western culture, Picasso constituted a stroke of luck. Is "stroke" the suitable term? This colloquialism connotes *good* luck. But the luck, the magic, the fetish-form that Picasso introduced, is neither good nor bad in any customary sense. To impose an evaluative standard on Picasso's art would convert his superstitious mentality to orthodoxy, whether religious, social, or aesthetic. It would immobilize the impress of his restless hands.

Interpreters should avoid encasing within cultural history the full extent of Picasso's effect, whether in approval or disapproval. Explain this and that contingent aspect—contextual issues keep arising—but let the generative core stand as a singularity, undiminished by comparison. During his final years, Picasso realized that the practice of pictorial representation had hardly evolved beyond its prehistoric beginnings; so much remained to be discovered.[78] Evaluative interpretation, by reinforcing existing cultural standards, becomes an impediment to future realization. Leave Picasso's creativity to the future of chance.

1 For essential aid in research, I thank John Semlitsch, Sheila Schwartz, Pepe Karmel, and Judit Geskó. In cases where no translator is indicated, the translations are mine. In keeping with the position of the Société Cezanne (www.societe-cezanne.fr), I do not include an acute accent in my own references to the surname of the artist Paul Cezanne.

2 Yve-Alain Bois, "Painting as Trauma," in *Picasso's Les Demoiselles d'Avignon*, ed. Christopher Green (Cambridge, 2001), p. 41 (emphasis added).

3 On Picasso's varied responses to Casagemas's death, see John Richardson, *A Life of Picasso: 1881–1906* (New York, 1991), pp. 209–14.

4 Natasha Staller, *A Sum of Destructions: Picasso's Cultures and the Creation of Cubism* (New Haven and London, 2001), p. 305, fig. 287; p. 312, fig. 295. See Staller's commentary, p. 313. Richardson (*A Life of Picasso: 1881–1906*, p. 283) dates the Manet parody to the year 1903.

5 As an example, see Bois 2001 (see note 2), p. 40.

6 Sigmund Freud, *Psychopathology of Everyday Life*, trans. A. A. Brill (New York, n. d.), p. 144.

7 Pierre Daix, *Picasso, Life and Art*, trans. Olivia Emmet (New York, 1994), p. 393n8. Originally published as *Picasso créateur: la vie intime et l'œuvre* (Paris, 1987). Daix was referring to speculations by Mary Matthews Gedo and Leo Steinberg. Mary Matthews Gedo, "Art as Exorcism: Picasso's *Demoiselles d'Avignon*," *Arts Magazine* 55 (October 1980), pp. 70–83. For Steinberg's various essays on Picasso, with authorized revisions and emendations, see Leo Steinberg, *Picasso: Selected Essays*, ed. Sheila Schwartz (Chicago, 2022).

8 Robert Rosenblum, "The *Demoiselles* Sketchbook No. 42, 1907," in *Je suis le cahier: The Sketchbooks of Picasso*, ed. Arnold Glimcher and Marc Glimcher (Boston and New York, 1986), p. 53. Freud's general view of the superstitious mentality accords with Lydia Gasman's assessment of Picasso: "Picasso's artistic magic was based on his tendency to attribute external reality to his inner desires and phantasies and was a crucial aspect of his deep seated superstitiousness"; Lydia Gasman, *Mystery, Magic and Love in Picasso, 1923–1938: Picasso and the Surrealist Poets* (Ann Arbor, 1981), p. 449.

9 Picasso, quoted in André Malraux, *Picasso's Mask*, trans. June Guicharnaud with Jacques Guicharnaud (New York, 1976), p. 13.

10 Julius Meier-Graefe, *The Spanish Journey*, trans. J. Holroyd-Reece (London, 1926), pp. 352–54. Originally published as *Spanische Reise* (Berlin, 1910). Compare with Paul Lafond, writing on El Greco in 1906: "His figures . . . shock us like apparitions. . . . His harmonies, almost too acute and capricious and jumbled, give a fever, as it were." Paul Lafond, "Domenikos Theotokopuli dit El Greco," *Les Arts* 58 (October 1906), p. 4, quoted in Jonathan Brown, "El Greco: The Man and the Myths," in *El Greco of Toledo*, ed. Jonathan Brown, exh. cat. Museo del Prado, Madrid, et al. (Boston, 1982), p. 27.

11 I could have no inkling that this image would be celebrated as the frontispiece for the catalogue of the 1982 exhibition *El Greco of Toledo* (ibid.).

12 Based on the existing documentation and his own notes of conversations with Picasso (1970–72), Rubin concluded that "there is not only no better but *no other* candidate" for essential changes in the *Demoiselles d'Avignon* "than the Trocadéro visit that the artist himself called a 'shock' and a 'revelation'" (original emphasis). William Rubin, "Picasso," in *"Primitivism" in Twentieth-Century Art: Affinity of the Tribal and the Modern*, ed.

William Rubin (New York, 1984), vol. 1, p. 256. See also Rubin's similar wording in his essay "The Genesis of *Les Demoiselles d'Avignon*," in *Les Demoiselles d'Avignon*, ed. John Elderfield, special issue of *Studies in Modern Art* 3 (New York, 1994), p. 105.

13 Among many interpretive accounts, see Richard Shiff, "Sensation Abstracted," in *Cezanne to Malevich: Arcadia to Abstraction*, ed. Judit Geskó, exh. cat. Szépművészeti Múzeum (Budapest, 2021), pp. 29–41.

14 Scholars have often invoked the negative response to *Les Demoiselles d'Avignon* among Picasso's contemporaries. For documentation, see Hélène Seckel, "Anthology of Early Commentary on *Les Demoiselles d'Avignon*," trans. Alexandra Bonfante-Warren, in *Les Demoiselles d'Avignon* (New York, 1994), pp. 226–56. On Gertrude Stein's reaction as an exception, see Tamar Garb, "'To Kill the Nineteenth Century': Sex and Spectatorship with Gertrude and Pablo," in Green 2001 (see note 2), pp. 55–76.

15 Rubin 1984 (see note 12), pp. 254–55, 335n46. In Christian Zervos's account, provided by Seckel, Picasso "was curious enough to push the door across the way." Seckel 1994 (see note 14), p. 216.

16 Rubin 1984 (see note 12), pp. 254–55.

17 Gertrude Stein rationalized Picasso's discovery by invoking an ethnic Moorish inheritance: "The Arabs created both civilization and culture for the negroes and therefore African art which was naïve and exotic for Matisse was for Picasso, a Spaniard, a thing that was natural, direct, and civilized"; Gertrude Stein, *Picasso* (Boston, 1959), p. 22. Originally published in 1938 (London and Paris). On the Moorish connection, see Rubin 1984 (see note 12), pp. 241, 334n3.

18 An example is Roland Penrose's objection to the fully articulated quotations included in Françoise Gilot's 1964 memoir *Life with Picasso*: "Picasso . . . never made speeches but let fall his most profound and surprising remarks in brief elliptical phrases which usually took the form of a paradox." Roland Penrose, *Picasso: His Life and Work* (Berkeley and Los Angeles, 1981), p. 455. By Penrose's criteria, the halting cadence of Malraux's quotation of Picasso connotes authenticity. On "quoting Picasso," see also William Rubin, "From Narrative to 'Iconic' in Picasso: The Buried Allegory in *Bread and Fruitdish on a Table* and the role of *Les Demoiselles d'Avignon*," *Art Bulletin* 65 (December 1983), p. 643.

19 Picasso, quoted in Malraux 1976 (see note 9), pp. 10–13.

20 An early example is Ron Johnson, "Picasso's *Demoiselles d'Avignon* and the Theater of the Absurd," *Arts Magazine* 55 (October 1980), p. 107. See the summary account of the scholarship in Rubin 1994 (see note 12, "Genesis"), pp. 98–103. Leo Steinberg objects to the impulse to argue by formal analogy. Steinberg, "Retrospect: Sixteen Years After," postscript to the reprint of his 1972 essay "The Philosophical Brothel," *October* 44 (Spring 1988), pp. 71–73.

21 Paul Lefort, "Dominico Theotocopuli, surnommé Le Greco," in *Histoire des peintres de toutes les écoles: École espagnole*, ed. Charles Blanc (Paris, 1869), pp. 7–8 within the eight-page fascicule on El Greco.

22 Picasso, quoted in Malraux 1976 (see note 9), p. 10.

23 Ibid., pp. 10–13. Consulting the French edition, I have altered the translation: Malraux, *La Tête d'obsidienne* (Paris, 1974), p. 18. On Europeans' regarding African objects as "malefic and threatening" while Oceanic objects were "luxuriant, unthreatening," see Rubin 1994 (see note 12, "Genesis"), p. 138n227. Suzanne Preston Blier—citing a photograph of the *Demoiselles* in an

(apparently) incomplete state with two of the five figures already bearing an "African" character—argues against the prevailing view that Picasso's introduction of mask-like faces was impulsively triggered rather than part of an orderly scheme; see her *Picasso's* Demoiselles: *The Untold Origins of a Modern Masterpiece* (Durham and London, 2019), pp. 60–68. At least two material facts undermine Blier's position: first, the only five-figure preliminary study for the *Demoiselles* lacks this "African" feature; second, the seemingly incomplete appearance of the painting in its photographic reproduction is likely a factor of orthochromatic film, standard at the time. Regardless of the nature of the documentation, scholars choose temperamentally between accepting chance as a "cause" (Picasso's unexpected experience at the Trocadéro) and insisting on reason as a cause (tracing Picasso's plan for the painting). Rubin gives a multifaceted account in Rubin 1994 (see note 12, "Genesis"), pp. 58, 69, 87, 94, 125n67, 136n224. (For an instance of Rubin's use of "not by chance," see p. 58.) Picasso's anachronistic reference to the "unconscious," potentially both Freudian and Lacanian, should not invalidate his 1937 recollection of 1907. For a contrary opinion, see Christopher Green, "'Naked Problems'? 'Sub-African Caricatures'? *Les Demoiselles d'Avignon*, Africa, and Cubism," in Green 2001 (see note 2), p. 138.
24 André Salmon, "Histoire anecdotique du cubisme" (1912), reprinted in Edward Fry, *Le Cubisme* (Brussels, 1968), p. 82.
25 Picasso, as recalled by Romuald Dor de la Souchère, *Picasso in Antibes*, trans. W. J. Strachan (New York, 1960), pp. 5, 18. See also Stein 1959 (see note 17), p. 9: "Picasso said once that [the inventor] does not know what he is going to invent."
26 Rubin refers to Picasso's introduction of the Africanized visages—that is, his appropriation—as "both a singular and a private act." Rubin 1994 (see note 12, "Genesis"), p. 116.
27 All three potential causes are extensively discussed in the analytical, historical literature. On the interpretive turn from formal causes to social and biographical causes as a way of isolating meaning in Picasso, see Steinberg, "The Philosophical Brothel," *October* 44 (Spring 1988), pp. 7–9, 71–74; Rubin 1994 (see note 12, "Genesis"), pp. 17–34; and Christopher Green, "An Introduction to *Les Demoiselles d'Avignon*," in Green 2001 (see note 2), pp. 1–14.
28 On the "hideousness of the faces," see for example Salmon 1912 (see note 24), p. 84.
29 In 1943, Picasso referred to Paul Cezanne as a protection, presumably not in the spiritual sense of the non-Western objects but in form, as a precedent for structural liberties (like El Greco): "I spent years studying his paintings. . . . He protected us." Picasso, quoted in Brassaï, *Conversations avec Picasso* (Paris, 1964), p. 113.
30 Steinberg 1988 (see note 27), p. 63. On Steinberg's sexualized metaphors, see my introduction to the essays collected in Steinberg 2022 (see note 7), pp. xi–xvi.
31 See Rubin 1994 (see note 12, "Genesis"), pp. 36–37.
32 Joris-Karl Huysmans, *À rebours* (1884), translated anonymously as *Against the Grain* (New York, 1931), pp. 151, 154.
33 On the colonialist context, see Patricia Leighten, "Colonialism, *l'art nègre*, and *Les Demoiselles d'Avignon*," in Green 2001 (see note 2), pp. 77–103.
34 Having searched for a specific mask as a source for the Africanized faces in the *Demoiselles*, Rubin, as well as others, found none. Rubin 1994 (see note 12, "Genesis"), pp. 106–08. Undaunted by his own due diligence, Rubin argued that "Picasso plumbed his unconscious and searched his memory for

the most terrifying faces he had ever seen"— which would have included "the ravaged and distorted heads of some congenital syphilitics." Rubin 1994, p. 116.
35 Rubin, quoted in Steinberg 1988 (see note 27), p. 65.
36 Steinberg 1988 (see note 27), p. 63.
37 The event occurred in 1906; see the several accounts from Max Jacob, quoted in Seckel 1994 (see note 14), p. 233. See also Rubin 1984 (see note 12), p. 296.
38 Jaime Sabartés, "Thoughts about Picasso" (1955) in Jaime Sabartés and Wilhelm Boeck, *Picasso* (New York, 1961), p. 25.
39 Rosamund Bernier, *Matisse, Picasso, Miró as I Knew Them* (New York, 1991), p. 122.
40 William Rubin, quoted in Milton Esterow, "Visits with Picasso at Mougins," *Art News* 72 (Summer 1973), p. 42.
41 Alexander Liberman, "Atelier of Pablo Picasso," *Vogue* (November 1956), p. 133.
42 Picasso, quoted in Malraux 1976 (see note 9), p. 11. On Picasso's paranoid suspicion of a hostile world—in psychoanalytic terms, a regressive primitivism—see Gasman 1981 (see note 7), pp. 503–09.
43 In his several references to a "revelation," Rubin, informed by his conversations with Picasso, uses the quotation marks, implying that it was the artist's term. See, for example, Rubin 1984 (see note 12), p. 255.
44 Salmon 1912 (see note 24), p. 84.
45 See André Salmon, "L'Anniversaire du Cubisme," *L'Art vivant* 36 (June 15, 1926), p. 445. Elsewhere Salmon implied that the lineage was one of equals, a contemporaneity that ignored chronology, with El Greco embedded among the others. He listed the primary figures in this order: "Cézanne, *les nègres* [African and Oceanic art], le Douanier Rousseau, le Greco, Ingres, Seurat." André Salmon, "Cubisme," *L'Art vivant* (Paris, 1920), p. 115. On an autonomy of form, compare with Georges Braque, who wrote, "The goal is not to reconstitute an anecdotal fact but to constitute a pictorial fact." Braque, "Pensées et réflexions sur la peinture," *Nord–Sud* (December 1917), p. 4. As Picasso himself put it in 1926, "I understood that painting had an intrinsic value, independent of the actual representation of objects. . . . Given that painting has its own, independent beauty, one could create an abstract beauty, as long as it remained pictorial (that is, depicting something). The statement appeared in the illustrated magazine *Ogoniok* (Moscow) and was quoted and translated by John Elderfield, who checked the original Russian publication against the later French translation. See Elderfield, "Picasso's Extreme Cézanne," in *Cézanne and Beyond*, ed. Joseph J. Rishel and Katherine Sachs, exh. cat. Philadelphia Museum of Art (Philadelphia and New Haven, 2009), p. 213.
46 Within the existing critical tradition, Steinberg wrote in 1972, the *Demoiselles* signified "a triumph of form over content." Steinberg 1988 (see note 27), p. 9.
47 Leo Steinberg, "The Algerian Women and Picasso at Large," in *Other Criteria: Confrontations with Twentieth-Century Art* (New York, 1972), p. 173.
48 Ibid., pp. 167, 201, 229.
49 Picasso, quoted by Liberman 1956 (see note 41), p. 134.
50 Compare with Steinberg's account in his essay on the Algerian Women in Steinberg 1972 (see note 47), pp. 189–91.
51 I find references to a "cinematic" view or method in Picasso, although suggestive, ultimately too limiting with respect to his imagination. But the analogy proves fruitful for interpreters committed to establishing context. See Staller 2001 (see note 4), pp. 137–60; Bernice B. Rose, *Picasso, Braque, and Early Film in Cubism* (New York, 2007).

52 See the related account of *Bather* in Pepe Karmel, *Picasso and the Invention of Cubism* (New Haven and London, 2003), p. 62: "Picasso seems to circle around the model."
53 See Picasso's statement in Françoise Gilot and Carlton Lake, *Life with Picasso* (New York, 1964), p. 219.
54 Paul Cezanne, letter to his son Paul, September 8, 1906, *Paul Cézanne, correspondence*, ed. John Rewald (Paris, 1978), p. 324. On Cezanne's thickened edges, see also Paul Smith, *Interpreting Cézanne* (London, 1996), pp. 44–46; Paul Smith, "Cézanne's Un-constructive Line," in Geskó 2021 (see note 13), p. 52.
55 I stress this aspect of Cezanne rather than the far more commonly invoked matter of (in French) *passage,* the suppression of precise contours that affords "passage" from one spatial plane to another. A focus on *passage* encourages viewing Cezanne's spatial effect as flattening; a focus on contours that turn emphasizes the volumetric potential.
56 Picasso (July 8, 1948), quoted in Daniel-Henry Kahnweiler, "Entretiens avec Picasso," in *Picasso: propos sur l'art*, ed. Marie-Laure Bernadac and Androula Michael (Paris, 1998), p. 80.
57 Meier-Graefe 1926 (see note 10), p. 352.
58 Picasso might justify such a feature as "independent . . . abstract beauty." (See his remark from 1926 quoted in note 45, above.)
59 On such observations, compare Steinberg 1972 (see note 47), pp. 157–59, 167–69, 205; Steinberg 1988 (see note 27), pp. 56–58; see also Richard Shiff, "Turn," in *Picasso Black and White,* ed. Carmen Giménez, exh. cat. Solomon R. Guggenheim Museum (New York, 2012), p. 54.
60 Imagine a closed, symmetrical, four-sided figure, a square. If it gains a fifth side, it is a pentagon. If it gains an infinite number of additional sides while maintaining its complete symmetry, it is a circle.
61 Steinberg, Gasman, Rubin, and no doubt others precede me in this line of interpretation.
62 See Michael Crichton, *Jasper Johns* (New York, 1994), p. 56.
63 This description nevertheless oversimplifies *Voice 2*, which manifests many other forms of displacement. Need this qualifier be stated? In an art like Johns's, or Picasso's, or perhaps anyone's, any interpretation introduces limits and risks oversimplification.
64 See the discussion of Johns's *Corpse and Mirror II* (1974) in Richard Shiff, "Constructing Physicality," *Art Journal* 50 (Spring 1991), pp. 46–47.
65 Discussing his relation to Duchamp, Johns has a backtracking, not-by-chance moment. He denies that Duchamp was the cause and he, Johns, the effect, but then invokes a play of "sympathy" (as surrogate cause) that "refreshes your attitude towards your own work." Johns, quoted in conversation with Ann Hindry (1989), in *Jasper Johns: Writings, Sketchbook Notes, Interviews*, ed. Kirk Varnedoe (New York, 1996), p. 227.
66 See Leo Castelli, Johns's dealer, statement to Edmund White (1996), in ibid., p. 304.
67 Johns, in Grace Glueck, "The 20th-Century Artists Most Admired by Other Artists" (1977), in ibid., p. 166.
68 Johns, quoted and described by Amei Wallach (1988), in ibid., p. 226.
69 Johns, interviewed by Roberta Bernstein (1980), in ibid., p. 201 (emphasis eliminated). Being unconscious would not prevent thought from being logical and structured—*raisonnable,* as Picasso supposedly said of fetish objects, African and Oceanic. See Salmon 1912 (see note 24), p. 82.
70 Johns, sketchbook note, ca. 1960, in Varnedoe 1996 (see note 65), p. 50.

71 Johns, statement to Michael Crichton, late 1991 or early 1992, in Crichton 1994 (see note 62), p. 71.
72 Grünewald created his altarpiece for a hospital. Interpreters concerned with historical context have often associated Johns's interest in this imagery with the AIDS crisis of the nineteen-eighties.
73 The sheet is dated the same day as *Woman in a Straw Hat* (May 1, 1936). Its studies represent a woman, head thrown back, seemingly asleep in a chair, reclining but not necessarily recumbent; see William Rubin, ed., *Picasso and Portraiture: Representation and Transformation,* exh. cat. The Museum of Modern Art (New York, 1996), p. 72.
74 See Crichton 1994 (see note 62), p. 71, on the possibility of multiple sources for Johns's experimentation with migrating facial features. See also Richard Shiff, "Preference without a Cause," in *Past Things and Present: Jasper Johns Since 1983*, ed. Joan Rothfuss, exh. cat. Walker Art Center (Minneapolis, 2003), pp. 18–19 and idem., "Johns Metanoid, Metanoid Johns," in *Jasper Johns: Gray,* ed. James Rondeau and Douglas Druick, exh. cat. The Art Institute of Chicago (New Haven, 2007), p. 138.
75 A typical Johnsian visual pun: a figure derived from Grünewald in the nominal background of *The Bath* shares aspects of the Picasso face to its right. The posture of the Grünewald figure, with the head thrown back, sends nose, eyes, and mouth toward the periphery of an oddly contorted (diseased) visage, seen from behind and above.
76 See Johns, interview by Amei Wallach (1988), in Varnedoe 1996 (see note 65), p. 226.
77 Cezanne actively joined the chain of exchanges relevant to this essay. Around 1885, he studied a black-and-white engraved magazine illustration of (what was then considered as) an El Greco portrait (see cat. 22), painting a liberal copy in color. See John Rewald, "Une Copie par Cézanne d'après Le Greco," *Gazette des beaux-arts* 6 (February 1936), pp. 118–21. On the affinity of Cezanne and El Greco, see Meier-Graefe 1926 (see note 10), p. 458. On the recent reassignment of the El Greco painting's authorship, see the BBC news release, November 12, 2019, "Lady in a Fur Wrap: Mystery of Glasgow Painting Revealed," https://www.bbc.com/news/uk-scotland-glasgow-west-50388375 (accessed March 18, 2022).
78 See Pierre Daix, "L'arrière-saison de Picasso ou l'art de rester à l'avant-garde," *XXe siècle* 41 (1973), p. 13.

Elective Affinities: Picasso and El Greco

Qu'est-ce que, au fond, un peintre? C'est un collectionneur qui veut se constituer une collection en faisant lui-même les tableaux qu'il aime chez les autres. (In essence, what is a painter? A collector who wants to make a collection by doing paintings that he likes by others.)

— Picasso to Daniel-Henry Kahnweiler, "Huit Entretiens avec Picasso," *Le Point* 42 (October 1952), pp. 22–30.

Pablo Picasso's enthusiasm for El Greco began at an early age, although the Old Master from Crete was still a controversial artist in Spain—and elsewhere—at the turn of the twentieth century. Picasso visited the Museo del Prado whenever he was in Madrid, and El Greco was among the painters he copied in his sketches. This was especially the case during his years at Madrid's Real Academia de Bellas Artes de San Fernando, which he attended from 1897. One drawing from 1899 is even signed "Yo El Greco" (cat. 5). As is clear from the pairings in the exhibition, Picasso was particularly intrigued by El Greco's portraits, a fascination that lasted a lifetime. "What I really like in his work are the portraits, all those gentlemen with pointed beards,"

he told Kahnweiler in the mid 1950s. "His religious pictures—the Trinity, the Virgin and so on—all that is Italian, decorative. But the portraits!"* While his dialogue with El Greco at the beginning of his career and in the subsequent Blue and Rose Periods (1901–06) is widely acknowledged, this exhibition seeks to broaden the perspective. Picasso's engagement with El Greco was not only more intense but also considerably more prolonged than is commonly assumed. In his writing and in his art, sometimes implicitly and sometimes quite directly, Picasso referenced El Greco throughout his entire life. A rich array of formal affinities with the Old Master can be traced across all his creative phases.

* Daniel-Henry Kahnweiler, "Entretiens avec Picasso au sujet des Femmes d'Alger" (1955), translated by P. S. Falla in *A Picasso Anthology*, ed. Marilyn McCully (Princeton, 1982), p. 251.

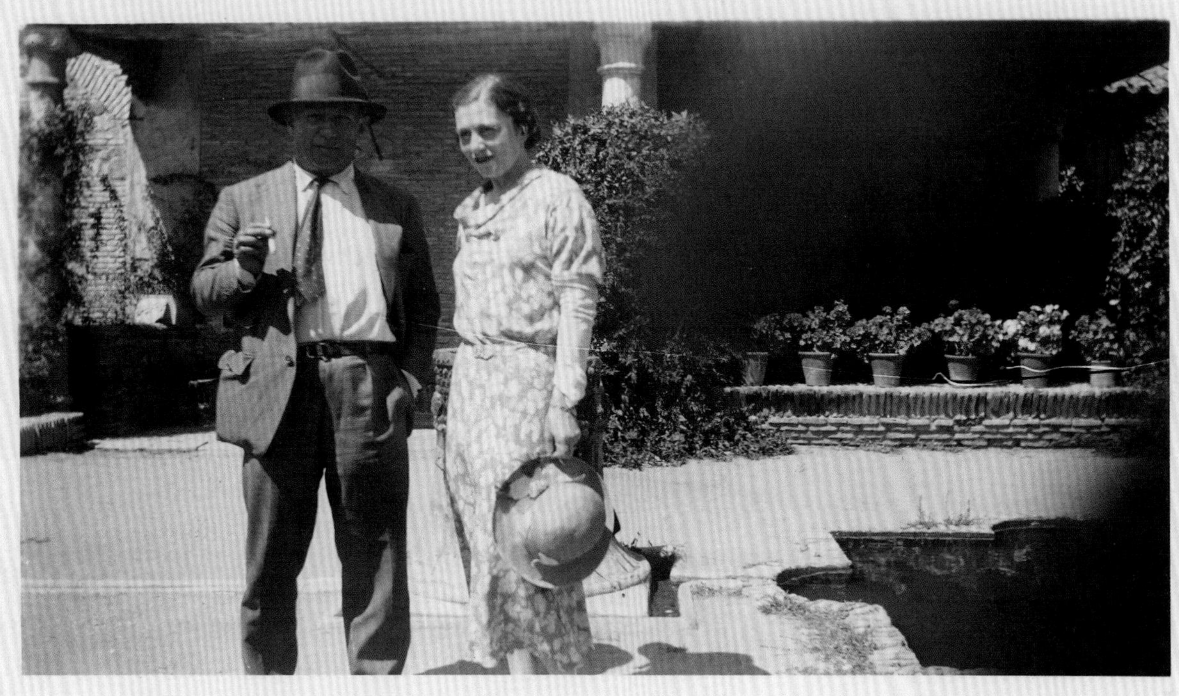

Olga and Pablo Picasso visiting the
house of El Greco in Toledo, 1934
Silver gelatin print, 6.9 × 11.7 cm

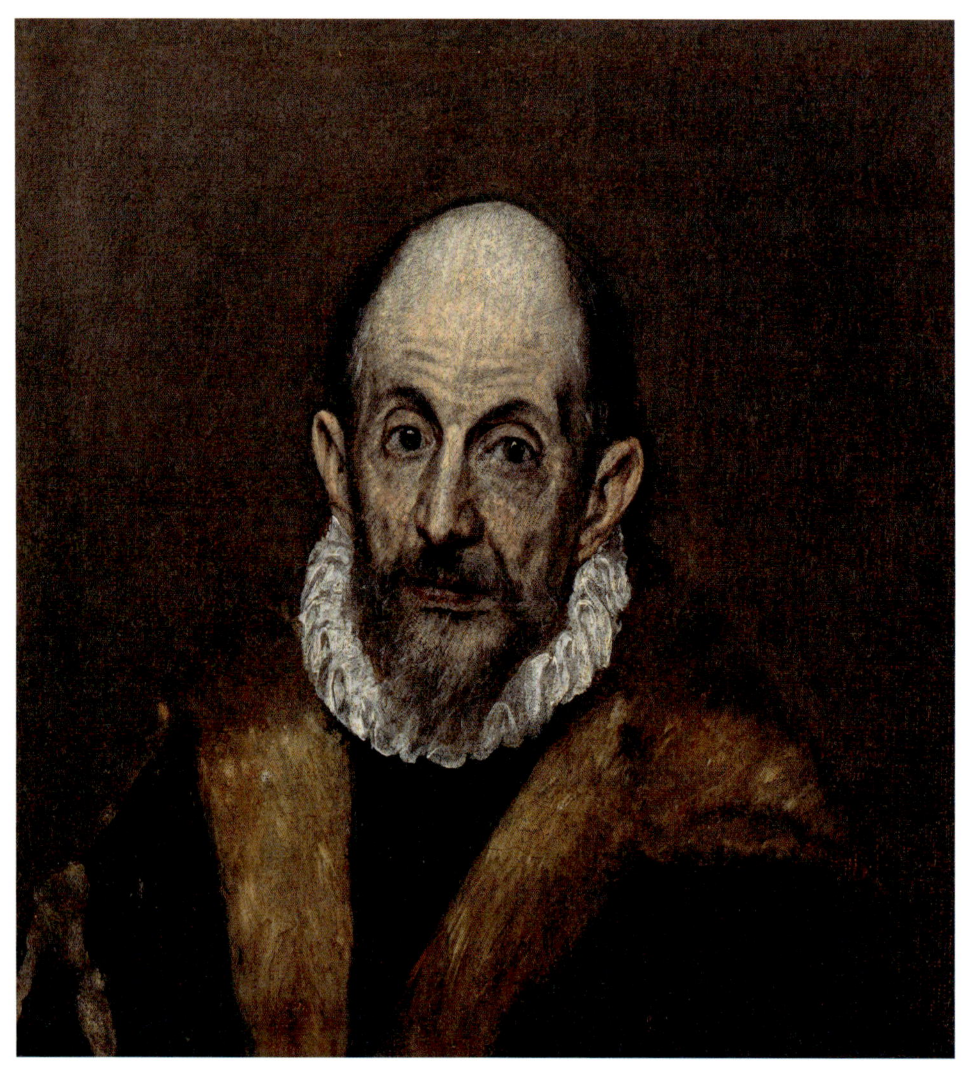

El Greco, *Portrait of an Old Man,* ca. 1595–1600

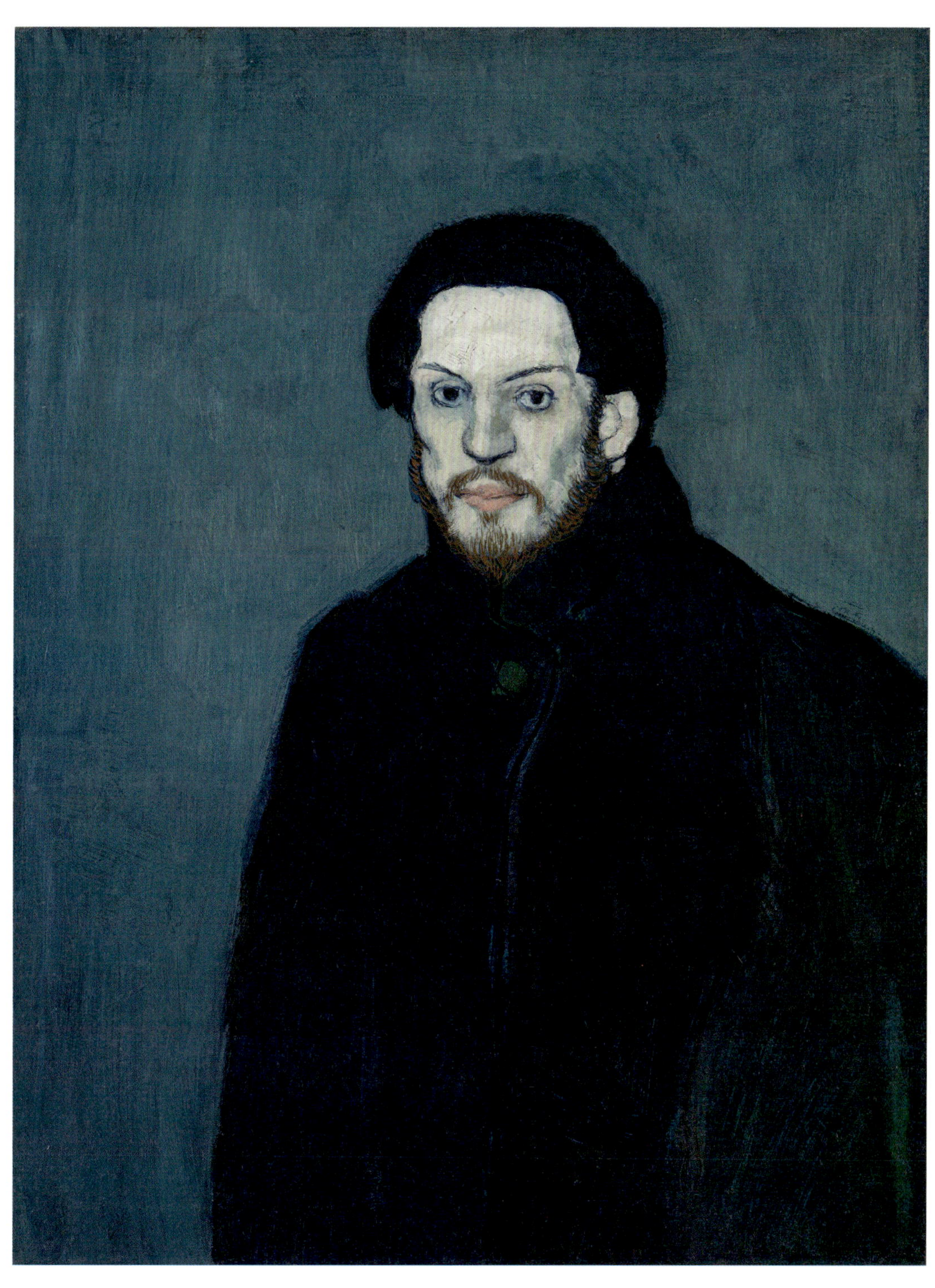

Pablo Picasso, *Autoportrait,* 1901

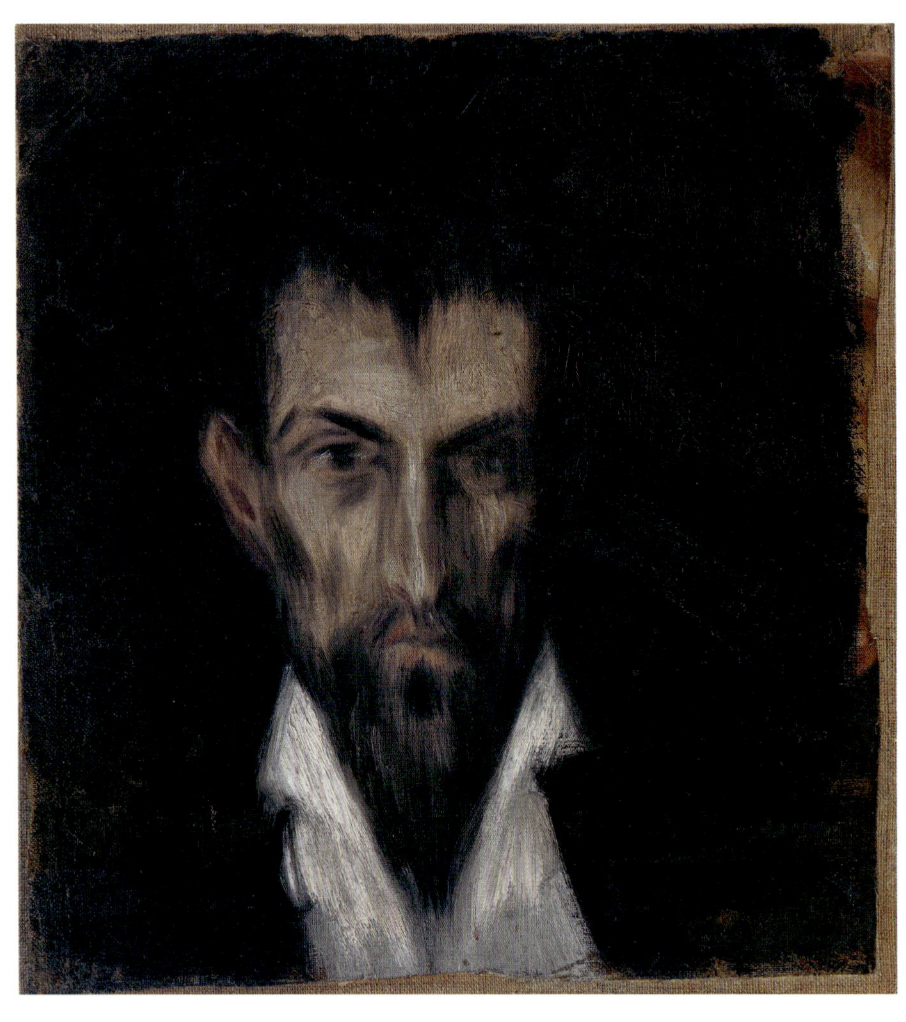

Pablo Picasso, *Man, after El Greco,* ca. 1899

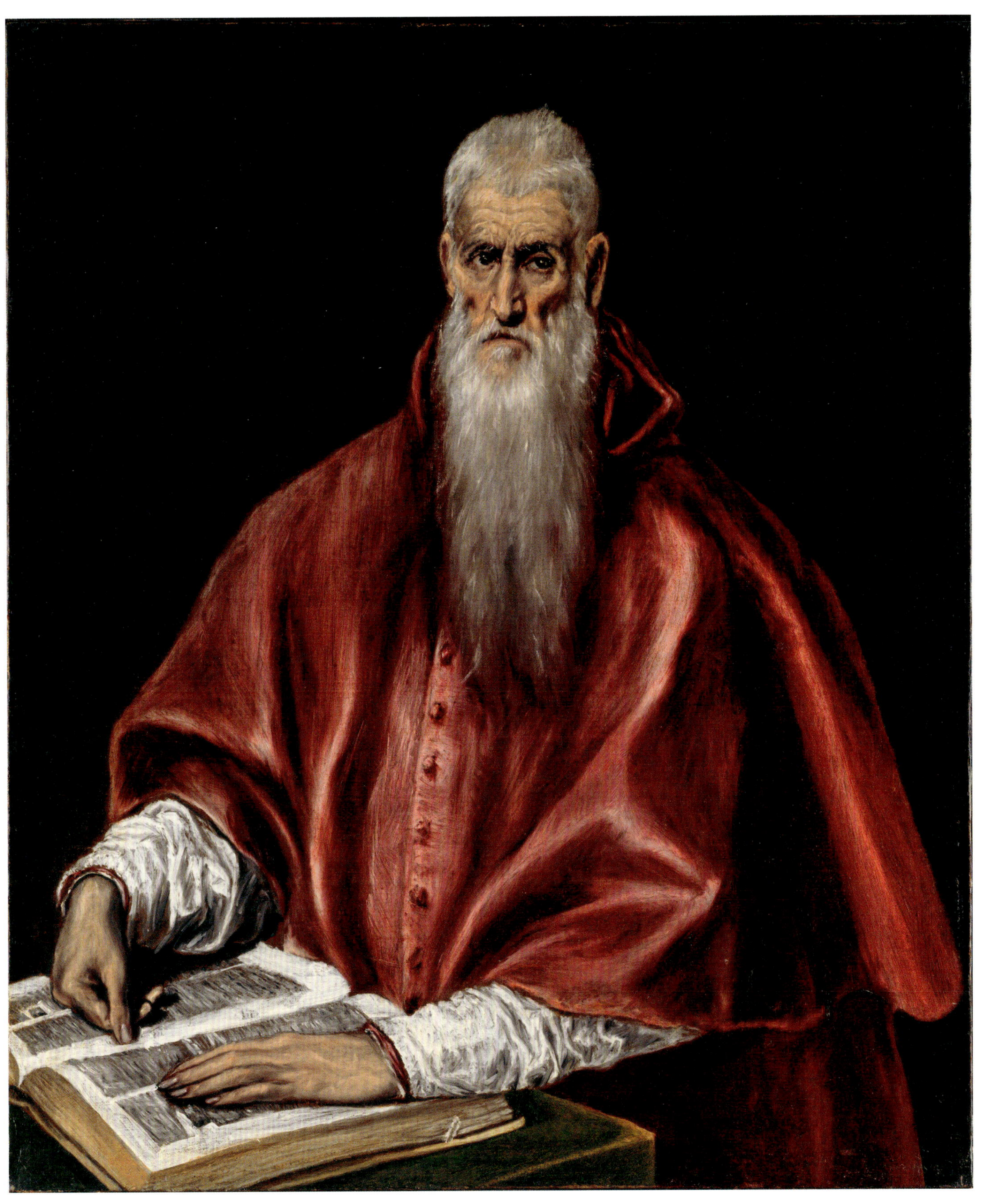

El Greco, *Saint Jerome as Scholar*, ca. 1610

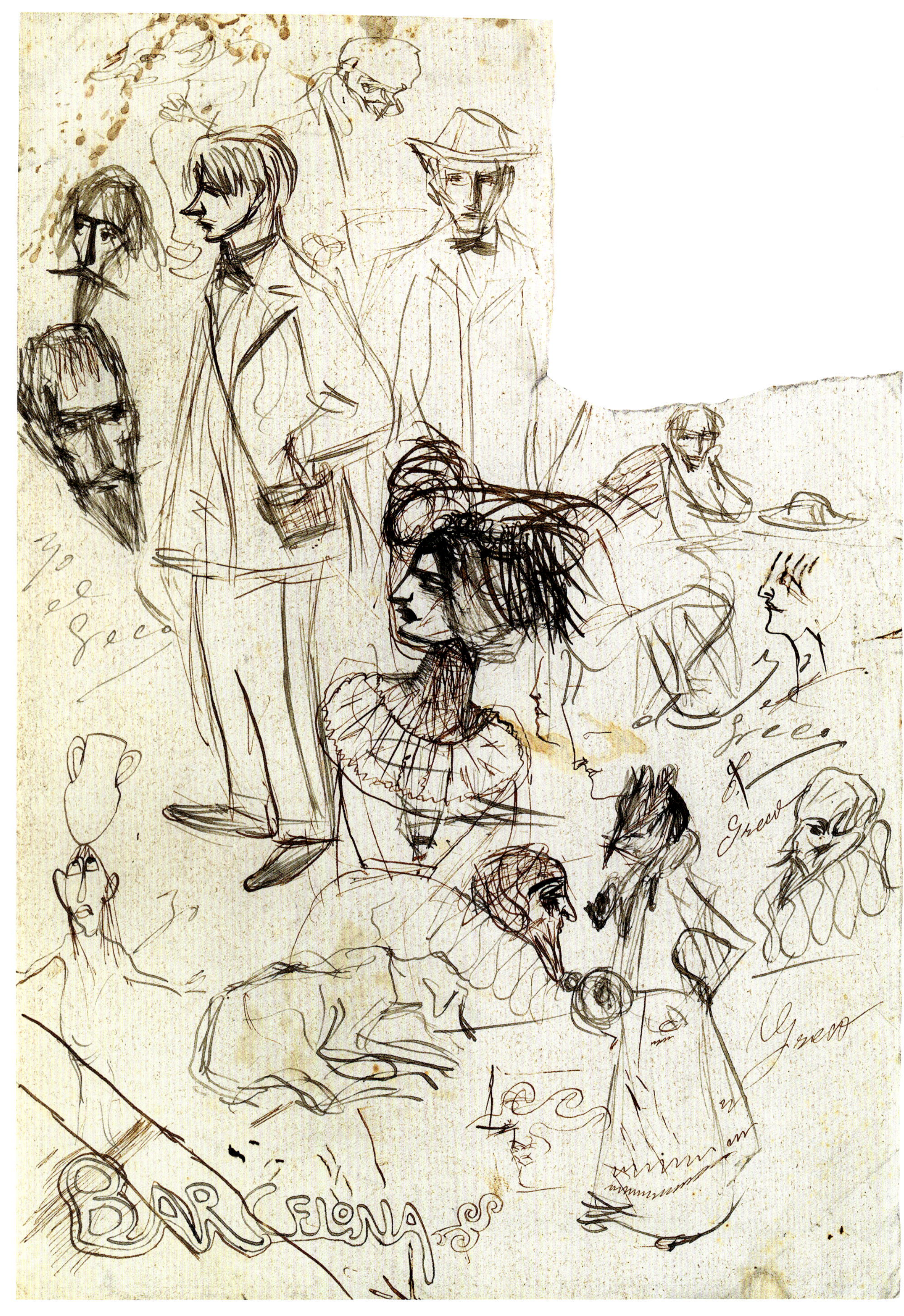

[Cat. 5]
Pablo Picasso, "*Yo El Greco*," ca. 1899

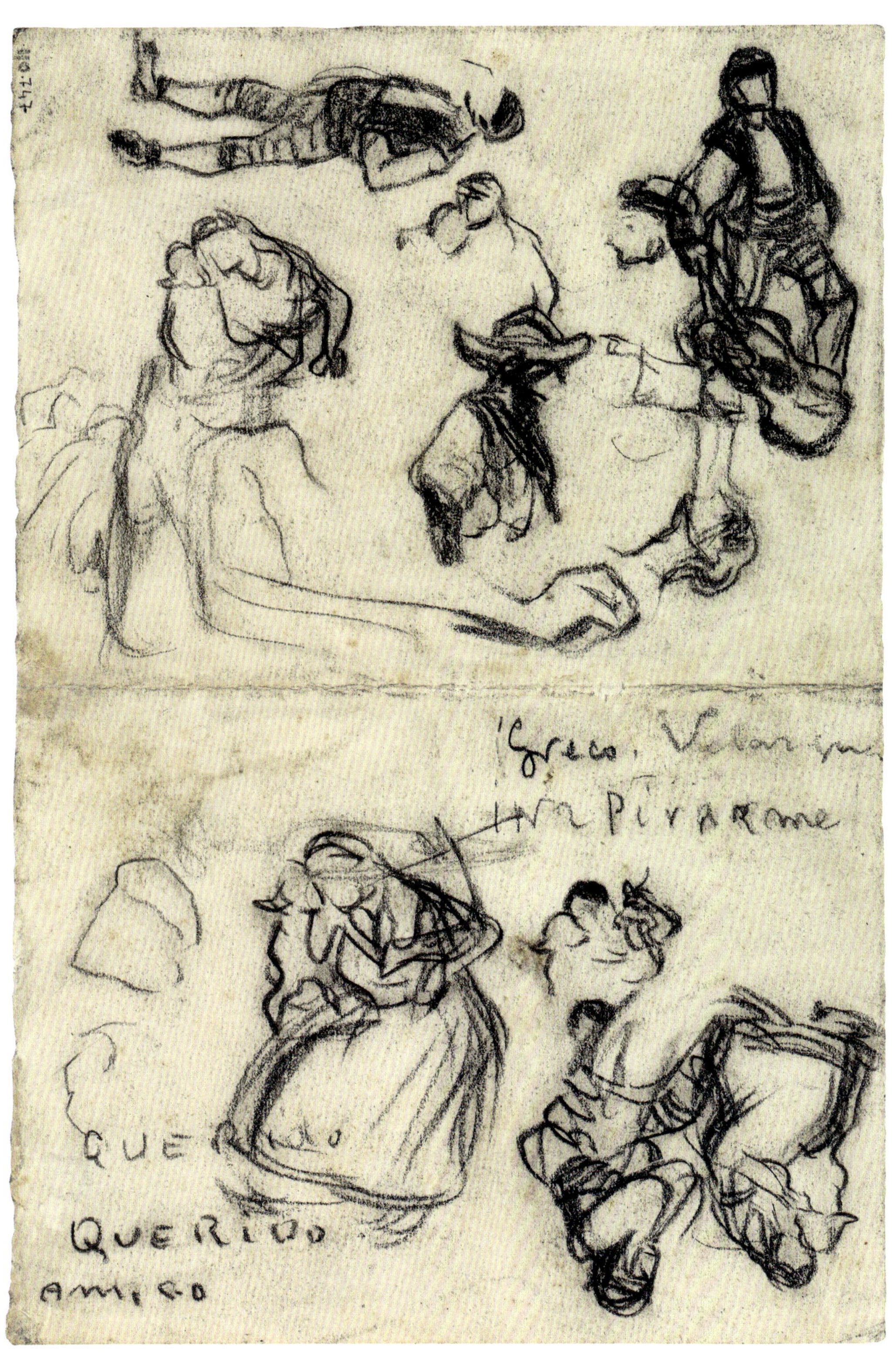

Pablo Picasso, *"Greco, Velázquez, INSPIRARME" (Several Horta Types)*, 1898–99

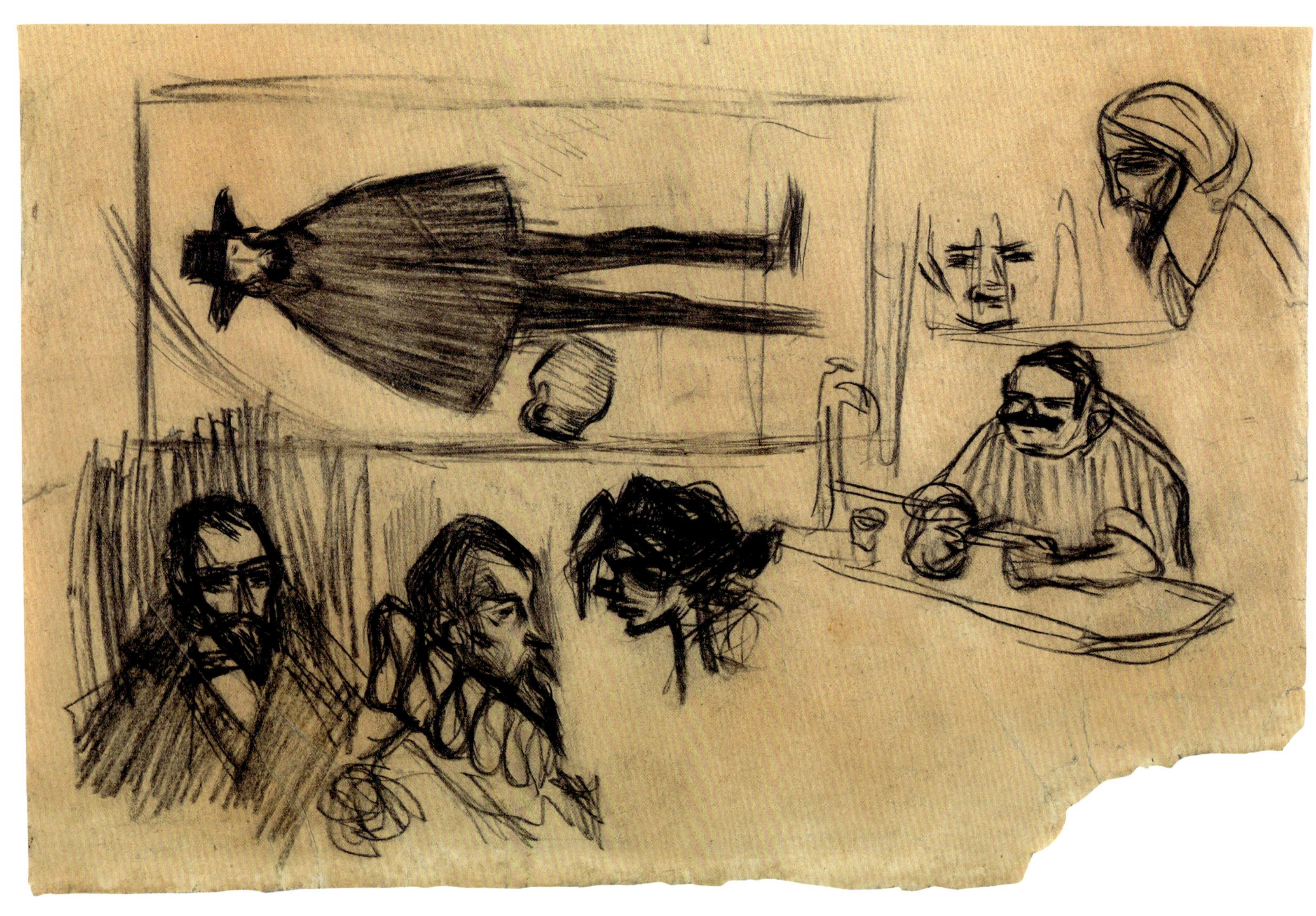

Pablo Picasso, *Pere Romeu and Other Sketches,* ca. 1899

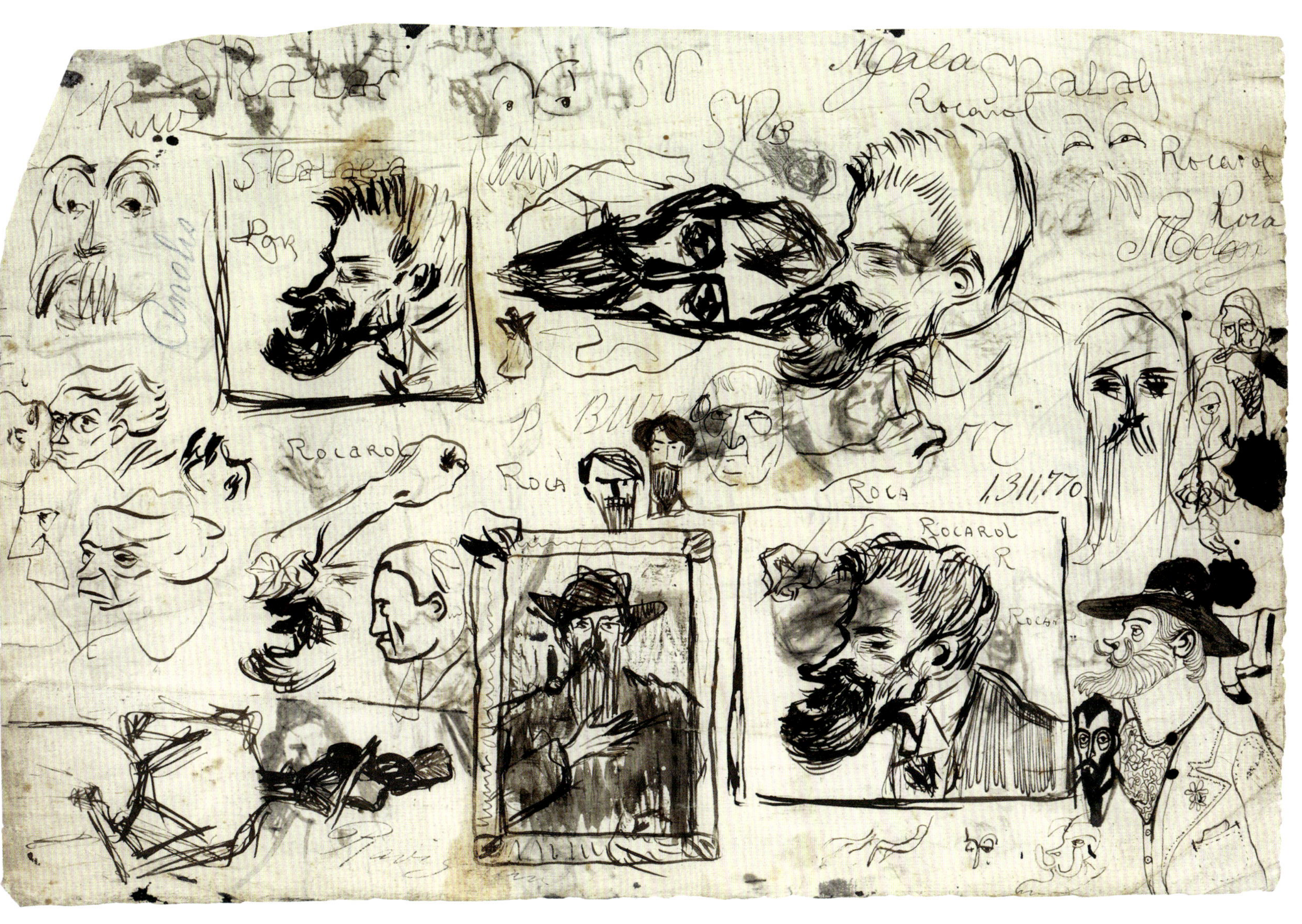

[Cat. 8]

Pablo Picasso, *Santiago Rusiñol Caricatured as* The Nobleman with His Hand on His Chest *by El Greco, Josep Rocarol i Faura, and Other Sketches,* 1899–1900

89

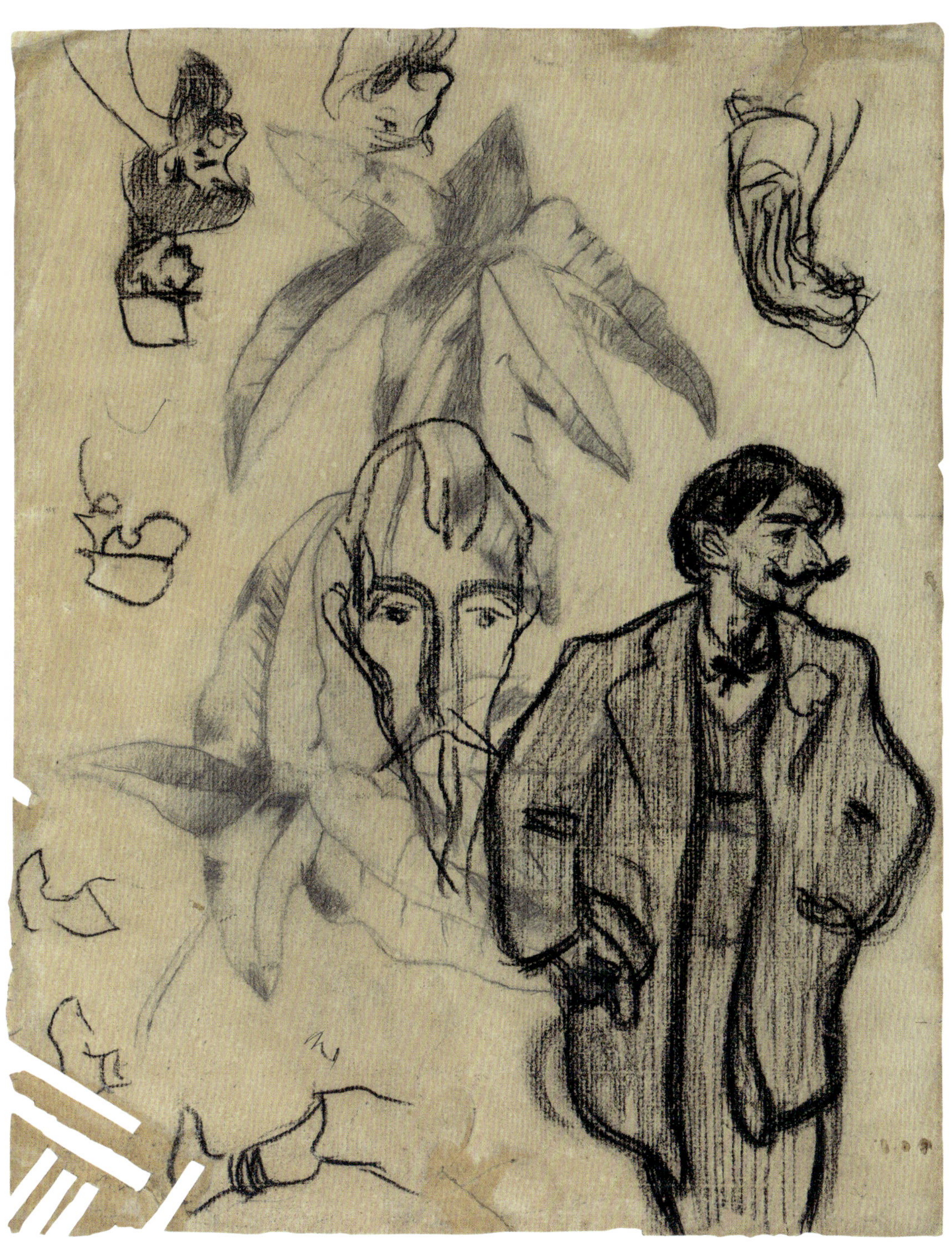

[Cat. 9]
Pablo Picasso, *Various Sketches,* ca. 1899

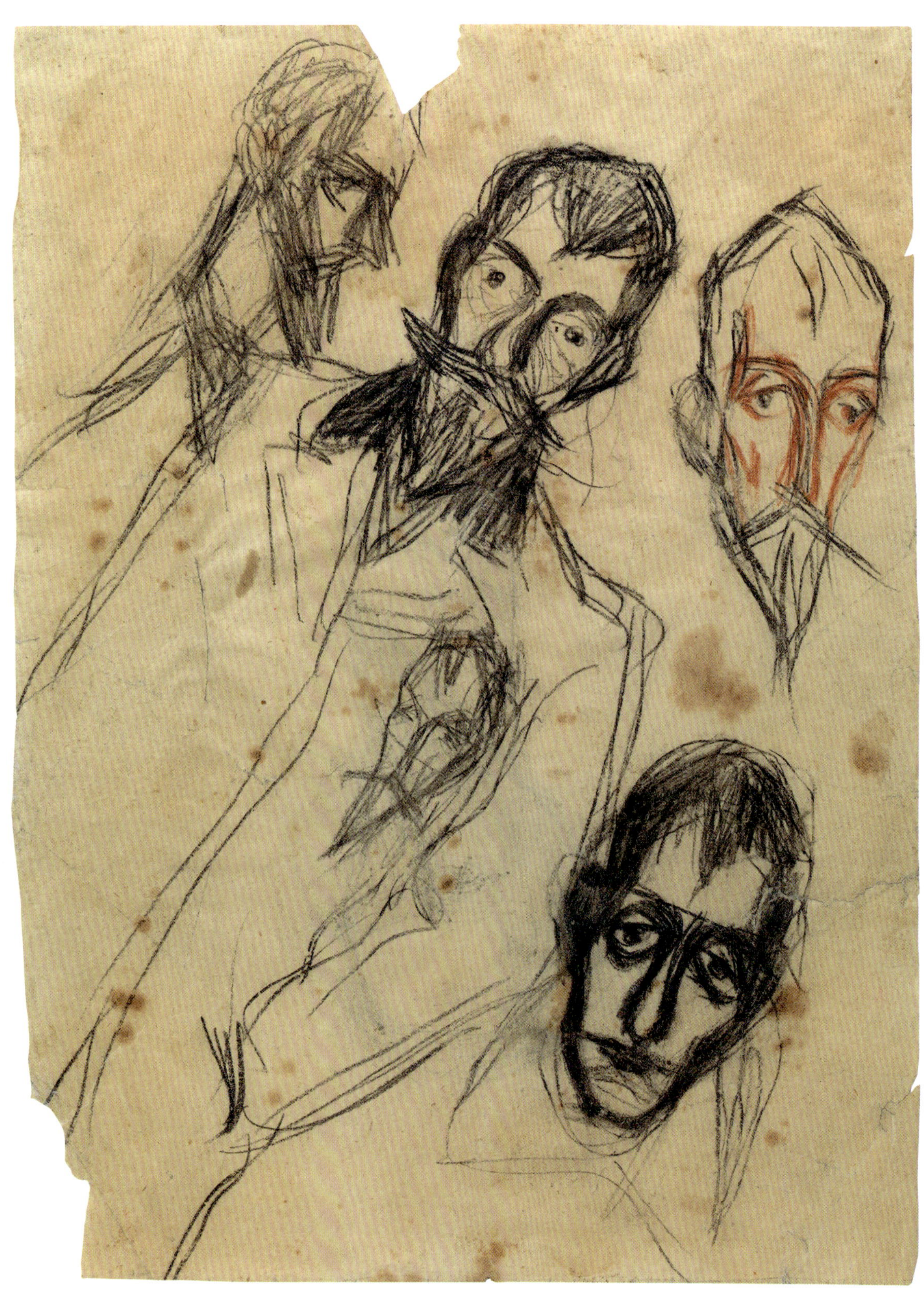

[Cat. 10]
Pablo Picasso, *Five Sketches of Grecoesque Figures,* ca. 1899

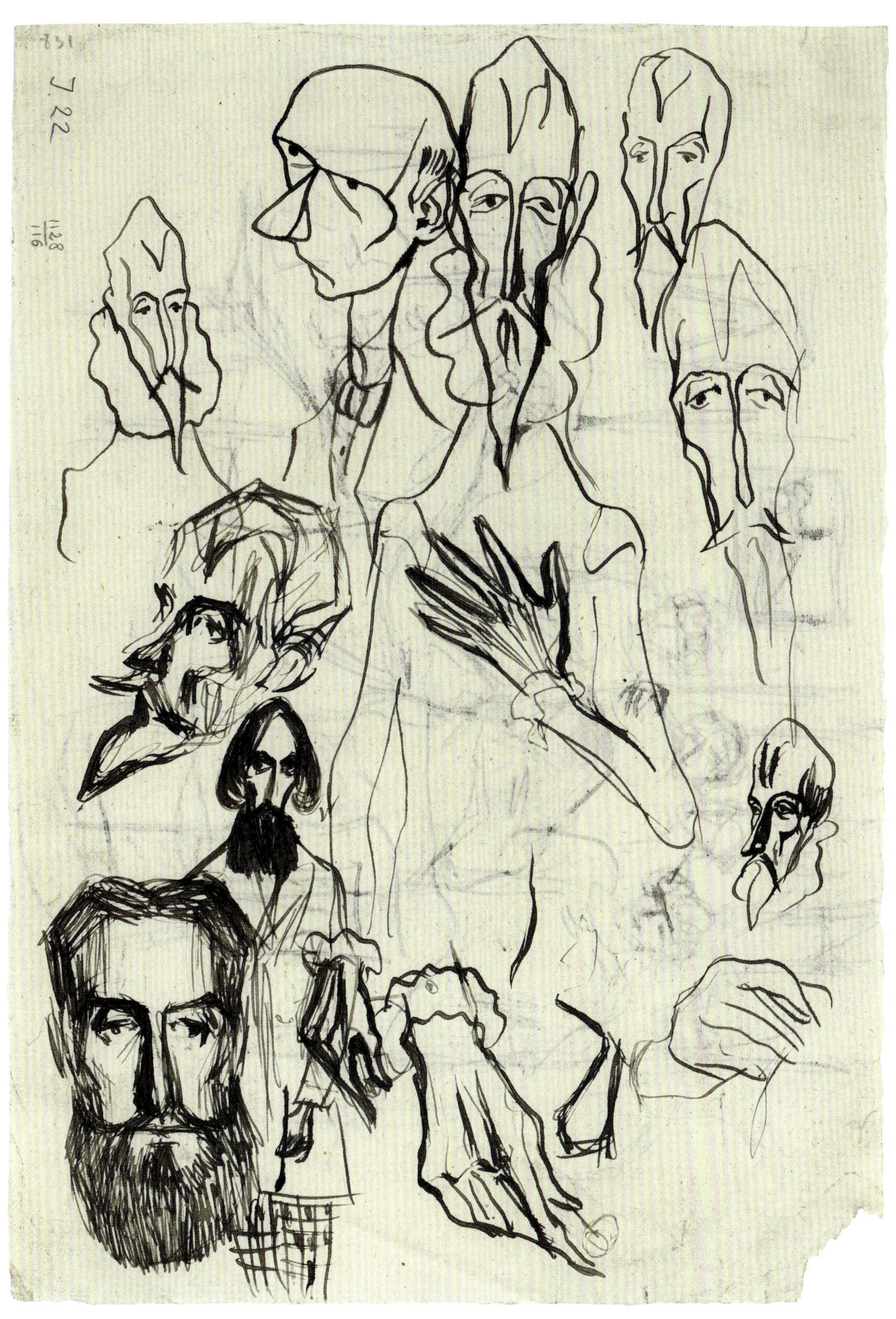

[Cat. 11]
Pablo Picasso, *Figures in El Greco Style, and Other Sketches,* 1899

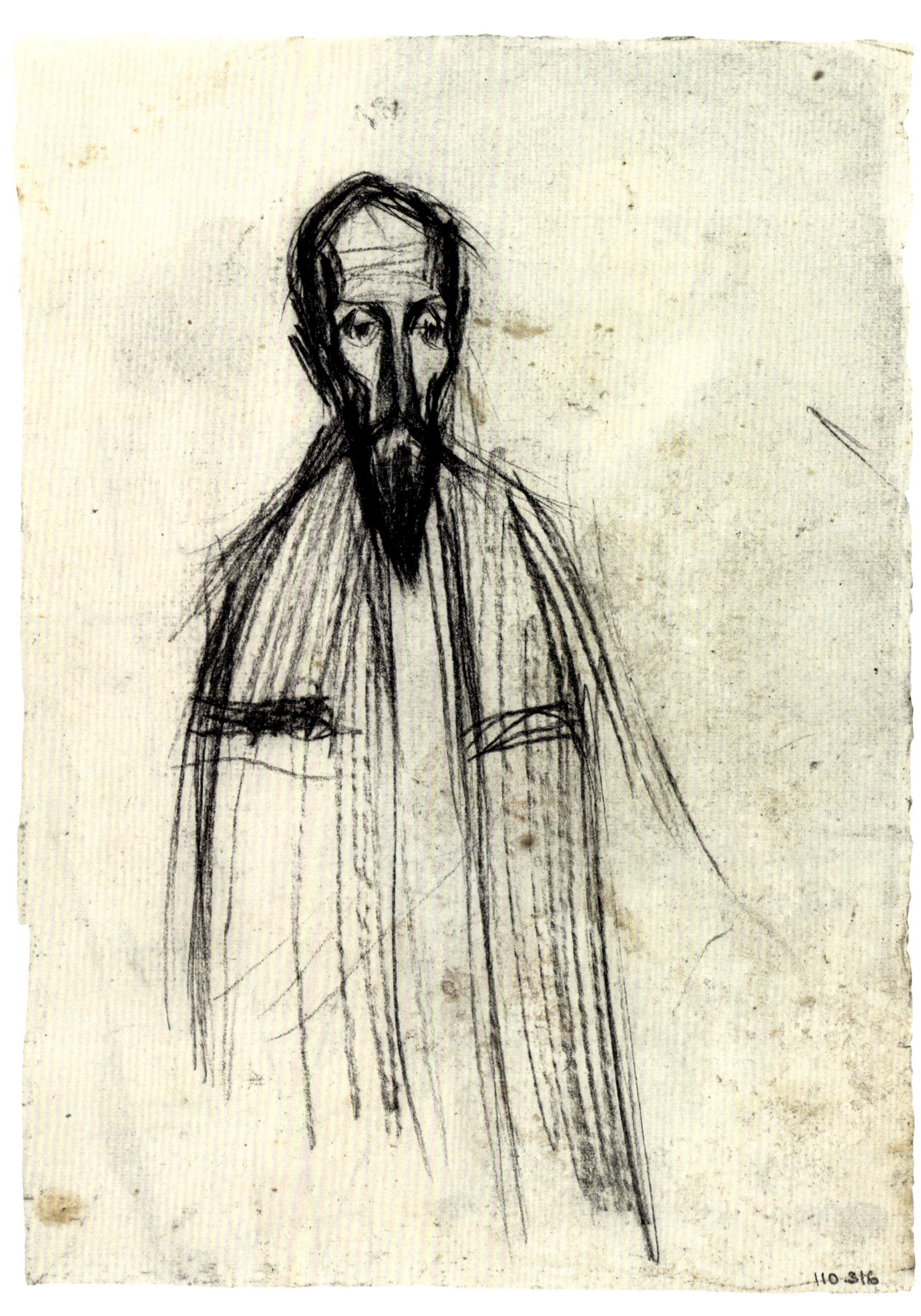

[Cat. 12]
Pablo Picasso, *Grecoesque Figure,* ca. 1899

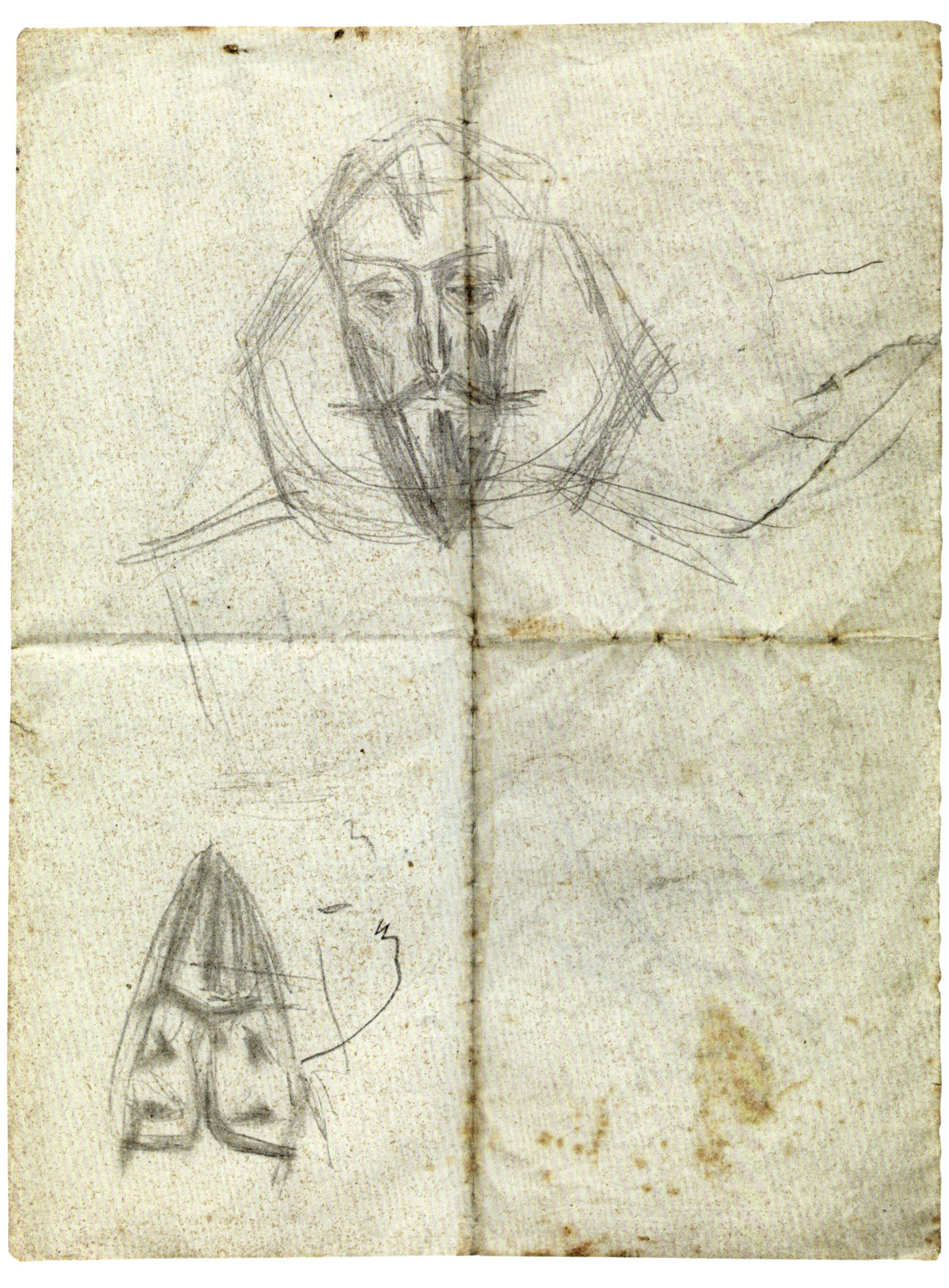

Pablo Picasso, *Two Heads, after El Greco,* ca. 1899

Elective Affinities: Picasso and El Greco

[Cat. 1] **El Greco**
Portrait of an Old Man
ca. 1595–1600
Oil on canvas, 52.7 × 46.7 cm
The Metropolitan Museum of Art, New York
Purchase, Joseph Pulitzer Bequest, 1924
Inv. 24.197.1

[Cat. 2] **Pablo Picasso**
Autoportrait (Self-Portrait)
Paris, 1901
Oil on canvas, 81 × 60 cm
Musée national Picasso, Paris
Inv. MP4

[Cat. 3] **Pablo Picasso**
Man, after El Greco, Barcelona, ca. 1899
Oil on canvas, 34.7 × 31.2 cm
Museu Picasso, Barcelona
Gift of Pablo Picasso, 1970
Inv. MPB 110.034

[Cat. 4] **El Greco**
Saint Jerome as Scholar, ca. 1610
Oil on canvas, 108 × 89 cm
The Metropolitan Museum of Art, New York
Robert Lehman Collection, 1975
Inv. 1975.1.146

[Cat. 5] **Pablo Picasso**
"Yo El Greco" (I, El Greco)
Barcelona, ca. 1899
Pen and ink on paper, 31.5 × 21.8 cm
Museu Picasso, Barcelona
Gift of Pablo Picasso, 1970
Inv. MPB 110.678

[Cat. 6] **Pablo Picasso**
"Greco, Velázquez, INSPIRARME"
(Several Horta Types)
Horta de Sant Joan, 1898–99
Conté crayon on paper, 24.3 × 16.2 cm
Museu Picasso, Barcelona
Gift of Pablo Picasso, 1970
Inv. MPB 110.747 R

[Cat. 7] **Pablo Picasso**
Pere Romeu and Other Sketches
Barcelona, ca. 1899
Conté crayon on paper, 31.5 × 21.4 cm
Museu Picasso, Barcelona
Gift of Pablo Picasso, 1970
Inv. MPB 110.659

[Cat. 8] **Pablo Picasso**
Santiago Rusiñol Caricatured as
The Nobleman with His Hand on
His Chest by El Greco, Josep Rocarol
i Faura, and Other Sketches
Barcelona, 1899–1900
Ink, wash, and graphite pencil on paper
23 × 33.4 cm
Museu Picasso, Barcelona
Gift of Pablo Picasso, 1970
Inv. MPB 110.683

[Cat. 9] **Pablo Picasso**
Various Sketches, Barcelona, ca. 1899
Graphite pencil and Conté crayon on
paper, 31 × 23.8 cm
Museu Picasso, Barcelona
Gift of Pablo Picasso, 1970
Inv. MPB 110.571

[Cat. 10] **Pablo Picasso**
Five Sketches of Grecoesque Figures
Barcelona, ca. 1899
Conté crayon and sanguine on paper
30.6 × 22 cm
Museu Picasso, Barcelona
Gift of Pablo Picasso, 1970
Inv. MPB 110.671

[Cat. 11] **Pablo Picasso**
Figures in El Greco Style, and Other
Sketches, 1899
Black ink on vellum paper, 21.5 × 31.5 cm
Fundación Almine y Bernard Ruiz-Picasso
para el Arte, Madrid
Inv. 00054V

[Cat. 12] **Pablo Picasso**
Grecoesque Figure, Barcelona, ca. 1899
Conté crayon on paper, 21.8 × 15.5 cm
Museu Picasso, Barcelona
Gift of Pablo Picasso, 1970
Inv. MPB 110.316 R

[Cat. 13] **Pablo Picasso**
Two Heads, after El Greco
Barcelona, ca. 1899
Graphite pencil on paper, 22 × 16.4 cm
Museu Picasso, Barcelona
Gift of Pablo Picasso, 1970
Inv. MPB 110.729

[Cat. 14] **Pablo Picasso**
Head of a Man, after El Greco, and Other
Sketches, Barcelona, ca. 1899
Conté crayon on laid paper, 24 × 16.1 cm
Museu Picasso, Barcelona
Gift of Pablo Picasso, 1970
Inv. MPB 110.641

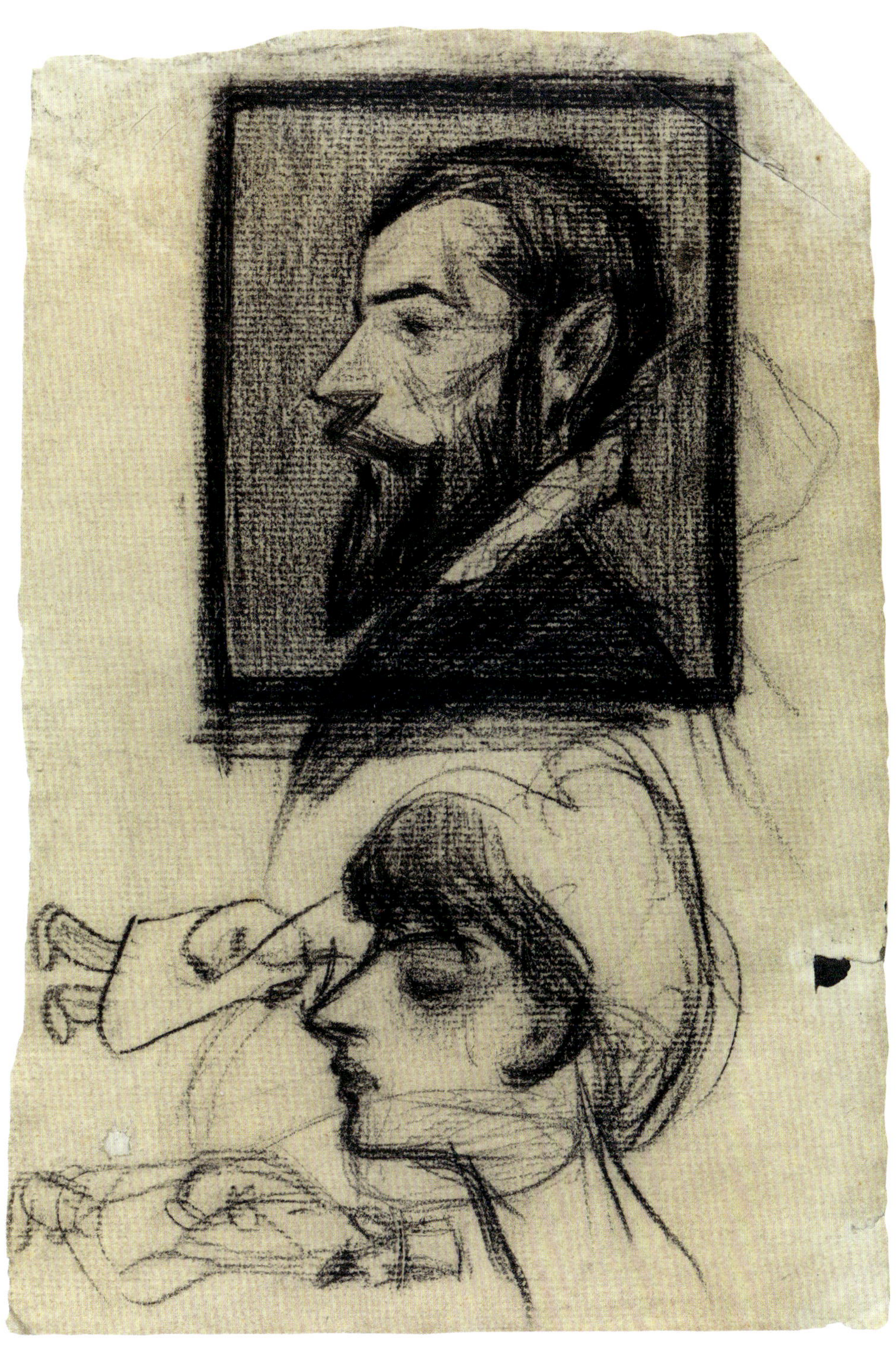

Pablo Picasso, *Head of a Man, after El Greco, and Other Sketches,* ca. 1899

Blue and Rose Periods: *The Burial of Casagemas* and Subsequent Works

People gather in crowds in front of it, they argue and discuss and lose their tempers. . . . they talk about it as they might talk about some contemporary picture, a thing with which they have a right to feel delighted or infuriated as the case may be—it is not like most old pictures, a thing classified and museumified, set altogether apart from life, an object for vague and listless reverence, but an actual living thing, expressing something with which one has to agree or disagree . . . That the artists are excited—never more so—is no wonder, for here is an old master who is not merely modern but actually appears a good many steps ahead of us, turning back to show us the way.

—Roger Fry, "El Greco," in *Vision and Design* (London, 1920), p. 138. (Fry is referring to El Greco's *Agony in the Garden of Gethsemane*, first displayed in the National Gallery in London in 1919.)

Picasso first met Carles Casagemas in Barcelona in 1899 when he was eighteen and Casagemas a year older. Young, elegant, and eccentric, Casagemas came from a well-to-do family and was a keen anarchist and Catalan nationalist. He and Picasso shared an apartment, travelled back and forth between France and Spain, and were regulars—together with Manuel Pallarès, Jaume (Jaime) Sabartés, and the brothers Mateu and Angel Fernandéz de Soto—at the Barcelona café Els Quatre Gats, the vibrant meeting place of the Catalan *modernistes*. In their shared studio in Paris, Casagemas, Picasso, and Pallarès led a wild life with their lovers and models, but Casagemas's drug habit and rapidly deteriorating mental health were an increasing strain on their friendship. Tragedy struck in February 1901, while Picasso was away in Spain: Casagemas shot himself in the Hippodrome café because of his unhappy love affair with Germaine Gargallo, one of their models. Picasso was deeply shaken by the suicide. Six months later, his Blue Period began when he started to process the incident in his art, painting a series of portraits of Casagemas with a shadowy bullet hole in his temple (cat. 15). This process of coming to terms with his friend's death culminated in *Evocation (The Burial of Casagemas)* (cat. 17). The sharp distinction between heavenly and earthly spheres, like the expressive gestures of the mourners, are clearly inspired by El Greco, especially his monumental canvas *The Burial of the Count of Orgaz* painted around 1588 for the church of Santo Tomé in Toledo (fig. p. 14). Both elements are also present in his versions of *Adoration of the Name of Jesus* (cats. 17, 18) and of *The Agony in the Garden* (cats. 19, 20). The heavenly sphere toward which Casagemas ascends has little to do with the Christian imaginary, however. Picasso's entire Blue Period is clearly marked by El Greco's influence, which extends into the Rose Period—for example in Picasso's *Madame Canals*, a portrait of the wife of his friend Ricardo Canals that is clearly inspired by the *Lady in a Fur Wrap*, which was attributed to El Greco until the mid-twentieth century (cats. 21, 22).

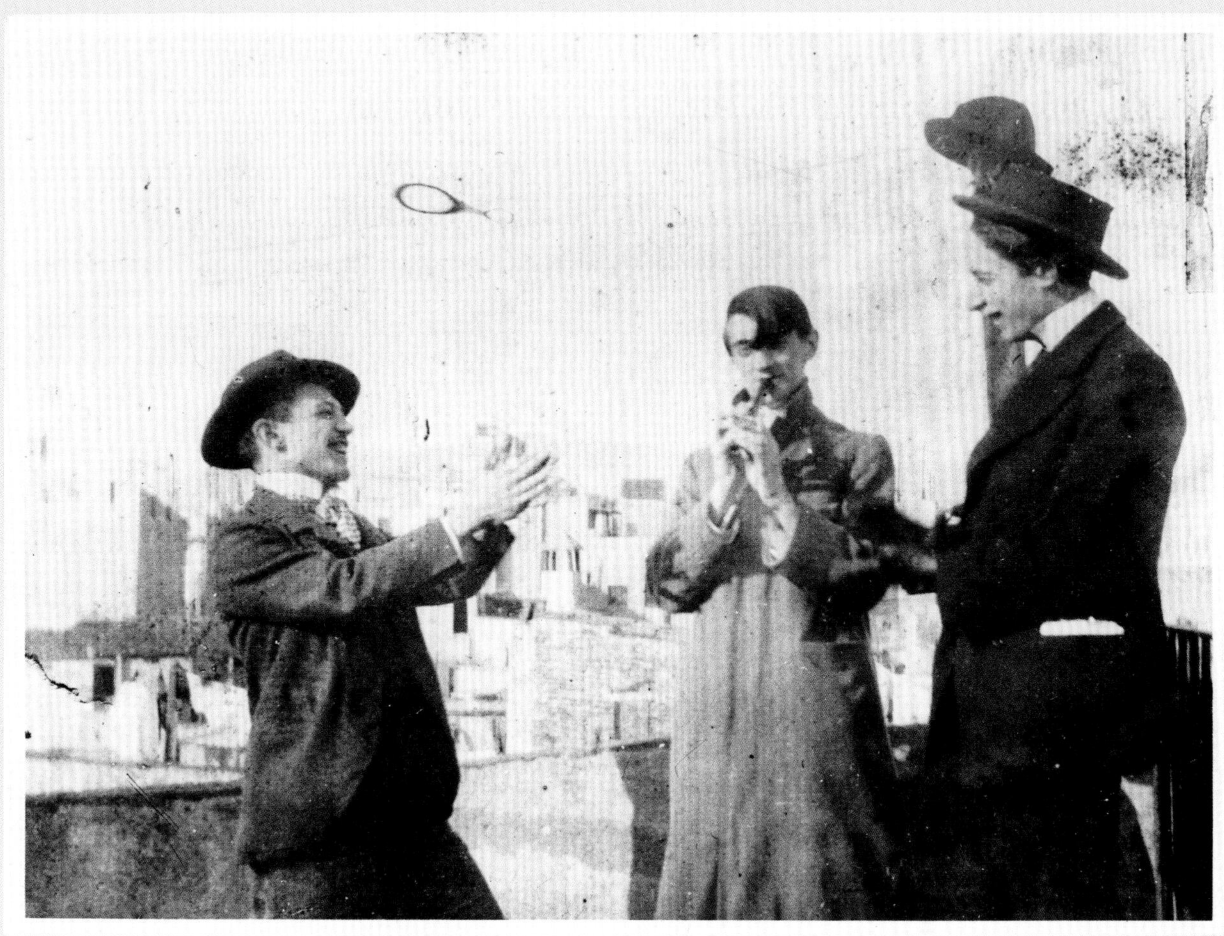

Manuel Pallarès i Grau
Picasso, Àngel Fernández de Soto, and
Carles Casagemas on the terrace of
3 Plaza de la Merced in Barcelona, ca. 1900
Musée national Picasso, Paris

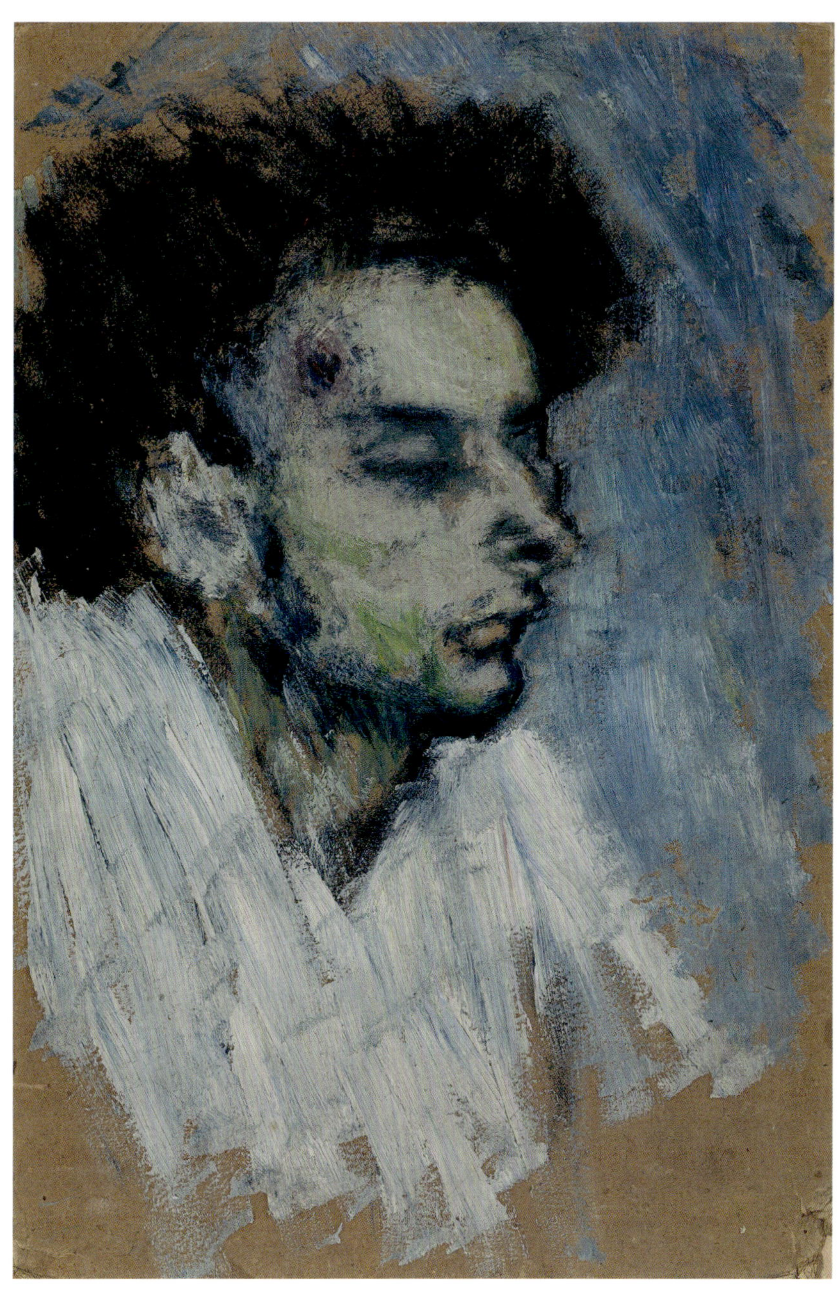

[Cat. 15]
Pablo Picasso, *Casagemas mort,* 1901

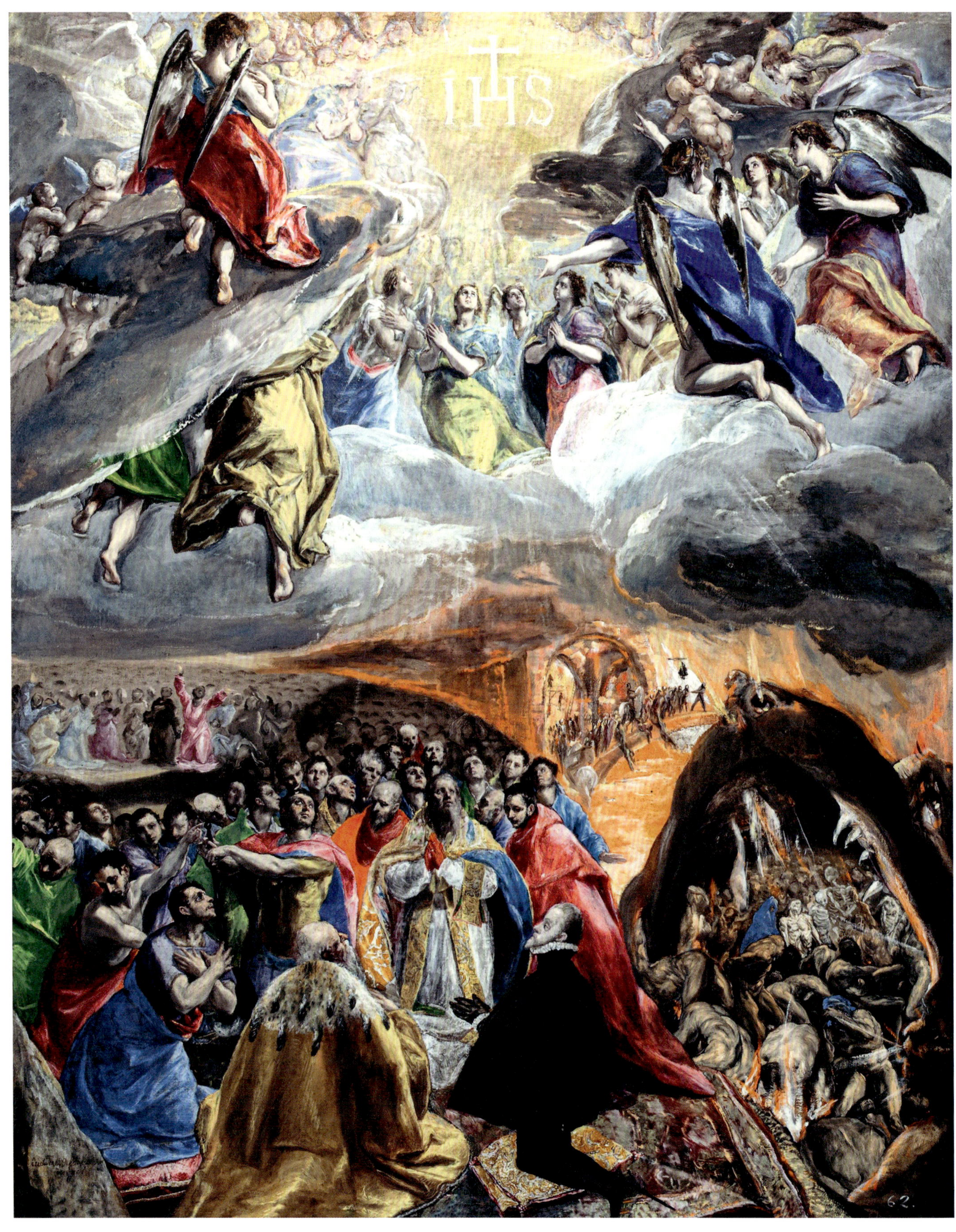

[Cat. 16]
El Greco, *The Adoration of the Name of Jesus,* ca. 1577–79

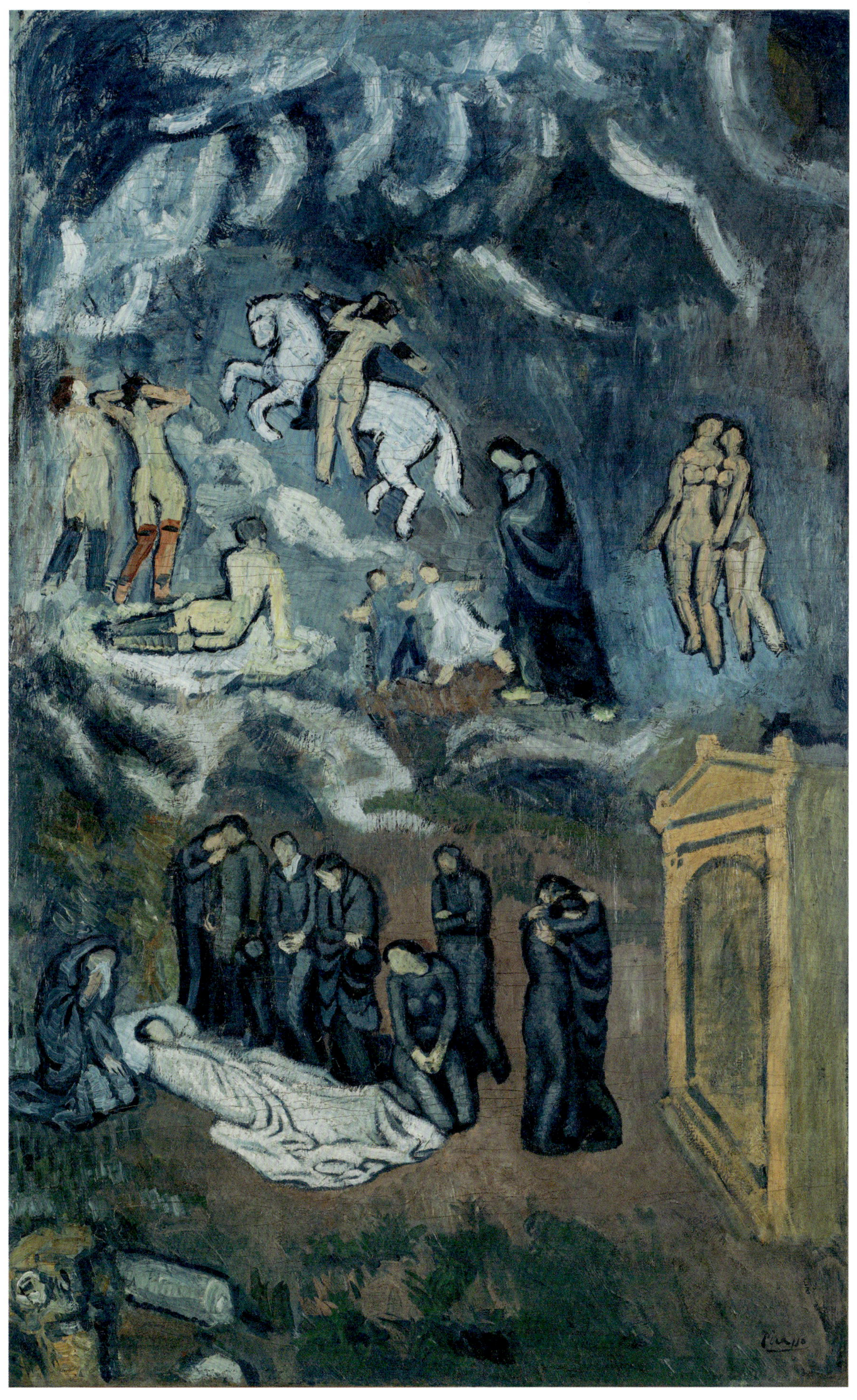

[Cat. 17]
Pablo Picasso, *Evocation (The Burial of Casagemas)*, 1901

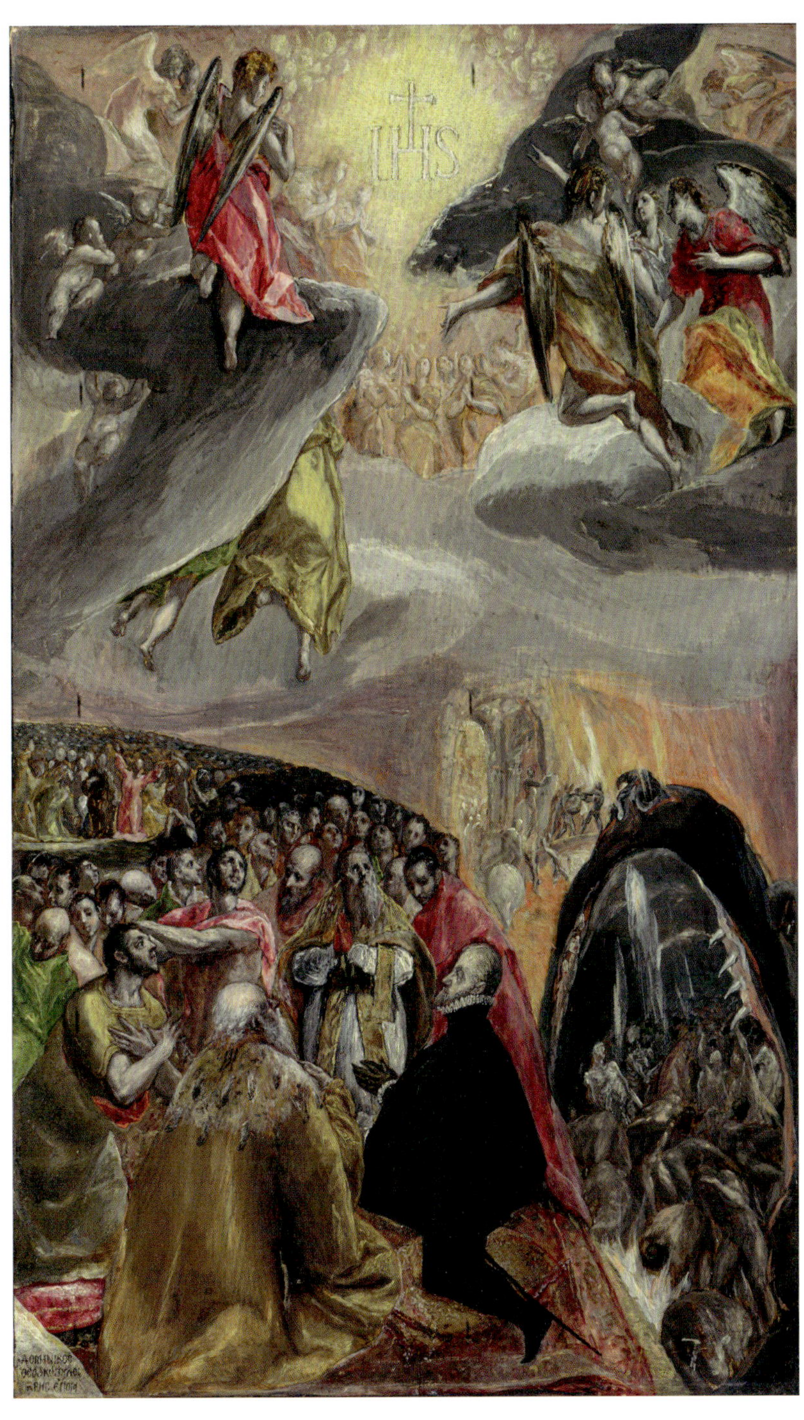

[Cat. 18]

El Greco, *The Adoration of the Name of Jesus,* late 1570s

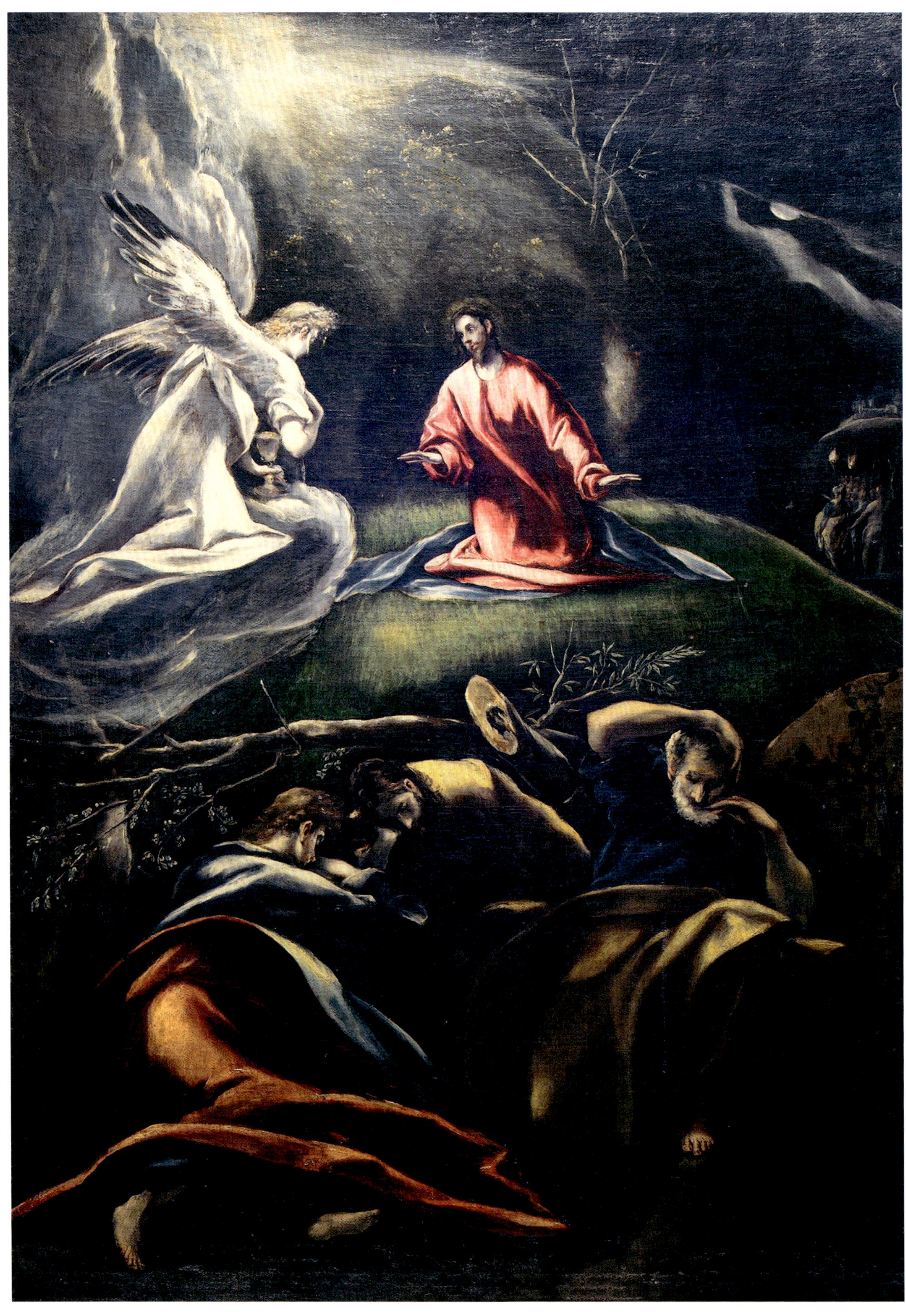

El Greco, *The Agony in the Garden,* ca. 1597–1607

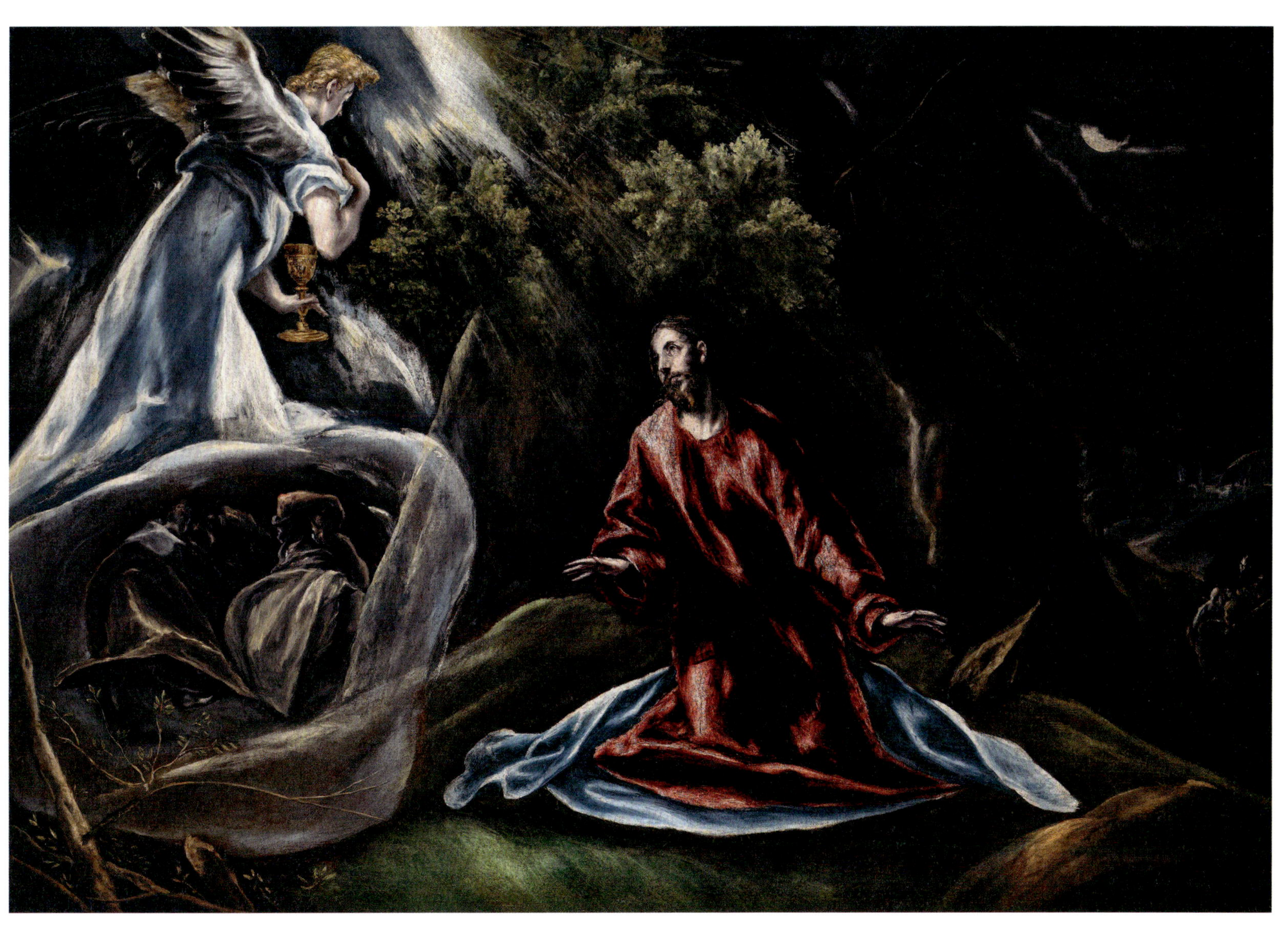

[Cat. 20]
El Greco, *The Agony in the Garden,* ca. 1600

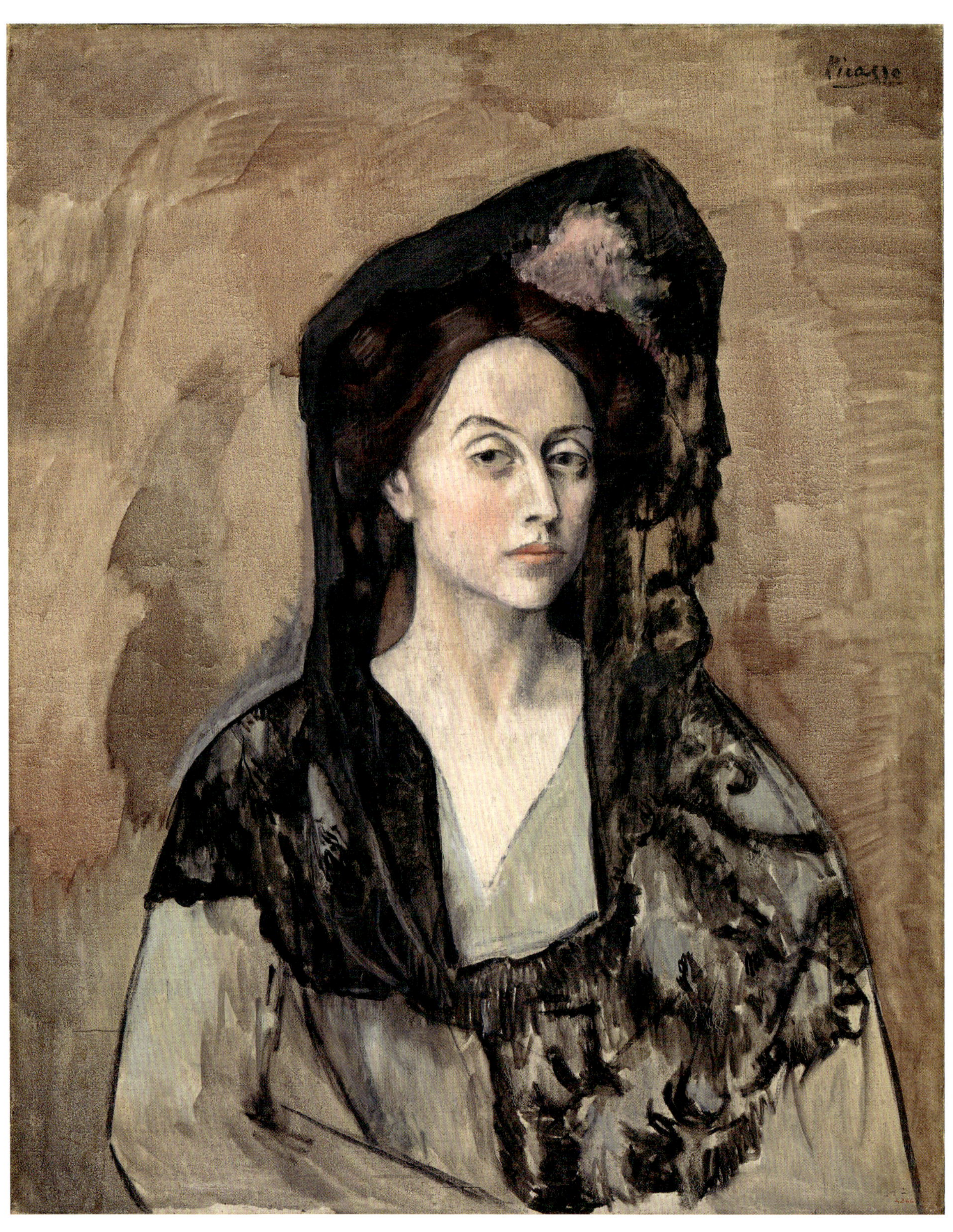

[Cat. 21]
Pablo Picasso, *Madame Canals (Benedetta Bianco)*, 1905

108

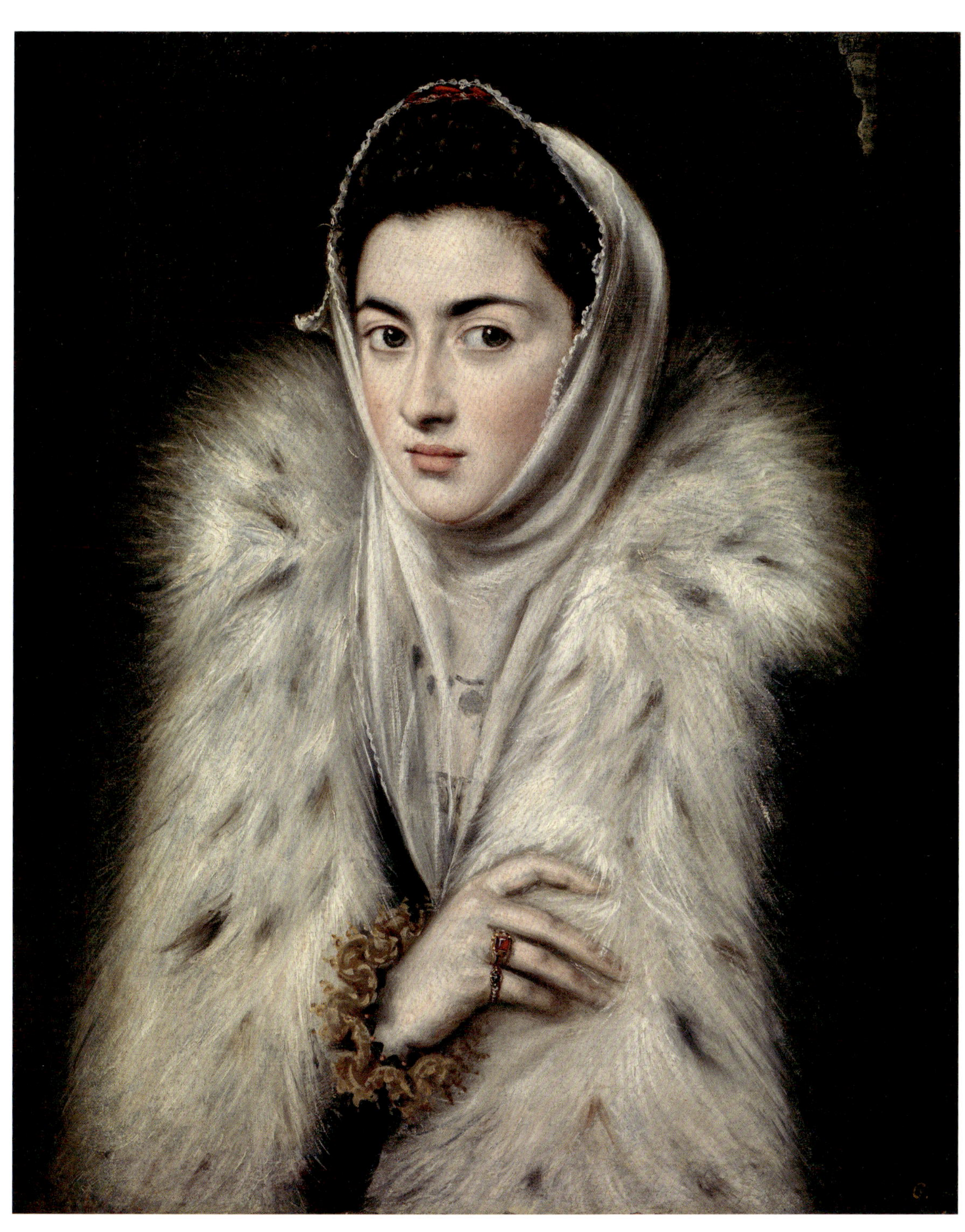

Alonso Sánchez Coello (formerly attributed to El Greco), *Lady in a Fur Wrap,* ca. 1580–88

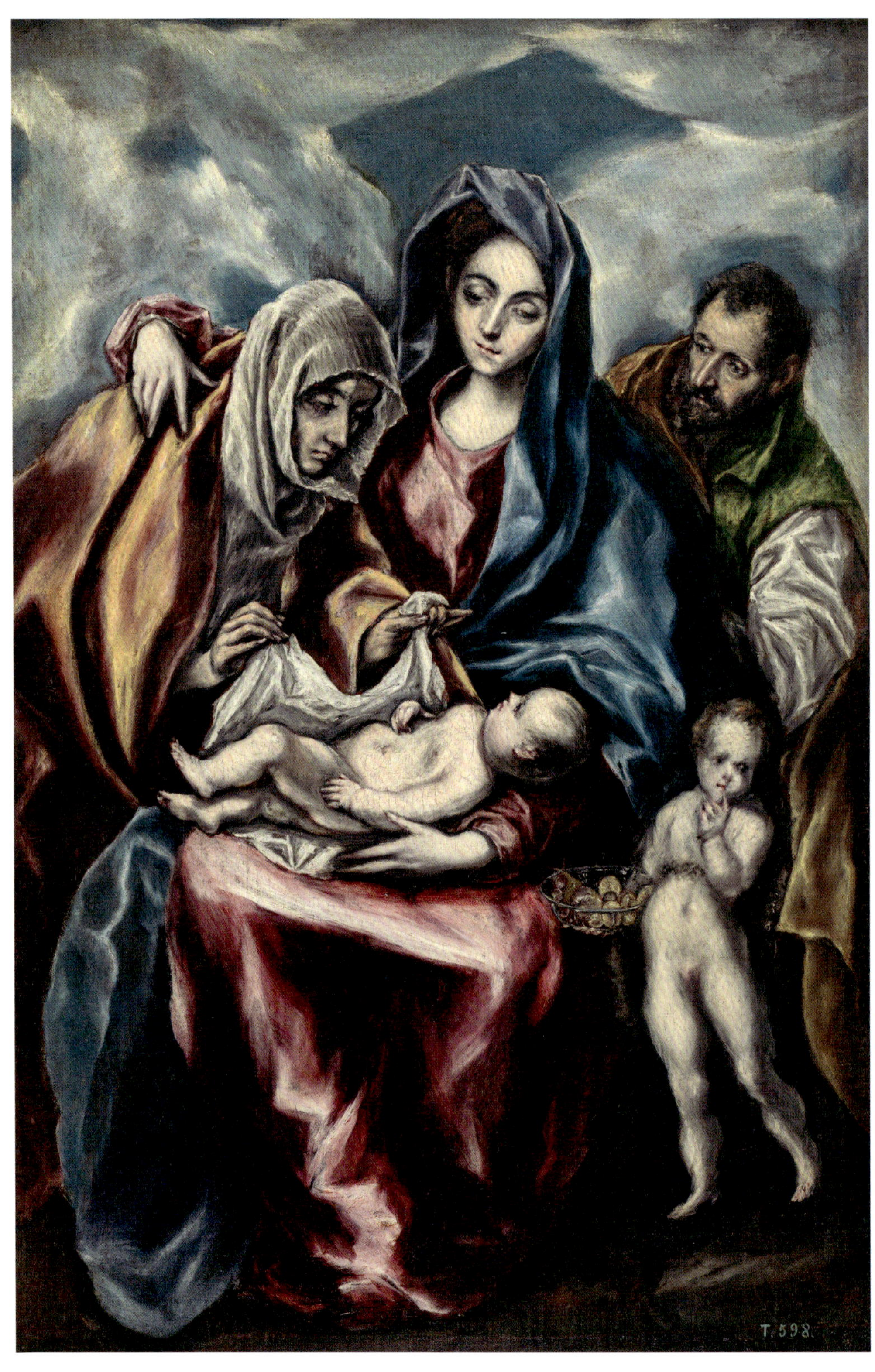

[Cat. 23]

El Greco, *The Holy Family with Saint Anne and the Infant Saint John,* ca. 1600

110

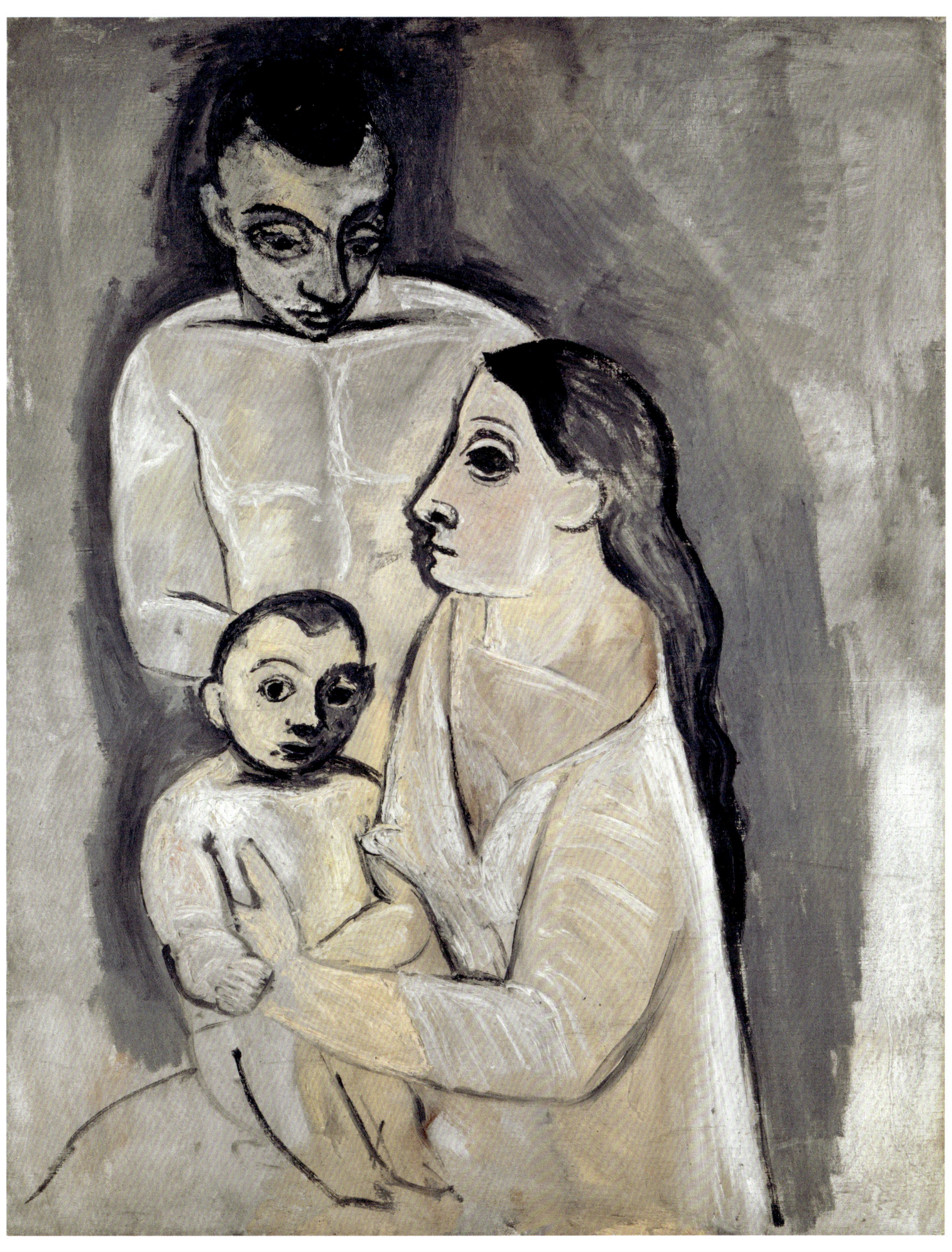

[Cat. 24]
Pablo Picasso, *Homme, femme et enfant,* 1906

Blue and Rose Periods: *The Burial of Casagemas* and Subsequent Works

[Cat. 15]
Pablo Picasso
***Casagemas mort* (Casagemas dead)**
Paris 1901
Oil on cardboard, 52 × 34 cm
Fundación Almine y Bernard Ruiz-Picasso
para el Arte, Madrid
Inv. 12048

[Cat. 16]
El Greco
The Adoration of the Name of Jesus
ca. 1577–79
Oil on canvas, 140 × 109.5 cm
Patrimonio Nacional, Real Monasterio de
San Lorenzo de El Escorial
Inv. 10014683

[Cat. 17]
Pablo Picasso
Evocation (The Burial of Casagemas)
Paris, 1901
Oil on canvas, 150 × 90.5 cm
Musée d'Art Moderne de la Ville de Paris
Inv. AMVP 1133

[Cat. 18]
El Greco
The Adoration of the Name of Jesus
late 1570s
Oil and egg tempera on pine
55.1 × 33.8 cm
The National Gallery, London
Inv. NG 6260

[Cat. 19]
El Greco
***The Agony in the Garden,* ca. 1597–1607**
Oil on canvas, 169 × 112 cm
Parroquia de Santa Maria la Mayor, Andujar
(Diocese of Jaén, Spain)

[Cat. 20]
El Greco
***The Agony in the Garden,* ca. 1600**
Oil on canvas, 100 × 143 cm
The Pittas Collection – El Greco

[Cat. 21]
Pablo Picasso
Madame Canals (Benedetta Bianco)
Paris, (autumn) 1905
Oil and charcoal on canvas, 90 × 70 cm
Museu Picasso, Barcelona
Acquisition Plandiura, 1932
Inv. MPB 4.266

[Cat. 22]
Alonso Sánchez Coello
(formerly attributed to El Greco)
***Lady in a Fur Wrap,* ca. 1580–88**
Oil on canvas, 62 × 50 cm
Glasgow Museums, Stirling Maxwell Collection,
gifted, 1967
Inv. PC.18

[Cat. 23]
El Greco
The Holy Family with Saint Anne
***and the Infant Saint John,* ca. 1600**
Oil on canvas, 107 × 68.5 cm
Museo Nacional del Prado, Madrid
Inv. P000826

[Cat. 24]
Pablo Picasso
Homme, femme et enfant
(Man, Woman, and Child)
Paris, fall 1906
Oil on canvas, 116 × 89 cm
Kunstmuseum Basel, gift of the artist to the
municipality of Basel; permanent loan from
the City of Basel, 1967
Inv. G 1967.11

[Cat. 25]
Pablo Picasso
***Self-Portrait with Palette,* 1906**
Oil on canvas, 91.9 × 73.3 cm
Philadelphia Museum of Art:
E. Gallatin Collection, 1950
Inv. 150-1-1

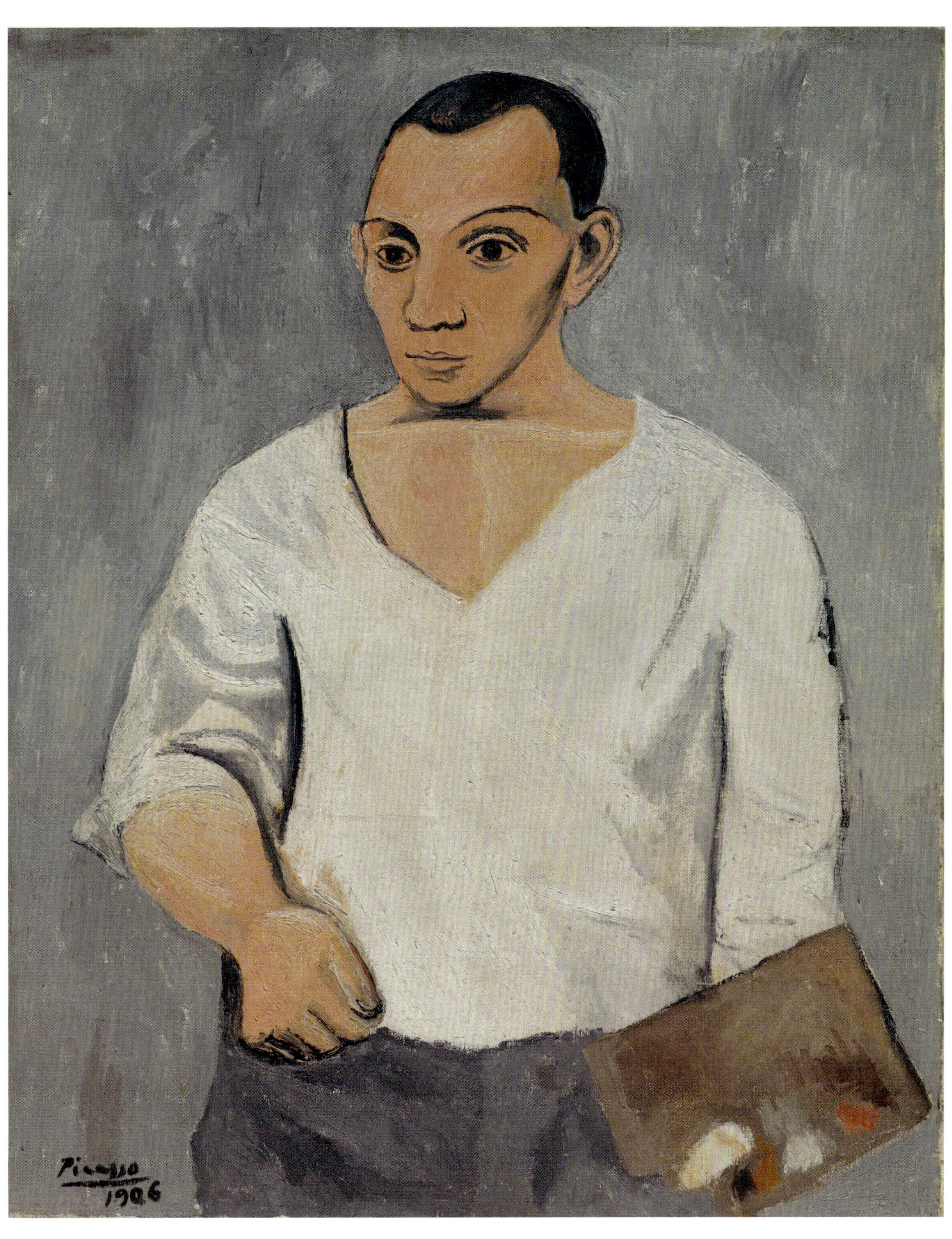

[Cat. 25]
Pablo Picasso, *Self-Portrait with Palette*, 1906

113

Toward Cubism

*It is true that Cubism is Spanish in origin, and it was
I who invented Cubism. We should look for Spanish
influence in Cézanne. . . . Observe El Greco's influence on
him. A Venetian painter but he is a Cubist in construction*

– Picasso, as recalled by Romuald
Dor de la Souchère, *Picasso in
Antibes* (New York, 1960), p. 14.

Picasso subscribed to the theory that Cubism originated in Spain. In that he was not alone. The American writer and publisher Gertrude Stein, one of his earliest collectors and supporters, claimed that Cubism was "a part of the daily life in Spain." But while Stein was talking about the way Spanish architecture cut the lines of the landscape without being in harmony with it,* Picasso was arguing from an art-historical perspective. His evocation of El Greco's influence was no mere turn of phrase; Picasso saw himself as the true heir of El Greco, Rembrandt, Velázquez, Paul Cézanne, and Henri Matisse. Although Cubism made a radical break with tradition, it also stood for a renewal of painting that fully acknowledged European art history. However innovative and adventurous Picasso was, he often worked with traditional motifs and genres: portraits and self-portraits, still lifes, nudes. After settling in Paris in 1904, he expanded his formal vocabulary to include forms from African and ancient Iberian art. We see this clearly in the faces of the prostitutes in *Les Demoiselles d'Avignon* (1907), his first large Cubist painting (see fig. p. 60). Here, too, however, the influence of El Greco should not be underestimated, as is evident in the echoes (especially of motif) of *The Vision of Saint John* (ca. 1608–14; fig. p. 67). A comparison of El Greco's *Coronation of the Virgin* (cat. 26) with Picasso's 1907 sketches for the *Demoiselles* (cats. 27, 28) or his *Harvesters* from the same year (cat. 29) also reveals some astonishing similarities: the exalted gestures, the elongated proportions of the figures, and the tendency to reduce the pictorial space and fracture the forms into separate planes of color.

*   Gertrude Stein, *Picasso*
(New York, 1984), p. 28.

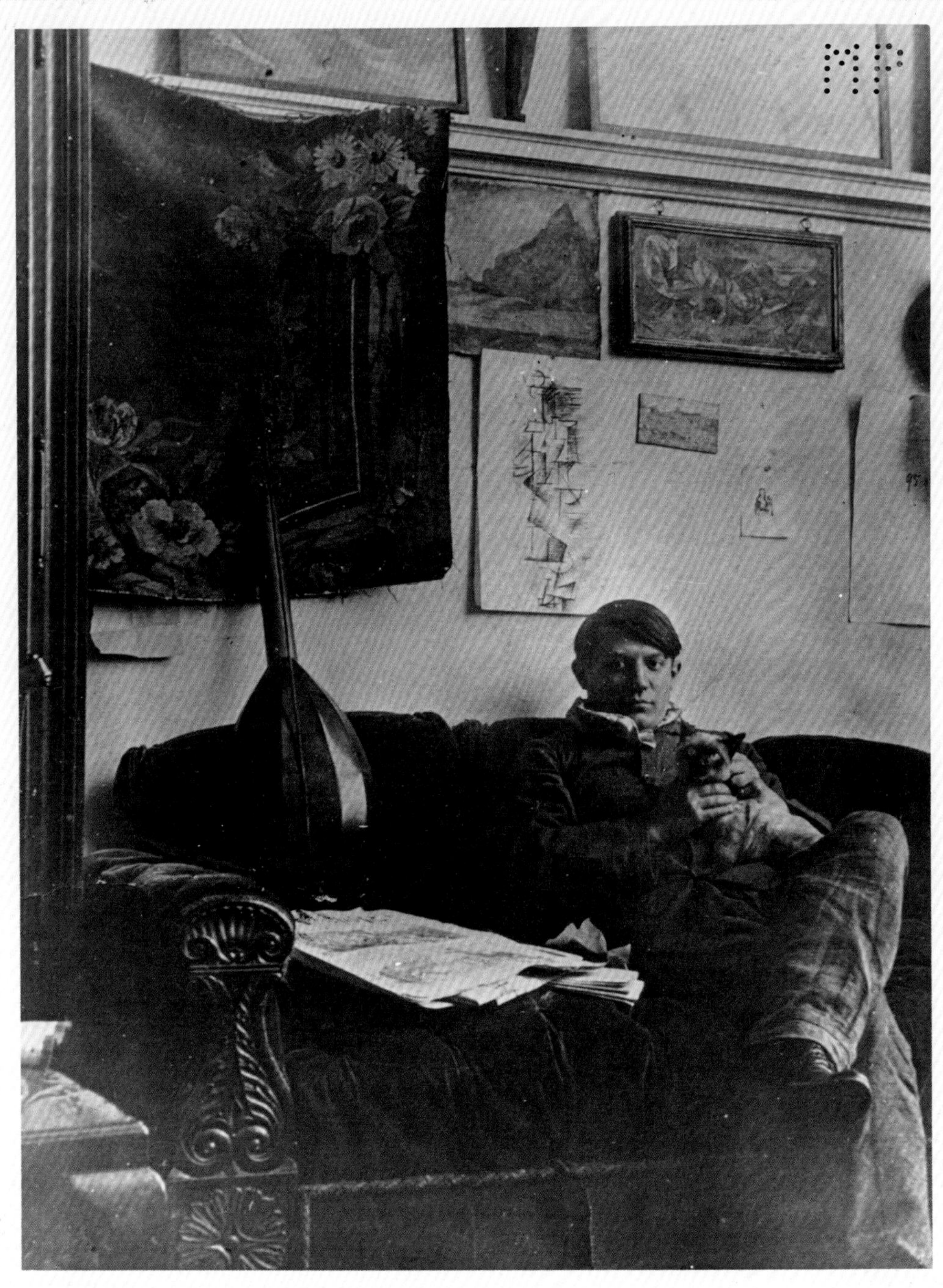

Picasso with a cat in his studio at 11 boulevard
de Clichy, Paris, December 1910
Silver gelatin print (contact print), 23.3 × 17.1 cm
Musée national Picasso, Paris

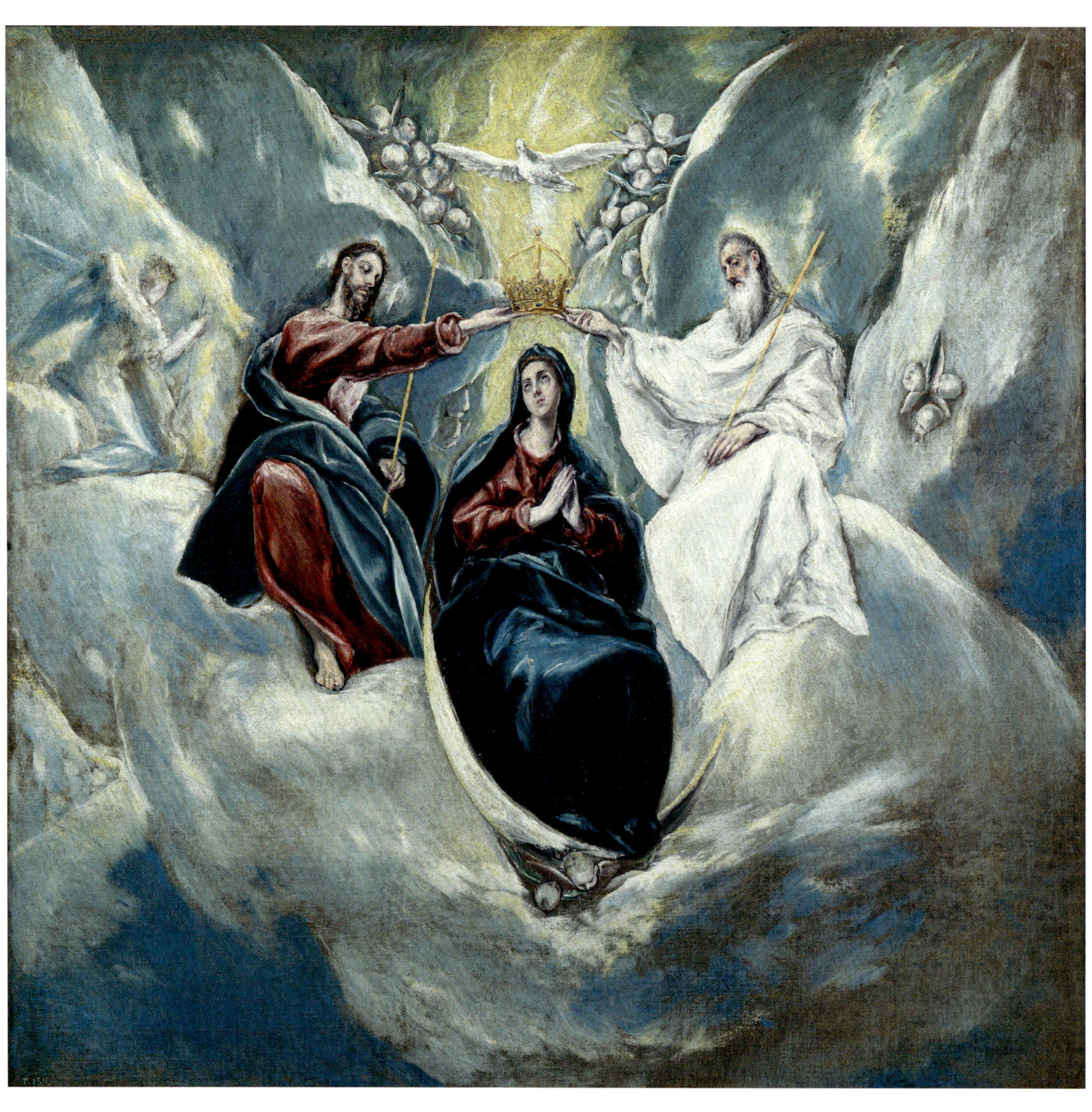

[Cat. 26]
El Greco, *The Coronation of the Virgin,* ca. 1592

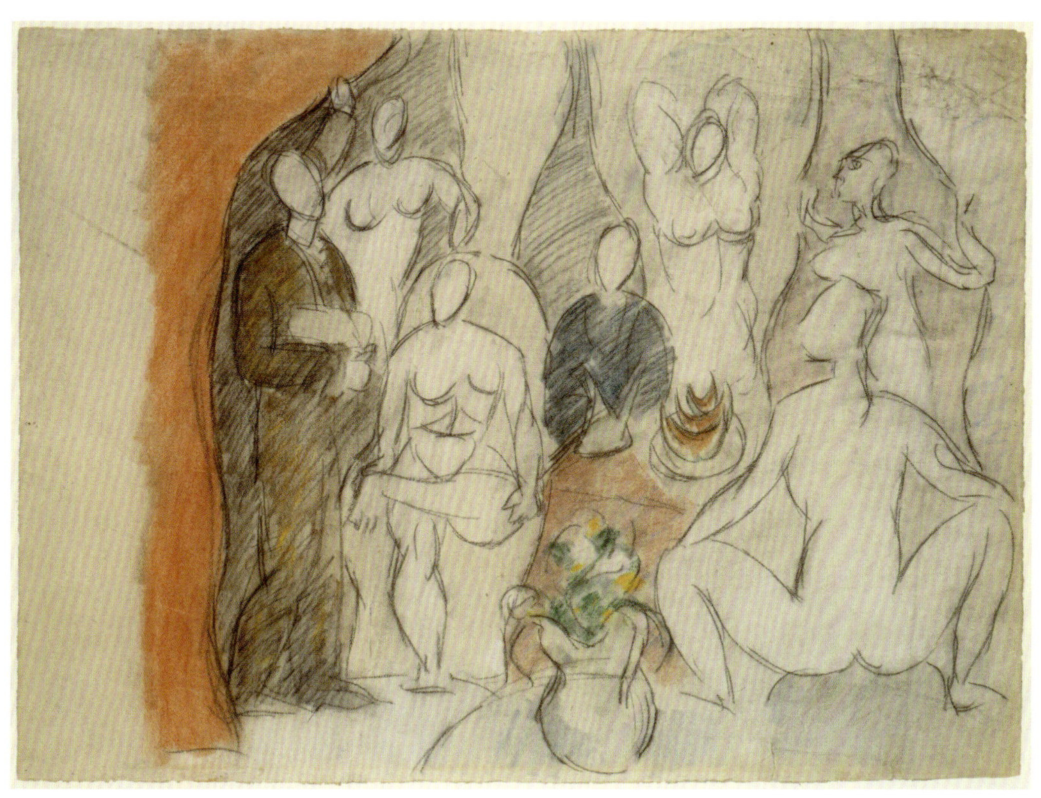

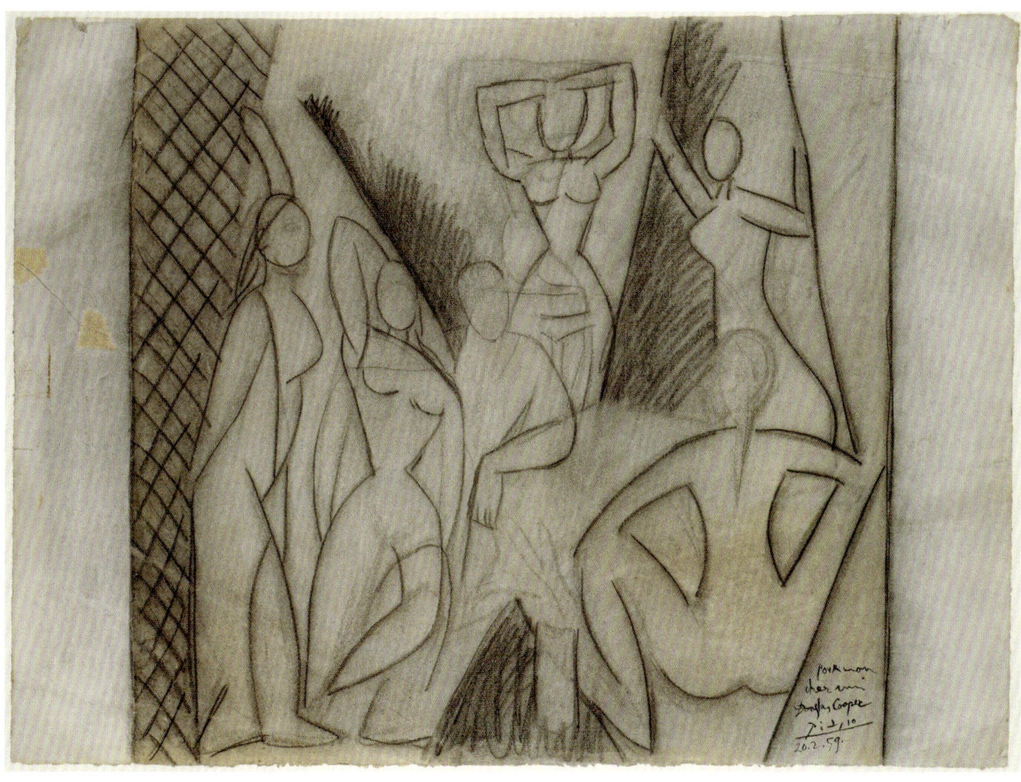

[Cat. 27]
Pablo Picasso, *Esquisse pour "Les Demoiselles d'Avignon,"* 1907
[Cat. 28]
Pablo Picasso, *Étude pour "Les Demoiselles d'Avignon,"* 1907

117

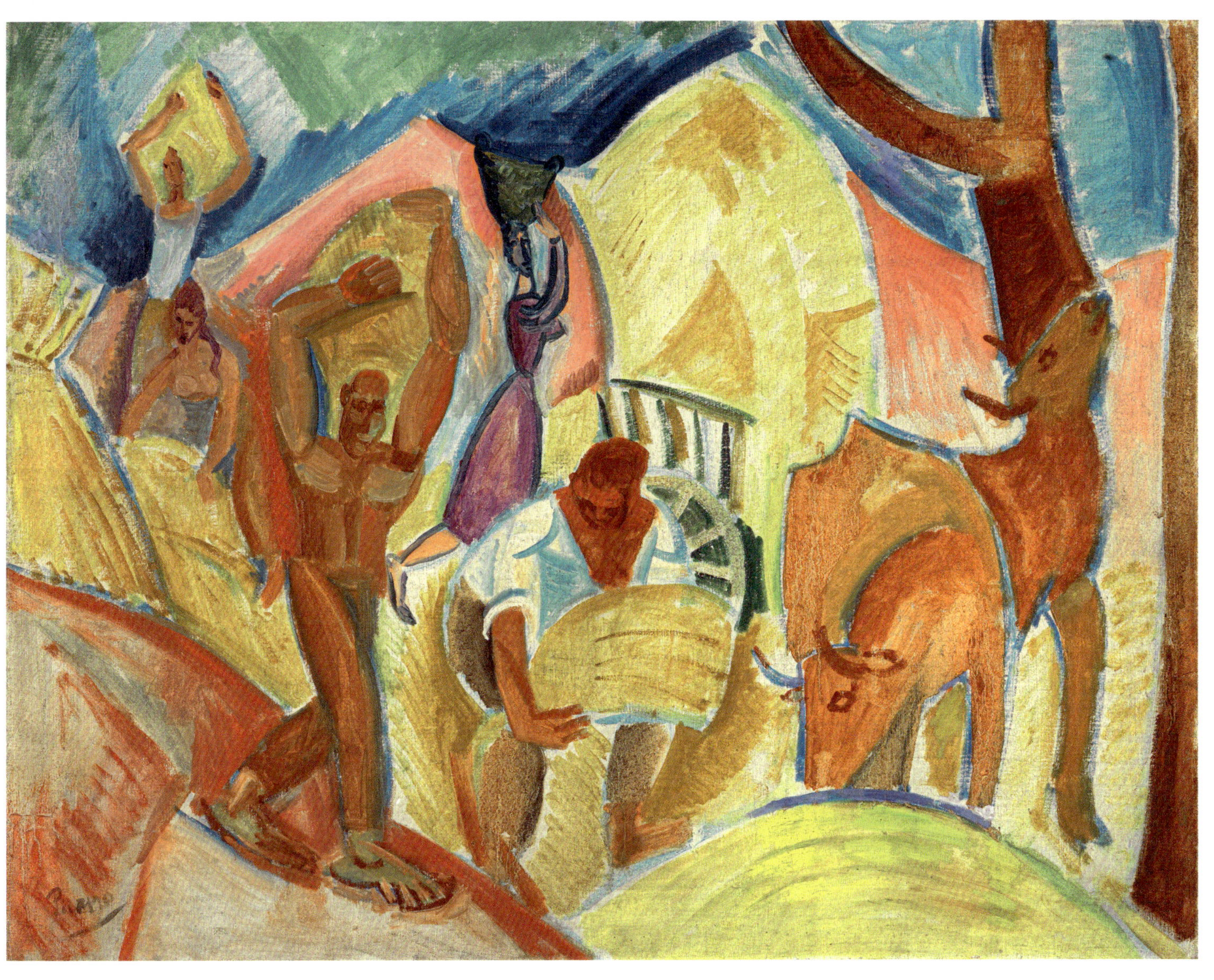

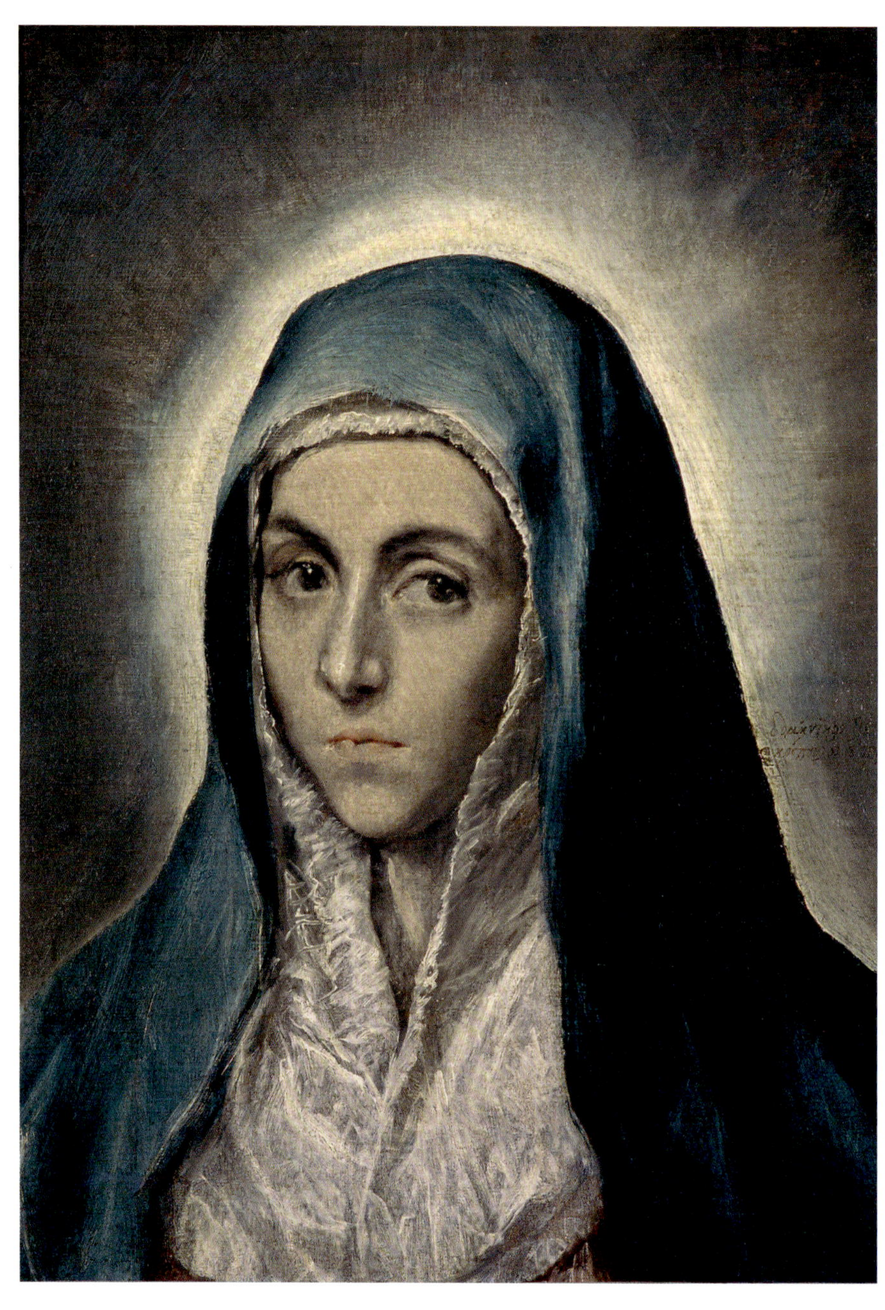

[Cat. 30]
El Greco, *The Virgin Mary,* ca. 1590

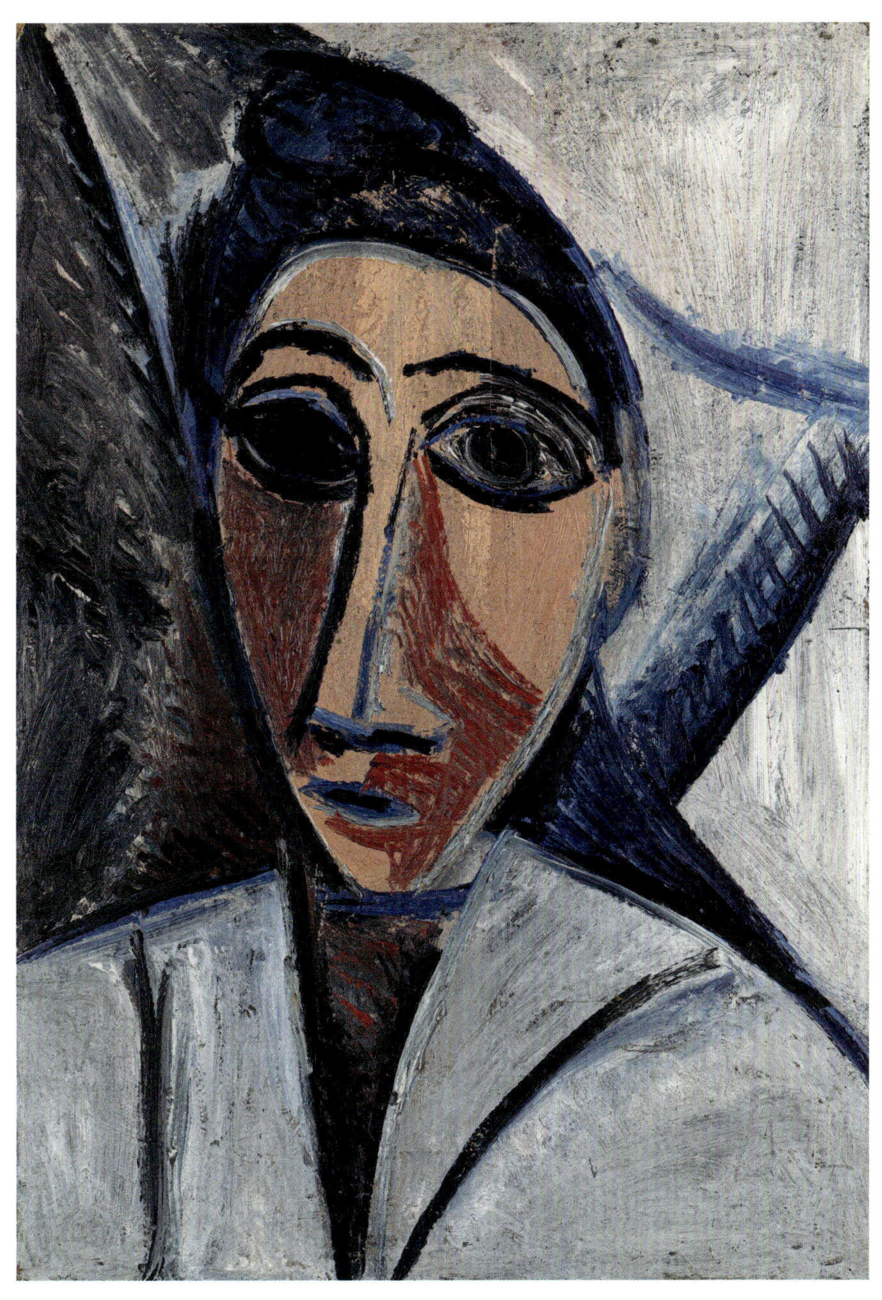

Pablo Picasso, *Buste de femme ou de marin (Etude pour les Demoiselles d'Avignon)*, 1907

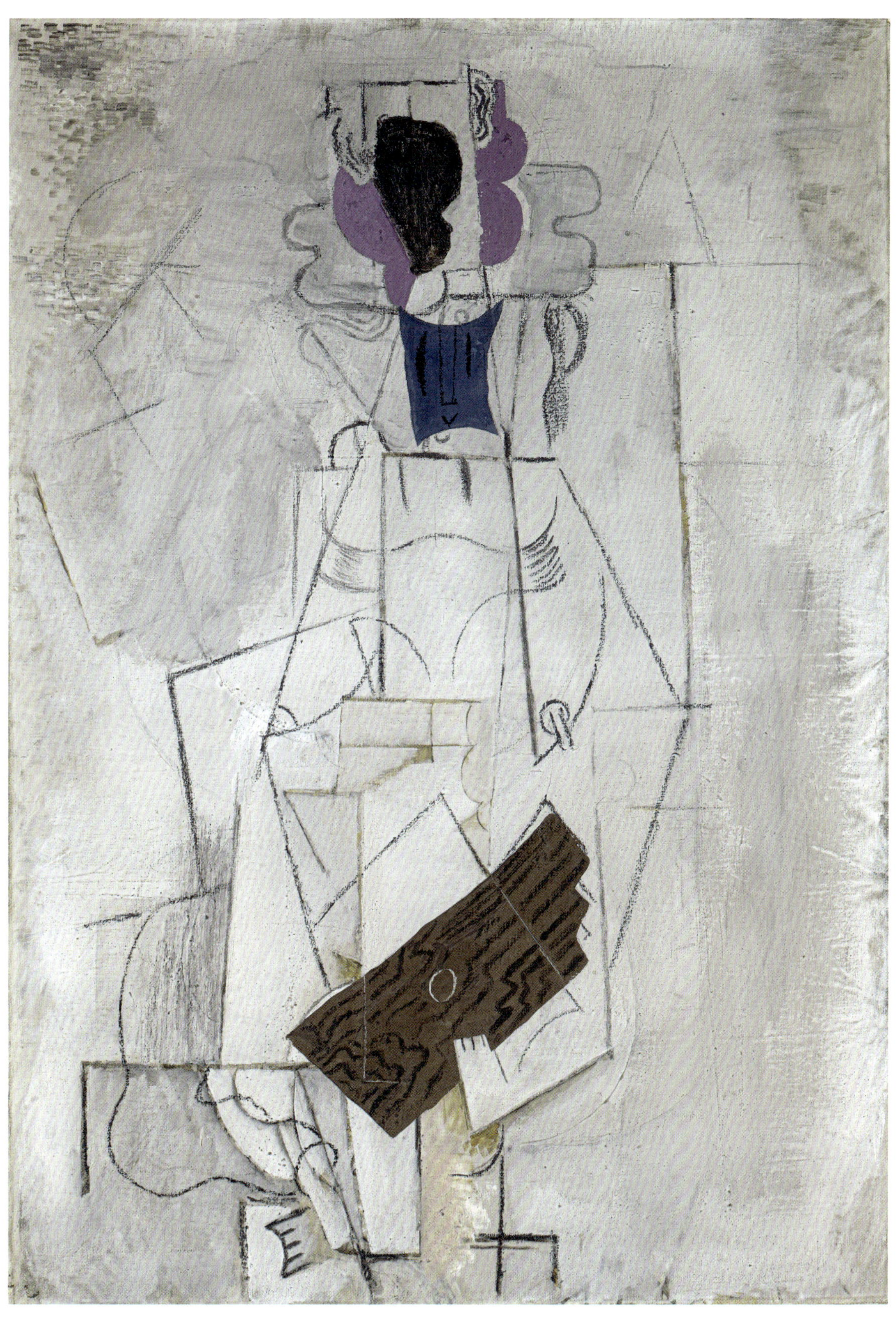

Pablo Picasso, *Femme à la guitare,* 1911–14

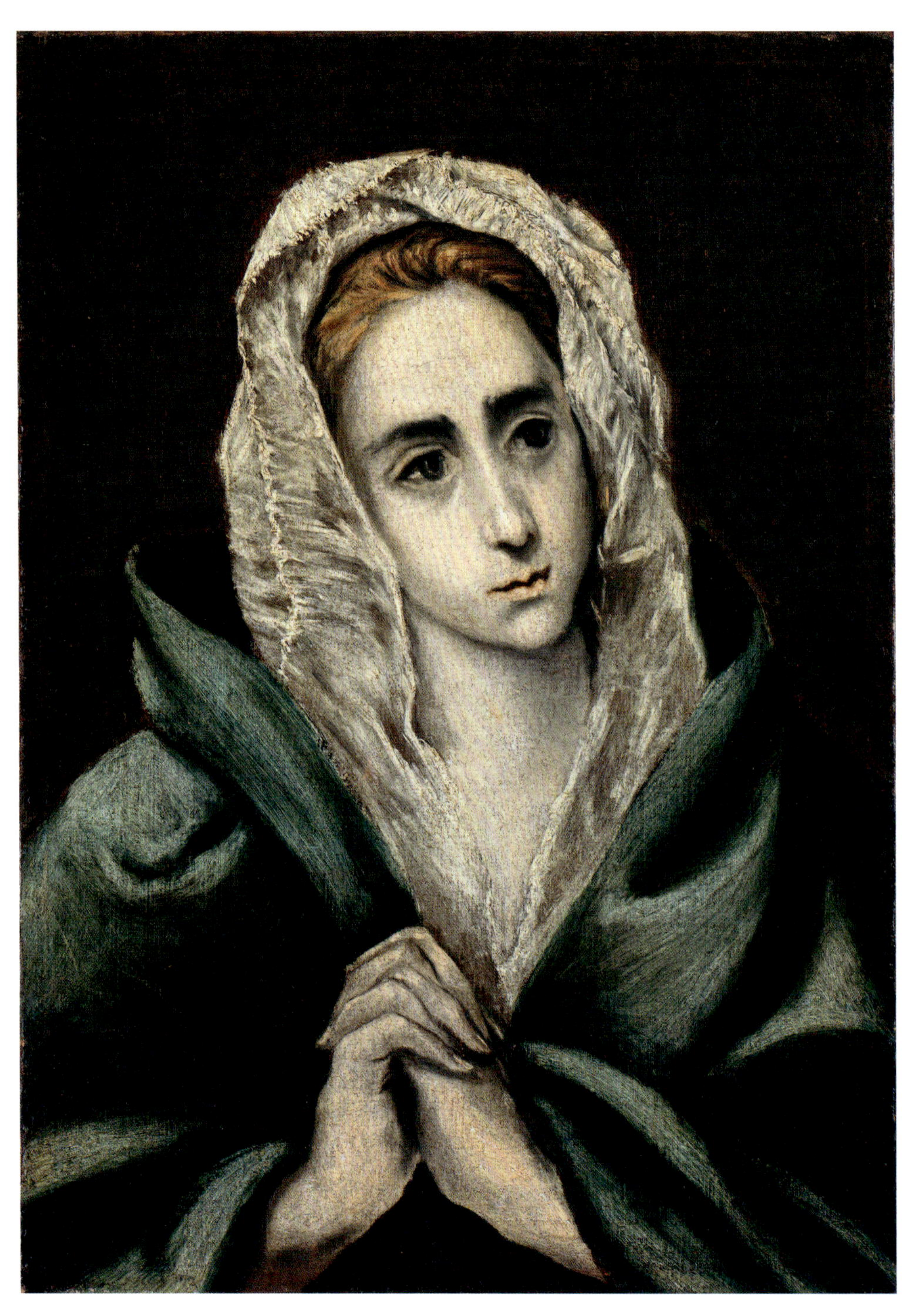

El Greco (Workshop), *Mater Dolorosa*, ca. 1587–90

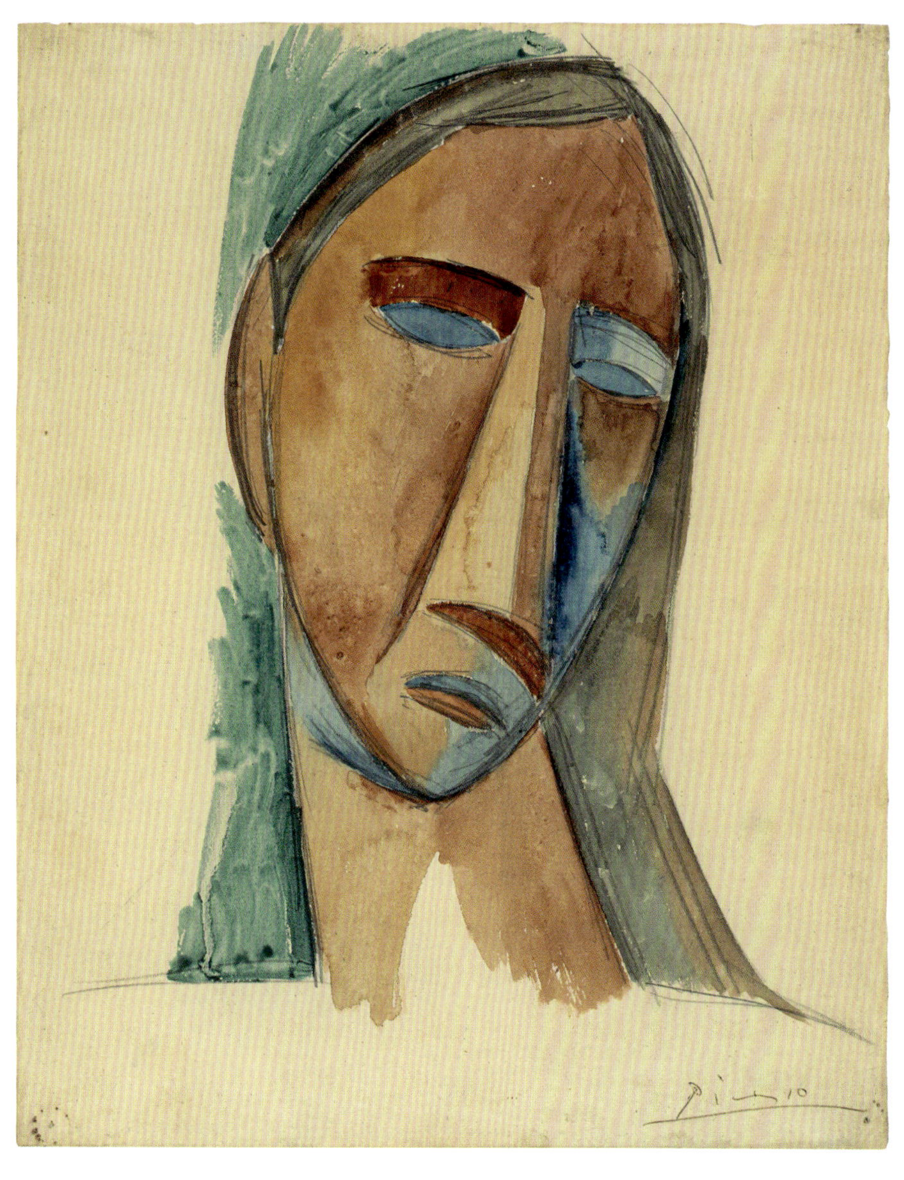

Pablo Picasso, *Tête de femme,* 1908

[Cat. 26] **El Greco**
The Coronation of the Virgin, ca. 1592
Oil on canvas, 99 × 101 cm
Museo Nacional del Prado, Madrid
Inv. P002645

[Cat. 27] **Pablo Picasso**
Esquisse pour "Les Demoiselles d'Avignon" (Compositional Study for *Les Demoiselles d'Avignon*), March/April 1907
Black chalk and pastel over pencil on Ingres paper, 47.7 × 63.5 cm
Kunstmuseum Basel, Kupferstichkabinett
Gift of the artist to the municipality of Basel; permanent loan from the City of Basel, 1967
Inv. 1967.106

[Cat. 28] **Pablo Picasso**
Étude pour "Les Demoiselles d'Avignon" (Study for "Les Demoiselles d'Avignon"), May 1907
Charcoal on paper, extended on either side, 47.6 × 63.7 cm
Kunstmuseum Basel, Kupferstichkabinett
Gift of Douglas Cooper, Paris, 1984
Inv. 1984.494

[Cat. 29] **Pablo Picasso**
Les Moissonneurs (The Harvesters) 1907
Oil on canvas, 65 × 81.5 cm
Museo Nacional Thyssen-Bornemisza, Madrid – Carmen Thyssen Collection
Inv. CTB.1979.39

[Cat. 30] **El Greco**
The Virgin Mary, ca. 1590
Oil on canvas, 53 × 37 cm
Musée des Beaux-Arts de Strasbourg
Inv. 276

[Cat. 31] **Pablo Picasso**
Buste de femme ou de marin (Etude pour les Demoiselles d'Avignon) (Bust of a Woman or a Sailor [Study for *Les Demoiselles d'Avignon*]), spring 1907
Oil on cardboard, 53.5 × 36.2 cm
Musée national Picasso, Paris
Inv. MP15

[Cat. 32] **Pablo Picasso**
Femme à la guitare (Woman with a Guitar), 1911–14
Oil on canvas, 130.2 × 90.1 cm
Kunstmuseum Basel, donated by Dr. h.c. Raoul La Roche, 1952
Inv. 2307

[Cat. 33] **El Greco (Workshop)**
Mater Dolorosa, ca. 1587–90
Oil on canvas, 62 × 42 cm
Staatliche Museen zu Berlin – Preussischer Kulturbesitz, Gemäldegalerie
Inv. 4/63

[Cat. 34] **Pablo Picasso**
Tête de femme (Woman's Head) Paris, 1908
Watercolor and pencil on paper, 34 × 21 cm
Staatliche Museen zu Berlin – Preussischer Kulturbesitz, Nationalgalerie, Museum Berggruen, private loan

[Cat. 35] **Pablo Picasso**
Portrait of Nusch Éluard February 9, 1938
Charcoal and pencil on canvas, 96 × 72 cm
Private collection

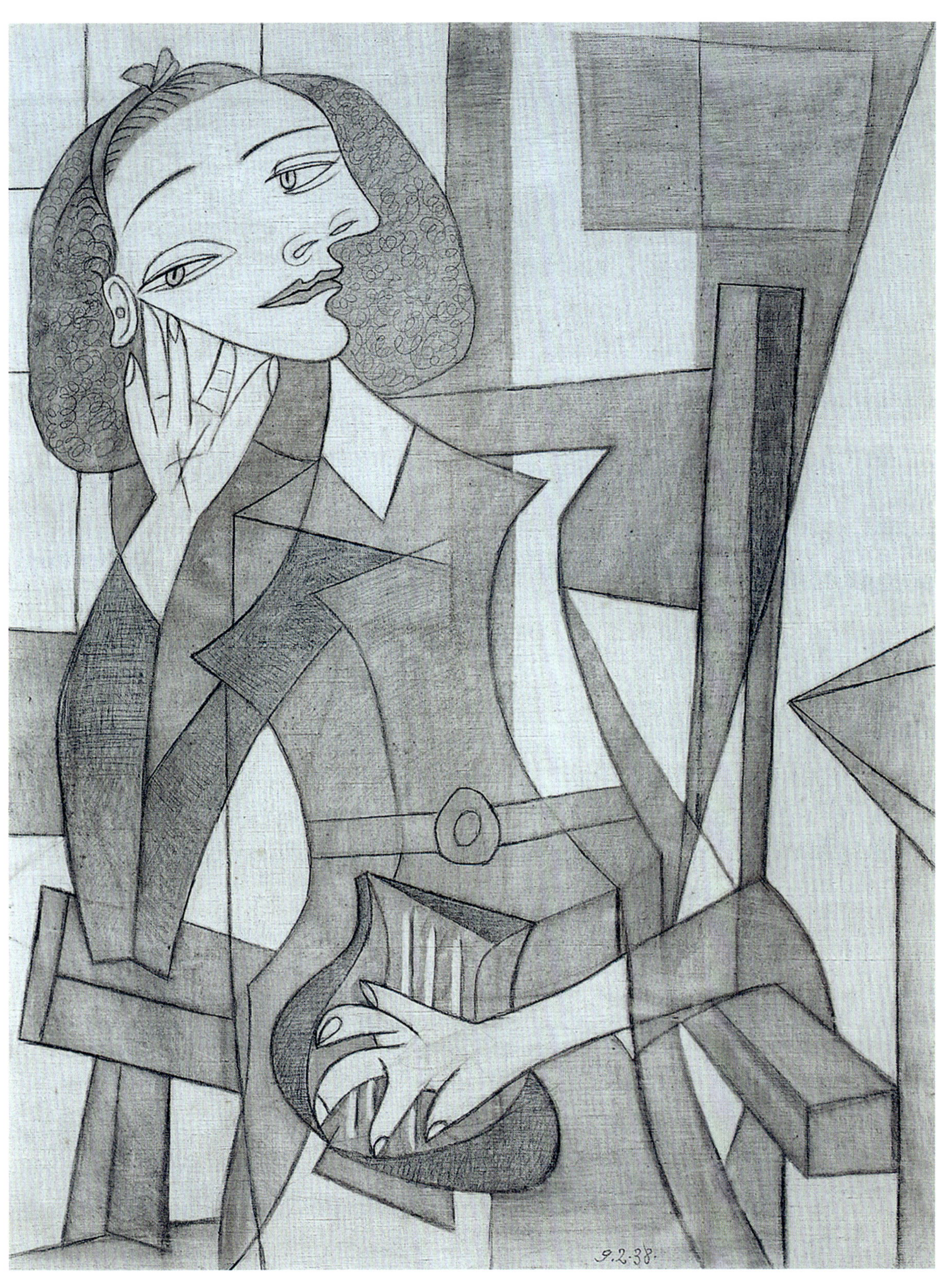

Pablo Picasso, *Portrait of Nusch Éluard*, 1938

El Greco and Cubism after 1910

I have a feeling that Delacroix, Giotto, Tintoretto, El Greco, and the rest, as well as all the modern painters, the good and the bad, the abstract and the non-abstract, are all standing behind me watching me at work.

– Picasso, as quoted by Hélène Parmelin in *Picasso Plain* (London, 1959), p. 77.

As a type, the *Apostolado*, or set of thirteen paintings depicting Christ and his twelve apostles, was a successful product of El Greco's studio, although most of these sets have since been scattered. The intact series of apostles from the Museo del Greco in Toledo, painted at the end of his life, is of particularly high quality and is thought to be his own work (cats. 22, 24, 26). A comparison of his apostles and other religious images with works from Picasso's Analytical Cubist phase reveals some at times surprising compositional echoes. These include not only similarities in pose (cats. 38–41) but also some more fundamental visual parallels: the reduction of pictorial space, the monochrome backgrounds, and the fragmentation of forms into jagged, different-colored planes that push up against one another with hard, clear edges, coming together to make up the sky, a rockface, the crease of a cloak. When we look at El Greco's astonishingly free and idiosyncratic style, the subtly overlapping brushstrokes only hinting at certain details, it is not difficult to grasp why Picasso and his generation found in him a kindred spirit. Although there is no hard evidence of direct, conscious allusions to El Greco in the works on display here, it is likely that the Toledan painter remained an important source of inspiration to Picasso around 1910 and in the decade that followed. Picasso's loose references to El Greco also demonstrate a powerful urge to make sure that the Old Masters were not left to languish in the museums but were kept alive through ever more radical transformations.

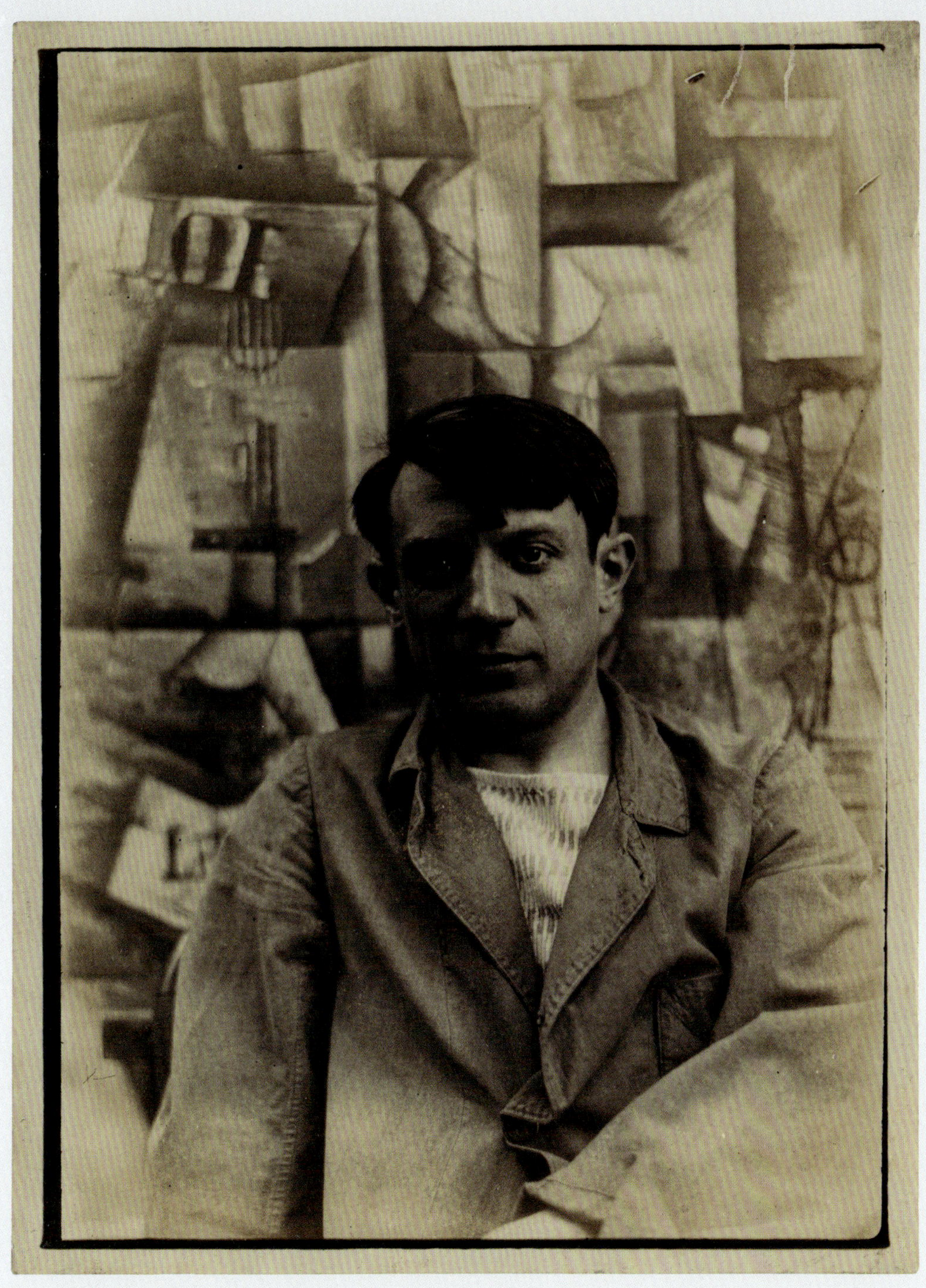

George de Zayas
Portrait of Pablo Picasso in front
of the painting *L'Aficionado* in his studio
on rue Schoelcher, Paris, ca. 1914
Silver gelatin print, 18.1 × 11.3 cm
Musée national Picasso, Paris

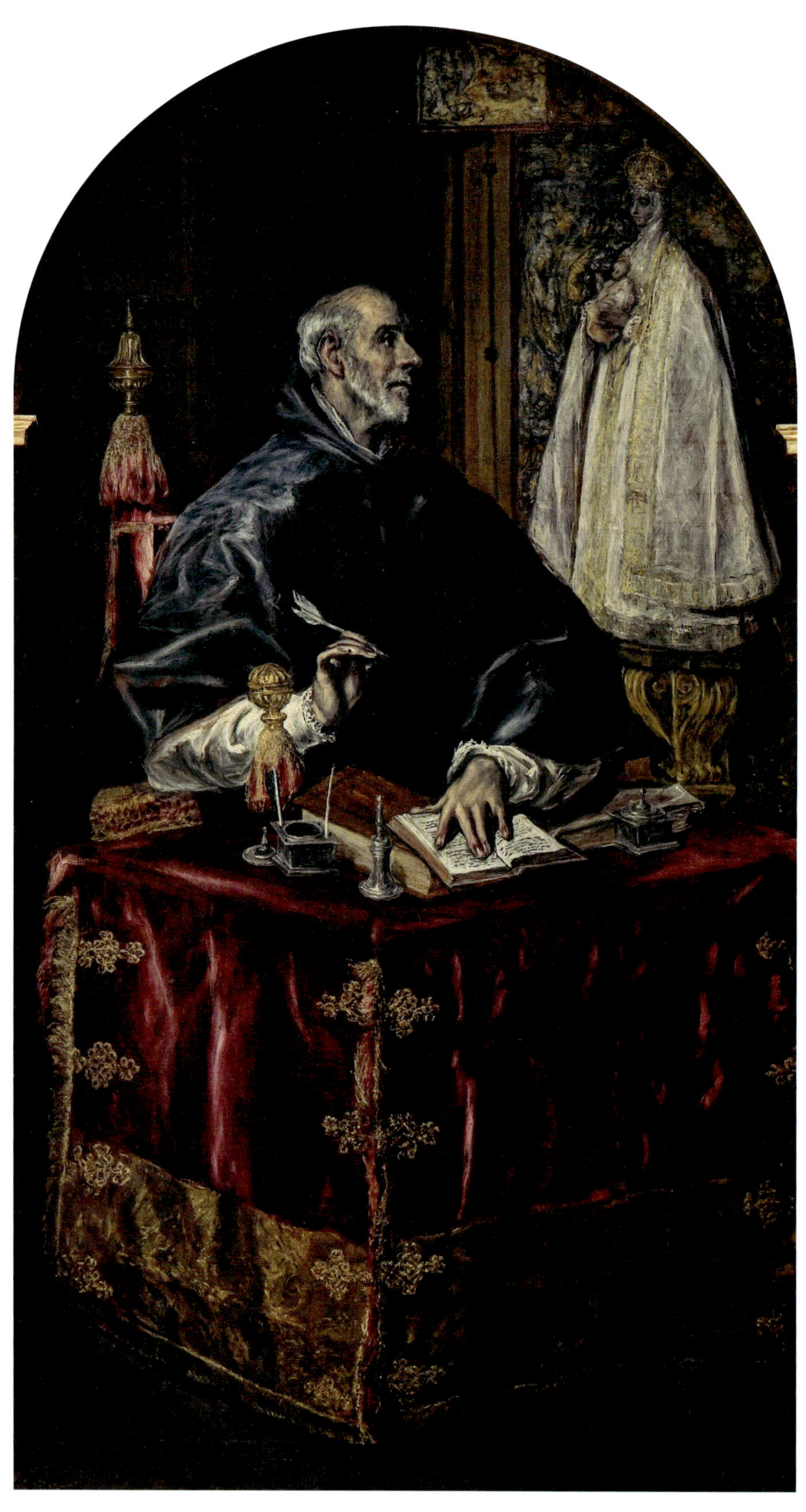

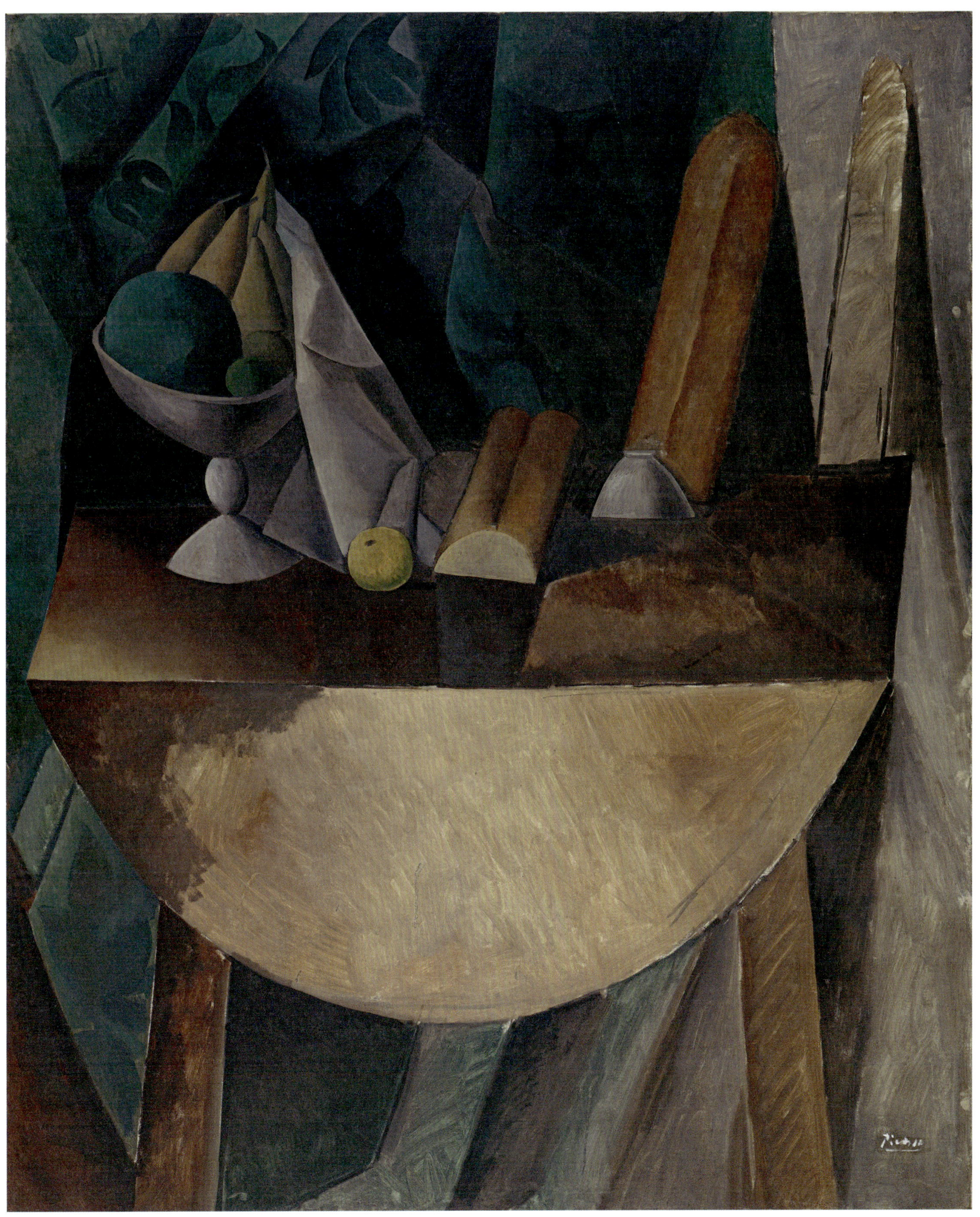

Pablo Picasso, *Pains et compotier aux fruits sur une table,* 1908–09

131

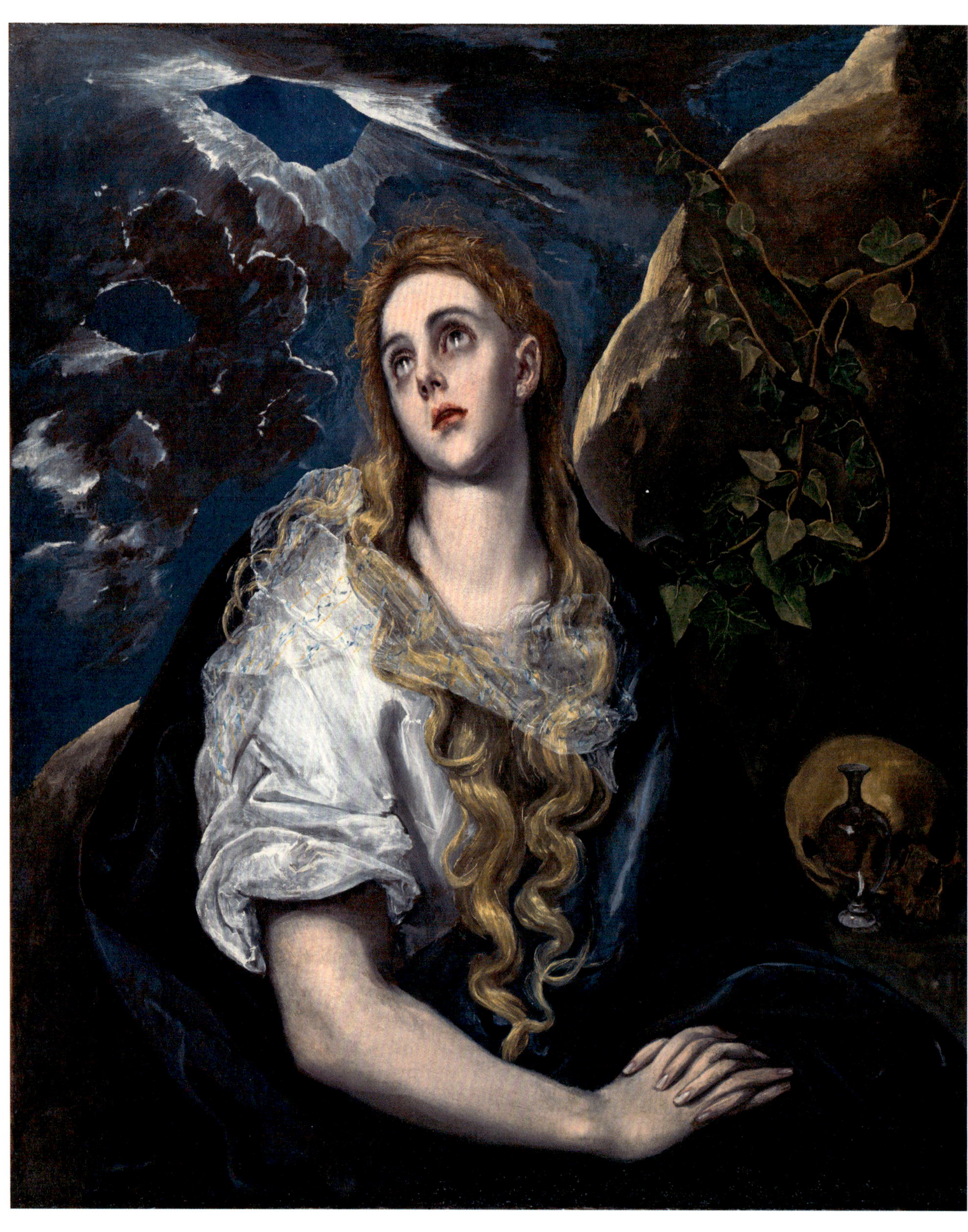

El Greco, *The Penitent Magdalene,* ca. 1580–85

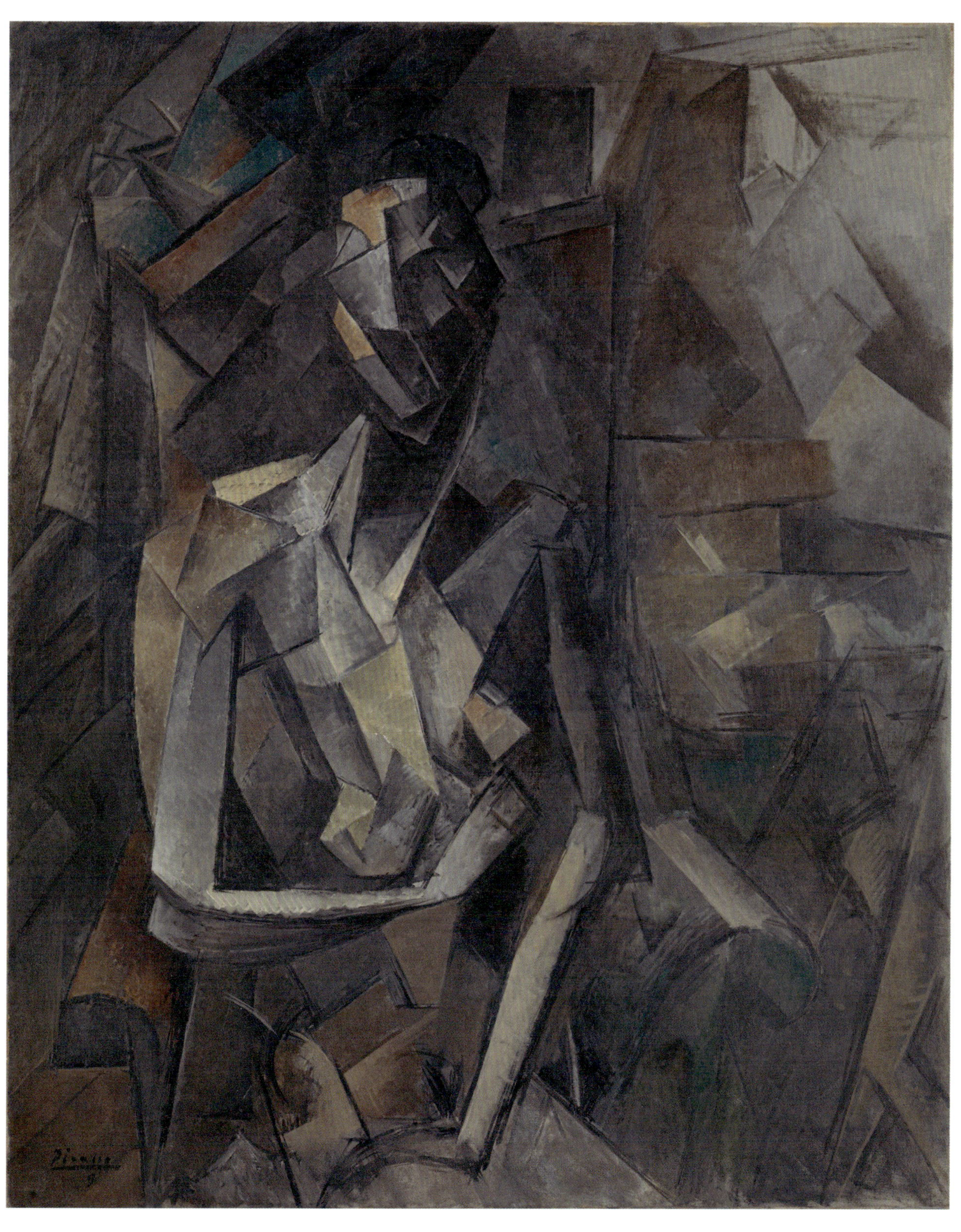

[Cat. 39]
Pablo Picasso, *Nu assis,* 1909–10

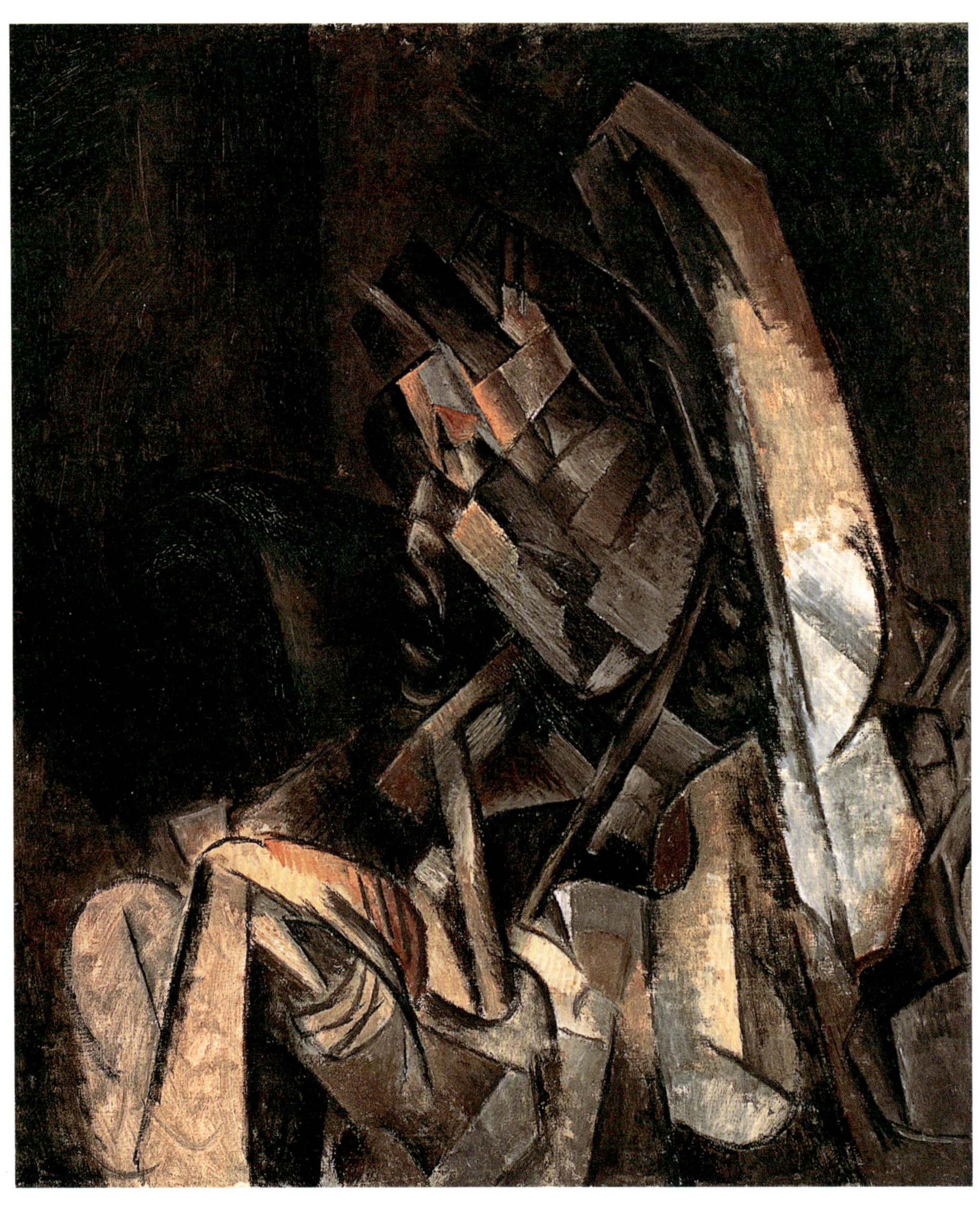

Pablo Picasso, *Femme assise dans un fauteuil,* **1910**

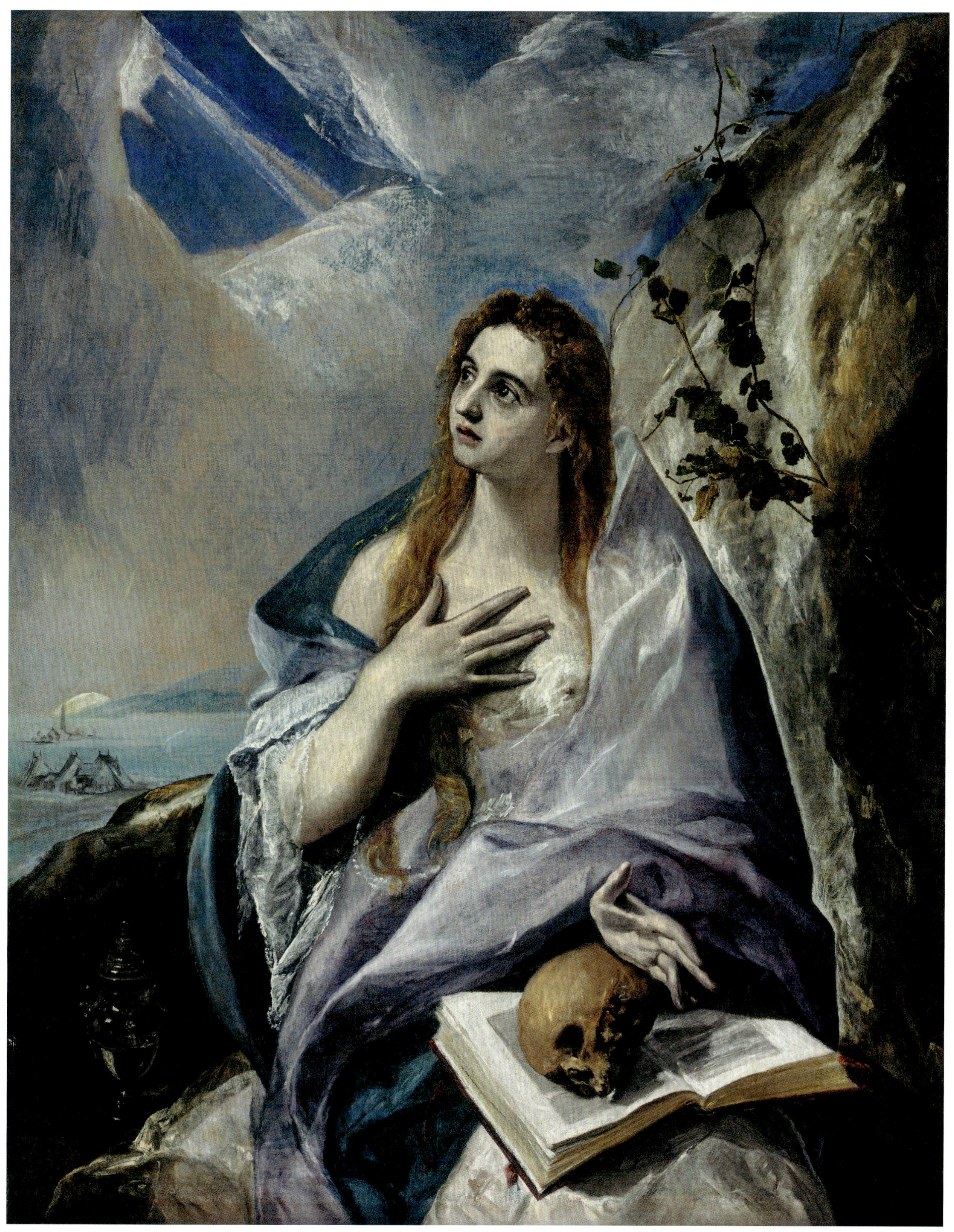

El Greco, *The Penitent Magdalene*, ca. 1576–77

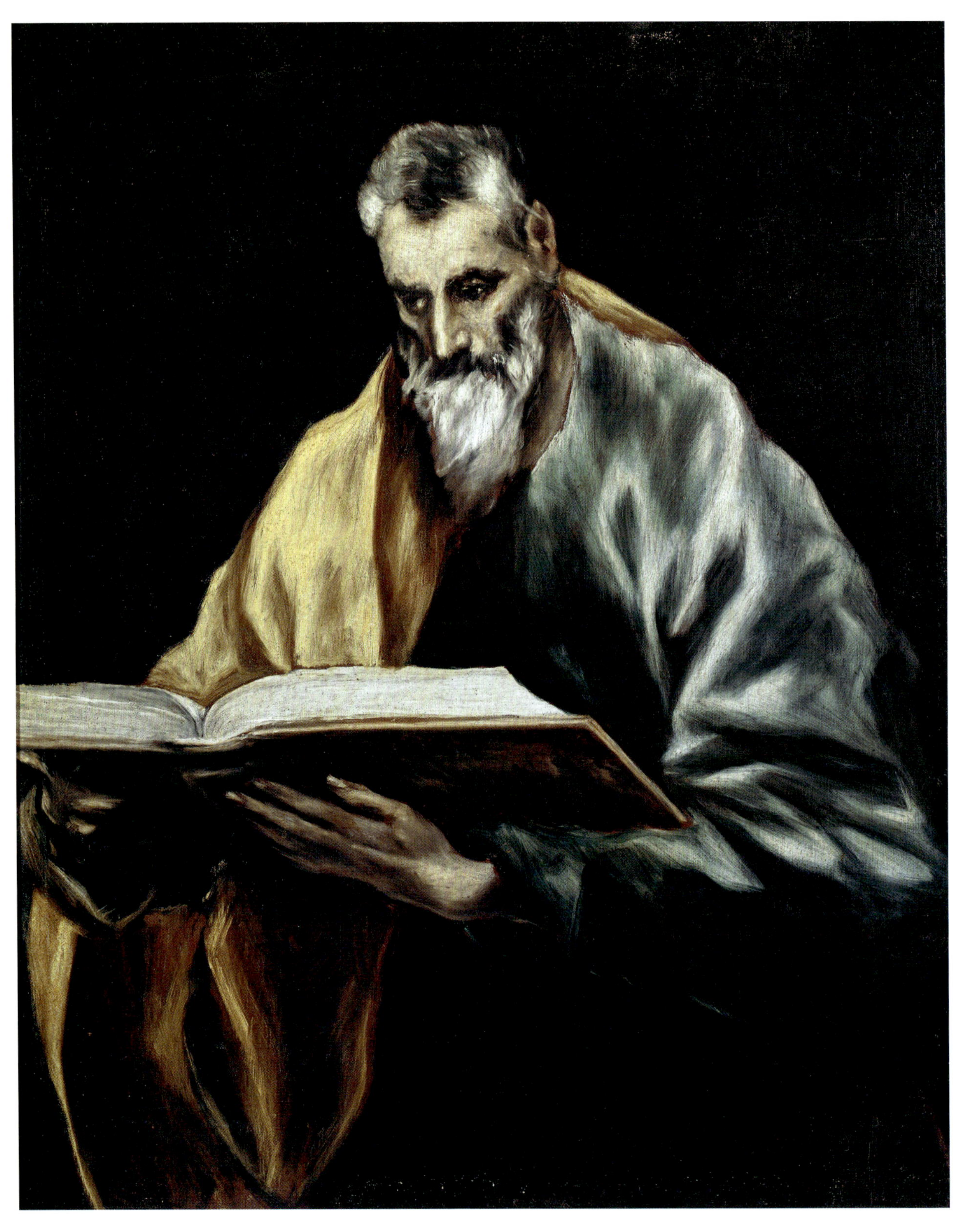

El Greco, *Saint Simon,* ca. 1610–14

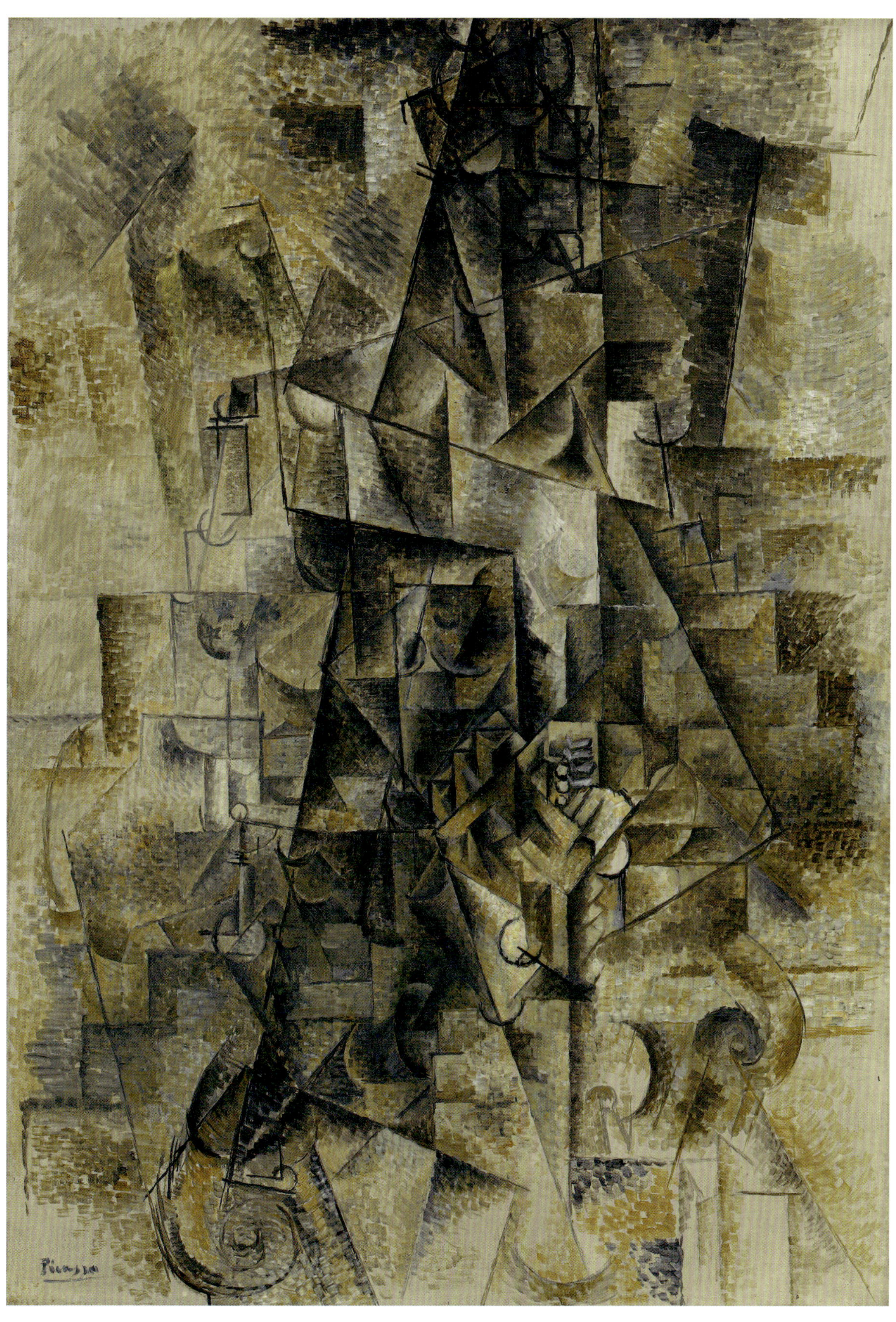

[Cat. 43]
Pablo Picasso, *L'Accordéoniste*, 1911

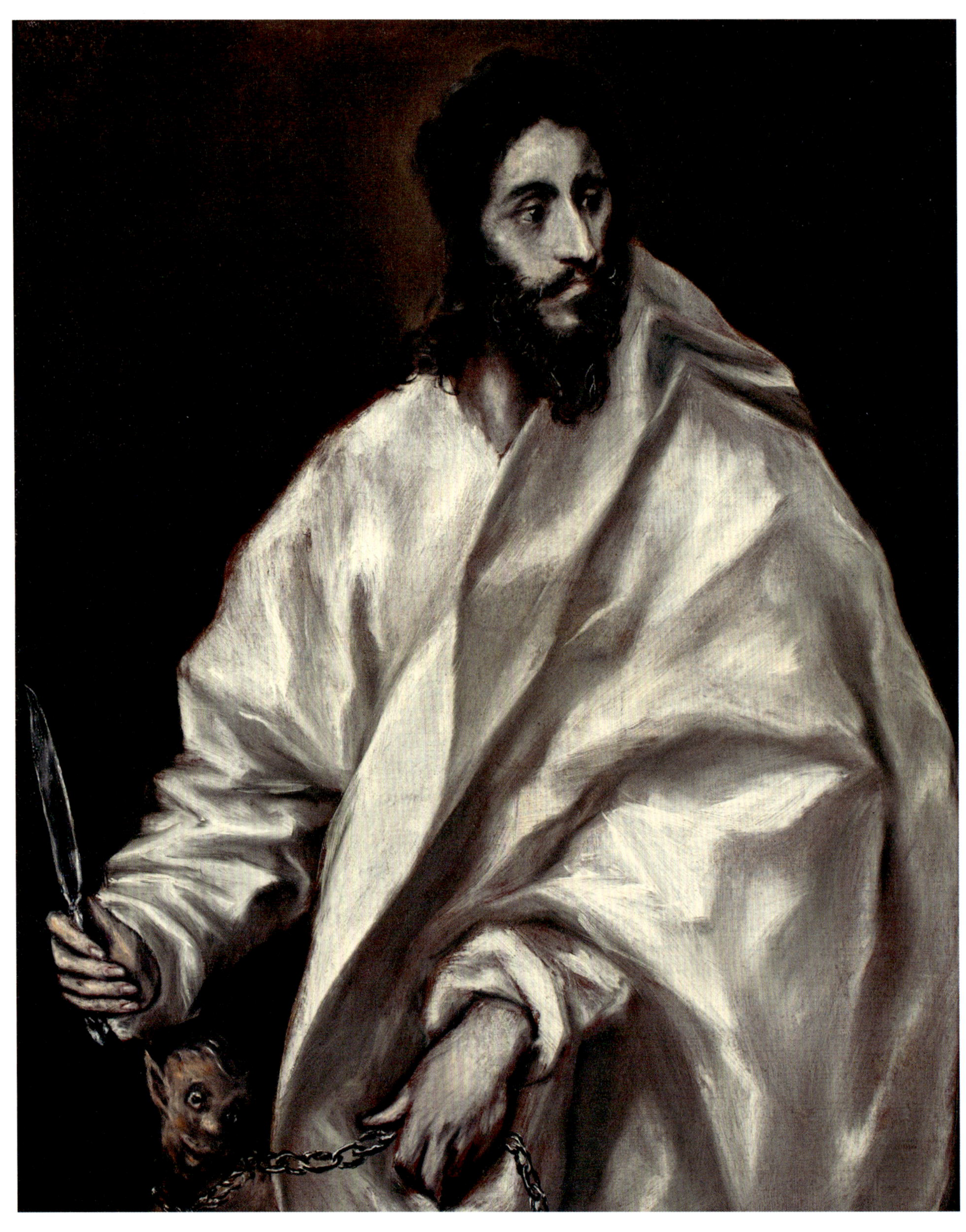

El Greco, *Saint Bartholomew*, ca. 1610–14

138

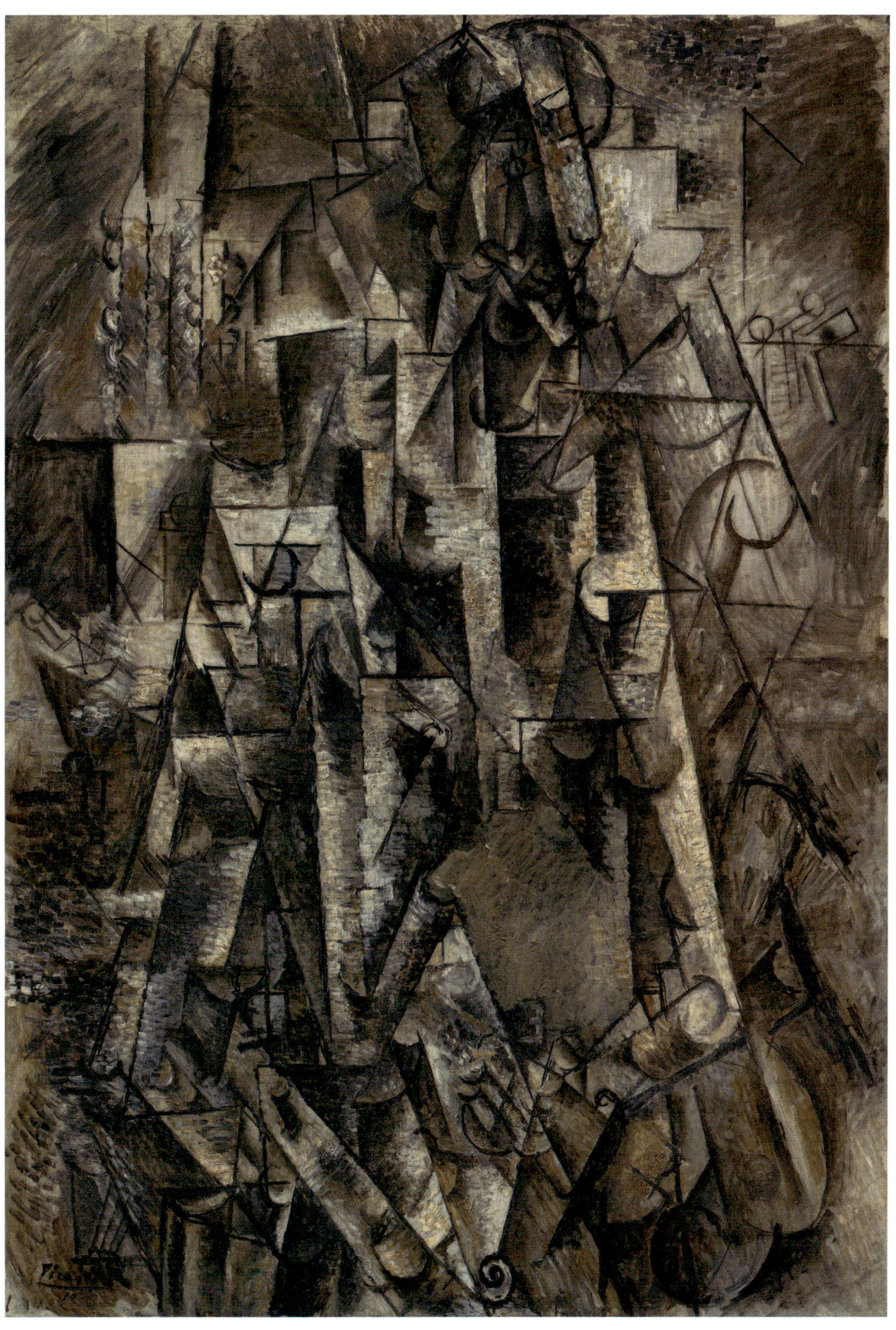

[Cat. 45]
Pablo Picasso, *Le Poète*, 1911

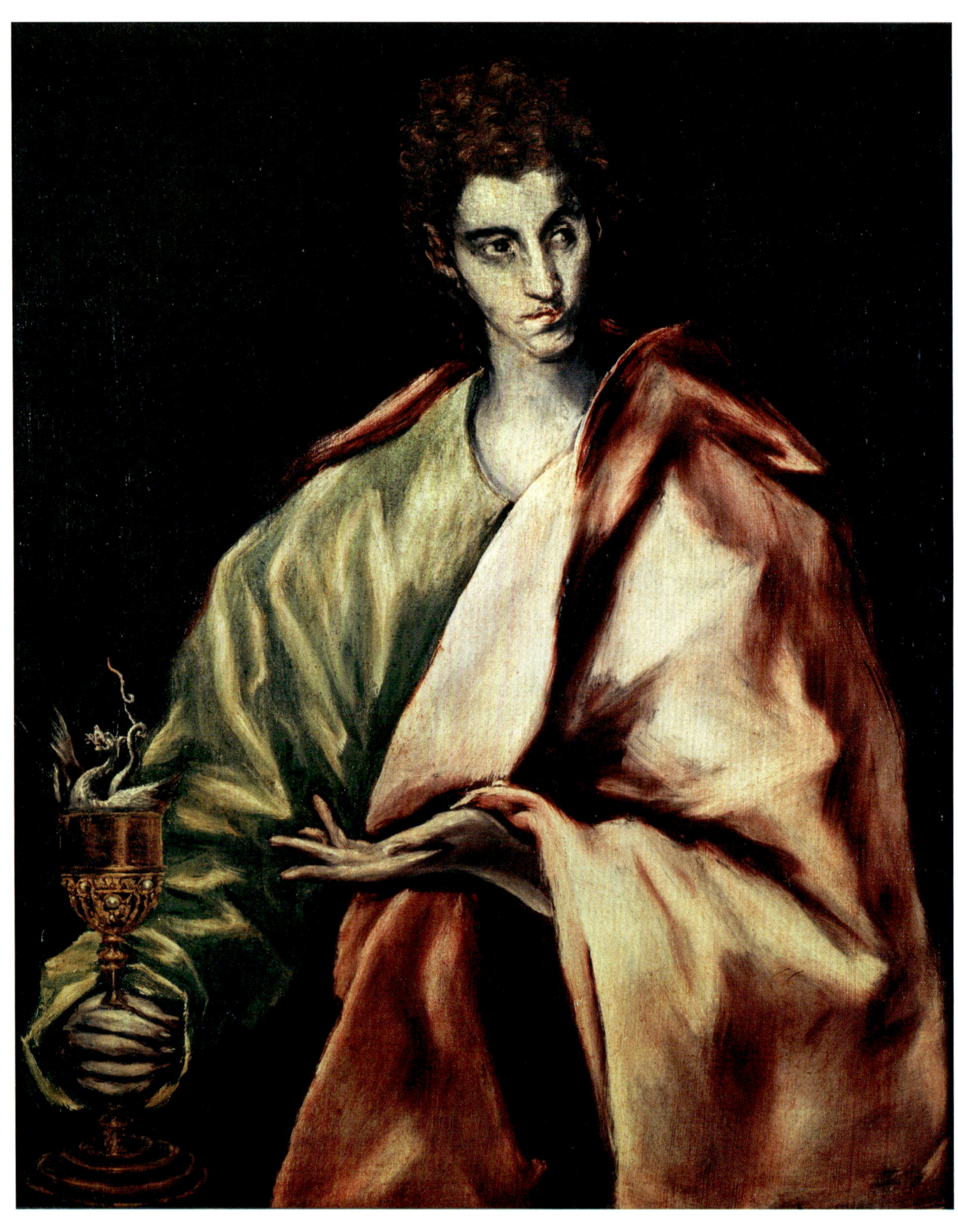

El Greco, *Saint John the Evangelist,* ca. 1610–14

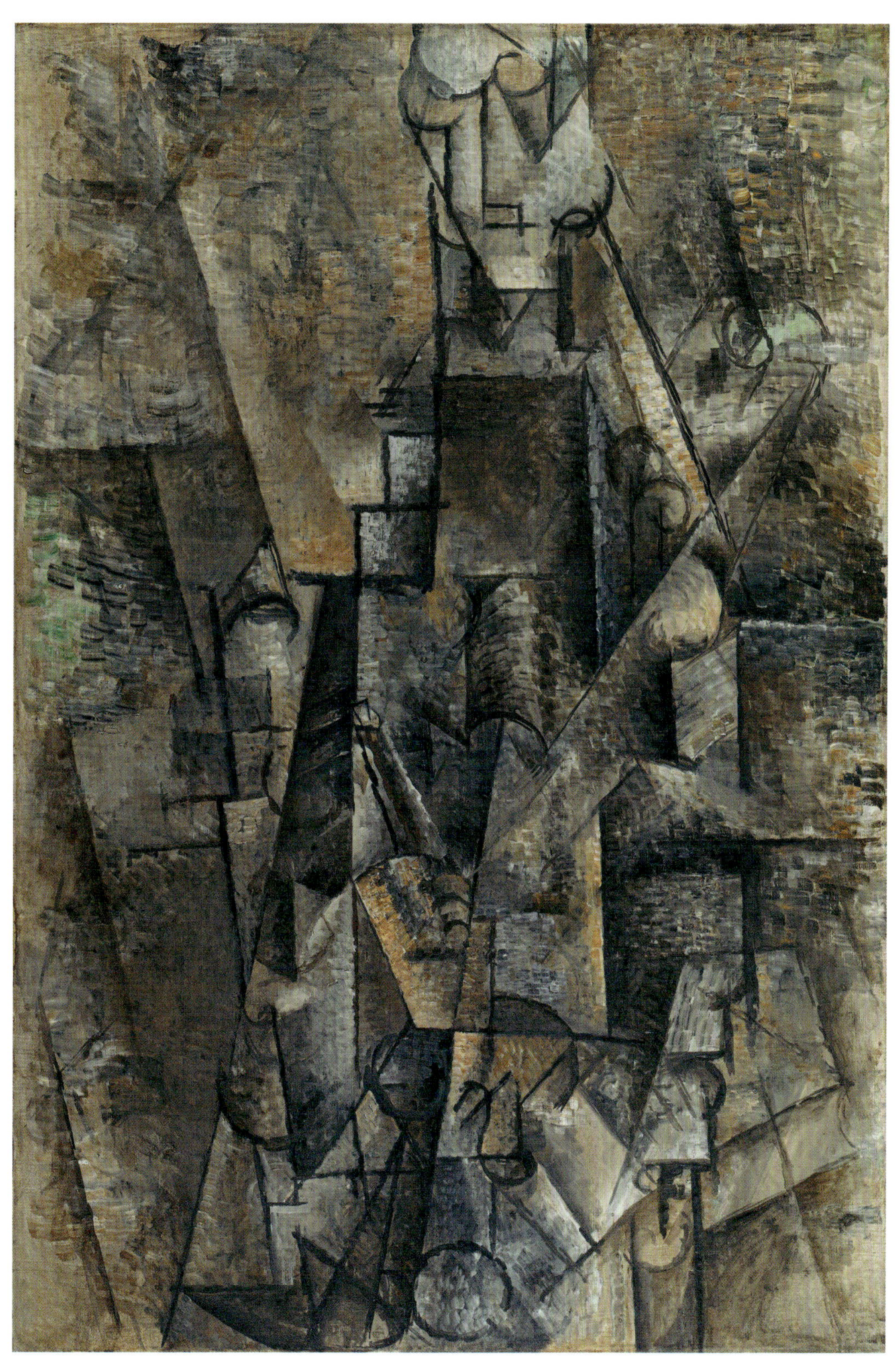

[Cat. 47]
Pablo Picasso, *Homme à la clarinette,* 1911–12

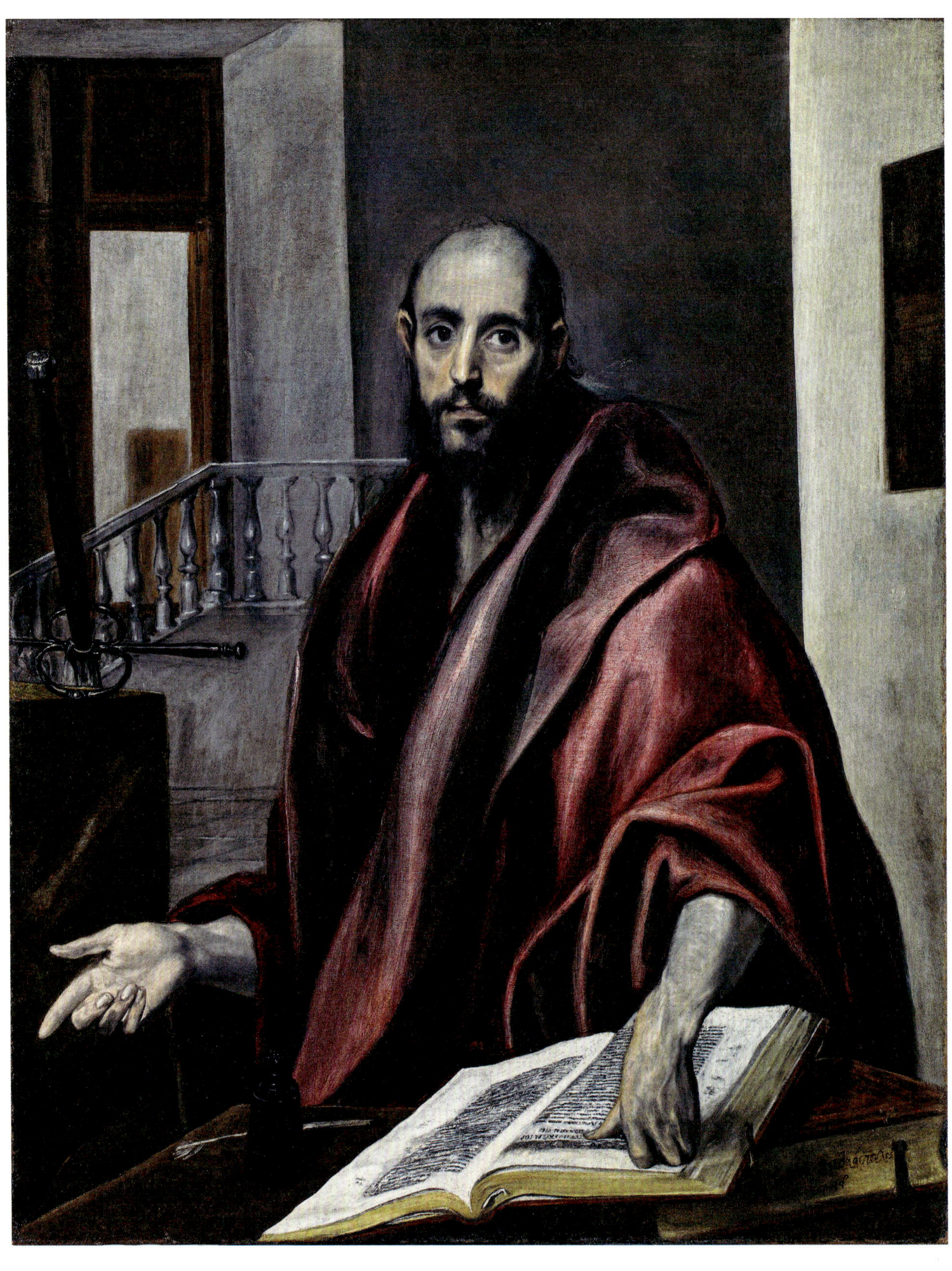

[Cat. 48]
El Greco, *Saint Paul,* ca. 1585

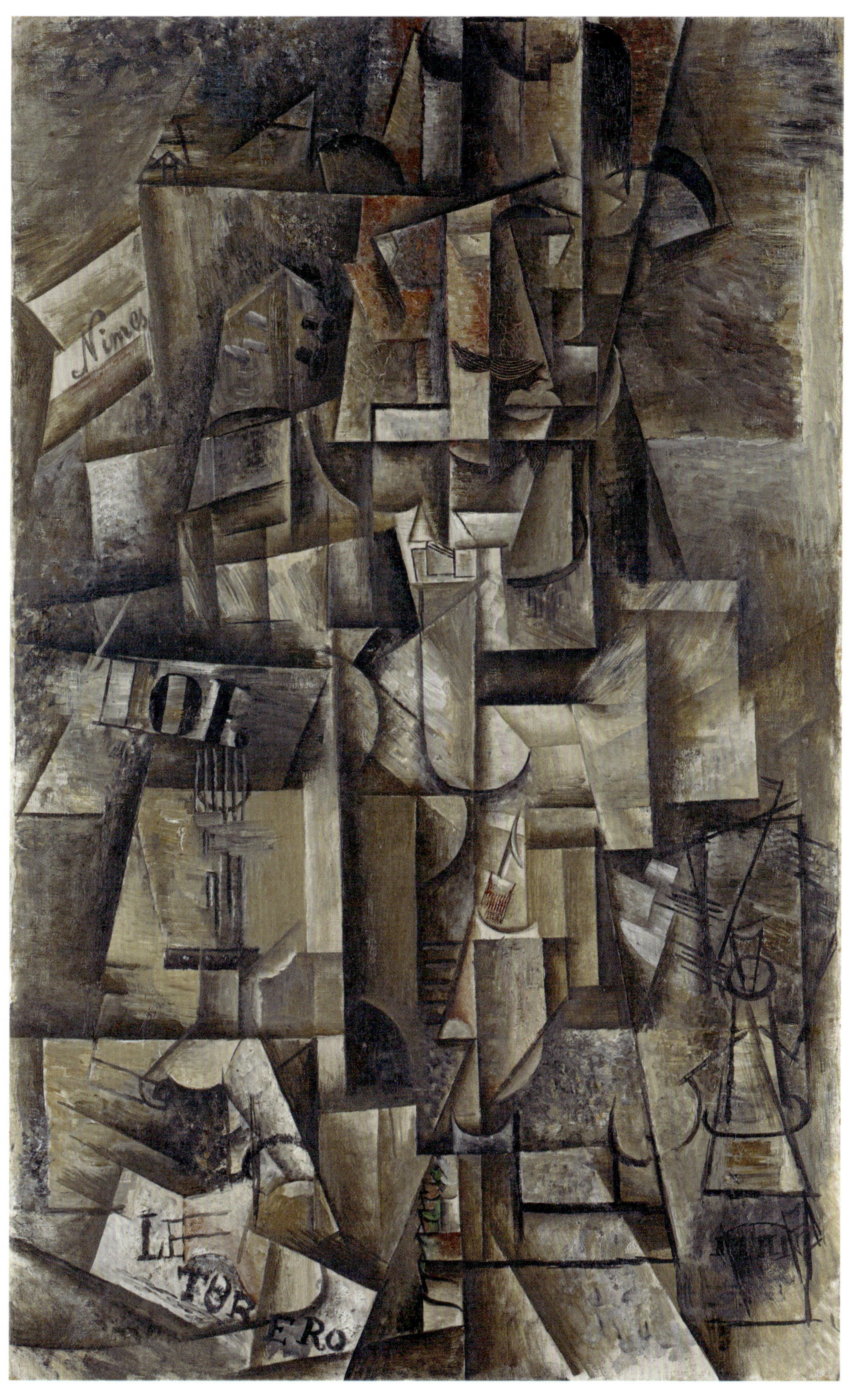

[Cat. 49]
Pablo Picasso, *L'Aficionado*, 1912

143

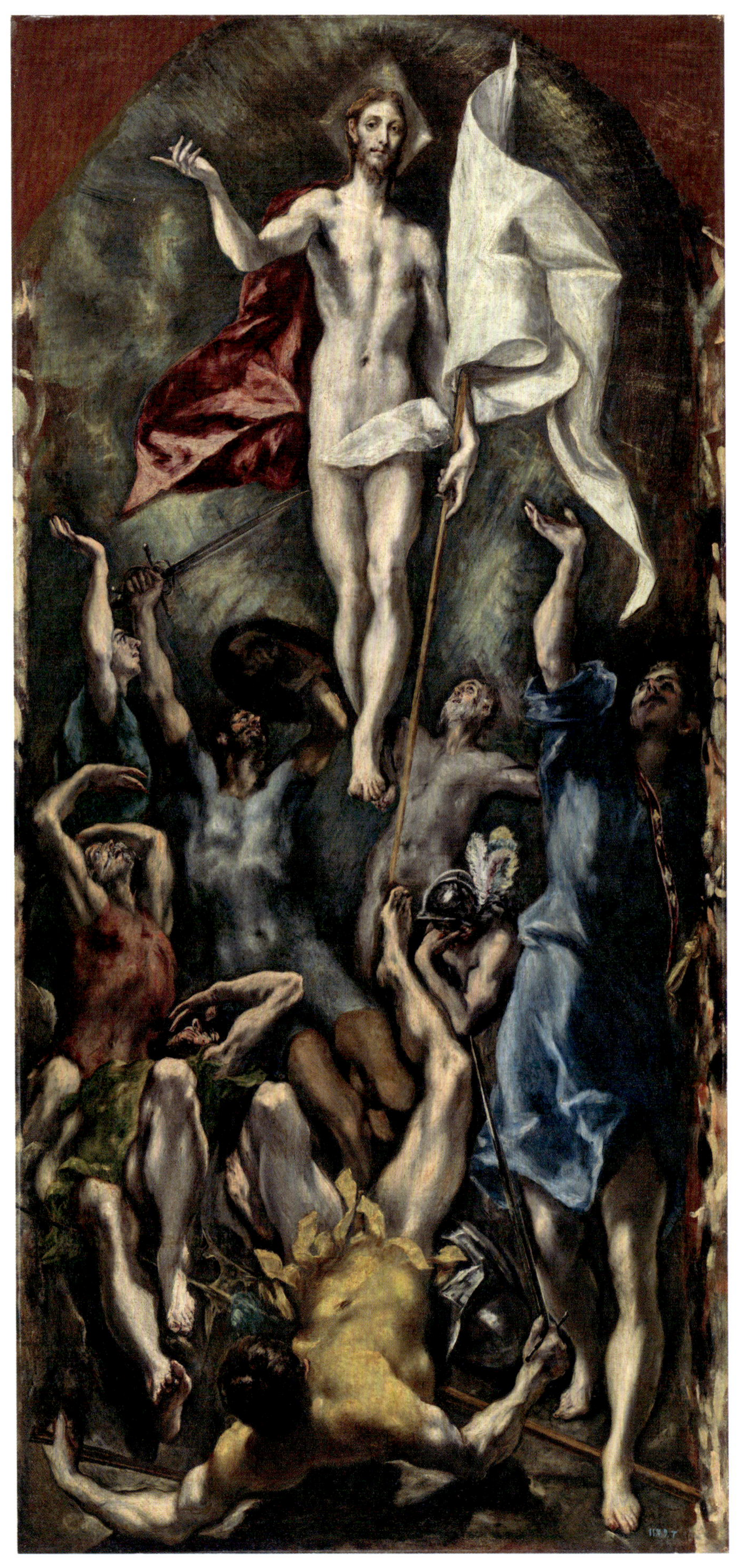

El Greco, *The Resurrection*, 1597–1600

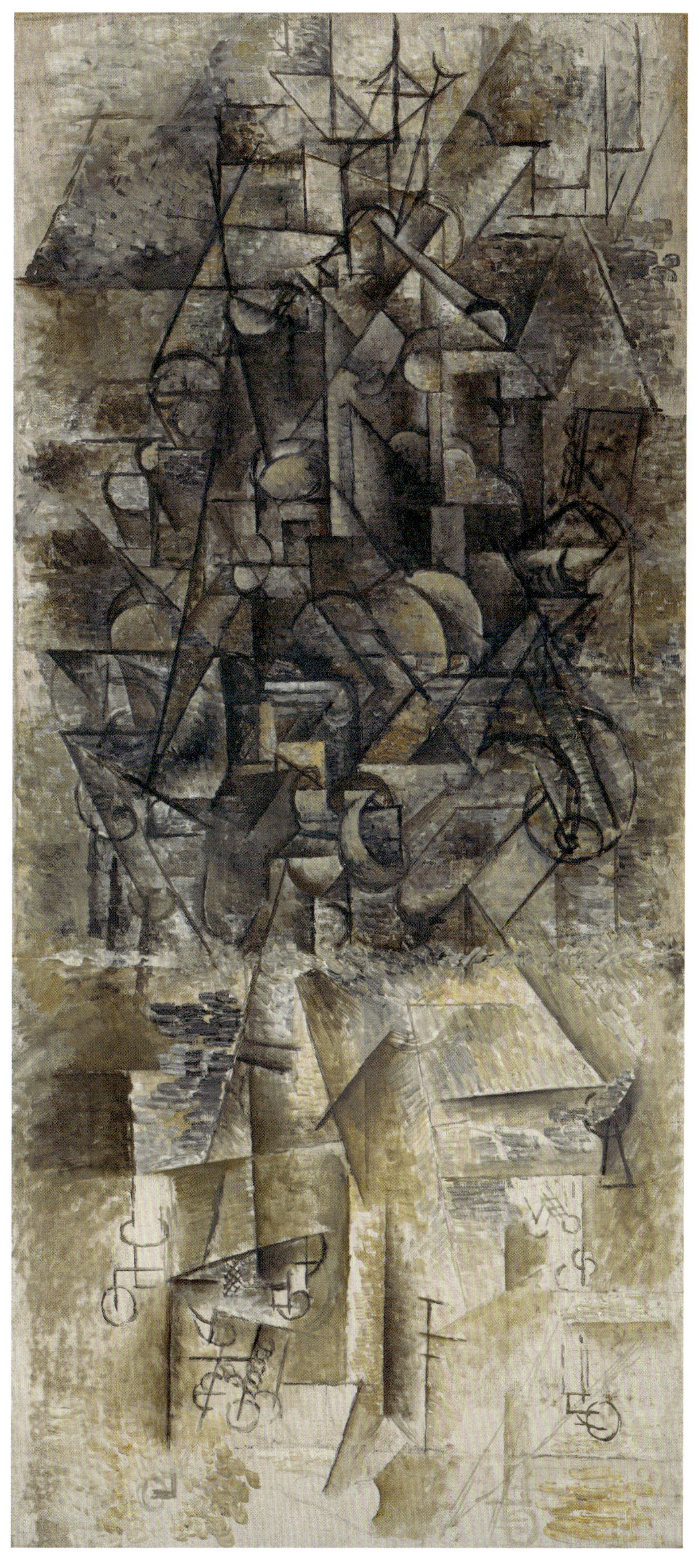

[Cat. 51]

Pablo Picasso, *Homme à la mandoline,* 1911

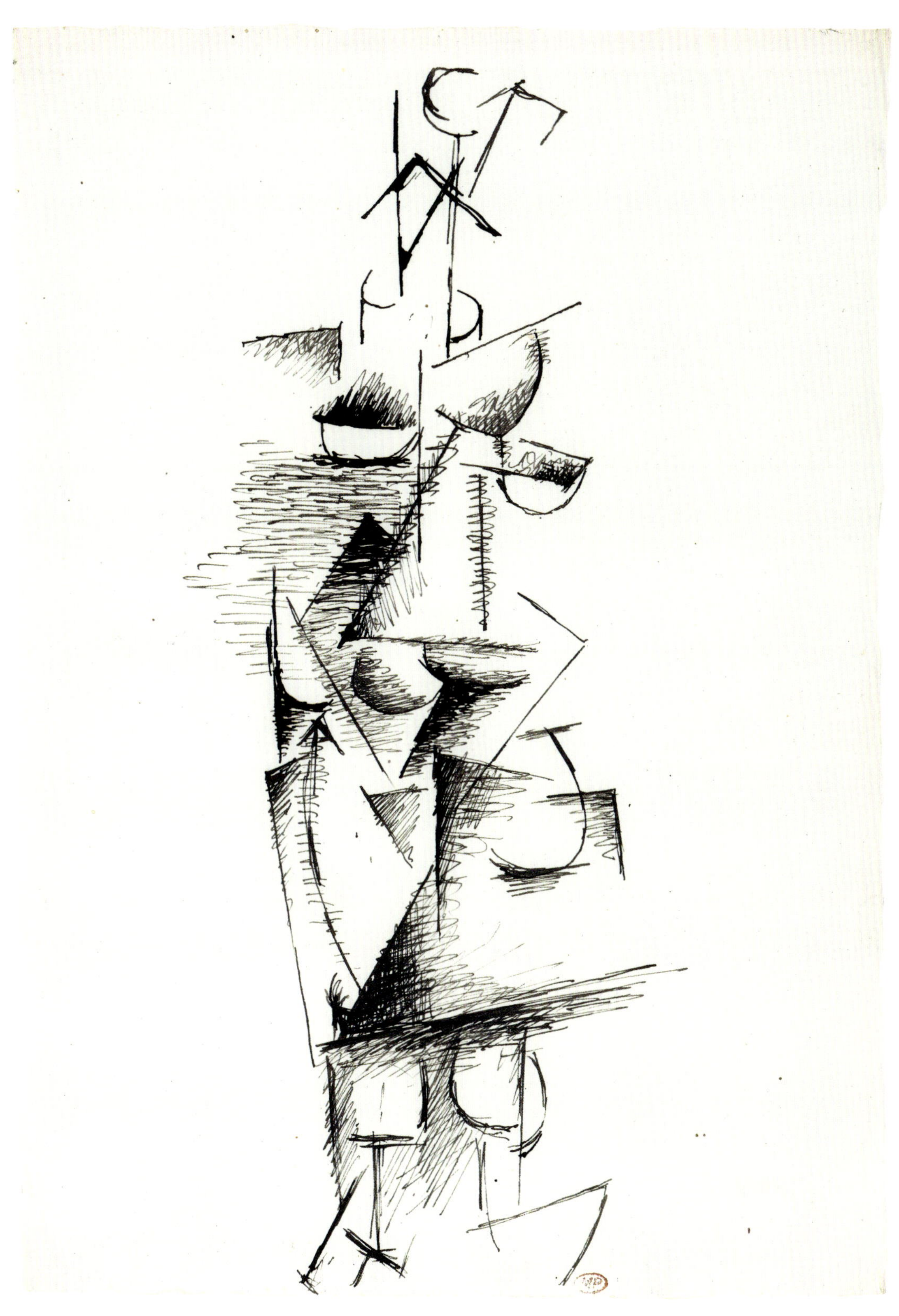

Pablo Picasso, *Nu debout,* 1910

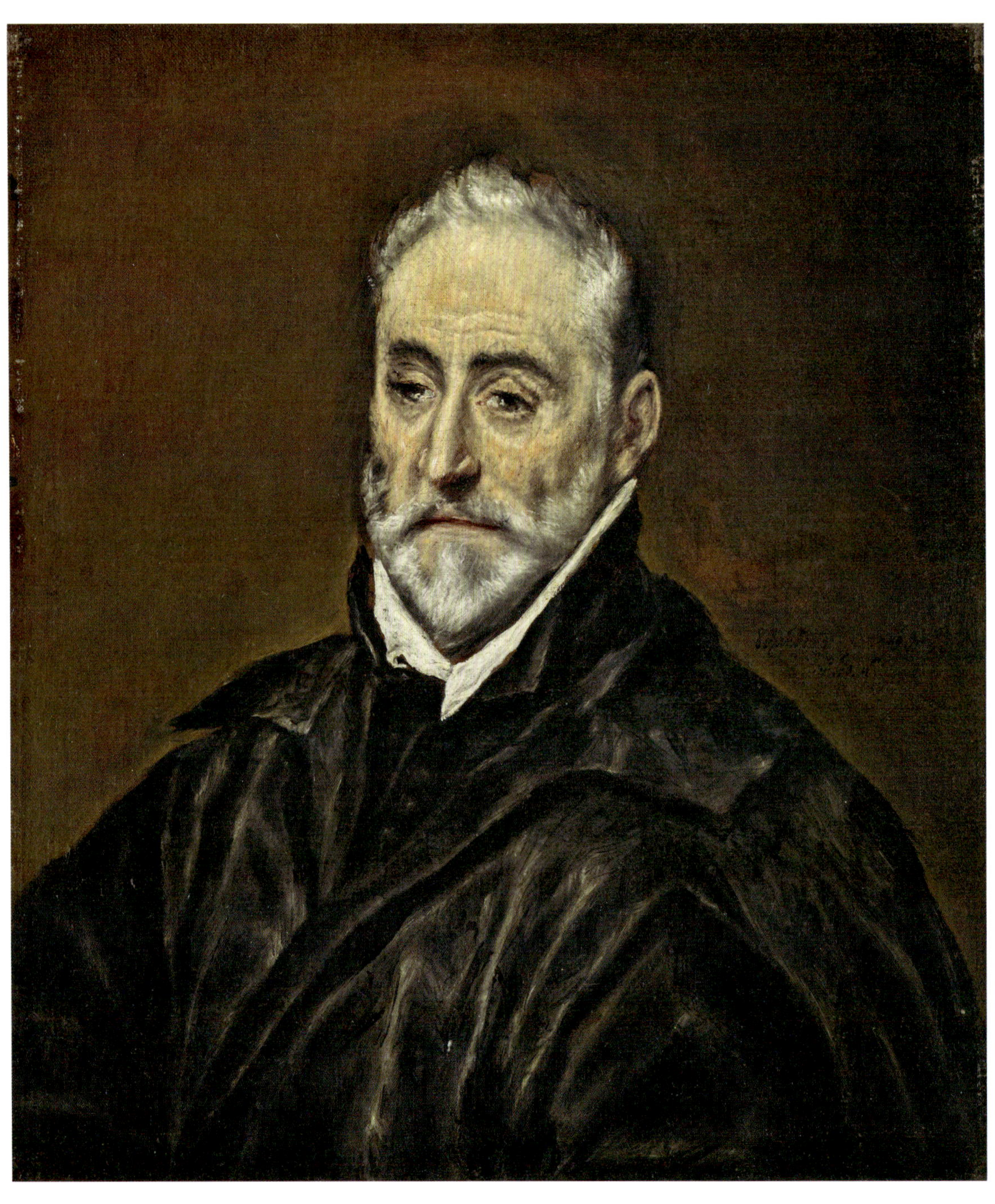

El Greco, *Portrait of Antonio de Covarrubias y Leiva*, ca. 1597–1600

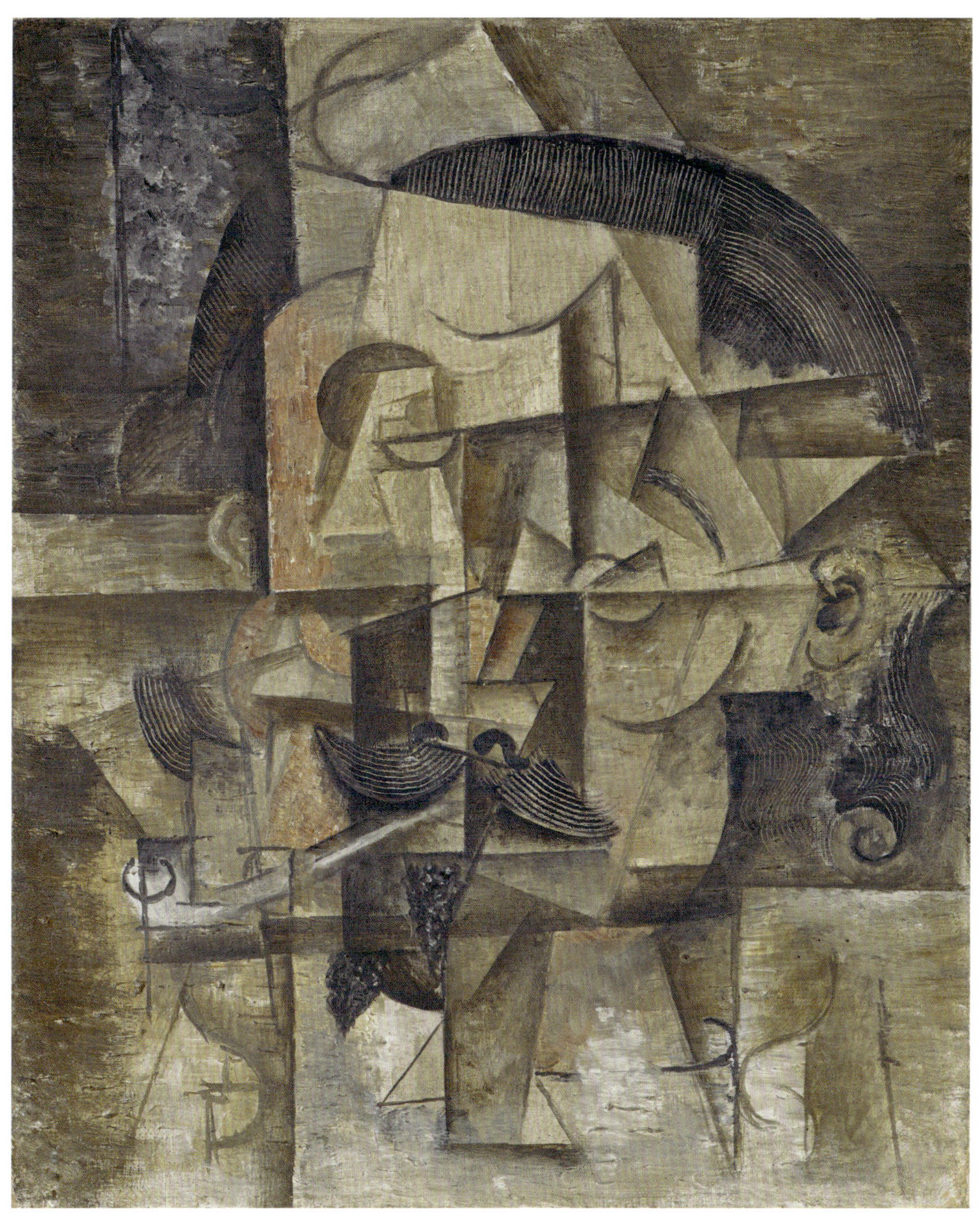

[Cat. 54]

Pablo Picasso, *Le Poète,* 1912

El Greco and Cubism after 1910

[Cat. 36] **El Greco**
Saint Ildefonsus, ca. 1603–05
Oil on canvas, 112 × 64 cm
Fundación Hospital Ntra. Sra. de La Caridad –
Memoria Benéfica de Vega (FUNCAVE)

[Cat. 37] **Pablo Picasso**
*Pains et compotier aux fruits sur une
table* (Bread and Fruit Dish on a Table)
1908–09
Oil on canvas, 163.7 × 132.1 cm
Kunstmuseum Basel, purchased with a contribution
from Dr. h.c. Richard Doetsch-Benziger 1951
Inv. 2261

[Cat. 38] **El Greco**
The Penitent Magdalene, ca. 1580–85
Oil on canvas, 101.6 × 81.9 cm
The Nelson-Atkins Museum of Art, Kansas City,
Missouri, Purchase: William Rockhill Nelson Trust
Inv. 30-35

[Cat. 39] **Pablo Picasso**
Nu assis (Seated Nude), 1909–10
Oil on canvas, 92.1 × 73 cm
Tate, London, purchased 1949
Inv. N05904

[Cat. 40] **Pablo Picasso**
Femme assise dans un fauteuil (Seated
Woman in an Armchair), 1910
Oil on canvas, 73.2 × 60.2 cm
Fondation Beyeler, Riehen/Basel, Beyeler Collection
Inv. 99.3

[Cat. 41] **El Greco**
The Penitent Magdalene, ca. 1576–77
Oil on canvas, 156.5 × 121 cm
Szépművészeti Múseum, Budapest
Inv. 5640

[Cat. 42] **El Greco**
Saint Simon, ca. 1610–14
Oil on canvas, 101 × 81 cm
Museo del Greco, Toledo
Inv. CE00008

[Cat. 43] **Pablo Picasso**
L'Accordéoniste (Accordionist)
Céret, summer 1911
Oil on canvas, 130.2 × 89.5 cm
Solomon R. Guggenheim Museum, New York
Solomon R. Guggenheim Founding Collection
By gift
Inv. 37.357

[Cat. 44] **El Greco**
Saint Bartholomew, ca. 1610–14
Oil on canvas, 101 × 81 cm
Museo del Greco, Toledo
Inv. CE00006

[Cat. 45] **Pablo Picasso**
Le Poète (The Poet)
Céret, August 1911
Oil on canvas, 131.2 × 89.5 cm
Peggy Guggenheim Collection, Venice (Solomon R.
Guggenheim Foundation, New York)
Inv. 76.2553 PG 1

[Cat. 46] **El Greco**
Saint John the Evangelist, ca. 1610–14
Oil on canvas, 101 × 81 cm
Museo del Greco, Toledo
Inv. CE00004

[Cat. 47] **Pablo Picasso**
Homme à la clarinette (Man with a
Clarinet), 1911–12
Oil on canvas, 106 × 69 cm
Museo Nacional Thyssen-Bornemisza, Madrid
Inv. 710(1982.35)

[Cat. 48] **El Greco**
Saint Paul, ca. 1585
Oil on canvas, 120 × 92 cm
Private collection

[Cat. 49] **Pablo Picasso**
L'Aficionado (The Aficionado), 1912
Oil on canvas, 134.8 × 81.5 cm
Kunstmuseum Basel, donated by
Dr. h.c. Raoul La Roche 1952
Inv. 2304

[Cat. 50] **El Greco**
The Resurrection, 1597–1600
Oil on canvas, 275 × 127 cm
Museo Nacional del Prado, Madrid
Inv. P000825

[Cat. 51] **Pablo Picasso**
Homme à la mandoline
(Man with a Mandolin)
Paris, autumn 1911
Oil on canvas, 162 × 71 cm
Musée national Picasso, Paris
Inv. MP35

[Cat. 52] **Pablo Picasso**
Nu debout (Standing Nude)
Cadaqués, summer 1910
Pen and black ink on paper
31.5 × 21.5 cm
Musée national Picasso, Paris
MP 645

[Cat. 53] **El Greco**
*Portrait of Antonio de Covarrubias y
Leiva*, ca. 1597–1600
Oil on canvas, 68 × 58 cm
Musée du Louvre, Paris
Inv. RF 1941 32

[Cat. 54] **Pablo Picasso**
Le Poète (The Poet), Sorgues, 1912
Oil on canvas, 59.9 × 47.9 cm
Kunstmuseum Basel, gift from Maja Sacher-Stehlin to
the municipality of Basel; on permanent loan from the
City of Basel, 1967
Inv. G 1967.14

[Cat. 55] **El Greco (Workshop)**
Saint James the Elder, ca. 1600–04
Oil on canvas, 102.4 × 83.2 cm
Kunstmuseum Basel
Inv. 1644

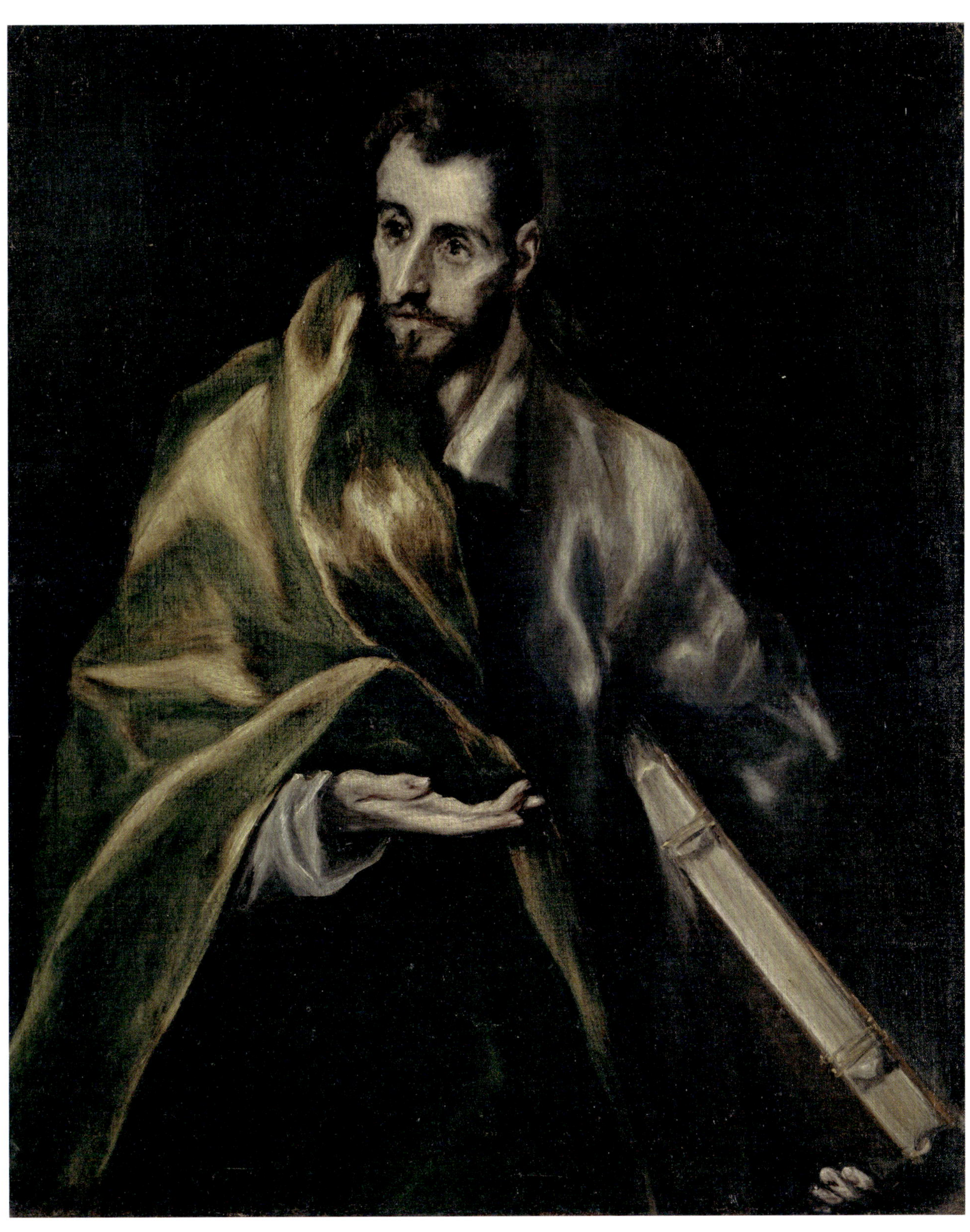

El Greco (Workshop), *Saint James the Elder,* ca. 1600–04

The Late Picasso: Wrestling with the Old Masters

Repeatedly I am asked to explain how my painting evolved. To me there is no past or future in art. If a work of art cannot live always in the present it must not be considered art at all. The art of the Greeks, of the Egyptians, of the great painters who lived in other times, is not an art of the past; perhaps it is more alive today than it ever was.

— Picasso, from an interview with Marius de Zayas; excerpted in Herschel B. Chipp, *Theories of Modern Art* (Berkeley and Los Angeles, 1984), p. 264.

Although many of the Old Masters are important reference points for the later phases of Picasso's work, El Greco's specific influence is less evident at this stage. In the last decade of Picasso's career, his dealer Daniel-Henry Kahnweiler noted that Picasso felt closer to Velázquez.* Whether or not his admiration for El Greco actually dwindled, he continued to have great esteem for his portraits. Picasso repeatedly affirmed his own place in the genealogy of the Old Masters and carried on the tradition in his own way; the historical costumes in the portrait of his friend and secretary Jaume (Jaime) Sabartés (1939, cat. 59) or the late *Bust of a Man* (November 8, 1970; cat. 68) are a case in point. But however many and varied Picasso's influences, the inscription on the back of the 1967 *Musketeer* (cat. 66) demonstrates the unerring presence of El Greco in his personal pantheon of Old Masters: "Domenico Theotocopulos van Rijn da Silva" is an explicit allusion to Picasso's three most revered masters, El Greco, Rembrandt van Rijn, and Diego Rodríguez de Silva y Velázquez. Clearly, Picasso continued late into his career to wrestle with his historical role models (whom he said he saw as contemporaries, whose presence he could feel as he worked). But whereas in his earlier years he had used the Old Masters as a compass to help him find his bearings as an artist, his late works show the supreme confidence of an artist who has himself become an Old Master—an artist who is aware of his status and communicates it through his paintings.

* Brassaï, *Conversations with Picasso*, trans. Jane Mary Todd (Chicago and London, 1999), p. 348.

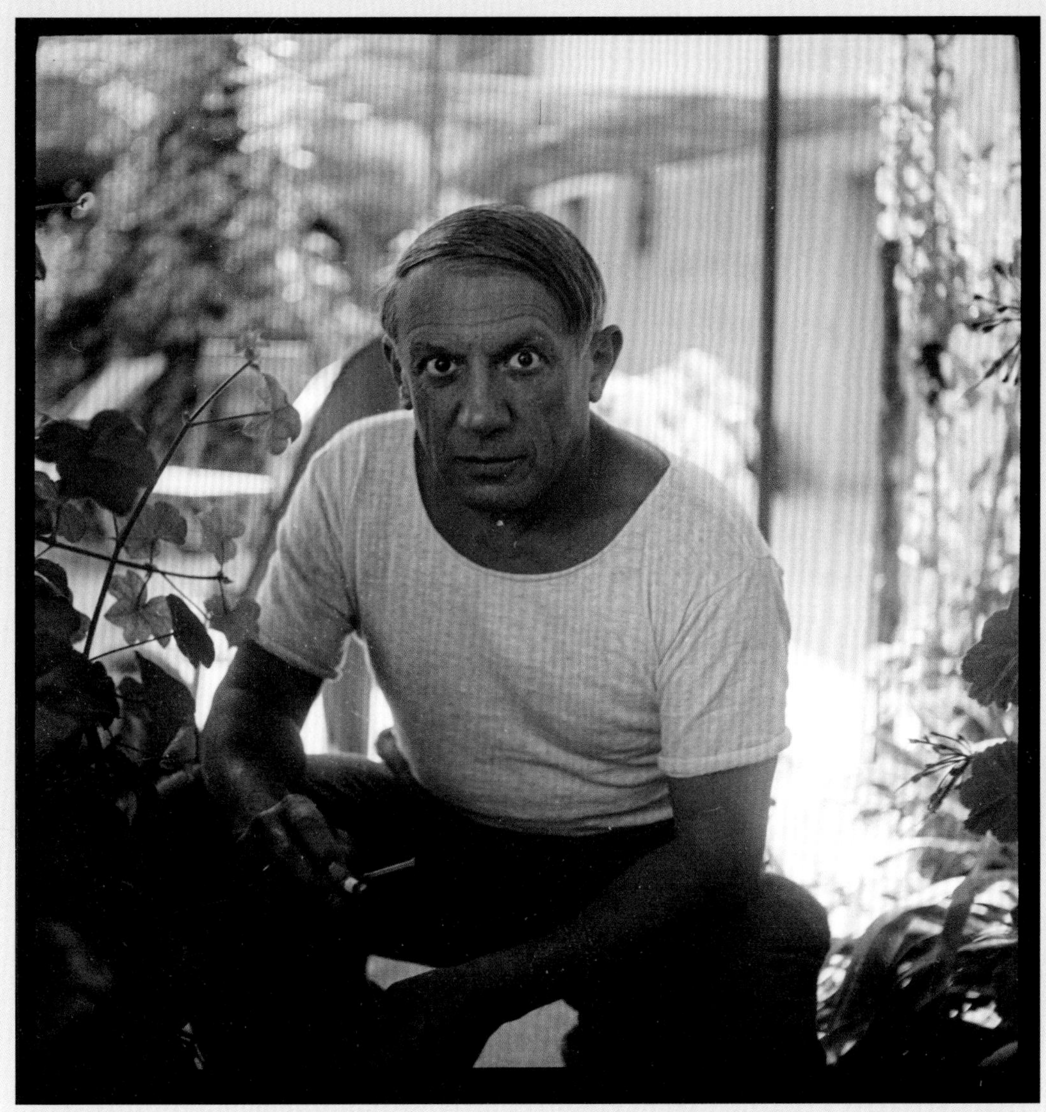

Dora Maar
Picasso in Mougins, 1937
Autochrome, 6 × 6 cm
Centre national d'art et de culture Georges-Pompidou, Paris

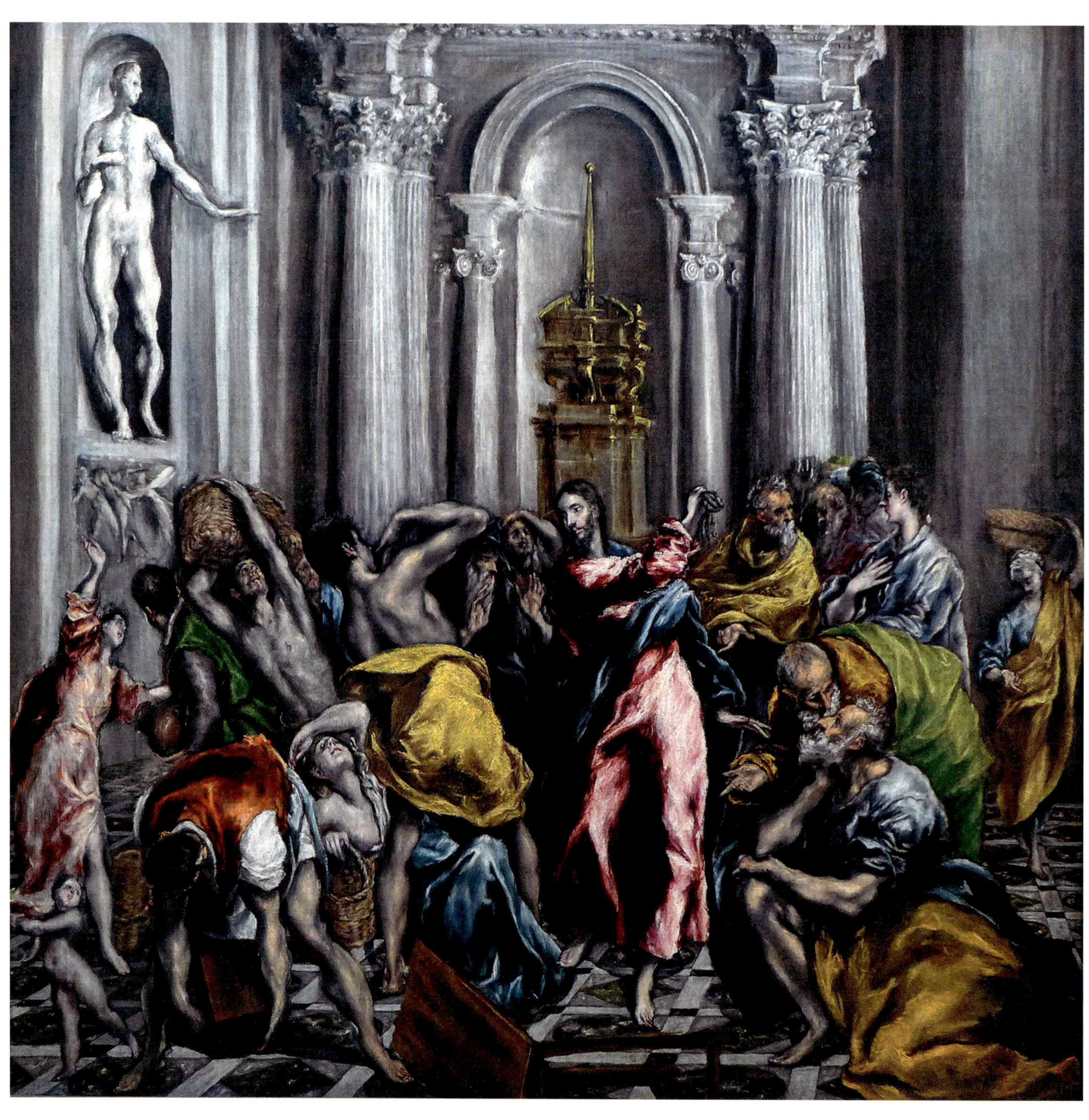

[Cat. 56]

El Greco, *Christ Driving the Traders from the Temple,* ca. 1610–14

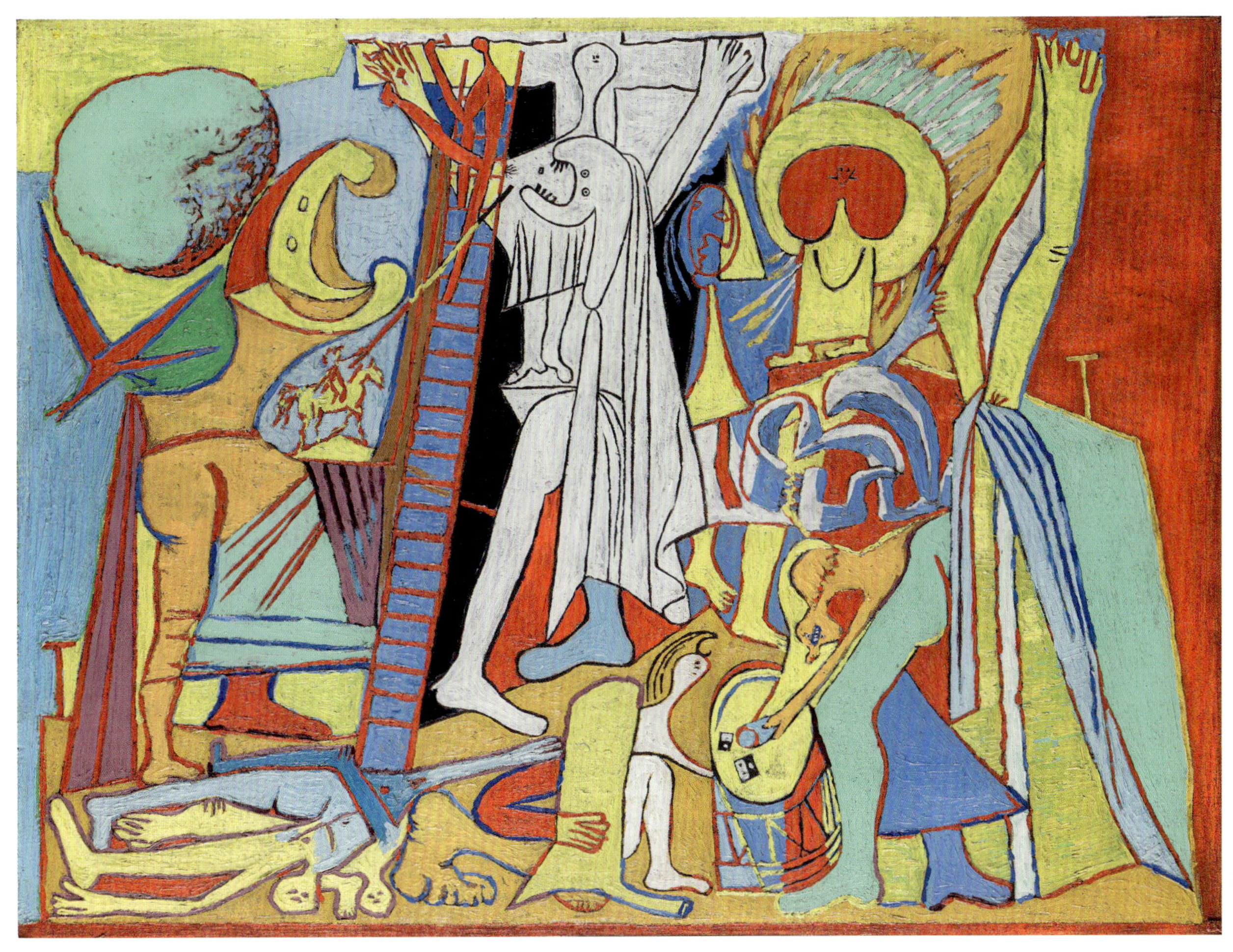

Pablo Picasso, *The Crucifixion,* 1930

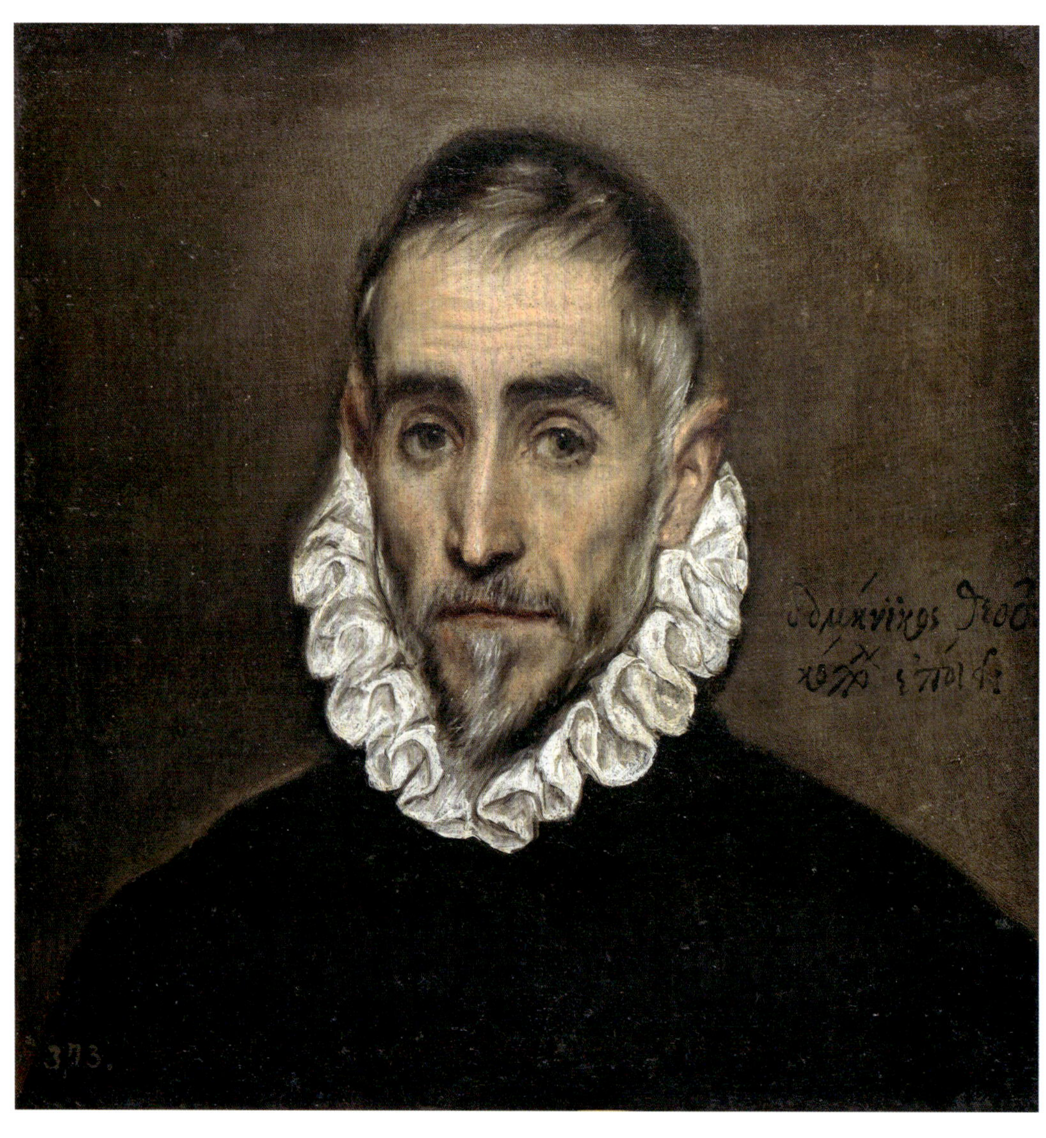

[Cat. 58]
El Greco, *An Elderly Gentleman*, 1587–1600

156

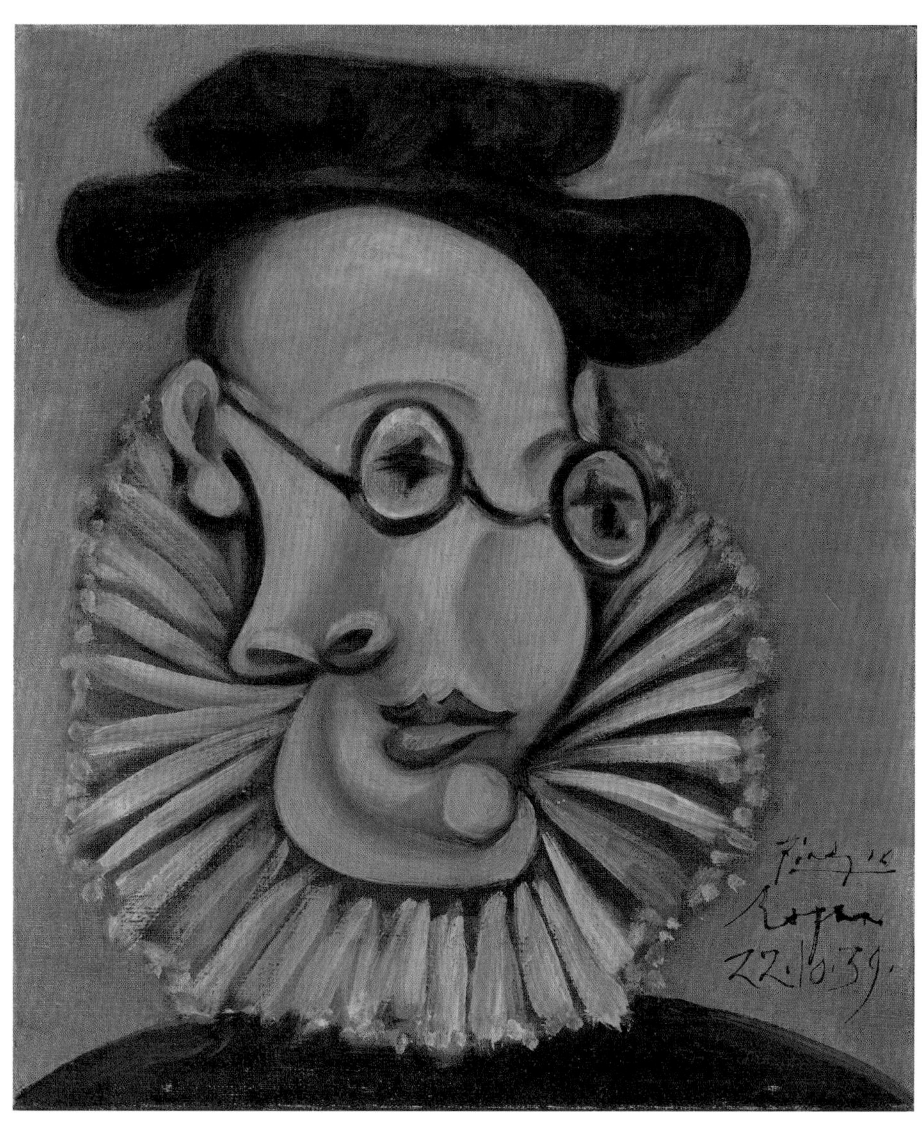

[Cat. 59]
Pablo Picasso, *Jaume Sabartés with Ruff and Bonnet,* 1939

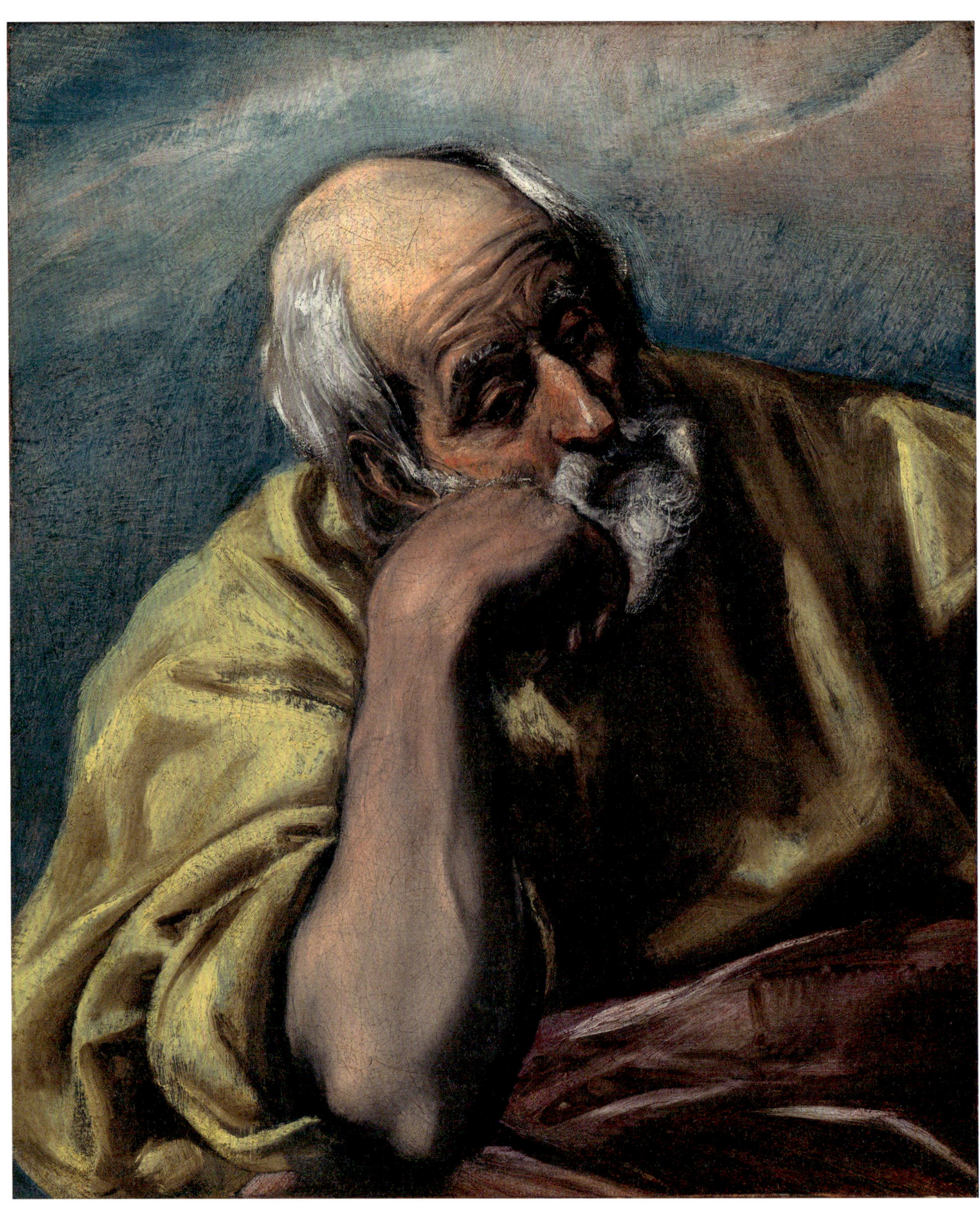

El Greco, *Saint Joseph,* ca. 1577–80

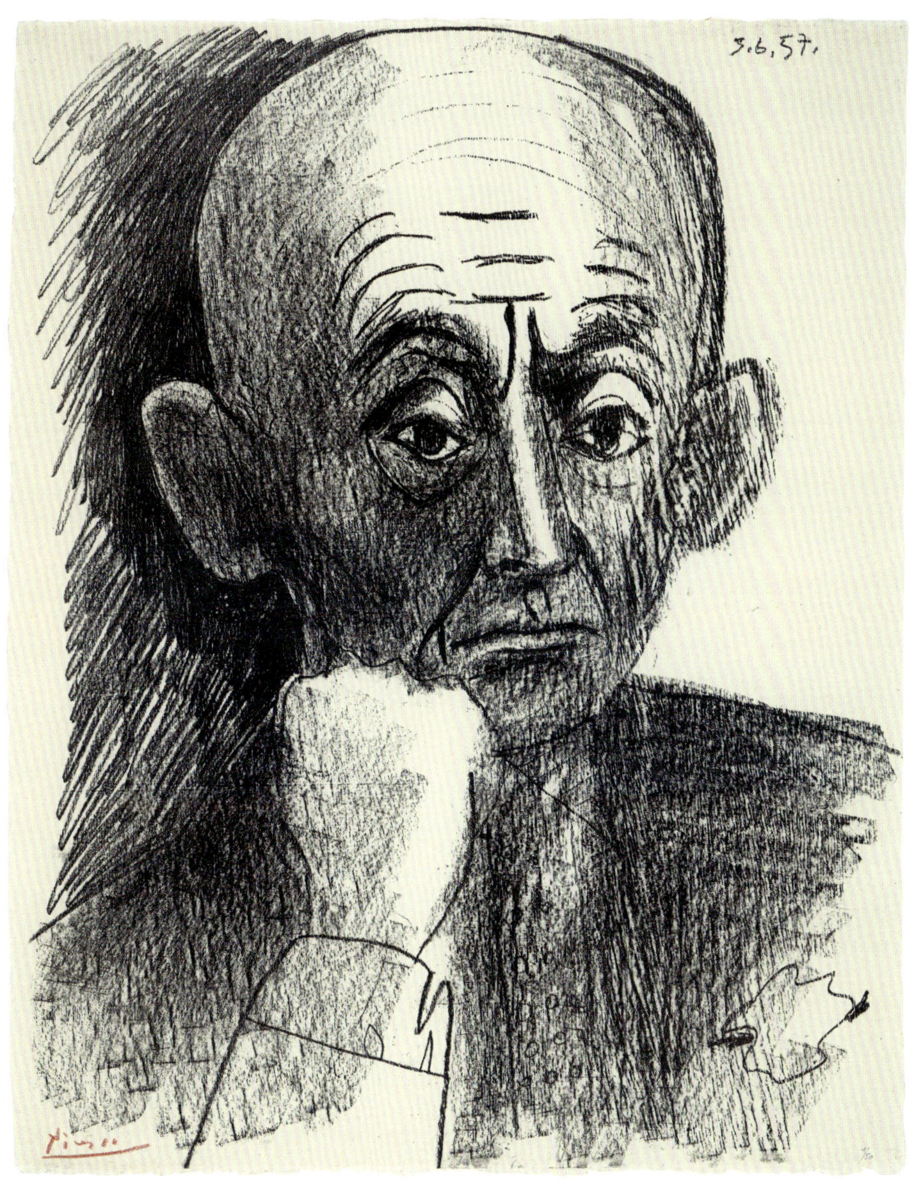

[Cat. 61]
Pablo Picasso, *Portrait de D. H. Kahnweiler, II,* 1957

159

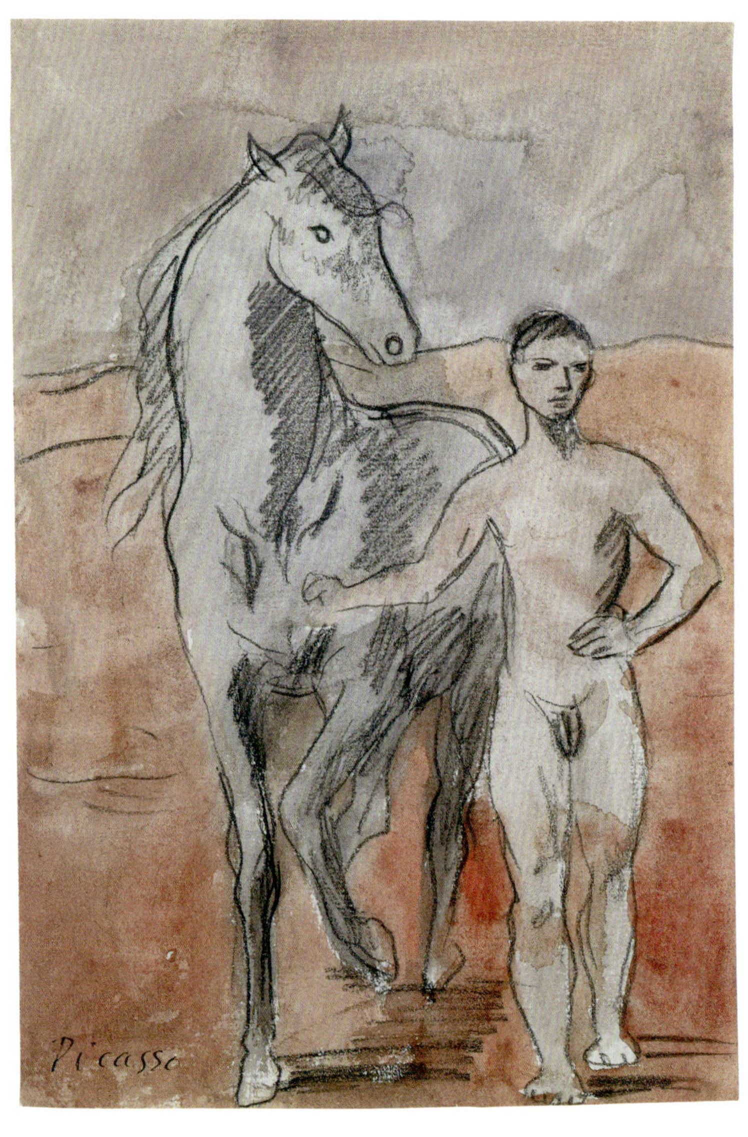

[Cat. 62]
Pablo Picasso, *Boy Leading a Horse,* 1905–06

160

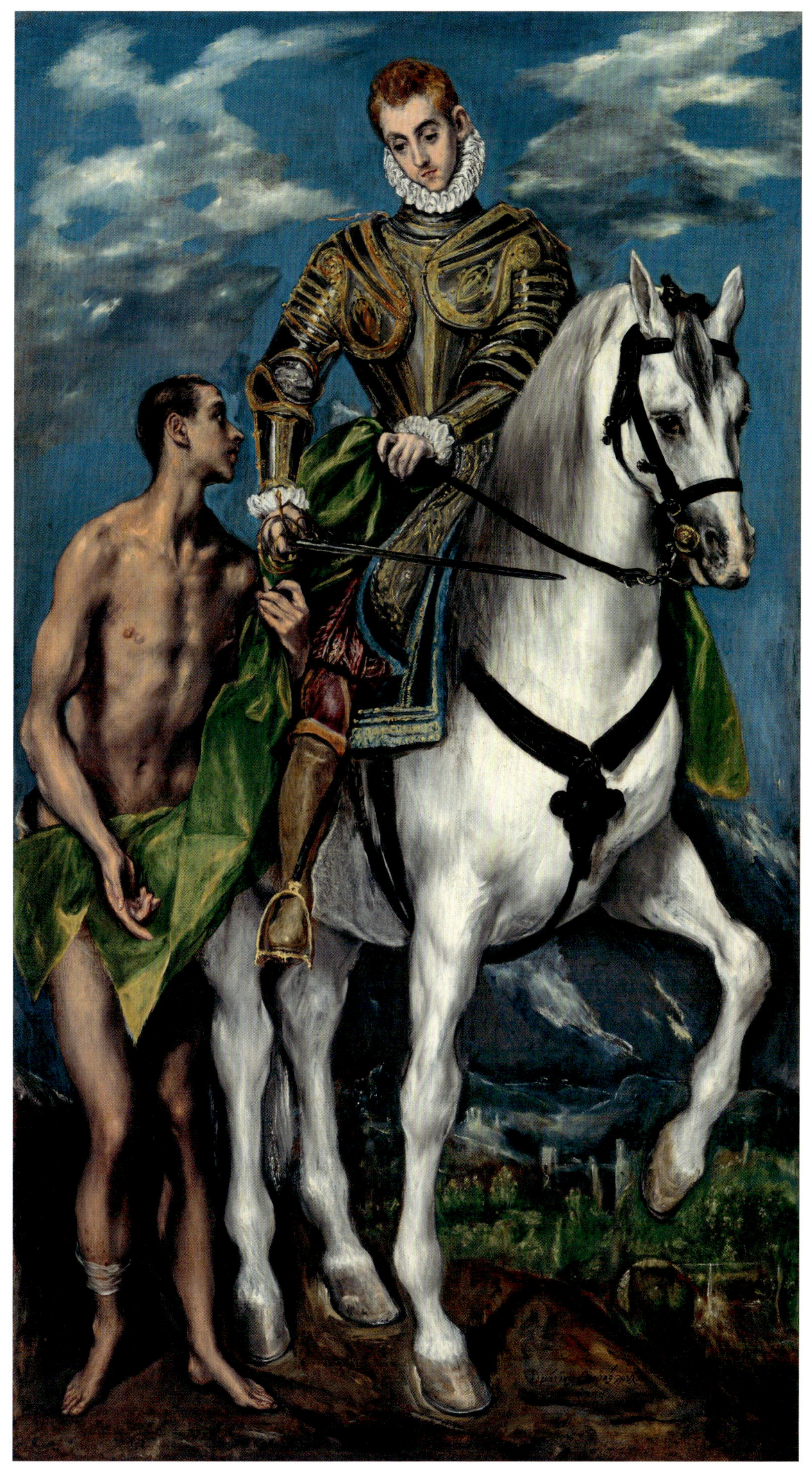

El Greco, *Saint Martin and the Beggar,* 1597–99

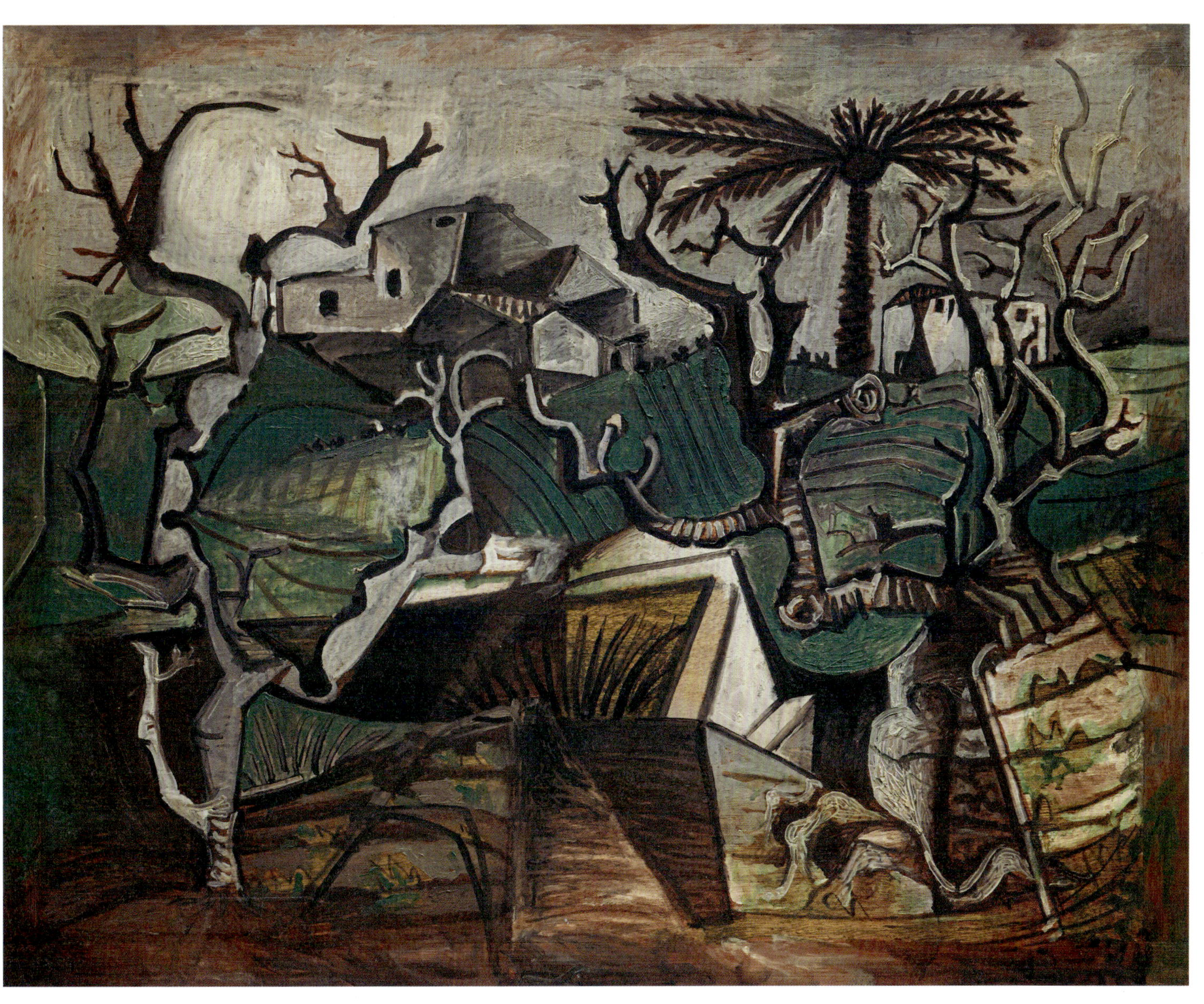

[Cat. 64]
Pablo Picasso, *Paysage d'hiver, Vallauris,* 1950

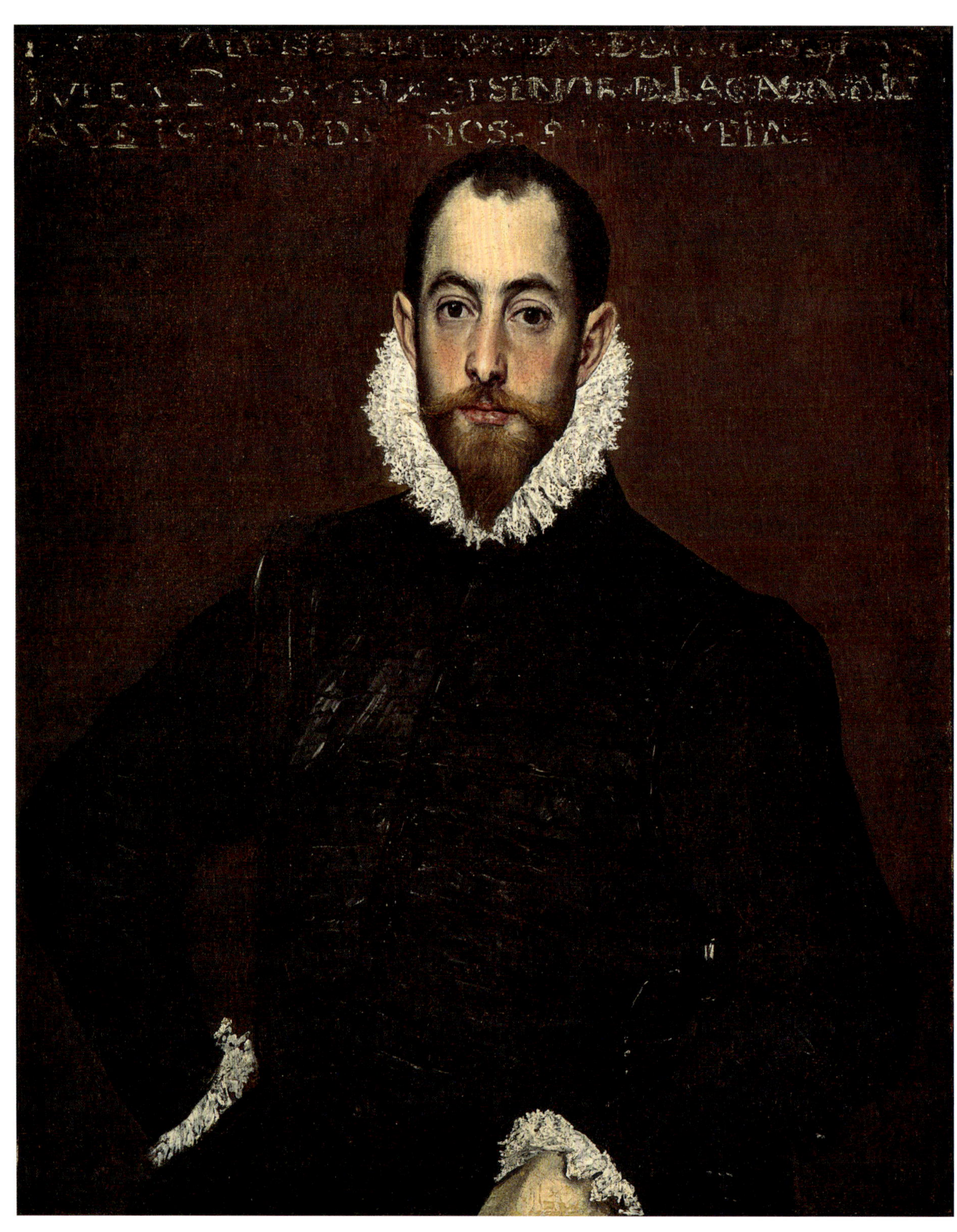

[Cat. 65]

El Greco, *Portrait of a Man of the House of Leiva,* ca. 1580–85

164

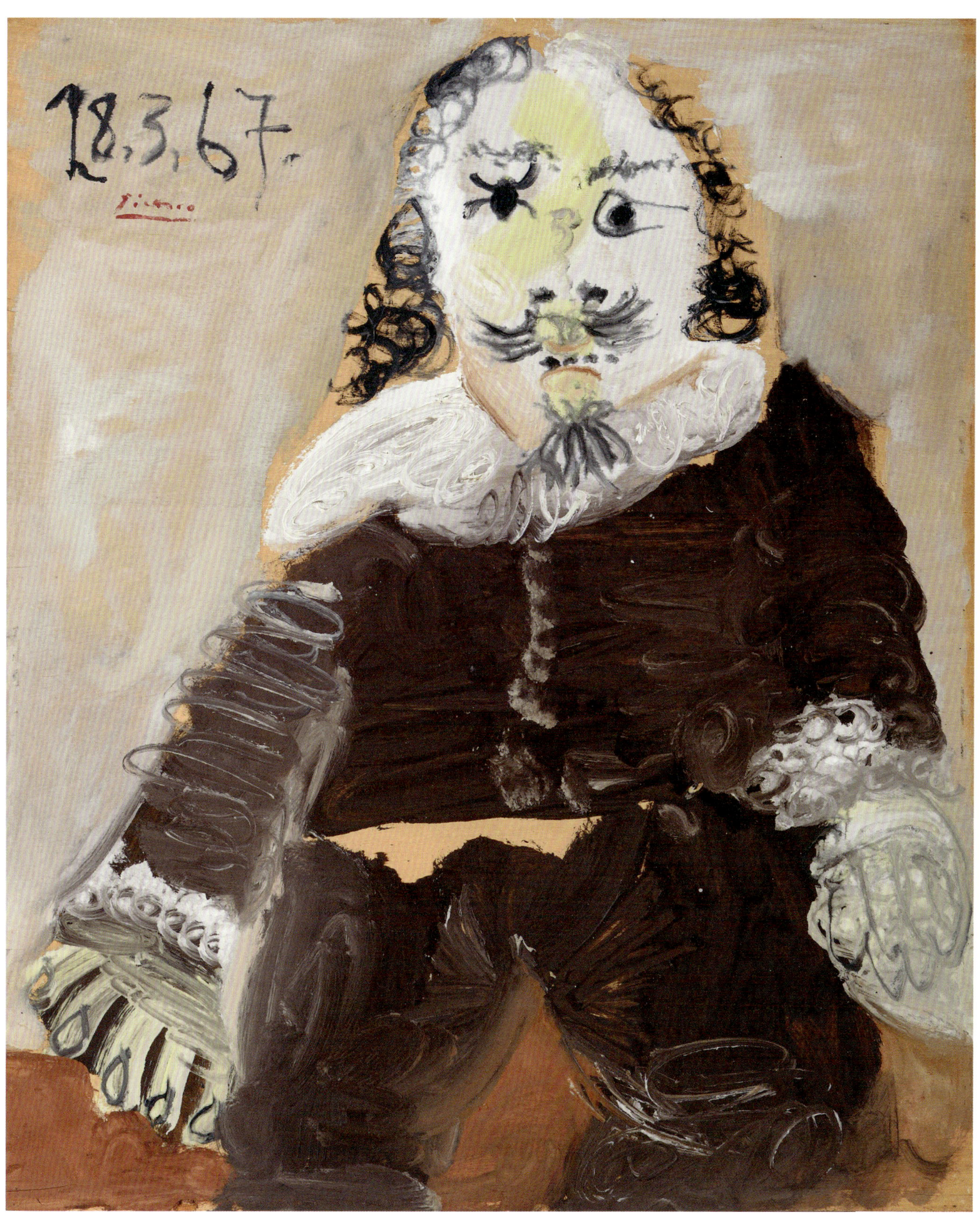

[Cat. 66]
Pablo Picasso, *The Musketeer (Domenico Theotocopulos van Rijn da Silva)*, 1967

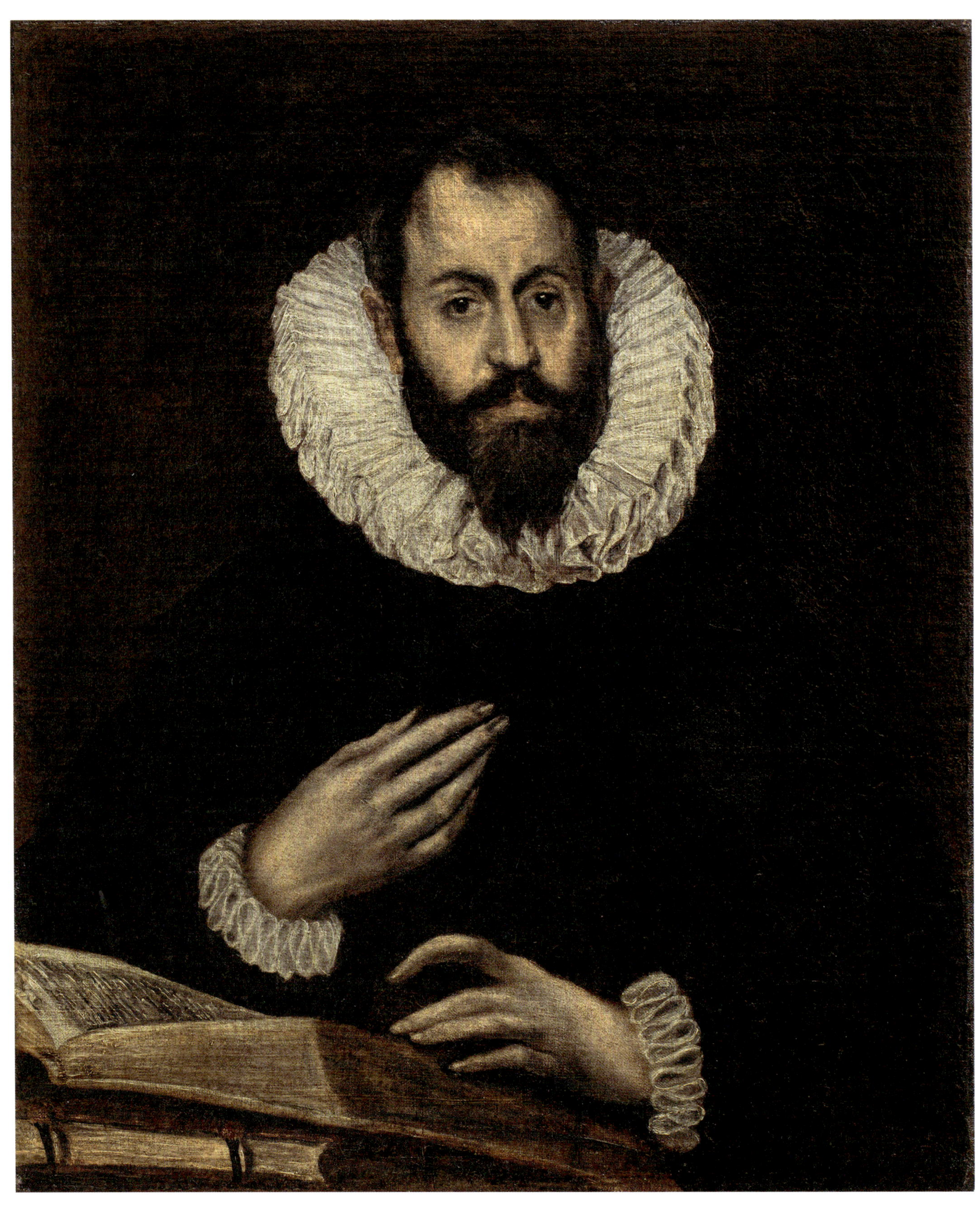

El Greco, *Portrait of a Man*, ca. 1600–10

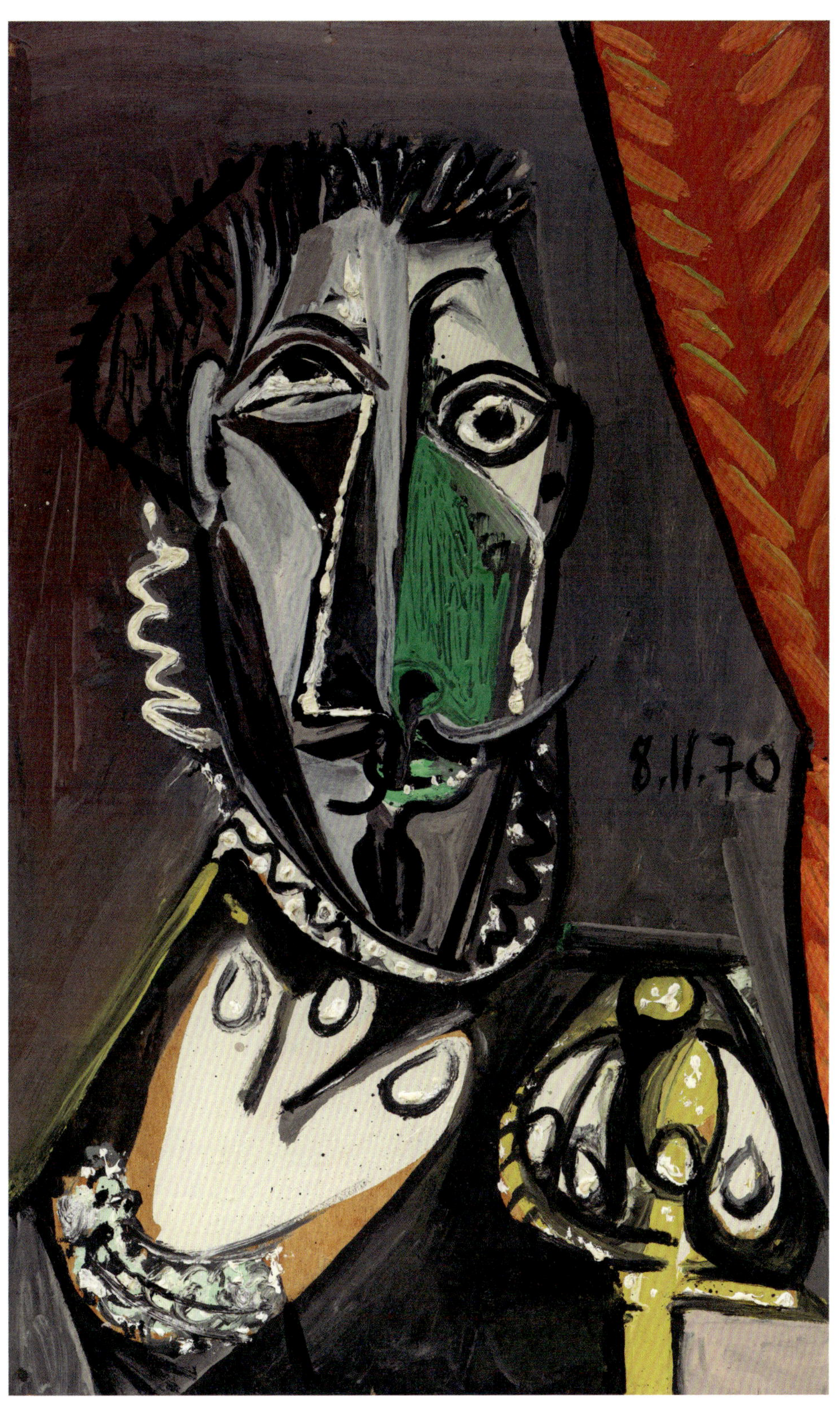

[Cat. 68]
Pablo Picasso, *Buste d'homme,* 1970

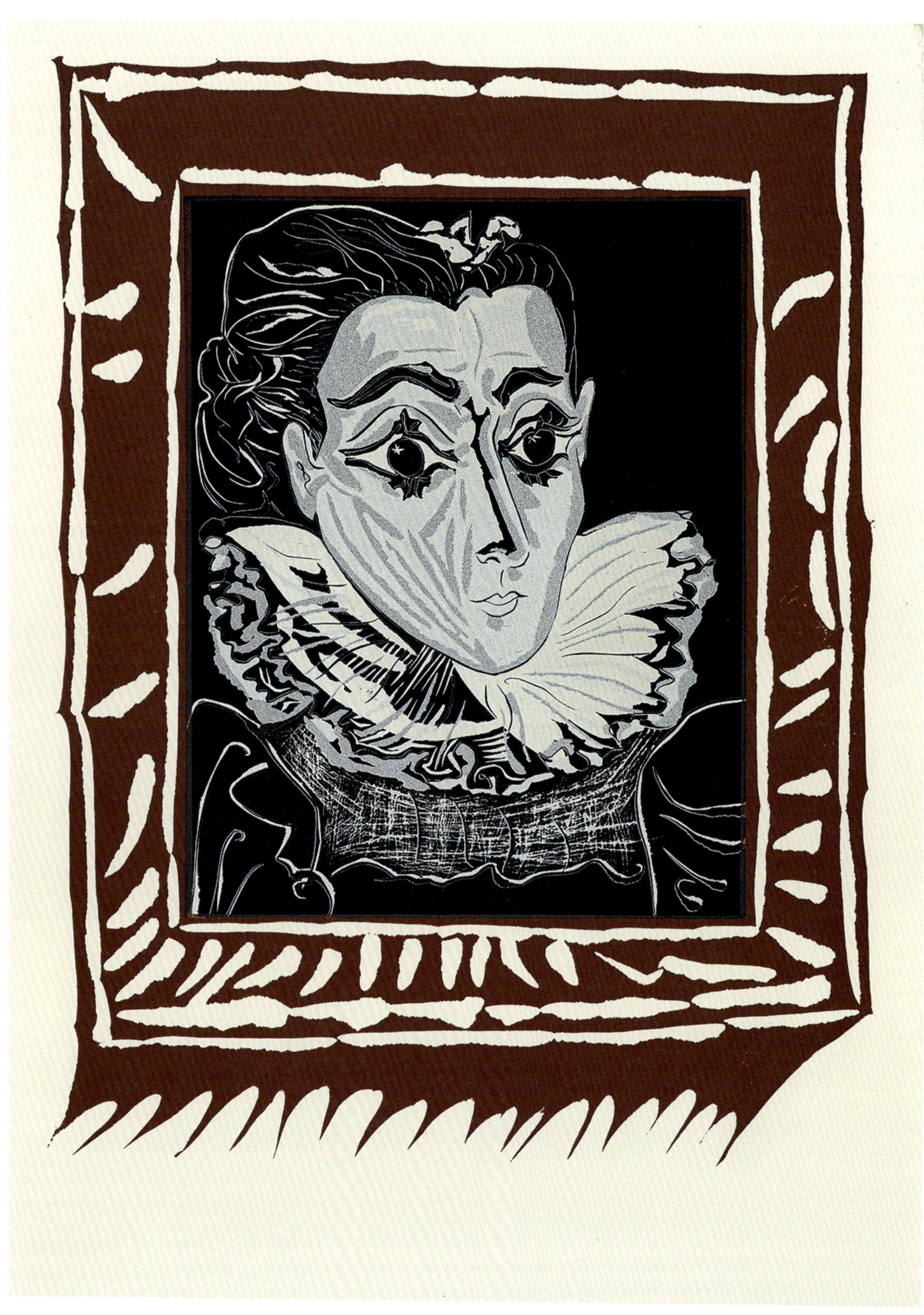

Pablo Picasso, *Portrait de Jacqueline à la fraise*, 1962

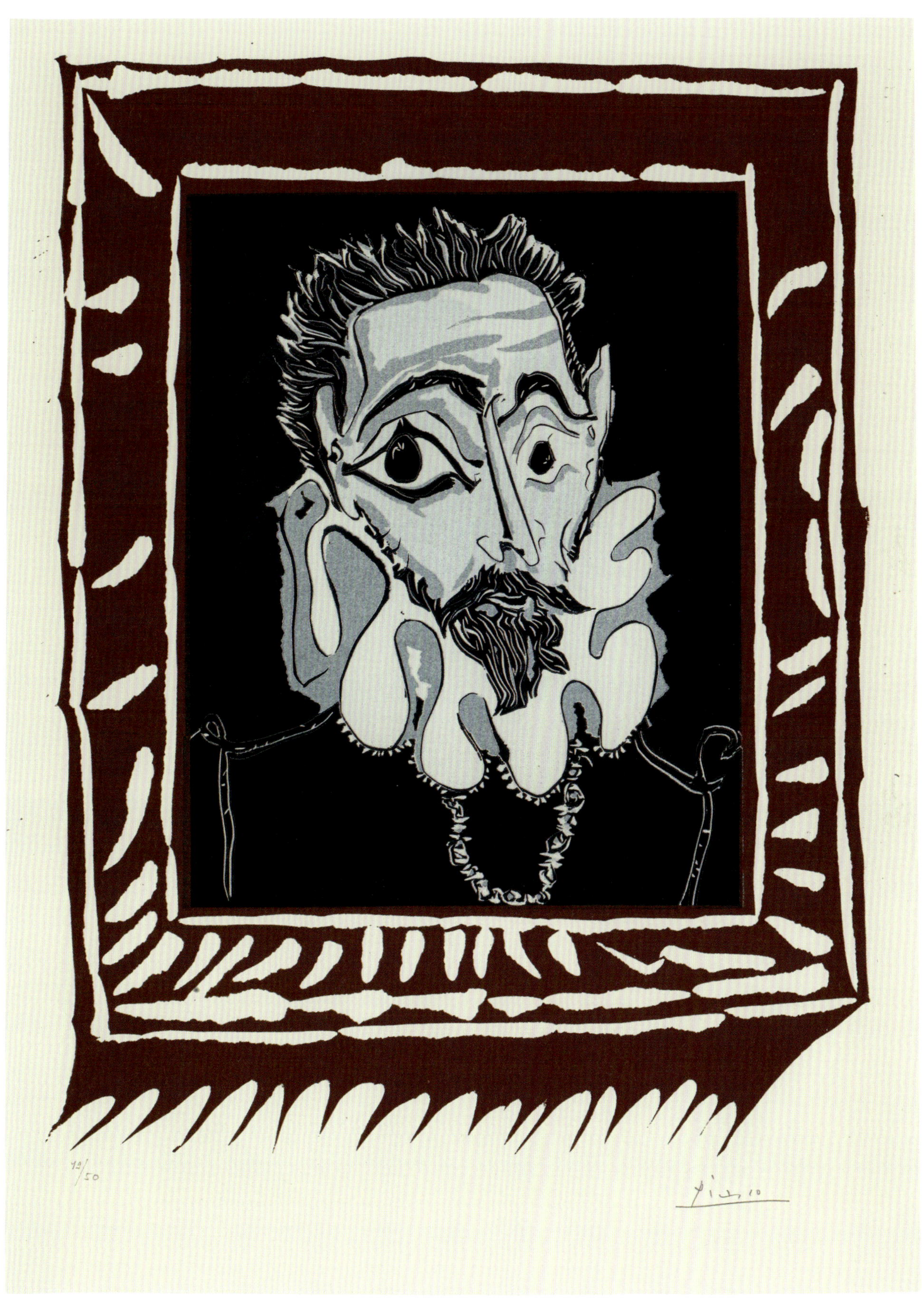

[Cat. 70]
Pablo Picasso, *L'Homme à la fraise,* 1962

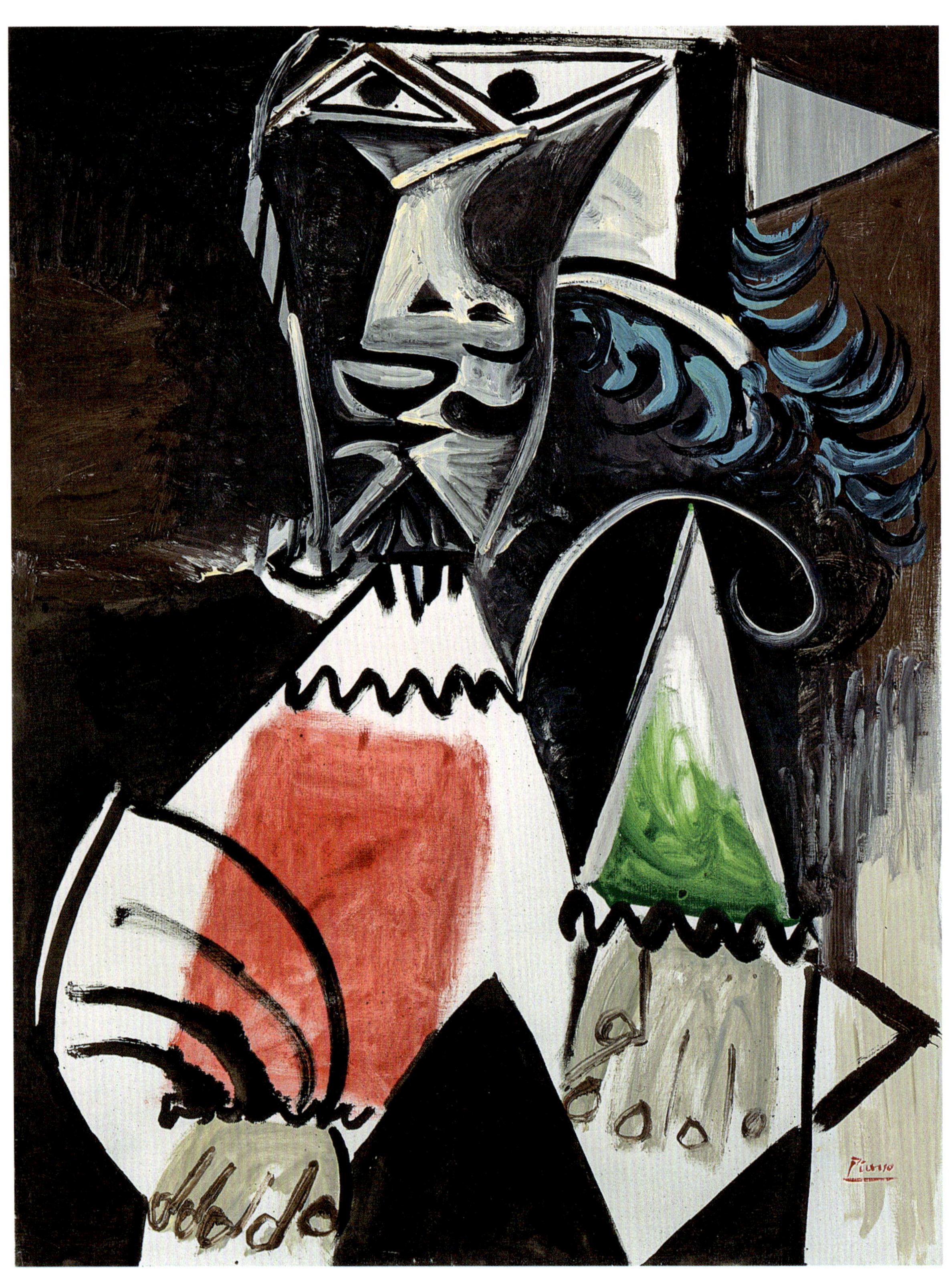

[Cat. 71]
Pablo Picasso, *Buste d'homme*, 1969

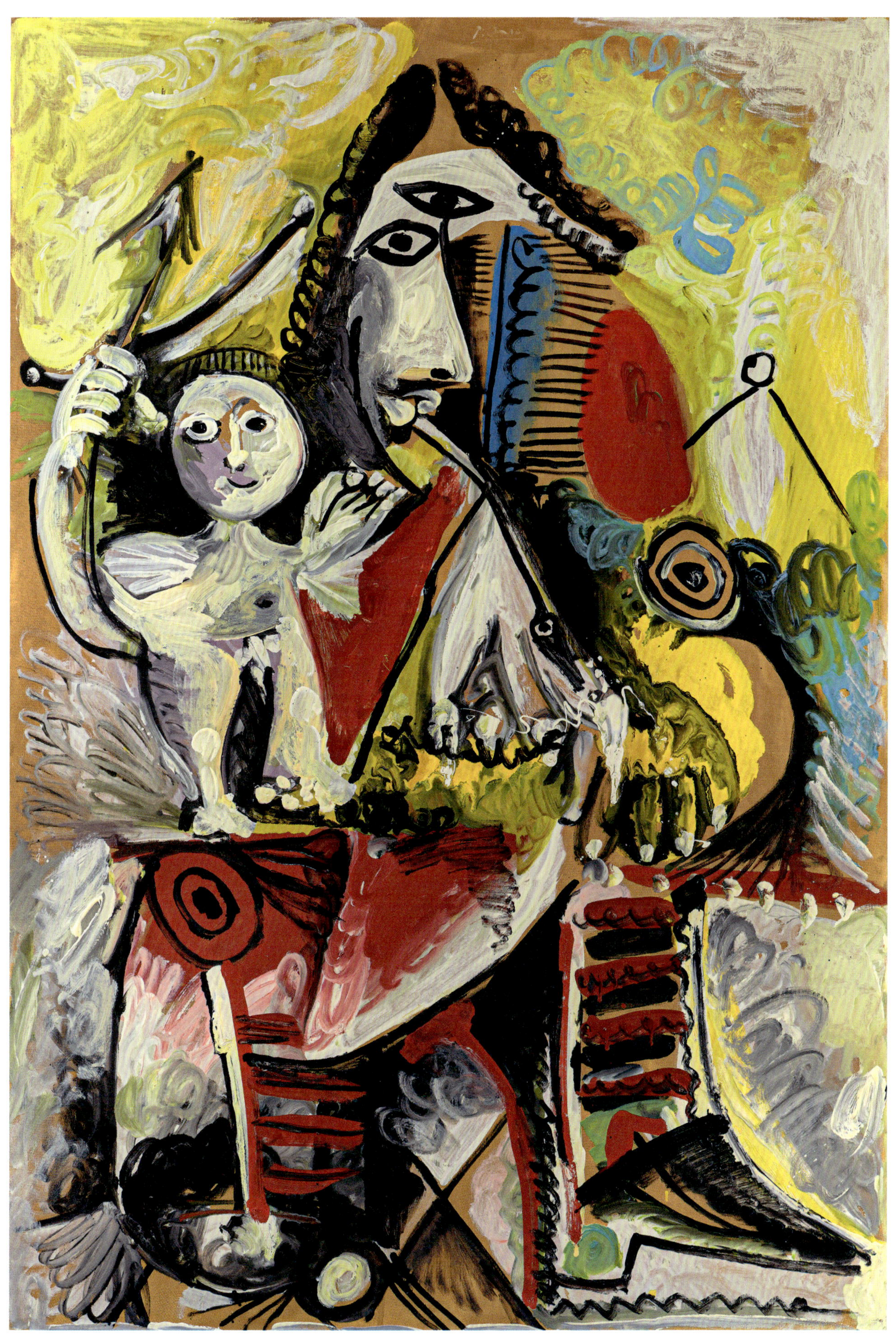

[Cat. 72]
Pablo Picasso, *Mousquetaire et amour,* 1969

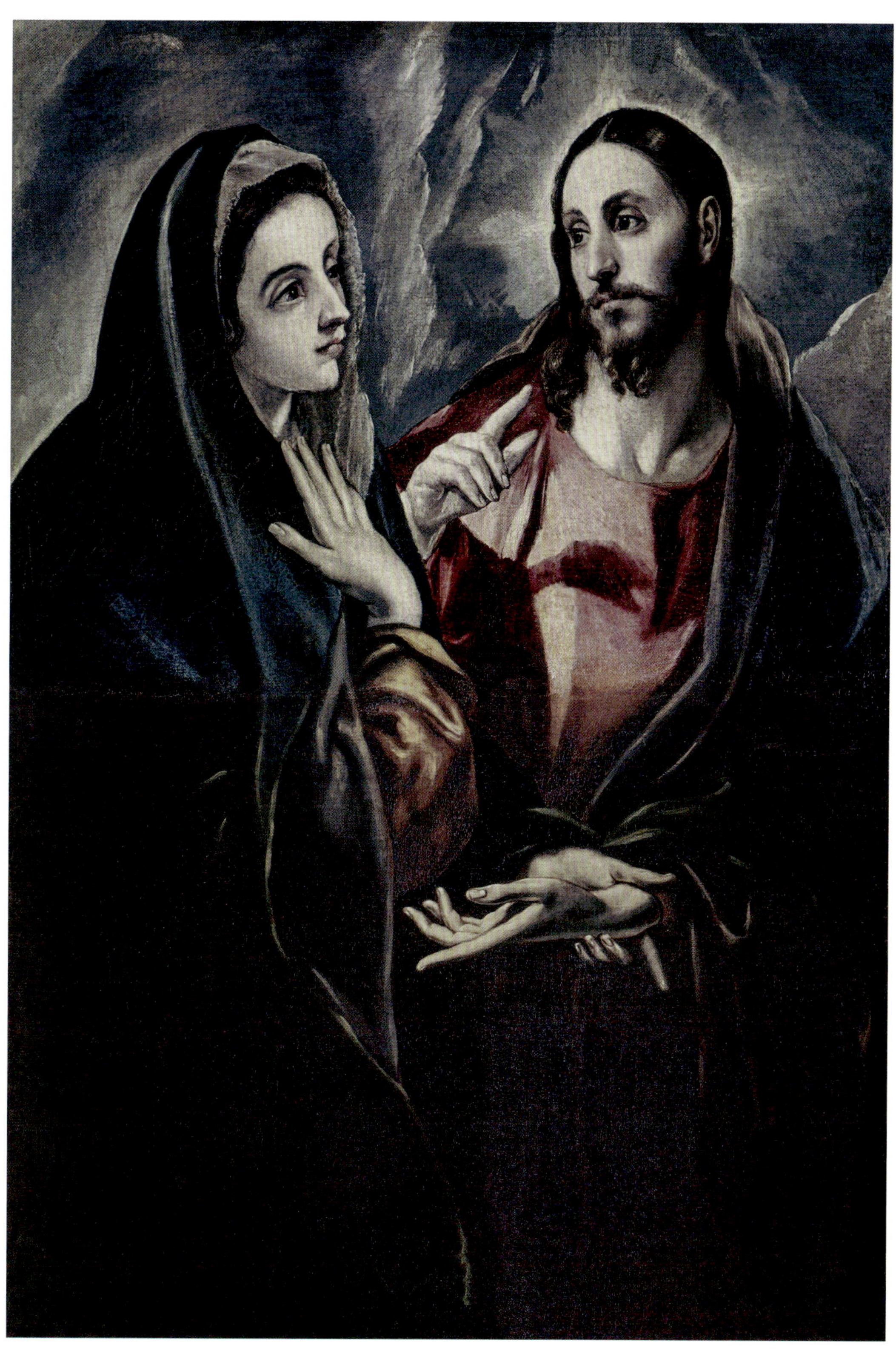

El Greco (Workshop), *Christ Taking Leave of His Mother*, ca. 1595

The Late Picasso: Wrestling with the Old Masters

[Cat. 56] **El Greco**
Christ Driving the Traders from the Temple, ca. 1610–14
Oil on canvas, 106 × 104 cm
Real Parroquia de San Ginés de Arles –
Archidiócesis Metropolitana de Madrid

[Cat. 57] **Pablo Picasso**
The Crucifixion
Paris, February 7, 1930
Oil on plywood, 51.5 × 66.5 cm
Musée national Picasso, Paris
Donated in 1979
Inv. MP122

[Cat. 58] **El Greco**
An Elderly Gentleman, 1587–1600
Oil on canvas, 46 × 43 cm
Museo Nacional del Prado, Madrid
Inv. P000806

[Cat. 59] **Pablo Picasso**
Jaume Sabartés with Ruff and Bonnet Royan, October 22, 1939
Oil on canvas, 46 × 38 cm
Museu Picasso, Barcelona
Gift of Jaume Sabartés, 1962
MPB 70.241

[Cat. 60] **El Greco**
Saint Joseph, ca. 1577–80
Oil on canvas, 68 × 56 cm
Private collection

[Cat. 61] **Pablo Picasso**
*Portrait de D. H. Kahnweiler, II
(Portrait of D. H. Kahnweiler, II)*
June 3, 1957
Edition Galerie Louise Leiris
Transfer lithograph (chalk, wood
structure from the wooden support
to which the transfer paper was
attached), printed on Vélin d'Arches
49.5 × 65 cm
Printed by Atelier Mourlot, Paris
Kunstmuseum Basel, Kupferstichkabinett
On permanent loan from the Gottfried Keller-
Stiftung, Bundesamt für Kultur, Bern
Inv. GKS 1093.196

[Cat. 62] **Pablo Picasso**
Boy Leading a Horse, 1905–06
Watercolor and Conté crayon
on paper, 23.5 × 15.6 cm
The Baltimore Museum of Art: The Cone Collection,
formed by Dr. Claribel Cone and Miss Etta Cone of
Baltimore, Maryland
Inv. BMA 1950.12.492

[Cat. 63] **El Greco**
Saint Martin and the Beggar, 1597–99
Oil on canvas, 193.5 × 103 cm
National Gallery of Art, Washington, D.C.
Widener Collection
Inv. 1942.9.25

[Cat. 64] **Pablo Picasso**
*Paysage d'hiver, Vallauris
(Winter Landscape, Vallauris)*
December 22, 1950
Oil on wood panel, 102.9 × 125.7 cm
Kate Ganz Family Trust, New York

[Cat. 65] **El Greco**
Portrait of a Man of the House of Leiva,
ca. 1580–85
Oil on canvas, 87.8 × 69.5 cm
The Montreal Museum of Fine Arts
Adaline Van Horne Bequest
Inv. 1945.885

[Cat. 66] **Pablo Picasso**
The Musketeer (Domenico Theotocopulos van Rijn da Silva)
March 18, 1967
Oil on plywood, 101 × 81.5 cm
Ludwig Museum – Museum of Contemporary
Art, Budapest
Inv. LML.1991.88.1

[Cat. 67] **El Greco**
Portrait of a Man, ca. 1600–10
Oil on canvas, 79.7 × 64.7 cm
Collection des Musées d'Amiens
Inv. M.P.Lav.1894-215

[Cat. 68] **Pablo Picasso**
Buste d'homme (Bust of a Man)
Mougins, November 8, 1970
Oil on plywood, 96.5 × 57.5 cm
Fundación Almine y Bernard Ruiz-Picasso
para el Arte, Madrid
Inv. 13712

[Cat. 69] **Pablo Picasso**
*Portrait de Jacqueline à la fraise
(Portrait of Jacqueline with Collar)*
Mougins, April 10, 1962
Linoleum: gouge and scraper on two
sheets of linoleum, stamped in six
passages on Arches vellum paper
62.5 × 44 cm
Museo Picasso Málaga
Donation of Bernard Ruiz-Picasso
Inv. MPM2.153

[Cat. 70] **Pablo Picasso**
*L'Homme à la fraise
(Portrait of a Man in a Ruff)*
Mougins, April 9, 1962
Edition Galerie Louise Leiris (1963)
Color linocut, using a gauge; print with
five colors on black background on
Vélin d'Arches, frame in brown printed
from a second sheet of linoleum
62.5 × 44 cm
Kunstmuseum Basel, Kupferstichkabinett
Ankauf 1963
Inv. 1963.171

[Cat. 71] **Pablo Picasso**
Buste d'homme (Bust of a Man)
September 22, 1969
Oil on canvas, 130 × 97 cm
Museum Frieder Burda, Baden-Baden
Inv. 571

[Cat. 72] **Pablo Picasso**
*Mousquetaire et amour
(Musketeer and Amor)*
Mougins, February 18, 1969
Oil on canvas, 194.5 × 130 cm
Museum Ludwig, Cologne, donation Sammlung
Ludwig 1976
Inv. ML 01019

[Cat. 73] **El Greco (Workshop)**
Christ Taking Leave of His Mother
ca. 1595
Oil on canvas, 131 × 92 cm
Property of the parish church of San Nicolás de Bari
– Archdiocese de Toledo, Spain; on permanent loan
to the Museo de Santa Cruz de Toledo

[Cat. 74] **Pablo Picasso**
Le Couple (The Couple)
June 10, 1967
Oil on canvas, 195 × 130 cm
Kunstmuseum Basel, gift of the artist to the
municipality of Basel; permanent loan from
the City of Basel, 1967
Inv. G 1967.13

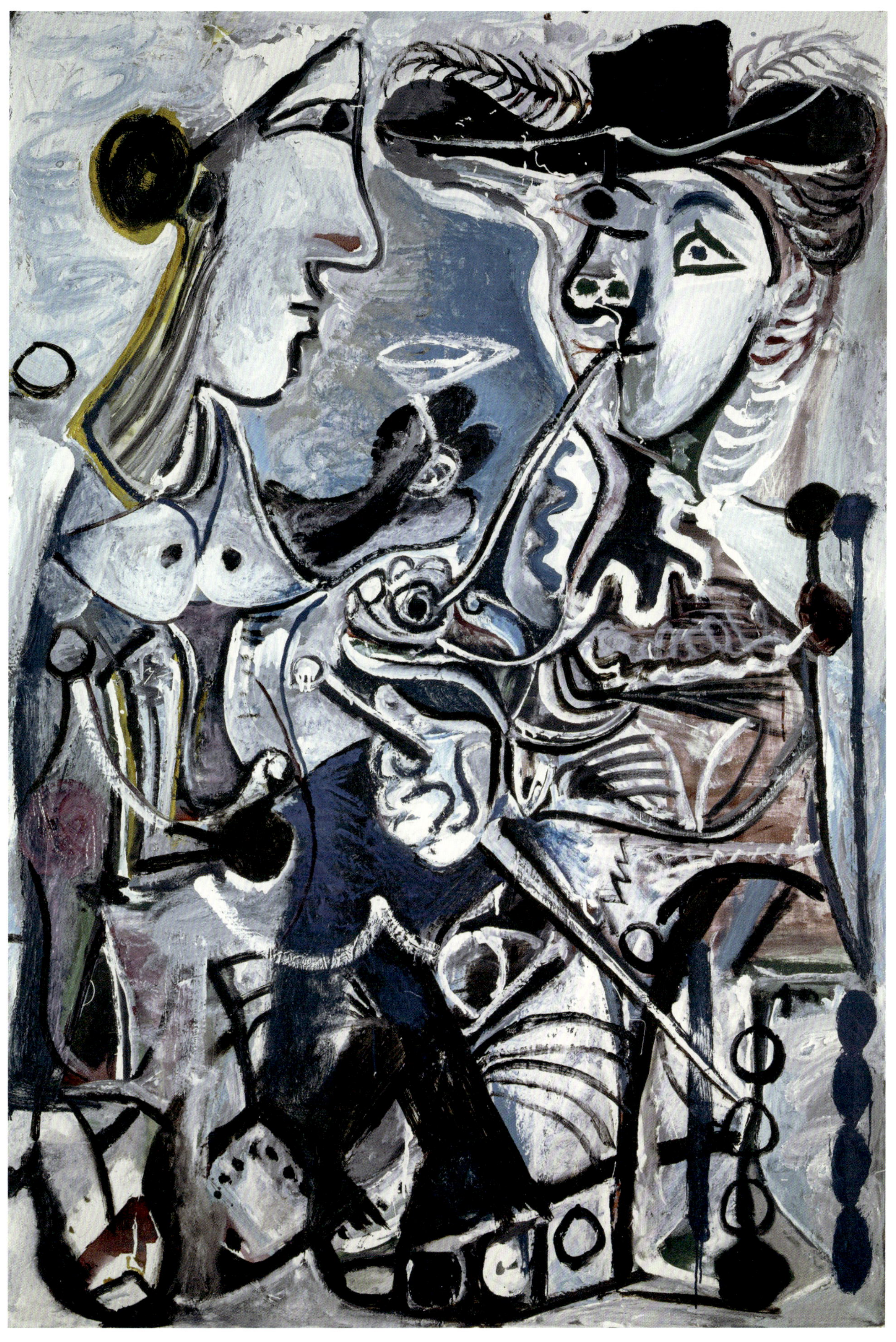

[Cat. 74]
Pablo Picasso, *Le Couple,* 1967

Chronology

El Greco

1541

Domenikos Theotokopoulos is born in Candia (modern Heraklion), capital of the island of Crete, which is under Venetian rule at the time. His family belongs to the Greek Orthodox middle class; his father, Georgios Theotokopoulos, is a tax collector for the Venetian authorities. The year of El Greco's birth has been calculated from a 1606 document in which he states that his age is sixty-five.

1556

Philip II (1527–1598) is crowned king of Spain.

1561

Philip II moves his court from Toledo to Madrid.

1563

A document dated September 28 names El Greco as "maestro Domengo Theotocopuli," evidence that he had completed his training as an icon painter by this point.

The Roman Catholic Church concludes its Council of Trent, which has met since 1545 to plan Counter-Reformation strategies in response to the Protestant Reformation. Of particular importance to Catholic art is the discussion about religious images; countering the Protestant charge of idolatry, the Council instead emphasizes the role of devotional images in supporting Catholic pedagogy and building faith. The bishops are tasked with inspecting all church art for "profane" content and, if necessary, censoring it. The Council's decrees allow Pope Pius V (pontificate 1566–72) to lay down strict rules and strengthen the power of the papacy; these rules significantly influence Rome and Catholic Europe in the late 1560s and early 1570s.

Building work begins on the Escorial, Philip II's new residence fifty kilometers northwest of Madrid. This vast complex, one of the largest late Renaissance constructions in Europe, is dominated by the basilica at its center and combines the functions of palace, monastery, and royal burial vaults (the Pantheon).

1564

Michelangelo (1475–1564) dies in Rome and is buried in Florence in the church of Santa Croce.

1566

On December 26, El Greco agrees to sell an icon, *The Passion of Christ*, in a lottery. Georgios Klontzas (1540–1608), one of Crete's most highly regarded icon painters at the time, appraises it at an impressive seventy ducats.

1568

El Greco is in Venice. Scholars dispute whether he actually worked in the studio of Titian (ca. 1488–1576), though the miniaturist Giulio Clovio (1498–1578) later claims this in a letter written from Rome to Cardinal Alessandro Farnese (1520–1589). El Greco's intense engagement with Venetian artists—including Titian, Jacopo Tintoretto (1518–1594), Jacopo Bassano (ca. 1510–1592), and Paolo Veronese (1528–1588)—will have an important impact on his subsequent work.

The Eighty Years' War begins, with the Seventeen Provinces of the Habsburg Netherlands fighting for independence from Spain (1568–1648).

1570

El Greco leaves Venice and travels through Italy to Rome. Thanks to the good offices of Giulio Clovio, El Greco joins Cardinal Farnese's household at Palazzo Farnese. Here he is part of a distinguished circle of artists, collectors, and humanist scholars, among them Fulvio Orsini (1529–1600), who has close ties to Spanish dignitaries. The contacts that El Greco makes in Rome are probably crucial to his later move to Spain.

1571

The Battle of Lepanto on October 7 results in the defeat of the Ottoman fleet in the Gulf of Patras by the Holy League – an alliance of Spain, the Papal States, Venice, and other Italian states – under the command of Philip II's half-brother, Don John of Austria.

In late October, El Greco's elder brother Manusso Theotokopoulos, a mariner, travels to Venice to ask permission to engage in piracy against the Ottomans.

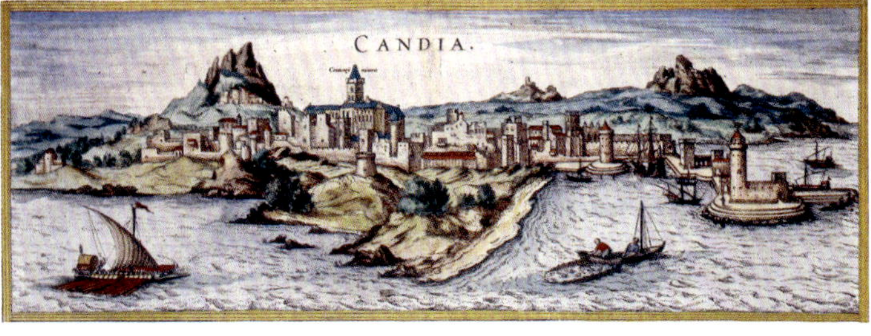

Georg Braun (1542–1622) and
Franz Hogenberg (ca. 1540–ca. 1590)
View of Candia, ca. 1572
Copperplate engraving

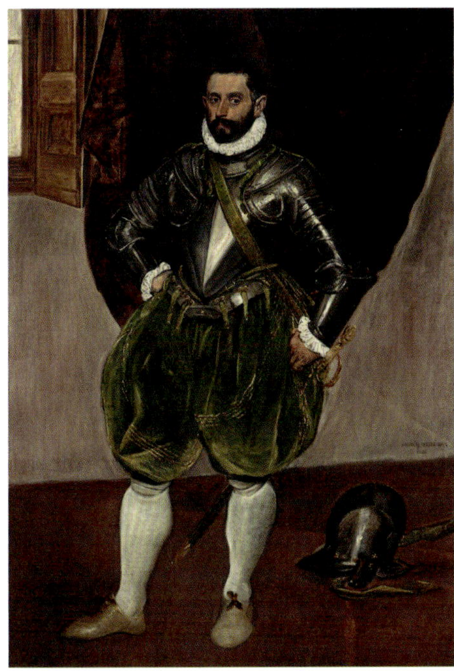

El Greco
Vincenzo Anastagi, ca. 1575
Oil on canvas, 188 × 126.7 cm
The Frick Collection, New York

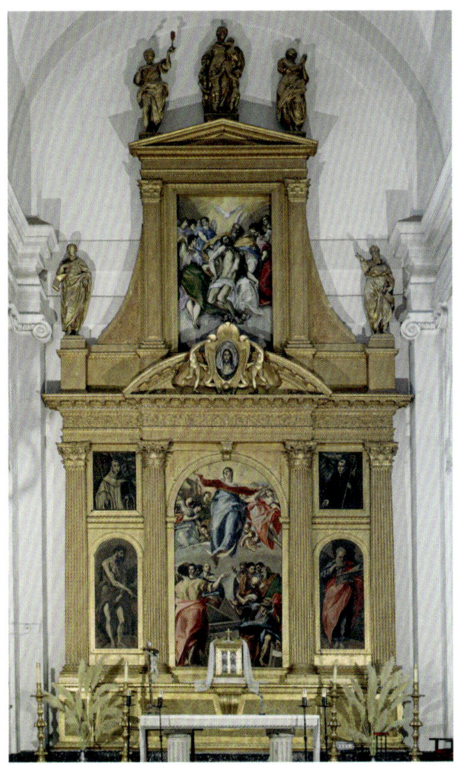

The main altarpiece of the convent church of Santo Domingo El Antiguo, which El Greco executed between 1577 and 1579. Many of the component paintings were subsequently dispersed and have been substituted with copies; only *Saint John the Baptist* and *Saint John the Evangelist* (lower right and lower left, respectively) remain in situ.
Iglesia de Santo Domingo El Antiguo, Toledo

1572

El Greco is expelled from Palazzo Farnese for unknown reasons. In a letter to the cardinal dated July 6, he complains of the injustice of the accusations against him. Later (circa 1620), Giulio Mancini relates that El Greco had affronted the artists of Rome by offering to paint a new, improved version of the *Last Judgment* in the Sistine Chapel for the stringent Pope Pius V. (Even before its completion in 1541, Michelangelo's fresco had been criticized for nudity and lack of "decorum.") Mancini's account cannot be confirmed, nor if proven, would it be possible to say whether El Greco's dismissal from Cardinal Farnese's employ had anything to do with insulting Michelangelo's reputation.

On September 18, El Greco joins the Roman painters' guild, the Compagnia di San Luca, and opens his own studio shortly afterward. He employs as his assistant the painter Lattanzio Bonastri da Lucignano (ca. 1550–1590).

1574

A second assistant Francesco Preboste (or Prevoste, 1544–1607) joins the studio. Preboste will later accompany El Greco to Spain and remain in his workshop until the end of his life.

1575

In May, a Knight of Malta named Vincenzo Anastagi (1531–1586) is appointed Sergeant Major of the Castel Sant'Angelo in Rome, and El Greco is commissioned to paint his portrait.

1576

El Greco and Preboste leave Rome for Spain (probably at the end of the year and certainly by the spring of 1577). El Greco presumably hopes for commissions at the Escorial, where several artists are in Philip II's employ.

Death of Titian in Venice.

1577

In June, El Greco signs contracts in Toledo. Diego de Castilla, dean of Toledo Cathedral (and father of his friend Luis de Castilla), commissions *The Disrobing of Christ* (fig. p. 41) for the cathedral sacristy as well as eight altarpieces for the monastery of Santo Domingo el Antiguo. In the same period, El Greco paints *The Adoration of the Name of Jesus* (cat. 16), possibly an allegory of the 1571 Battle of Lepanto. This painting, which contains a portrait of Philip II, is presumably an attempt to garner favor with the king.

1578

Birth of El Greco's son Jorge Manuel Theotocopuli (1578–1631) to Jeronima de las Cuevas, about whom nothing is known. The boy is named after El Greco's father and brother. He will later become a painter like his father and will take over his studio in Toledo after his death.

1579

Completion of *The Disrobing of Christ*.

On June 15, El Greco meets with Archbishop Garcia de Loaysa Giron, head architect of the cathedral of Toledo, for an appraisal of the painting. This leads to the first of the legal disputes that will mark almost all El Greco's important commissions. While El Greco's appraisers value the painting at 900 ducats, the cathedral representatives put it at only 227 ducats. They also raise several theological objections (see p. 41).

On July 23, the painting is appraised again and valued at 317 ducats, but no agreement is reached.

Not until December 8, 1581 will El Greco accept a payment of 350 ducats, but he does not undertake the changes that the authorities request.

The altarpieces for Santo Domingo el Antiguo are installed in time for the monastery's consecration on September 22, 1579.

1579–80

Philip II commissions El Greco to paint *The Martyrdom of Saint Maurice and the Theban Legion* (fig. p. 42) for the altar of a side chapel in the basilica of the Escorial. The contract stipulates that the artist is responsible for procuring his own materials and must find supporters to bear the costs. When El Greco fails to raise the necessary sum, the king writes a letter to the prior of the Escorial on April 25, 1580, instructing him to put the money at El Greco's disposal.

1582

Death of Carmelite mystic Teresa de Ávila (1515–1582). She is beatified in 1614, declared a patroness of Spain in 1617, and canonized in 1622.

1583

The *Martyrdom of Saint Maurice* is valued at 800 ducats, but despite this unusually high price, the painting fails to win the king's approval and is relegated to a less prominent place in the basilica. A replacement work is commissioned from Italian artist Romulo Cincinnato (ca. 1502–1593), an arbitrator at the appraisal of El Greco's painting.

1584

El Greco is commissioned to design a frame for *The Disrobing of Christ*; he is paid 570 ducats upon its completion in 1587.
Completion of the Escorial.

1585

After settling in Toledo permanently, El Greco rents three apartments in the Marques de Villena's palace on September 10. Here he has his studio and lives with his son Jorge Manuel. Because of the high costs of running the workshop and the frequent delays in payment resulting from lengthy lawsuits, El Greco is in debt for long periods of his life.

1586

The Roman painter Federico Zuccari (1539–1609) visits Toledo. It is believed to be during this visit that he gives El Greco his annotated 1568 copy of Giorgio Vasari's *Lives of the Artists*. El Greco's extensive marginalia provide much useful information about his views on art.
On March 18, parish priest Andrés Núñez de Madrid commissions El Greco to paint *The Burial of the Count of Orgaz* for the church of Santo Tomé in Toledo. The painting is to depict the legendary appearance of Saints Augustine and Stephen at the burial in 1327 of the philanthropist Gonzalo Ruiz de Toledo, Count of Orgaz. El Greco includes portraits of several contemporary Toldean dignitaries. There are debates to this day as to whether one of the men looking out of the painting is a self-portrait, but there is no proof either way.

1587

The relics of an early Christian martyr, Saint Leocadia of Toledo, are ceremonially transferred to Toledo Cathedral. El Greco designs two triumphal arches for the related procession, which is attended by Philip II.

1588

On July 1, El Greco and Preboste send two pictures of saints to art dealers Jerónimo González and Pedro López de Párraga in Seville, with permission to collect payment for them. Later, El Greco will often put paintings from his studio on the art market.
Three years into the Anglo-Spanish War (1585–1604), Philip II sends a highly armed fleet – the Spanish Armada – toward England, but it suffers a crushing defeat.

1589

On December 27, El Greco signs a contract, renewing his rental agreement. The document names him as a resident of Toledo.

1591

On February 14, El Greco is commissioned to make a side altar for the church of San Andrés in Talavera la Vieja (Cáceres). The painting and sculptures are completed and installed in 1592.

1594

Death of Jacopo Tintoretto in Venice.

1595

Pedro Salazar de Mendoza (ca. 1549–1629), administrator of the Hospital de Tavera and canon of Toledo's cathedral, commissions El Greco to make a tabernacle. The work includes statues of four Latin fathers of the church and *Risen Christ*. El Greco will work for the Hospital de Tavera again at the end of his life.

1596

In December, the Council of Castile commissions El Greco to create a monumental multipart altarpiece (now dispersed) for the church of the Augustinian seminary of Doña María de Aragón in Madrid, including a *Resurrection of Christ* (cat. 50). Although the list of sponsors mentioned in the contract suggests a large network of supporters, El Greco is obliged

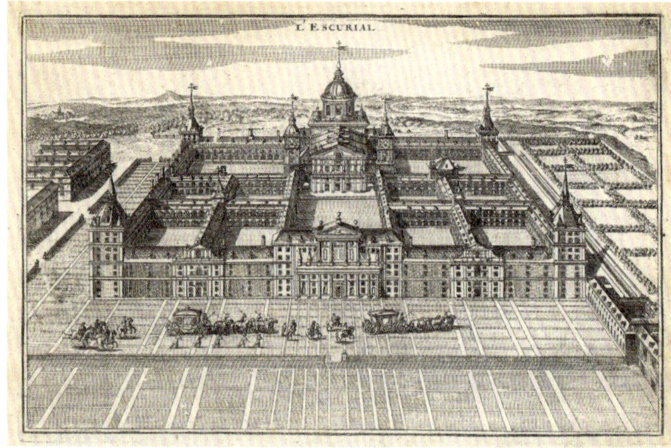

Seventeenth-century bird's-eye view of the Palace-Monastery of San Lorenzo de El Escorial (built between 1563 and 1684)
Engraving

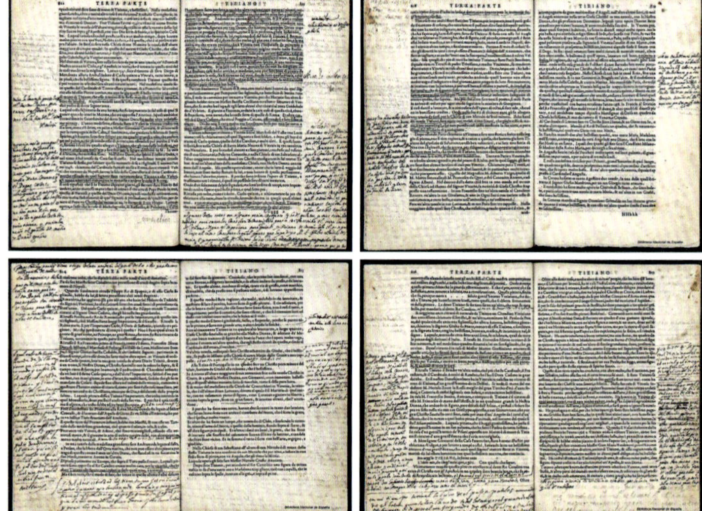

El Greco's annotations to the entry "Tiziano" in the second edition of Giorgio Vasari's *Le vite de' più eccellenti pittori, scultori, e architettori* (Florence, 1568), pp. 812–19
Biblioteca Nacional de España, Madrid

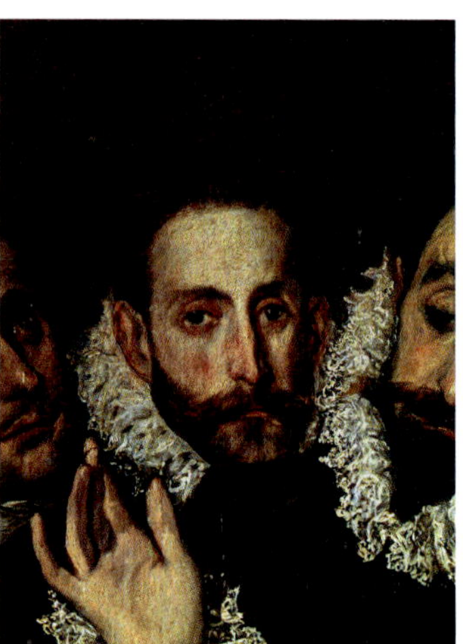

El Greco
The Burial of the Count of Orgaz (detail), 1586–88
Oil on canvas, 480 × 360 cm
Iglesia de Santo Tomé, Toledo
(See fig. p. 14)

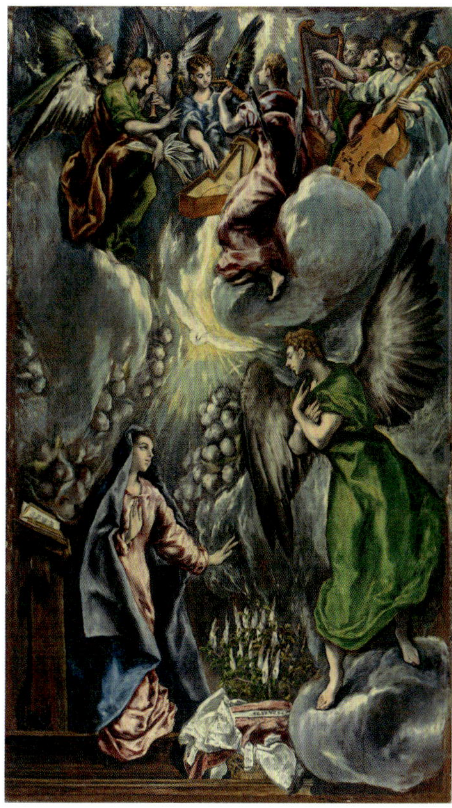

El Greco
The Annunciation, ca. 1597–1600
Oil on canvas, 315 × 174 cm
Museo Nacional del Prado, Madrid

to obtain court orders in 1597 and 1599 for the advance of two thousand ducats stipulated in his contract. There are further delays in payment even after the work has been completed, transported to Madrid, and appraised at six thousand ducats.

1597

On April 16, El Greco is commissioned to make the high altar for the royal monastery of Santa María de Guadalupe southwest of Toledo. He is offered a staggering sum of sixteen thousand ducats for the work, which is to be completed within eight years. In case of his death, the altar is to be finished by Preboste and Jorge Manuel.

A document from May 24 shows that El Greco and Preboste send more paintings to dealers in Seville.

On November 9, Martín Ramírez de Zayas commissions El Greco to paint three altarpieces for his private family chapel of San José in Toledo.

1598

Death of Philip II on September 13. Philip III (1578–1621) is crowned king of Spain.

Birth of Gian Lorenzo Bernini (1598–1680).

1599

On December 13, the altarpieces for the chapel of San José are valued at 2,848 ducats. El Greco's client, Ramírez de Zayas, agrees to pay only after a second appraisal has confirmed the valuation. But he does pay 636 ducats to El Greco's creditors: 136 ducats to a draper and 500 ducats to the still-life painter Juan Sánchez Cotán (1560–1627).

Birth of Diego Velázquez (1599–1660).

1600

On December 12, a certain Luis Pantoja Portocarrero issues El Greco a receipt for rental payment, suggesting that the artist has moved to new accommodations.

1603

El Greco is commissioned to paint an altarpiece for the Franciscan college of San Bernardino de Siena in Toledo. For this he is paid about

275 ducats in total, receiving his final payment on September 10, 1604.

Jorge Manuel, now about twenty-five years old, is beginning to assume more responsibility in the studio, appearing in documents as El Greco's assistant and business partner, witnessing contracts, and collecting fees for his father (fig. p. 26). It is he who secures the contract for the paintings in the chapel of the Hospital Nuestra Señora de la Caridad in Illescas.

Luis Tristán de Escamilla (ca. 1585–1624), later one of Toledo's most important painters, enters El Greco's studio as an apprentice and remains until about 1606.

1604

On August 5, El Greco again rents twenty-four rooms in the Marques de Villena's palace at an annual rent of 175 ducats. He will remain here until his death in 1614.

1605

A two-year-long dispute arises over the payment of the altarpiece for the chapel of the Hospital de la Caridad. Complaints are made on three counts: cracks in the woodwork, El Greco's failure to meet the deadline, and the presence of contemporary figures in the painting, which are deemed likely to distract viewers from their devotion (fig. p. 40).

1606

In connection with the dispute over the altarpiece for the Hospital de la Caridad, El Greco requests a tax exemption, which is granted to him. It is the first time that an artist in Spain is exempt from taxation.

On August 25, El Greco and Jorge Manuel are offered 900 ducats to paint an altarpiece for Juan Bautista de Úbeda's family chapel in the parish church of San Ginés in Madrid.

On November 7, Jorge Manuel accepts a commission in his father's name to paint the main altarpiece and two side altars of the parish church of San Martín de Montalbán, near Toledo.

Miguel de Cervantes (1547–1616) publishes the first part of his novel *Don Quixote.*

The Spanish court returns to Madrid after a spell in Valladolid.

1607

In April and May, two documents name Preboste and Jorge Manuel as El Greco's representatives in all matters; Jorge Manuel holds the more important position in the studio. As these are the last written documents concerning Preboste, it seems likely that he died later in the year.

On November 28, El Greco is commissioned to complete a work in the Oballe Chapel in San Vicente, Toledo after the death of artist Alejandro Semín (ca. 1551–1607). Various changes are to be made, including enlarging the altarpiece, replacing the frescoes with oil paintings, and adding a framed scene of the *Visitation* (fig. p. 19). A document from December 12 notes that the sum of 1,280 ducats has been agreed upon as payment.

On April 25, the Spanish Armada suffers a final and devastating defeat in the Battle of Gibraltar at the hands of a Dutch fleet.

1608

On November 16, El Greco takes on his last big commission: three elaborate altarpieces with several paintings and sculptures for the Hospital de Tavera in Toledo. The work, which is incomplete at his death in 1614, will be continued by his son Jorge Manuel.

1610

Death of Michelangelo Merisi, known as Caravaggio (1571–1610), in Porto Ercole.

1611

Francisco Pacheco (1564–1644) visits El Greco in Toledo; he gives a detailed account of the visit in his posthumously published treatise *El arte de la pintura* (1649). Beside a description of the studio, Pacheco's text contains information about El Greco's views on art—his preference, for example, for the Venetian art of Titian over that of Michelangelo.

The Toledo city councilors commission El Greco and Jorge Manuel to design a monument for the funeral ceremony of Philip II's widow, Margaret of Austria (1584–1611). The memorial is extolled in a sonnet by the Trinitarian monk Hortensio Félix Paravicino y Arteaga (1580–1633), a famous orator and poet (fig. p. 63).

1612

El Greco and Jorge Manuel buy a family tomb in the monastery church of Santo Domingo el Antiguo in Toledo. As part of the contract they agree to provide the church with an additional altarpiece, and El Greco starts work on *The Adoration of the Shepherds*, the last painting that he lives to complete (fig. p. 43). It will be installed in the church in 1614.

1613

El Greco completes his work for the Oballe Chapel and asks for an appraisal. The paintings, however, will not be installed in the chapel until 1615.

1614

A document from March 31 tells us that El Greco is confined to his bed; he gives his son and sole heir Jorge Manuel power of attorney to draw up his will, pay off his debts, and arrange his funeral. El Greco's old friend Luis de Castilla is to act as his executor.

El Greco dies in Toledo on April 7. After a funeral procession through the city and a sung mass in Santo Domingo el Antiguo, he is buried in the family tomb. In the days that follow, several other masses are held for El Greco in Toledo: three in Santo Domingo el Antiguo and a total of ten in the churches of San Pedro Mártir and Santísima Trinidad. In the months to come, Jorge Manuel will order another hundred masses for the soul of his dead father in the churches of Santo Tomé and Santo Domingo el Antiguo.

Beside various pieces of equipment from his studio, the inventory drawn up after El Greco's death includes 150 drawings, a similar number of paintings (some incomplete), and more than a hundred books in different languages and on subjects ranging from theory of art and architecture to theology.

1618

Beginning of the Thirty Years' War.

1619

After disputes over the payment of the family tomb in Santo Domingo el Antiguo arising from the lower-than-expected valuation of *The Adoration of the*

Shepherds, Jorge Manuel acquires a new burial vault in the church of San Torcuato in Toledo, and El Greco's remains are transferred there.

1621

Philipp IV (1605–1665) is crowned king of Spain.

A further inventory of El Greco's estate is made on the occasion of Jorge Manuel's second marriage.

1622

On April 18, representatives of the Hospital de Tavera try to have Jorge Manuel arrested for failing to complete the work commissioned from El Greco in 1608. Jorge Manuel refutes the charges, but some of his possessions are seized. A year later the paintings are delivered to the Hospital, but the legal disputes over further work and payment are still unresolved at Jorge Manuel's death nine years later.

1631

On March 28, Jorge Manuel Theotocopuli dies in Toledo. He is buried the following day in the family tomb in San Torcuato.

1641

Publication of *Obras posthumas, divinas y humanas*, a collection of poems by Hortensio Félix Paravicino, including four sonnets in praise of El Greco.

1648

The Thirty Years' War ends with the Peace of Westphalia. At the same time, the Dutch Republic is finally recognized as a sovereign state and the Eighty Years' War also comes to an end.

1649

Arte de la pintura, su antiguedad y grandeza by painter and art theorist Francisco Pacheco is published posthumously. The treatise contains a detailed account of his 1611 visit to El Greco's studio in Toledo. Pacheco's assessment of El Greco's artistic skills is ambivalent, oscillating between admiration and rejection. Although he finds words of praise for El Greco's portraits, he shows little understanding of his painting style, writing disparagingly of his "crueles borrones," (cruel stains, or rough blotches). Pacheco also disputes El Greco's opinion that Michelangelo was a good sculptor but did not know how to paint.

1659
The Peace of the Pyrenees ends the Franco-Spanish War (1635–59).

1661
Louis XIV (1638–1715), king of France since 1643, emerges from the regency of Anne of Austria and Cardinal Jules Mazarin to assume total control as "Sun King."

1724
Artist and biographer Antonio Palomino (1653–1726) publishes the third volume of his influential treatise *El museo pictórico y escala óptica*, which contains the biographies of many Spanish artists, including El Greco. Drawing on Pacheco's account, among others, Palomino writes admiringly of El Greco's portraits and lauds his efforts—by waging lawsuits against stingy clients—to defend the honor and freedom of art; but otherwise he has only faint praise and starts a number of rumors. He writes, for instance, that El Greco's "extravagant" style was part of an attempt to distinguish his own paintings from those of Titian. In his chapter on Velázquez, whom he considers the acme of Spanish painting, Palomino laments "the bizarreness into which [El Greco] fell at the end" and passes the damning verdict "that whatever he did well, no one did better, and what he did badly, no one did worse." These disparaging remarks will shape the public perception of El Greco until well into the nineteenth century.

1789
The Storming of the Bastille marks the beginning of the French Revolution.

1792
Outbreak of the French Revolutionary Wars, a series of military conflicts pitting France against the monarchies of Europe in shifting coalitions. From 1796, a young military leader named Napoleon Bonarparte (1769–1821) begins to distinguish himself on the battlefield.

1798
European Powers and the Ottoman Empire form the second coalition against France.

1799
Napoleon becomes First Consul of France and declares the revolution over. Conflict continues to engulf Europe and the Mediterranean. The subsequent Napoleonic Wars (1803–15) profoundly shape power politics throughout Europe, including Spain.

1804
Napoleon crowns himself emperor.

1807–08
Beginning of the Peninsular War, with Napoleonic troops encroaching on and then occupying Spanish territory. Francisco de Goya (1746–1828) documents the atrocities against the civilian population in his prints and paintings.

1812
Spain adopts its first liberal constitution – the Constitution of Cádiz – but it is revoked in 1814 with the return to absolute monarchy. The constitution is subsequently reinstated for two brief periods (1820–23, 1836–37) before being superseded by the Spanish Constitution of 1837, another short-lived constitution, which is revoked in 1845.

1815
Napoleon's defeat at Waterloo marks the end of the Napoleonic Wars. The Congress of Vienna establishes a new political order in Europe.

1821
Two years after the opening of the Museo del Prado, the catalogue lists only one work by El Greco, a portrait. It is displayed in the gallery alongside works of the Venetian masters Titian and Veronese.

1824
End of Spanish colonial rule in South America.

1832
The Prado now has ten works by El Greco in its possession, but there is still only one on display.

1833
Isabella II (1830–1904) ascends to the Spanish throne, reigning until 1868.

1838
In France, King Louis Philippe (1773–1850) presents his "Galerie espagnole" in five rooms of the Louvre. It is the first time that such an extensive collection of Spanish art has been on public display in Paris. Several paintings by El Greco are exhibited alongside works by Francisco de Zurbarán (1598–1664), Bartolomé Esteban Murillo (1617–1682), Jusepe de Ribera (1591–1652), and Velázquez. Among them are *Lady in a Fur Wrap* (cat. 22)—a work attributed to El Greco until a few decades ago—and the smaller version of the *Adoration of the Name of Jesus* (cat. 17). The collection is enthusiastically received, not only by artists and critics but also by the general public. El Greco, hitherto largely unknown, enjoys his first, modest popularity.

1848
The Louvre's Spanish gallery is disbanded after Louis Philippe's abdication; he takes the paintings with him into exile in England. After his death, the collection is auctioned in 1853 in London.

1849
Founding of the Democratic Party in Spain.

1865
Édouard Manet (1832–1883) travels to Madrid; in a letter to art critic Zacharie Astruc (1833–1907) he mentions not only Diego Velázquez and Francisco de Goya, but also El Greco.

1872
The Prado acquires fifteen additional works by El Greco, most of them religious paintings, when it incorporates the collections of the disbanded Museo de la Trinidad.

1873
On February 11, the First Spanish Republic is proclaimed, following the abdication of Amadeo I (1845–1890) after only two years on the throne. It lasts only until December 29, 1874, when the monarchy is restored.

Pablo Picasso

1881

Pablo Picasso is born on October 25 in Málaga, the first child of Don José Ruiz y Blasco (1838–1913), a painter of Basque origins, and María Picasso y Lopez (1855–1939) from Andalusia. His father works as a drawing teacher at the San Telmo School of Art in Málaga.

Most of the El Grecos on display in the Prado at this time are portraits. The museum director, Federico de Madrazo (1815–1894), tells art historian Carl Justi (1832–1912) that El Greco's religious paintings are "absurd caricatures" and laments being unable to get rid of them.

1883

Architect Antoni Gaudí (1852–1926) begins work on the Sagrada Família in Barcelona.

1884

Birth of Picasso's first sister, Dolores (Lola) on December 15.

1887

Birth of Picasso's second sister, Concepción (Conchita).

1888

Picasso's father gives him his first drawing lesson.

1888

Universal Exposition in Barcelona.

1891

After several attempts, Picasso's father is hired that April by the Instituto da Guarda in La Coruña to teach art. The family moves to La Coruña.

1892

At the age of eleven, Picasso enters the Escuela de Bellas Artes in La Coruña, which he attends alongside regular school and where his father teaches him drawing and ornament.

1893

Picasso moves up to the life-drawing class. He also draws war scenes, portraits of his family, and landscape sketches.

1894

Impressed by his son's success, Don José presents him with his palette, paints, and brushes and declares he will renounce his own career as an artist.

Catalan artist Santiago Rusiñol (1861–1931) buys two paintings by El Greco and carries them in a procession to his studio in Sitges.

1895

In the spring, Picasso pays his first visit to the Prado, where he makes two sketches inspired by Velázquez and discovers the work of Goya.

After the death from diphtheria of Picasso's seven-year-old sister Concepción, the family moves to Barcelona. His father starts to teach drawing at the art school La Llotja, and Picasso passes the entrance exam with flying colors and is accepted there as a student.

1896

At the age of fifteen, Picasso moves into his first studio on Calle de la Plata in Barcelona. He paints *The First Communion* for the Exposición de Bellas Artes é Industrias Artísticas, which opens on April 23. The picture, which shows his other sister, Lola, is one of his first attempts at religious genre painting. In the same year he receives his first paid commission: two paintings in the style of Murillo for a convent in Barcelona.

1897

Picasso is accepted at the Real Academia de Bellas Artes de San Fernando and moves to Madrid. He attends the academy from October 1897 until June 1898. During that time, he returns to the Prado to study the work of Velázquez and El Greco. He is particularly fascinated by El Greco, and together with some fellow students and his teacher José Moreno Carbonero, he travels to Toledo to see El Greco's masterpiece, *The Burial of the Count of Orgaz*. He makes a caricature of the painting, replacing El Greco's figures with his teachers from the Academia.

1898

Picasso falls ill with scarlet fever. When he is better, his best friend Manuel Pallarès (1876–1974) invites him to stay on the family farm in Horta de Sant Joan (Horta de Ebro) to recuperate. While there, Picasso paints studies

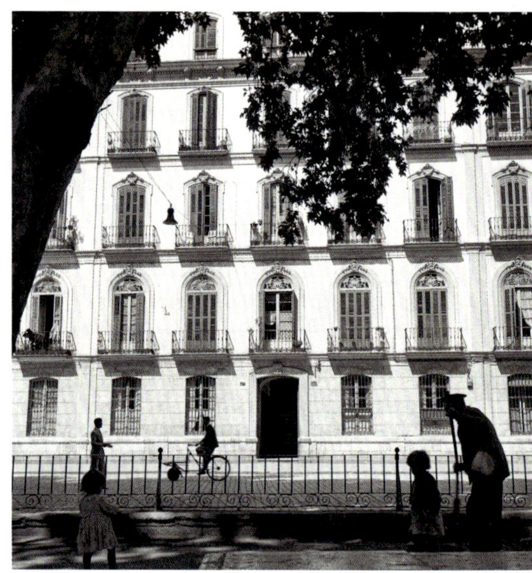

Herbert List
Picasso's birthplace in Malaga, 1951
Exposure of a 6-x-6-centimeter negative

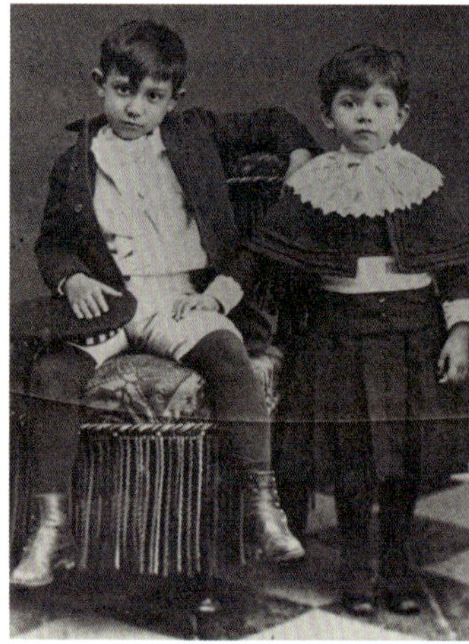

Picasso at the age of seven with his sister,
Lola Ruiz Picasso (1884–1958) in Malaga, 1888
From Pablo Picasso's private archive
Silver gelatin print, 12 × 9 cm
Musée national Picasso, Paris
Gift of the Picasso Estate, 1992

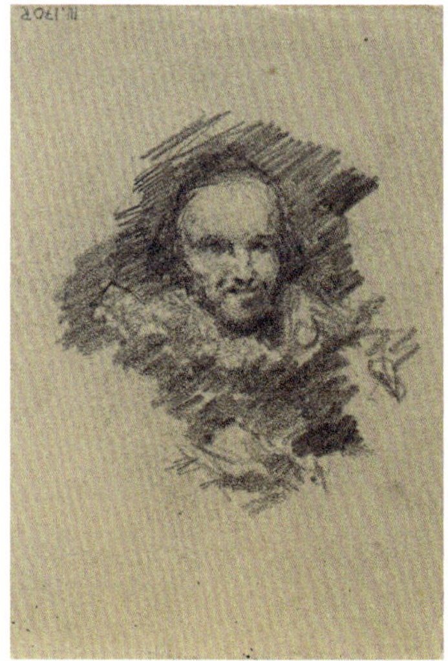

Pablo Picasso
Copy of *The Buffoon Calabacillas*
by Velázquez, April 16, 1895
Sketchbook page, graphite pencil on paper
12.2 × 8.1 cm
Museu Picasso, Barcelona
Gift of Pablo Picasso, 1970

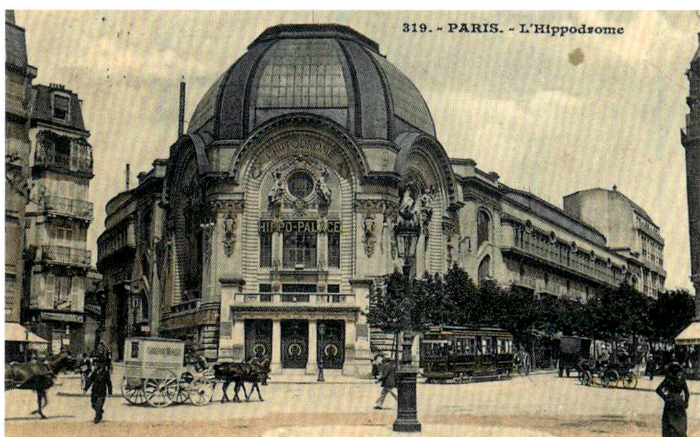

The Café de L'Hippodrome in Paris on the
boulevard de Clichy, ca. 1911
Postcard, 5.2 × 8.2 cm

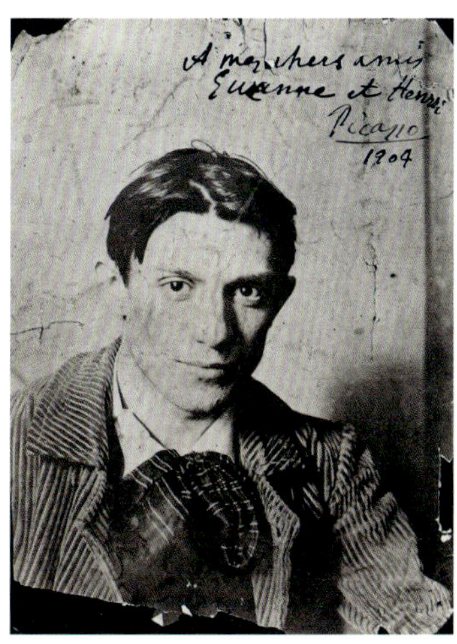

Ricardo Canals y Llambi
Photograph of the young Picasso with
handwritten dedication to Suzanne and
Henri Bloch, 1904
Silver gelatin print, dimensions unknown
Musée national Picasso

of nature and landscape, in which he begins to break with the academicism of his father.

A monument to El Greco is erected in the town of Sitges (fig. p. 56) at Rusiñol's instigation.

On April 23, the Spanish-American War breaks out. It ends on August 12 with the loss of Spain's last important colonies.

1899

In January, the seventeen-year-old Picasso returns to Barcelona, where he has a studio on Calle de Escudellers Blancs. He joins the large circle of avant-garde artists who meet in Els Quatre Gats, a cabaret and French café. Among them are painters Carles Casagemas (1880–1901), Isidre Nonell (1872–1911), and Sebastià Junyer-Vidal (1878–1966), and sculptors Julio González (1876–1942) and Manolo Martínez Hugué (1872–1945). Picasso also gets to know the writer Jaume (Jaime) Sabartés (1881–1968), who will later become his secretary (cat. 59). He becomes a member of the Cercle Artístic de Barcelona and is an increasingly enthusiastic devotee the Catalan Modernism movement.

Picasso "signs" one of his many El Greco-style sketches with the words "Yo El Greco" (cat. 5); in another, he draws inspiration from El Greco and Velázquez (cat. 6).

1900

The Art Nouveau-influenced journal *Juventud* (Youth) publishes Picasso's first illustrations.

In February, he holds his first exhibition of about 150 drawings at Els Quatre Gats. From now on he will sign his work with his mother's maiden name.

After renting a studio together on Riera de Sant Joan, Casagemas and Picasso travel to Paris in the autumn. Picasso immerses himself in the art scene of Montmartre and takes a keen interest in Impressionist and Post-Impressionist painting. He also meets journalist and poet Max Jacob (1876–1944).

1901

Casagemas commits suicide in the Hippodrome café because of a failed love affair. Picasso is deeply shaken by the loss of his friend. The news reaches

him while he is in Spain, and the month of February also includes travel to Toledo. He begins to processCasagemas's death in a series of pictures clearly influenced by El Greco (cats. 15, 17). These pictures also mark the beginning of Picasso's Blue Period—paintings dominated by a palette of blue and green tones, steeped in melancholy, and pervaded by themes of poverty, old age, and loneliness. Together with Francisco de Asís Soler, Picasso founds the journal *Arte Joven* in Madrid. When it folds after only four issues, he returns to Paris, where Max Jacob puts him up. On June 24, an exhibition showing sixty-four of Picasso's paintings opens in the gallery of Ambroise Vollard (1865–1939); many paintings are sold.

1902

The Prado dedicates its first solo exhibition to the work of El Greco, with a total of eighty-four paintings.

1903

In January, Picasso goes to Barcelona. This time he stays a year before returning to Paris.

Death of Paul Gauguin (1848–1903).

1904

On April 12, Picasso settles permanently in Paris. The art dealer Paul Durand-Ruel (1831–1922) finds him a studio at the Bateau-Lavoir in Montmartre at a monthly rent of fifteen francs. Picasso meets a great number of French poets and artists, among them Guillaume Apollinaire (1880–1918). He also meets Fernande Olivier (1881–1966), who models for him and will be his lover for seven years. After the Blue Period comes the brighter palette of the Rose Period, with its figures from the world of the circus: clowns, artistes, and jugglers.

1905

Picasso meets the Stein siblings —Leo Stein (1872–1947) and Gertrude Stein (1874–1946)—who will become great supporters and collectors of his work. He also gets to know Henri Matisse (1869–1954), André Derain (1880–1954), and art dealers Wilhelm Uhde (1874–1947) and Daniel-Henry Kahnweiler (1884–1979).

On February 26, an exhibition showing work by Picasso opens at Galeries Serrurier on boulevard Haussmann; paintings from the Rose Period are on view for the first time.

In spring, an exhibition of work by Vincent van Gogh (1853–1890) and Georges Seurat (1859–1891) is held at the Salon des Indépendants. The first Fauvist works by Matisse and Derain are shown at the new Salon d'Automne in the fall, along with a retrospective of Jean-Auguste-Dominique Ingres (1780–1867).

The Spanish painter Ignacio Zuloaga (1870–1945) acquires El Greco's *Vision of Saint John* (also called *The Opening of the Fifth Seal*) in Córdoba and brings it to Paris, where Picasso sees it (fig. p. 65).

1906

Picasso's palette shifts from pinks to terracottas and grays. He visits an exhibition at the Louvre of excavated Iberian sculptures from Osuna and travels to Gósol in the summer with Fernande Olivier. The influence of the Osuna figures is clear in the groups of nudes he paints at this time and in his sketches of peasants. His work is increasingly sculptural and abstract.

Ten works by Paul Cézanne (1839–1906) are exhibited at the Salon d'Automne, where there is also a retrospective of the work of Gauguin.

Death of Cézanne in Provence.

1907

Kahnweiler becomes Picasso's official dealer. Through Derain, Picasso meets Georges Braque (1882–1963), and the two painters are soon engaged in an intense artistic dialogue that will be crucial to the development of Cubism. Picasso starts work on *Les Demoiselles d'Avignon,* one of the founding works of this revolutionary new movement (fig. p. 60; cats. 27, 28). Beside artifacts from non-European cultures, such as African masks and sculptures, El Greco's *Vision of Saint John,* seen by Picasso in Zuloaga's studio, is a likely source of inspiration.

A Cézanne retrospective is held at the Salon d'Automne.

1908

At the beginning of his Cubist phase, Picasso steps up his work with Braque.

He is a keen collector of works by other artists and exhibits some of them in his studio in November. Guests include Apollinaire, Marie Laurencin (ca. 1883–1956), Leo and Gertrude Stein, Jacob, Braque, and Maurice Utrillo (1883–1955).

The Von der Heydt Museum in Wuppertal is the first German museum to acquire a painting by Picasso.

Spanish art historian Manuel B. Cossío (1857–1935) publishes his groundbreaking El Greco monograph.

Several El Grecos from Zuloaga's collection are exhibited at the Salon d'Automne.

1909

In May, Picasso and Fernande Olivier travel to Spain and spend the summer in Horta de Sant Joan. It is a productive time; Picasso paints a series of landscapes and several portraits of Fernande. These Cubist paintings are clearly influenced by Cézanne.

Back in Paris, he sells some of his work to important collectors and dealers such as Sergei Ivanovich Shchukin (1854–1936), Uhde, Vollard, and the Steins. His improved financial situation allows him and Fernande to move to 11 boulevard de Clichy in September.

An El Greco exhibition is held in the Real Academia de Bellas Artes de San Fernando in Madrid.

The journal *Revue bleue* publishes *Greco ou le secret de Tolède* (El Greco or the Secret of Toledo) in several installments; this text by French novelist and right-wing nationalist politician Maurice Barrès (1862–1923) will have an important influence on the reception of El Greco. The text will be published in book form in 1912 and translated into several languages.

1910

Exhibitions of Picasso's work are held for the first time in Germany, Budapest, and London. Picasso and Derain meet in Cadaqués in Spain. In September, Picasso returns to Paris.

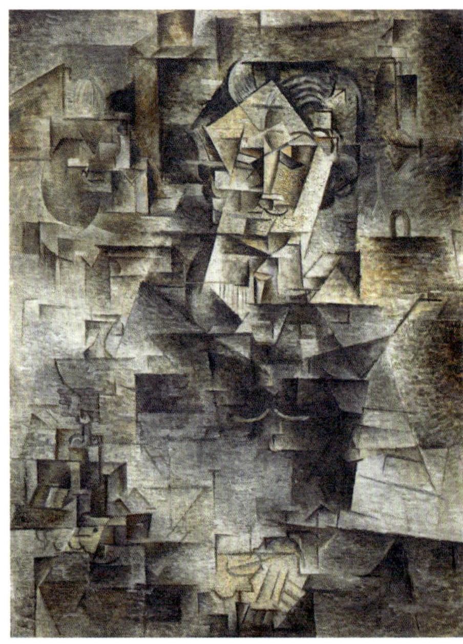

Pablo Picasso
Daniel-Henry Kahnweiler, 1910
Oil on canvas, 100.4 × 72.4 cm
The Art Institute of Chicago

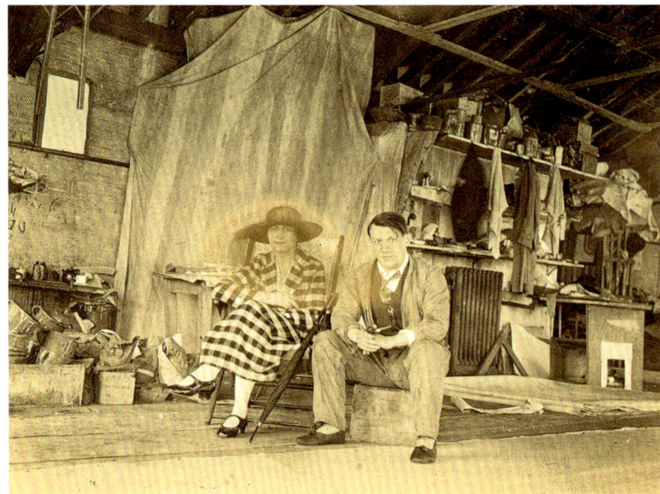

Olga Khokhlova (1891–1955) and Picasso seated in the theater workshop at Covent Garden, London, 1919
From Pablo Picasso's personal archive.
The photo album from 1919, sent by Vladimir and Elisabeth Violet Polunin, documents Picasso that summer painting the curtain for Diaghilev's ballet *Le Tricorne*
Photographic print, dimensions unknown
Musée national Picasso, Paris

The Casa y Museo de El Greco opens in Toledo. At the Prado in Madrid, almost thirty of El Greco's paintings are incorporated into the rooms of Spanish painting.

Julius Meier-Graefe (1867–1935) publishes *Spanische Reise* (*The Spanish Journey,* 1926), an at times effusive book extolling El Greco as a precursor of modern art. The book spurs, among other things, the enthusiastic reception of El Greco among the German Expressionists.

1911

In July, Picasso travels to Céret in the south of France, where Braque and Jacob visit him. His paintings show evidence of a new approach; the forms are dissected, though without reaching full-blown abstraction. This style will later be called Analytical Cubism.

On October 1, a Cubism room opens at the Salon d'Automne. Picasso is not represented, but he is mentioned in the press as one of the founders of the movement.

Picasso's work is exhibited in the United States for the first time, at Alfred Stieglitz's Gallery 291 in New York. Picasso gains increasing international recognition.

1912

Picasso's style develops toward Synthetic Cubism, characterized by flatter compositions and the return to a broader color palette. He experiments with collage and Braques's technique of papier collé, and completes his first three-dimensional constructions. His work is shown in several international exhibitions—in Cologne, Berlin, Munich, London, and Moscow.

Picasso ends his now tepid relationship with Fernande Olivier and moves into 242 boulevard Raspail with his new lover Eva Gouel (1885–1915), whom he had met a year before.

The almanac *Der Blaue Reiter* is published, including a pairing of El Greco's *Saint John the Baptist* across from a painting by Robert Delaunay (1885–1941) from his Eiffel Tower series.

1913

In February, Picasso's first big retrospective is held in the gallery of Heinrich Thannhauser in Munich: seventy-six paintings and thirty-eight watercolors.

Picasso's father José Ruiz dies on May 3.

Picasso is represented at the Armory Show in New York with eight works.

The collection of Marczell von Nemes is auctioned in Paris. It had previously been on display in several European cities such as Budapest, Munich, and Düsseldorf, with work by modern artists exhibited alongside paintings by El Greco. A total of twelve El Grecos come under the hammer, including the Saint Mary Magdalene now in Budapest (cat. 41).

1914

In June, Picasso moves to Avignon. World War I breaks out on July 28.

On August 1, France orders mobilization. As a foreigner, Picasso is exempt from French military service, but Braque is called up, and their collaboration on Cubism comes to an end. The war sparks off a general desire to abandon Modernism and return to classical traditions.

Picasso and Eva Gouel return to Paris in October.

Picasso's dealer Kahnweiler, like many German gallery owners in France, has his collection confiscated by the French government and his gallery closed. Thirty-six works by Picasso are among those confiscated.

1915

Picasso meets painter, writer, and director Jean Cocteau (1889–1963), who introduces him to impresario Sergei Diaghilev (1872–1929), founder of the Ballets Russes.

Eva Gouel dies on December 14 after contracting tuberculosis.

1916

Guillaume Apollinaire returns from the front with a head injury. Picasso makes several portraits of him. In June, five etchings and a drawing by Picasso are exhibited at the Cabaret Voltaire in Zurich, founded that February.

Soon afterward, Picasso moves to Montrouge, a southern suburb of Paris.

1917

Death of Edgar Degas (1834–1917).

At Diaghilev's request, Picasso agrees to collaborate on the ballet *Parade*. He and Cocteau travel to Rome, Naples, Pompeii, and Florence to work on the stage set and costumes. He falls in love with dancer Olga Khokhlova (1891–1955).

1918

An exhibition of works by Matisse and Picasso is held in Galerie Paul Guillaume at the beginning of the year.

On July 12, Picasso and Olga Khokhlova marry in the Russian church in Paris; witnesses are Cocteau, Jacob, and Apollinaire.

The newlyweds meet art dealer Paul Rosenberg (1881–1959) while spending the summer in Biarritz. Back in Paris in the winter they rent a duplex at 23 rue La Boétie, not far from Rosenberg's gallery. Picasso uses the upper floor as his studio.

On November 9, Guillaume Apollinaire dies of the Spanish flu. Death of Pierre-Auguste Renoir (1841–1919).

1919

Picasso enters his Classical Period, inspired by antiquity and Ingres.

In March, the young Joan Miró (1893–1983) visits him in his studio.

In May, Picasso goes to London to work on the stage set and costumes for another Ballets Russes production, *Pulcinella*.

Several exhibitions of Picasso's work are held in Rosenberg's gallery.

The Treaty of Versailles is signed on June 28.

1920

Death of Amedeo Modigliani (1884–1920).

Pulcinella premieres at the Théâtre de l'Opéra in Paris.

Picasso spends the summer in Juan-les-Pins and returns to Paris in September.

Solo exhibitions are held in Rome and Paris.

For the first time, a room in the Prado is dedicated exclusively to the work of El Greco.

1921

Birth of Paulo Picasso (1921–1975) on February 4.

Art historian Maurice Raynal (1884–1954) publishes the first ever Picasso monograph with the Delphin Verlag in Munich. The French translation comes out a year later.

In June, an auction is held of the art confiscated from Kahnweiler's gallery by the French government in 1914. Kahnweiler is able to buy back some of Picasso's work.

1922

Picasso is in the Breton coastal town of Dinard from June to September.

Jean Cocteau's *Antigone* premieres in December with a stage set designed by Picasso and Cocteau and costumes designed by Coco Chanel. Picasso meets the Dadaist—later Surrealist—poets André Breton (1896–1966), Louis Aragon (1897–1982), and Tristan Tzara (1896–1963).

1923

The May 19 issue of *The Arts* contains an interview of Picasso by Marius de Zayas (1880–1961).

Picasso spends the summer in Antibes, painting in both Cubist and classical styles.

The dictatorship of General Miguel Primo de Rivera (1870–1930) begins in Spain.

1924

Death of Léon Bakst (1866–1924), an artist associated with the Ballets Russes.

Picasso designs curtains, décor, and costumes for the ballet *Mercure*. An enlarged version of his 1922 painting *Two Women Running on the Beach* is used for the curtains of Cocteau's ballet *Le train bleu*.

Picasso returns to Juan-les-Pins for the summer.

He begins to engage with Surrealism in his art.

1925

In Paris for the first time, Salvador Dalí (1904–1989) visits Picasso.

The first Surrealist exhibition, *La Peinture surréaliste*, is held at Galerie Pierre in November; Picasso participates, along with Giorgio de Chirico (1888–1978), Max Ernst (1891–1976), and Joan Miró. But although certain aspects of Picasso's work bring him close to Surrealist principles, he would never feel that he belonged to the movement.

1926

Picasso spends the summer in Juan-les-Pins.

In October he spends a short time in Barcelona. Art historian Christian Zervos (1889–1970) founds *Cahiers d'Art*, a journal for contemporary art, and devotes several issues to Picasso. In 1932, Zervos and Picasso will work together on a catalogue raisonné of Picasso, which will eventually extend to thirty-three volumes.

1927

On January 8, Picasso meets the seventeen-year-old Marie-Thérèse Walter (1909–1977) at the Galeries Lafayette. She becomes his model and then his secret lover.

He spends the summer in Cannes, where he starts work on the *Bathers* cycle.

1928

Picasso begins to work together with sculptor Julio González.

The Picassos move to Dinard. Picasso continues to meet Marie-Thérèse Walter in secret.

1931

The Second Republic is proclaimed in Spain after the death of Miguel Primo de Riveras.

1932

Picasso paints a series of portraits of Marie-Thérèse Walter.

Another big Picasso retrospective opens in the Galeries Georges Petit on June 16. New are both the size of the exhibition (225 works) and the fact that it is curated by Picasso himself.

In the autumn, Picasso travels with his family to Zurich where his first museum exhibition opens in the Kunsthaus there.

1933

In Germany, Adolf Hitler becomes chancellor on January 30, marking the beginning of Nazi rule.

1934

Picasso travels to Spain with his wife and son, visiting among other sites, the house of El Greco in Toledo.

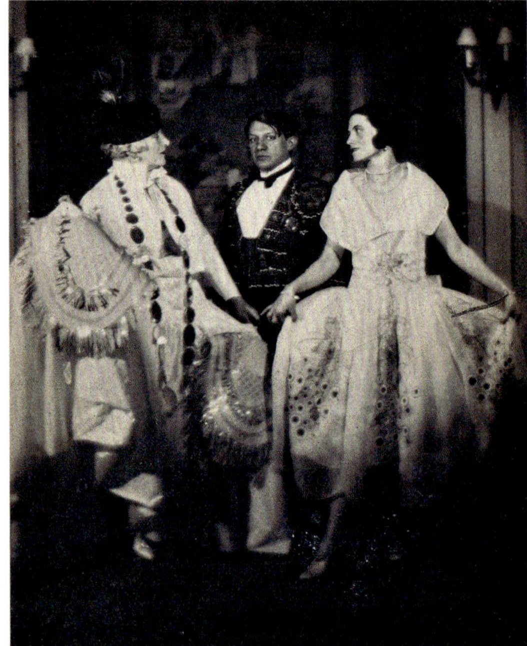

Man Ray
Picasso as a torero between Madame de Erraguyen and Olga at the costume ball of the Comte de Beaumont, 1924
Chlorobromide print, 21 × 16 cm
Museo National Centro de Arte de Reina Sofia, Madrid

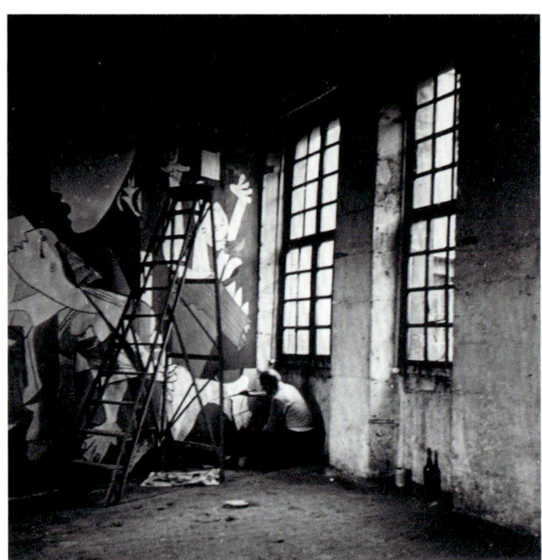

Dora Maar
Picasso working on *Guernica* while seated on the floor of his studio on rue des Grands-Augustins
May–June 1937
Silver gelatin print, 20.8 × 20.1 cm
Musée national Picasso, Paris

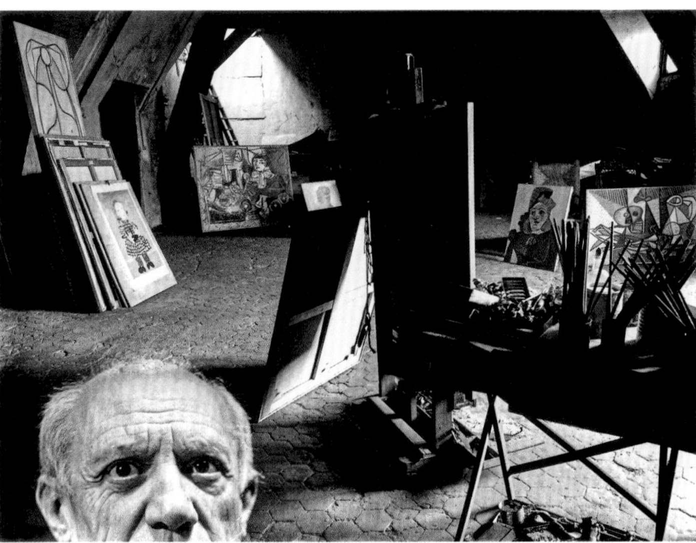

Robert Doisneau
Picasso in his studio on rue des
Grands-Augustins, 1956
Silver gelatin print, 17 × 22.2 cm
Atelier Robert Doisneau

1935

Olga discovers that Marie-Thérèse is pregnant and breaks up with Picasso. The child, Maya, is born on October 5 to Marie-Thérèse Walter and Picasso. During this time, Picasso writes several poems.

1936

The Spanish Civil War begins on July 17.

The Republicans appoint Picasso director of the Prado. Although he will never exercise this function in Madrid, he makes public appearances elsewhere in this role during the Civil War. The Prado collections are evacuated soon after the outbreak of war to protect them from destruction; after a long odyssey by train and truck they eventually reach Switzerland in February 1939. A selection of 175 masterpieces are exhibited in Geneva, among them twenty-five paintings by El Greco, including *The Resurrection* (cat. 50). Four-hundred thousand visitors attend the exhibition before the paintings are returned to Madrid later in the year.

Picasso meets photographer and painter Dora Maar (1907–1997), who becomes his lover. They spend the summer together in Mougins and Juan-les-Pins.

1937

Picasso paints the famous work *Guernica* for the Spanish pavilion at the Paris Universal Exposition; the painting's subject is the bombardment and destruction of the Basque town of Guernica by the German Condor Legion. This harrowing monumental painting is on display at the Universal Exposition from June until November, along with the Weeping Woman series and three sculptures by Picasso.

1939

Picasso's mother María dies in Barcelona on January 13.

The Spanish Civil War ends with the defeat of the Republicans and the victory of the putschists under General Francisco Franco (1892–1975). Thus begins the period of the Francoist dictatorship, which will continue until Franco's death. The evacuated Prado collections are returned to Madrid and handed over to the victors.

Picasso, a fierce opponent of the Franco regime, will never again set foot in his native Spain.

On September 1, Germany's invasion of Poland triggers World War II.

Picasso retreats to the villa Les Voiliers in Royan.

1940

A large Picasso retrospective is held at the Museum of Modern Art in New York.

Picasso spends the autumn in his Paris studio on rue des Grands-Augustins, devoting himself mainly to sculpture.

1943

Picasso meets Françoise Gilot (b. 1921) who becomes his lover and preferred model.

1944

Picasso joins the French Communist Party.

1945

The German army capitulates on May 8.

On August 6, a US bomber drops the world's first atomic bomb on Hiroshima. The attack on Nagasaki follows three days later.

On September 2, Japan capitulates, and World War II is officially over.

Picasso paints *The Charnel House* in response to the horrors of the concentration camps.

1946

Picasso moves to the Côte d'Azur.

1947

Picasso makes a large donation to the Musée National d'Art Moderne in Paris when it reopens after World War II.

A son, Claude, is born on 15 May to Françoise Gilot and Picasso.

1949

Picasso's *Dove* is selected for the poster of the World Peace Congress in Paris.

A daughter, Paloma, is born on April 19 to Françoise Gilot and Picasso.

1950

Françoise Gilot leaves Picasso and moves to Paris with their children. Picasso meets Jacqueline Roque (1927–1986), who becomes his next lover.

1953

Picasso produces a cycle of 180 drawings on the subject of painter and model. He also starts work on variations of masterpieces by Velázquez, Manet, and El Greco.

1956

The newly expanded Prado devotes three rooms to El Greco.

1957

Picasso completes a cycle of variations on Velázquez's 1656 painting *Las Meninas*. In 1968 he will donate it to the city of Barcelona in memory of his friend and secretary Sabartés (cat. 59).

In June Picasso begins his last poem, "El entierro del Conde de Orgaz," completed some time in 1959. The long, exalted prose poem imagines an orgiastic gathering at which Velàzquez and Goya also make their appearance and where the *Meninas* in their beds carry the Count of Orgaz to his grave. It is not published until 1969.

1958

Picasso buys the Château of Vauvenargues near Aix-en-Provence.

1961

Picasso and Jacqueline marry and move to Mougins.

1963

The Museu Picasso opens in Barcelona.

1966

A retrospective is held in the Grand Palais and the Petit Palais in Paris to celebrate Picasso's eighty-fifth birthday.

1967–68

Picasso makes two sketches parodying El Greco's *Burial of the Count of Orgaz*. In the first, the figures appear as clowns. In the second, he transforms the count's body into a roast chicken and replaces El Greco's portrait with a rather larger portrait of himself. He also paints *The Musketeer* (cat. 66), signing it on the back with the name "Domenico Theotocopulos van Rijn da Silva."

1970

Picasso makes a generous donation to the Museu Picasso in Barcelona.

An exhibition of his late work is held in the Palais des Papes in Avignon.

1971

The Louvre celebrates Picasso's ninetieth birthday with an exhibition in the Grande Galerie. It is the first time that such an honor has been bestowed on a single artist.

1973

Picasso dies in Mougins on April 8. He is buried on the grounds of the Château de Vauvenargues.

Compiled by Lara Baltsch, Gabriel Dette, and Olga Osadtschy

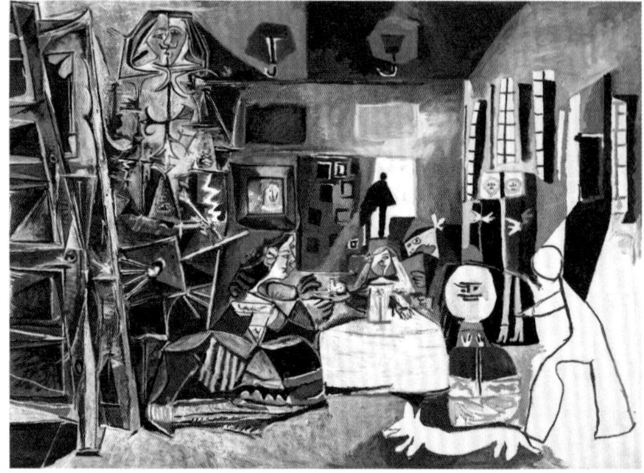

Pablo Picasso
Las Meninas (Study), Cannes, August 1, 1957
Oil on canvas, 194 × 260 cm
Museu Picasso, Barcelona, gift of Pablo Picasso, 1968

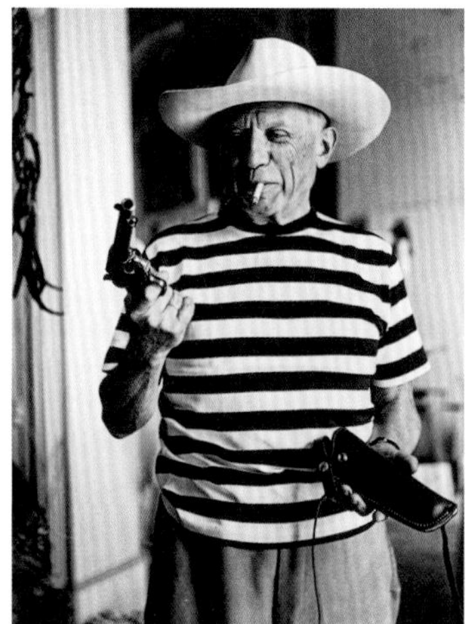

André Villers
Picasso with the revolver and hat given to him by Gary Cooper, Cannes, 1958
Silver gelatin print, 37 × 27 cm
Museum Ludwig, Cologne
Acquired with funds from the Peter and Irene Ludwig Stiftung, 2011

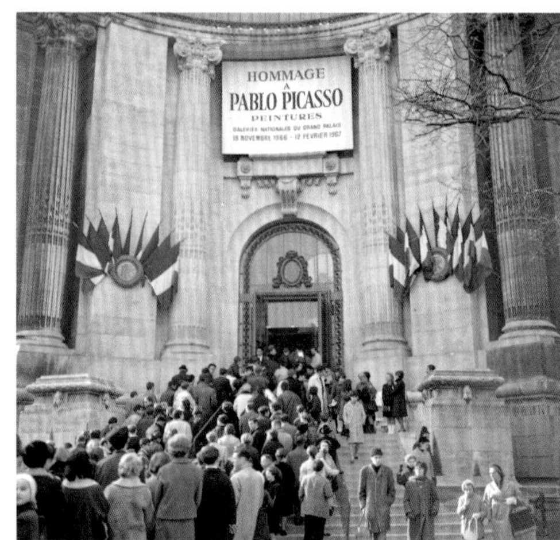

Visitors queuing for the *Hommage à Pablo Picasso* exhibition at the Grand Palais (November 18, 1966–February 12, 1967)
Paris, February 1967

Photo Credits

Pp. 14 & 38: akg images / Joseph Martin; p. 18: © Alexander Meledin / ©Succession Picasso / DACS, London 2022 / Bridgeman Images; pp. 19 & 60: © 2022 Dumbarton Oaks; pp. 20 (top) & 138: akg-images / André Held; pp. 20 (bottom): bpk | Scala, Florence; pp. 21 & 159: Courtesy National Gallery of Art, Washington; p. 24: ©RMN-Grand Palais (Musée national Picasso-Paris) / Mathieu Rabeau; p. 27: akg-images / Maurice Babey; p. 28: Edward Quinn, ©edwardquinn.com / ©Succession Picasso / 2020, ProLitteris, Zurich; p. 35: Wikimedia Commons, ©2012 by Benaki Museum, Athens; p. 36: akg-images / Mondadori Portfolio / Luciano Pedicini; p. 37: Minneapolis Institute of Art, The William Hood Dunwoody Fund / Public Domain (CC-PDM); p. 40: akg-images / Album / Oronoz; p. 41: Bridgeman Images; p. 42: bpk | Scala; p. 44: Digital Image CC0 Art Institute of Chicago; p. 49: akg-images / Album / Oronoz; pp. 52 & 177 (top): ©1998–2022 The Frick Collection; p. 54: Lightworks Media / Alamy Stock Photo; pp. 62 & 71: ©2022. Digital Image, The Museum of Modern Art, New York / Scala, Florence; pp. 63 & 65: Photograph ©2022 Museum of Fine Arts, Boston; p. 68: Photo ©RMN-Grand Palais (musée du Louvre) / Franck Raux; p. 73: akg-images / Erich Lessing; p. 75 (top): bpk / RMN - Grand Palais / Adrien Didierjean; p. 102: Patrimonio Nacional, Real Monasterio de San Lorenzo de El Escorial; p. 103: Photo ©Paris Musées, musée d'Art moderne, Dist. RMN-Grand Palais / image ville de Paris; p. 105: ©The National Gallery London, Picture Library; p. 106: Parroquia Santa María La Mayor, Andújar, Diócesis de Jaén España; p. 107: The Pittas Collection – El Greco; p. 109: ©CSG CIC Glasgow Museums and Libraries Collections; p. 113: Philadelphia Museum of Art, Image Library; pp. 119 & 141: ©Museo Nacional Thyssen-Bornemisza, Madrid; p. 120: ©Musées de Strasbourg, A. Plisson; p. 124: bpk / Gemäldegalerie, SMB / Jörg P. Anders; p. 125: bpk / Museum Berggruen, Private collection / Jens Ziehe; p. 127: ©2022. Digital Image M. Maurice Aeschimann; p. 130: Fundación Hospital Ntra. Sra. de La Caridad Memoria Benéfica de Vega (FUNCAVE); p. 132: ©John Lamberton; p. 133: ©Tate Images; p. 134: Fondation Beyeler, Riehen/Basel, Sammlung Beyeler; p. 135: Museum of Fine Arts - Hungarian National Gallery; p. 136: ©2022. White Images / Scala, Florence; pp. 137 & 139: ©2022. The Solomon R. Guggenheim Foundation, New York; p. 142: courtesy of the owner; p. 148: Photo ©RMN-Grand Palais (musée du Louvre) / Thierry Ollivier; p. 153: ©Centre Pompidou, MNAM-CCI, Dist. RMN-Grand Palais / image Centre Pompidou, MNAM-CCI; p. 154: ©Patrice Cartier / Bridgeman Images; p. 158: ©2022. Digital Image courtesy of the owner; p. 160: ©Baltimore Museum of Art, Mitro Hood; p. 163: courtesy Kate Ganz Family Trust, New York, photo Jerry L. Thompson; p. 164: The Montreal Museum of Fine Arts, Brian Merrett; p. 165: József Rosta / Ludwig Museum – Museum of Contemporary Art; p. 166: photo Michel Bourguet / Musée de Picardie; p. 168: Marc Domage ©Museo Picasso Málaga; p. 170: Museum Frieder Burda, Baden-Baden; pp. 171 & 188 (center): © Rheinisches Bildarchiv Köln; p. 176: Antiquarian Images / Mary Evans Picture Library; p. 178 (top): Grosvenor Prints / Mary Evans Picture Library; p. 178 (center): Biblioteca Nacional de España, Madrid; p. 182 (top): ©Herbert List Estate, M. Scheller, Hamburg / Agentur Focus; pp. 182 (center) & 183 (bottom): Photo ©RMN-Grand Palais (Musée national Picasso-Paris) / image RMN-GP; p. 183 (top): Wikimedia Commons; p. 184 (top): bpk / The Art Institute of Chicago / Art Resource, NY; p. 186 (top): Archivo Fotografico Museo Nacional Centro de Arte Reina Sofía; p. 187: ©Robert Doisneau / Gamma Photo; p. 188 (bottom): ©Roger-Viollet

akg images: pp. 16, 26, 53 (top), 75 (bottom), 138

Fundacion Almine y Bernard Ruiz-Picasso para el Arte: pp. 81, 93, 101, 167

Kunstmuseum Basel / Martin P. Bühler: pp. 76, 117, 123, 131, 143, 149, 151, 169, 175 (Martin P. Bühler); Jonas Hänggi: pp. 51, 74, 76, 111, 159

Digital Image CC0 The Metropolitan Museum of Art, New York: pp. 32, 34, 67, 82, 85

Museu Picasso Barcelona ©Fotogasull: pp. 47, 84, 86-88, 89, 91, 92, 94-95, 97, 108, 157, 182, 188 (top)

Photo ©RMN-Grand Palais (Musée national Picasso-Paris) / Adrien Didierjean: pp. 121, 129, 145, 186 (bottom); Mathieu Rabeau: pp. 83, 99, 115, 147, 155, 184 (bottom)

©Photographic Archive. Museo Nacional del Prado, Madrid: pp. 23, 43, 46, 50 (top), 53 (bottom), 54, 110, 116, 144, 156, 179

©2022. Album / Scala, Florence: pp. 173, 177 (bottom), 178 (bottom)

This book is published in
conjunction with the exhibition

Picasso – El Greco
Kunstmuseum Basel
June 11–September 25, 2022

Curated by Carmen Giménez
With Gabriel Dette, Josef Helfenstein,
and Ana Mingot

Catalogue:

Editors
Carmen Giménez
Josef Helfenstein

Managing Editors
Gabriel Dette
Olga Osadtschy

Picture Editors
Lara Baltsch
Olga Osadtschy

Project Manager
Richard Viktor Hagemann

Copy Editor
Miranda Robbins

Translations
Tony Beckwith
(Spanish: pp. 15–31; 47–57)
Imogen Taylor
(German: pp. 6–11; 33–45; 78;
96; 126; 112; 126; 150; 174–84)

Graphic design
Rutger Fuchs Amsterdam

Typeface
Monotype Plantin
Neue Haas Grotesk

Production
Thomas Lemaître

Reproductions
DruckConcept, Berlin

Printing and binding
Printer Trento s.r.l.

Paper
Garda Ultramatt, 150 g/m2

© 2022 for the reproduced works by Pablo
Picasso: Succession Picasso / ProLitteris,
Zurich / VG Bild-Kunst, Bonn
© 2022 for the reproduced works by
Robert Doisneau: Gamma Photo
For the reproduced works by Brassaï
© Estate Brassaï - RMN-Grand Palais
© 2022 for the reproduced works by
Jasper Johns: ProLitteris, Zurich / VG Bild-
Kunst, Bonn
For the reproduced works by Herbert List
© herbert list / Magnum Photos / Agentur
Focus
For the reproduced works by Dora Maar
© ADAGP, Paris / VG Bild-Kunst, Bonn
© 2022 for the reproduced works by
Man Ray: Man Ray 2015 Trust / ProLitteris
Zurich / VG Bild-Kunst, Bonn

Published by
Hatje Cantz Verlag GmbH
Mommsenstrasse 27
10629 Berlin
www.hatjecantz.com
A Ganske Publishing Group Company

ISBN 978-3-7757-5213-8
(English edition)
ISBN 978-3-7757-5212-1
(German edition)

Printed in Italy

Cover illustrations:
El Greco
An Elderly Gentleman,
1587–1600 (cat. 58)
Pablo Picasso
*Jaume Sabartés with Ruff
and Bonnet,* 1939 (cat. 59)

Exhibition:

KUNSTMUSEUM BASEL

Director
Josef Helfenstein

*Head of Art & Research,
Deputy Director*
Anita Haldemann

Head of Art Care
Werner Müller

*Head of Finance &
Operations*
Tim Kretschmer

*Head of Marketing &
Development*
Mirjam Baitsch

*Assistant Curator
Old Masters*
Gabriel Dette

*Assistant Curator
of the Director*
Olga Osadtschy

Intern
Lara Baltsch

*Head of Exhibition
Management*
Matthias Fellmann

*Head of Collection
Management*
Svenja Held

Registrar
Monique Meyer

Conservation
Sophie Eichner
Annette Fritsch
Esther Rapoport
Annegret Seger
Simone Wissel
Lina Wyss
Caroline Wyss Illgen

*Art Handling &
Technical Support*
Claude Bosch
Felix Böttiger
Sophie Brönnimann
Urs Cavelti
Dominique Gfeller
Philipp Gueniat

Photographer
Jonas Hänggi

Head of Communications
Karen N. Gerig

Marketing
Vera Reinhard
Christian Selz

Digital Media
Ana Brankovic

Curator of Programs
Daniel Kurjakovic

Art Education & Outreach:
Hanna Horst (Head)
Hanna Banholzer (Research
Assistant)
Marilena Raufeisen (Intern)

Technical Services
Urs Nachbur
Roland Schweizer

Shop
Nina Mösch
Simon Buikema
Sabina Gauch

KUNSTMUSEUM BASEL
St. Alban-Graben 16
CH-4010 Basel
Tel. +41(0) 61 206 62 62
Fax +41(0) 61 206 62 52
www.kunstmuseumbasel.ch